vegetables

REVISED EDITION

THE MOST AUTHORITATIVE GUIDE
TO BUYING, PREPARING, AND COOKING,
WITH MORE THAN 300 RECIPES

vegetables

James Peterson

TEN SPEED PRESS
Berkeley

Contents

Introduction

WHEN I SET OUT TO WRITE the first edition of *Vegetables* in 1996, I went to the local bookstore to look at other vegetable books. I almost gave up when I saw hundreds of books about vegetables and several shelves full of vegetarian books, which made up one of the largest sections in the store. But as I flipped through the books, and after giving my newly conceived vegetable project a little thought, I realized that what I wanted to write was different. In my perusal of the competition I found few recipes for the simplest dishes—things like glazed carrots, mashed potatoes, sautéed spinach, and steamed asparagus—dishes to cook on a Wednesday evening with a house full of kids and after a day at the office. Some of the books extolled the virtues of shopping at the local farmers' market (who could disagree?), but they didn't mention those winter days when the only source of vegetables may be the supermarket. And while it's great to cook with lovely fresh or even heirloom vegetables, it's more of a challenge to make something tasty out of a few beans or a bag of supermarket mushrooms. So I decided to write a book that would include not just new or unfamiliar dishes but also the tried-and-true dishes that many of us grew up with. I also wanted to liven up many of these dishes by adding new twists—like folding pesto or roasted garlic into mashed potatoes or pine nuts and raisins to sautéed spinach.

At the same time, I decided to include simple new ways (new to us but traditional in other places) to cook less-familiar vegetables, such as kale, Swiss chard, fennel, and escarole. Many of these dishes were based on memories of meals in great restaurants or of travels to foreign countries; some were last-minute inventions made up after out-of-control buying sprees at the farmers' market. The purpose of some of these recipes was, of course, to provide new tastes and combinations, but also to offer simple, flavorful, and lighter alternatives to "traditional" methods.

It's now fourteen years since the publication of the first edition of *Vegetables*, and as books do, *Vegetables* went out of print. I (along with my publisher, Ten Speed Press) saw an opportunity to republish *Vegetables* with full-color photography. We have now included photographs of most of the vegetables and many of the recipes.

In addition to new color photography, this revised edition contains more than thirty new vegetable entries, fifty new recipes, and a new section on herbs. Chopping and dicing have been more thoroughly explained, and the book now has a thirty-page techniques section that explains (and sometimes shows) every method you might need to cook a vegetable. The new vegetable entries are mostly for Asian vegetables, although a few European ones (salsify, crosnes) have made their way in. The herb section covers all the common herbs, as well as lesser-known varieties (rue, epazote).

In the years since *Vegetables* was first published, American tastes have changed. We have stirred away from a richer and more subtly flavored European-influenced cuisine, to the direct flavors, bold variations in texture, and bright colors of Asian cooking. To accommodate this, I have spent many a morning in Chinatown trying to unravel the mysteries of Asian vegetables. The results of these endeavors are found throughout the book as I've taken some of these exotic and not-so-exotic beans and lentils, gourds, herbs, and rhizomes home to my kitchen laboratory for experimentation. Many of them I have cooked using traditional techniques and flavorings, but others have called out for completely new treatments.

This new edition of *Vegetables* is divided into two sections, the extensive technique section followed by an alphabetical listing of the vegetables themselves. Once you've read the technique section, the techniques called for in the recipes should all be familiar. Hopefully, with the knowledge of those techniques, you'll be able to improvise with both familiar and unfamiliar vegetables. For example, the section on gratins—probably better known as casseroles—analyzes which liquids (cream, béchamel sauce, broth, coconut milk, and so on) are most appropriate. It shows how cooking times and temperatures influence the final result and how various toppings can be used to create a crust. Armed with this knowledge, a new idea or recipe for a gratin should be easily accommodated and mastered.

But the new *Vegetables* is not just about techniques. It also explores the flavor combinations used in many of the world's great cuisines. Unlike many fusion dishes that have no tradition behind them, the dishes in *Vegetables* are firmly grounded in the cultural habits of various peoples working in the kitchen.

In short, armed with this new edition, you can embark on new culinary adventures and feel free to improvise in the kitchen. Once you have the basic understanding of how each vegetable behaves, coupled with a familiarity with the techniques that are used in its preparation, your flights of fancy will be well grounded in the realities of those treatments best suited to your preparations.

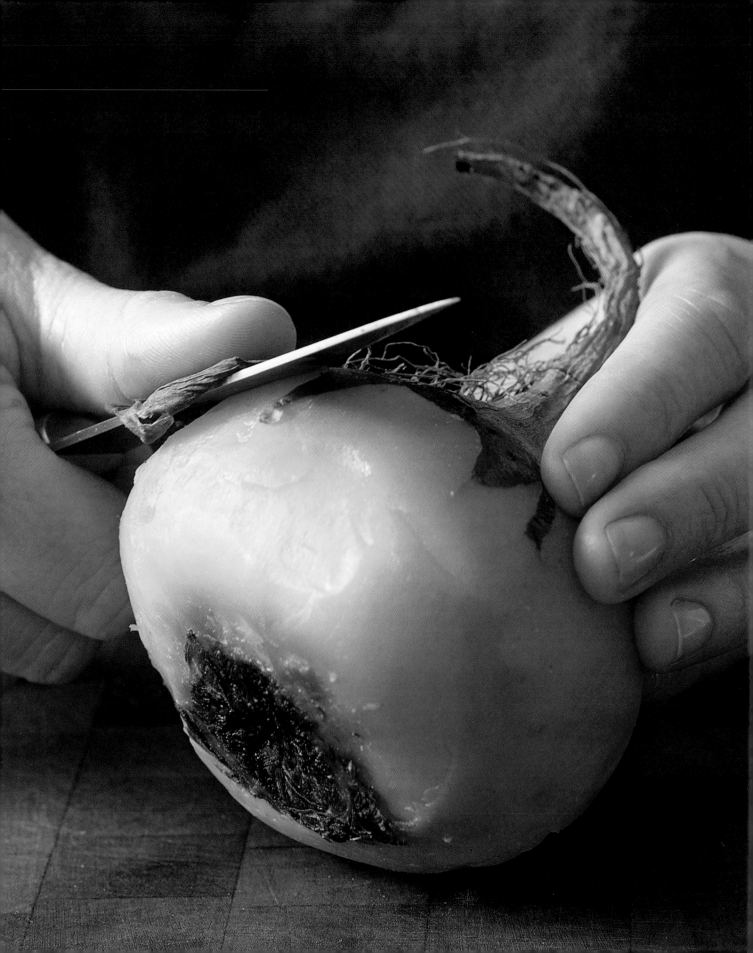

PART I

Techniques for Preparing and Cooking Vegetables

Knife Skills

BEFORE EMBARKING ON A RECIPE, improvised or otherwise, it's essential to have at least a rudimentary mastery of those most basic knife skills: chopping, finely chopping or mincing, cubing, and dicing.

Basic Chopping Techniques

Chopping is the most straightforward of knife skills. To chop a vegetable is to cut it in a random way. You're not dicing or cubing it, but rather simply hacking away at it until it has the size that you want.

To chop an herb such as parsley, use the longest knife you have. A long knife, because you can align what you're chopping next to the blade, is the most efficient tool because you end up chopping more at once. To chop an herb or small vegetable, hold the knife in your right hand (assuming you're right handed) with the end of the blade pressing against the cutting board. This pressure holds the knife in place and allows you to establish a kind of spring action in which the knife blade springs back as you chop. Use your left hand to continually feed what it is you're chopping under the knife blade. Don't use your left hand to hold down the top of the knife, a common error among even professional chefs. Some recipes call for fine versus coarse chopping. Fine chopping is used for vegetables that are meant to cook very quickly or to release the maximum of their flavor in a relatively small period of time. Vegetables are cut into cubes such as macédoine and brunoise when they show up in the finished dish and the dish is somewhat formal.

Onions and shallots require their own chopping methods. Halve the onion, cutting through the two ends—don't slice through the equator. First slice each half in two directions—one parallel with the length of the onion half, the other with the knife held sideways—with the slices left attached at the root end. Then slice across the two slices that you have already been made. The whole thing will fall apart (except for the little bit

Chopping parsley.
Mincing parsley.

of remaining root end). Then chop the diced onion more or less finely—anywhere from coarse chopping to mincing.

To cut turnips, celeriac, and other round vegetables into cubes, first cut off the sides so you arrive at a large cube (if you peel the vegetable first you can save the trimmings for soups and purees). Cut this cube into panels the thickness you want for the final cubes. Cut these panels—stack them if you feel comfortable—into sticks and then cut these sticks crosswise to arrive at cubes (see photos, page 351).

To cut elongated vegetables, such as carrots or parsnips, into perfect dice, cut them first into lengthwise pieces about 1 inch long. Trim the sides off these pieces and then cut the pieces into panels. Cut the panels into sticks—called "julienne" when about an $1/8$ inch thick, and "macédoine" when about $1/4$ inch—and then crosswise into cubes. Cutting elongated vegetables into a perfect dice requires considerable waste, and most of the time you're going to want to cut these vegetables in a way that takes advantage of the whole vegetable. To do this efficiently, cut the vegetable lengthwise into 3 wedge-shaped strips. Slice these crosswise into little triangles.

CUTTING CARROTS, SALSIFY, AND PARSNIPS INTO EVEN-SIZE PIECES

Peeling and slicing is the easiest way to prepare carrots and parsnips for cooking, but some of us like the crunch and savor of vegetables cut into larger pieces. To cut carrots, salsify, or parsnips, peel them and cut them into 1- to $1^1/2$-inch-long pieces. Because carrots and parsnips taper, some of the pieces will be too small and others too large to cook evenly. To make the pieces all the same size, leave the smallest sections whole. Stand the thicker pieces on end and cut them lengthwise in halves, thirds, or quarters, depending on their size, so all the pieces end up being about the same size. This makes them prettier to look at and will ensure they all cook in the same amount of time. You can also cut the woody core out of each of the pieces—a nice refinement but usually not necessary. If you're feeling conscientious, snap out the piece of wooden core in the center of each wedge by sliding a paring knife along where the core meets the orange outer part of the carrot and then gently twisting.

If you're really being fancy, you can trim the edges of the pieces to give them a smoother and rounder appearance with a technique called "turning."

TURNING VEGETABLES

This techniques takes a little time to learn, but once mastered (even a little) it will make presenting roasted and glazed vegetables all the more dramatic. Turning consists of rounding off the edges of vegetables, such

Cut carrots into equal-length pieces.
Cut each piece into halves or wedges.
Cut the cores out of each piece.

as turnips, carrots, and celeriac. To turn vegetables, they must first be cut into appropriate shaped and sized pieces, usually the shape of elongated footballs or garlic cloves, all the same size.

Hold the vegetable at one end between the thumb and forefinger of your left hand. With a small sharp knife (preferably one with a concave shape) in your right hand, rotate the vegetable against the knife blade, following the edges and smoothing off the edges and the ends.

SLICING CARROTS *EN PAYSANNE*

Unless you need carrots in perfect rounds, it's more efficient to cut the carrots into little triangles called slicing *en paysanne*. Cut the carrots lengthwise into quarters and then slice the quarters, bunched together.

GETTING AT THE FLAVOR: PEELING, CHOPPING, CRUSHING GARLIC

The easiest way to peel garlic is to just break the cloves off the garlic, cut off the tiny hard edge on one end of the clove with a paring knife, and crush them, one at a time, by laying the side of a chef's knife or cleaver over each clove and giving the knife a quick whack with your fist. The

⤳ SLICERS ⤳

Unless you're very handy with a knife, and few of us are, it's much faster and easier to slice certain vegetables with a vegetable slicer, either an inexpensive plastic slicer or a more expensive stainless steel mandoline.

Benriner is a popular brand of plastic slicer. Benriner slicers have razor-sharp blades and a plastic frame that you hold with one hand while sliding the vegetable against the blade with the other. When shopping for a plastic vegetable slicer, be sure to buy one with small nuts on the back for adjusting the exact thickness of the slices. Some brands allow you only two or three thicknesses, none of which ever seems to be the right one.

A mandoline is another kind of vegetable slicer. Mandolines are made of stainless steel and have legs for holding the slicing surface in place. Their main disadvantage is their expense—about five times as much as a plastic cutter. But if you slice or fry a lot of potatoes, a mandoline is almost indispensable; it not only slices but juliennes, cuts different size french fries, and is the only gadget for making ruffled potato chips.

A more rarified slicing gadget is the truffle slicer. A truffle slicer is small, usually made of stainless steel, and is hand-held. If you're slicing truffles at the table—say, over pasta—a truffle slicer is elegant to look at and can even be passed around with the truffle for guests to help themselves (if you trust your guests that much).

Slicers (but not truffle slicers) come with guards with which to hold the vegetable as you're slicing it. These inevitably get misplaced. A good alternative is to hold the vegetable with a towel, a habit I encourage for obvious reasons.

Slicing potatoes for french fries using a mandoline.

Cutting the hard end off the clove.

Crushing the clove to facilitate peeling.

Peeling the clove.

Slicing toward the root end.

Slicing laterally.

Mincing.

peel will just slip off. I never use a garlic press to extract the pulp or juice from garlic because most of the pulp gets stuck in the press and the press is difficult to clean.

Peeled garlic cloves can be chopped like any other vegetable, but some recipes require that the garlic pulp be worked to a paste. A large mortar and pestle are ideal, but few of us are so equipped—the requisite large marble mortar and pestle can cost more than a good food processor—but fortunately it's easy to crush garlic to a paste with a chef's knife. To make garlic paste, cut off the hard little end from the pointed end of the clove, give the clove a whack with the side of a cleaver to help loosen the peel, and chop the garlic before crushing it with the side of the knife. Keep pushing the knife along the surface of the garlic while leaning on the knife with your other hand—you can use a surprising amount of force.

Crushing minced garlic.

PEELING, SEEDING, AND SALTING TOMATOES

While many of us don't bother to peel tomatoes, much less seed them, peeling can make the tomato seem more tender if it's underripe and hard. Cooked tomatoes will also release the peel, in little curlycues, into the surrounding sauce. Tomatoes are seeded, especially when they are destined for salads, so the liquid doesn't dilute the vinaigrette.

PEELING. Plunge the ripe summer tomatoes in boiling water and leave for 30 seconds; leave firm or underripe tomatoes for 45 seconds. Drain the tomatoes in a colander and rinse with plenty of cold water. Cut out the section of stem still attached to the tomato and slip off the peel with your fingers or a paring knife. If you have only one or two tomatoes and a gas stove, you can roast the tomatoes over the flame with a long fork until the skin bubbles up, then rinse and slip off the peel. Remember that you don't need to peel tomatoes for sauces or soups that are going to be strained—the straining eliminates the peels and seeds.

SEEDING. To seed tomato wedges for salads, remove the seeds by sliding your finger along both sides of each wedge so the seeds fall out. To seed tomatoes that are being chopped or sliced, halve them crosswise and squeeze the seeds out of each half.

SALTING. Firm or underripe tomatoes you want to use in salads will be much tastier when sprinkled with coarse salt and drained. Peel the tomatoes, cut them into wedges, and seed the wedges. Toss thoroughly with 1 tablespoon of coarse salt per 6 tomatoes and drain in a colander for 30 minutes. A teaspoon or two of good kirsch helps bring out the tomatoes' naturally fruity flavor.

SEEDING CANNED TOMATOES. Because canned tomatoes have already been peeled, they need only to be drained and the seeds taken out before they are used. The easiest way to remove the seeds is to dig your thumb into each tomato in one or two places and give a gentle squeeze. Figure that one 28-ounce can of canned tomatoes yields about 2 cups drained and seeded pulp.

PEELING AND SEEDING TOMATOES

Cut out the stem by cutting a circle around it using a very sharp knife.

Plunge the tomatoes in boiling water and leave for about 30 seconds.

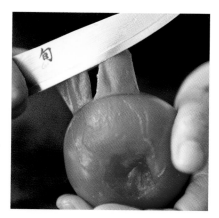

Drain in a colander, rinse immediately with cold water, and pull away the skin.

Halve the tomatoes through the equator.

Squeeze the seeds out of each of the halves.

When slicing tomatoes for a salad, cut vertically.

Then cut each of the halves into wedges.

Press the seeds out of each of the wedges.

CHARRING, PEELING, AND SEEDING BELL PEPPERS AND FRESH CHILES

Many recipes call for peppers that have been peeled. The peel, however, is so thin that it has to be charred and then pulled off with your fingers and scraped away with a paring knife. Peppers can be charred on the stove, over the grill, or under the broiler.

GAS STOVE METHOD. Arrange the peppers or chiles right over the burners with the flame turned on high. Turn them over every couple of minutes and cook until thoroughly charred and coated with black. If any section of the pepper becomes coated with white ash, you're overdoing it—move that part out of the flame.

GRILL METHOD. Don't build a charcoal fire just for grilling peppers or chiles, but if you're barbecuing anyway, just grill the peppers—turning them from time to time with tongs—until they are blackened on all sides.

BROILER METHOD. Arrange the peppers or chiles so they're about $1/2$ inch from the broiler flame. Rotate every minute or so with tongs so they blacken evenly. Watch the peppers carefully—some broilers will blacken them very quickly.

Put the charred peppers in a plastic bag for 10 minutes and then pull off the charred peels with your fingers. Scrape off any stubborn patches of peel with a paring knife. Quickly rinse the peppers or chiles under cold running water to eliminate any flecks of peel. Pat dry with paper towels. Cut out the stems with a paring knife and cut the peppers in half lengthwise. Spoon out the seeds and pull out any large pieces of white pulp.

Blacken bell peppers on the stove for peeling.

Scrape the peel away with a paring knife. Cut out the stems.

Remove the seeds.

Methods of Cooking

MOST OF US MANAGE TO COOK VEGETABLES, usually with a quick boil or sauté, but this severely limits what vegetables have to offer. Some vegetables do better boiled or steamed, while others may need the intense heat of the frying pan or a slow gentle oven. Once you understand a few basic principles, it's easy to figure out how to cook almost any vegetable without looking at a recipe.

Boiling

Boiling is the easiest and most obvious way to cook almost any ingredient. Green vegetables are often best when boiled. The intense heat of boiling water cooks them so quickly that they keep their fresh flavor and bright color. Usually when we boil vegetables, we add salt to the water to help preserve the vegetable's color. Green vegetables are plunged into the rapidly boiling water in a process called "blanching" or sometimes "parboiling." Sometimes we simmer vegetables, such as turnips (again, the technique is called "blanching" or "parboiling"), to extract and eliminate bitternesss or too strong a flavor, or we simmer vegetables such as potatoes to cook them evenly through.

BOILING ROOT VEGETABLES

With the exception of carrots, which are better glazed, root vegetables can be put in a pot of cold water and brought slowly to a simmer. If a large root vegetable or a potato is tossed into a pot of boiling water, the outside will overcook, and the inside will remain undercooked. Root vegetables and potatoes should never actually be boiled, they should be gently simmered—otherwise the vegetables may crack open. Strong-tasting root vegetables, such as old turnips are sometimes peeled and simmered (parboiled) to get rid of some of their strong flavor before they are cooked using other methods. Much of the time it doesn't matter, but if you want to take away some of the vegetable's flavor (such as bitterness in a turnip), remove the peel before boiling. If the vegetables are delicate, such as fresh

Potatoes prepared for boiling.

baby root vegetables, leave the peel on and either eat it or remove it after cooking. When parboiling root vegetables, it isn't necessary to add salt to the water.

BOILING GREEN VEGETABLES

Plunge green vegetables into a large pot of boiling water over the highest possible heat—a technique sometimes called blanching—to cook them quickly and keep them green and slightly crunchy. Use at least 6 quarts of water per pound of vegetables. If you use less, the water will cool down when you add the vegetables, and the vegetables will stew instead of cook quickly. Stewed green vegetables lose color and nutrients and become waterlogged. Add about 2 tablespoons of salt per 6 quarts of boiling water (don't measure, just dump some in). Using salt also keeps the vegetables bright green. And don't worry; the salt is poured off with the cooking water.

You'll save time by covering the pot as the water is coming to a boil, but green vegetables should be cooked uncovered. Green vegetables release volatile acids as they cook; if these acids are trapped in the pot, they'll cause the vegetables to wilt and lose their bright color.

Green beans.

> **⚙ SIMMERING AND BOILING: WHAT'S THE DIFFERENCE? ⚙**
>
> When water is heated, its temperature steadily rises until it reaches 212°F (100°C). As the temperature approaches the boiling point, the movement of the water molecules overpowers their tendency to hold together, and the water bubbles up and turns into steam. The energy supplied by the stove no longer contributes to making the water hotter but to making steam instead. Because of this, you can't make water hotter than 212°F unless you enclose it, such as in a pressure cooker, or add another ingredient, such as salt. Because of this, simmering water—water held slightly below the boil—will cook vegetables almost as quickly as boiling water. The surface of a pan of simmering water should shimmer—the French say it should smile—not roll. Boiling is typically called for when cooking green vegetables, while simmering is more appropriate for such ingredients as root vegetables or broth, which must be carefully skimmed to eliminate fat.

DON'T OVERCOOK OR UNDERCOOK

Don't rely too firmly on cooking times recommended in the recipes. While approximate times are provided, every vegetable is different, no time will be exact. To know when vegetables are done, fish one out of the pot with a slotted spoon, taste it, and decide if you like its texture. For most leafy vegetables, just drain the vegetables as soon as the leaves lose their stiffness and "melt"—spinach, for example, cooks in about 30 seconds. Tougher or stronger-tasting greens, such as kale, chard, or beet greens, need to be cooked longer to soften and to lose some of their "raw" vegetable flavor. The doneness of root vegetables, such as turnips or potatoes, is judged by the ease with which a fork or knife penetrates the vegetable. The best way to judge the doneness of green vegetables is simply to bite into a piece. Some vegetables, such as summer squash or mushrooms, that already contain a lot of water, should never be cooked in water.

The purpose of cooking vegetables quickly is to preserve their flavor, texture, and color. Hot vegetables shouldn't sit around once they're cooked, or they'll overcook and lose their freshness. Drain cooked vegetables immediately in a colander and serve them at once. If you're cooking vegetables to be served cold or to be reheated later, "refresh" them immediately by stirring them into a big bowl of ice water or, if you're short on ice, by rinsing them under rapidly running cold tap water until cool.

Steaming

Most vegetables that can be boiled can also be steamed. Frankly I've never found there to be much difference in steamed or boiled vegetables, and I find that most cooks veer toward one method or the other because it's what they've gotten used to or what's convenient.

While boiled vegetables are cooked submerged in water, steamed vegetables are held suspended above the water so they're cooked by the steam. To steam vegetables, you'll need a steamer or some improvised arrangement to keep the vegetables surrounded by steam. Most of us have encountered the folding metal steamers that fit into the pot and hold the vegetables suspended over a small amount of boiling water. These are perfectly fine unless you steam large amounts of vegetables, in which case you'll probably want to invest in a metal or Chinese bamboo steamer, neither of which is expensive. One kind of metal steamer—sometimes called a couscous maker—is simply a pot with another pot that fits on top. The pot on top has tiny holes on the bottom and a tight-fitting lid of its own. Water is brought to a boil in the lower pot and the vegetables are placed in the upper pot with the lid. Another kind of metal steamer is a cylindrically shaped metal basket with holes on its bottom and sides and small metal feet. The steamer is placed in a covered pot that contains a small amount of boiling water. A bamboo steamer works in a similar way except that you have to supply the bottom pot (often a wok) to hold the boiling water and then fit the steamer (which has its own lid) over the pot. One of the advantages of Chinese steamers is that you can stack together two or more at the same time, so if you're steaming different foods at once, you can keep them separate. Another option is a countertop steamer and rice cooker, which is convenient and easy to use.

When steaming, steam quickly. Make sure the water is boiling rapidly before adding the vegetables. Keep the lid tightly closed during steaming. Use enough water so it won't boil down to nothing during the steaming. If you're steaming a lot of vegetables over a long period, make sure the water in the steamer doesn't run dry—if it does, you'll know right away because the kitchen will start to fill with a very peculiar smell.

Serve the steamed vegetables right away; don't leave the vegetables sitting on the back of the stove or in the turned-off steamer or they'll overcook and lose their color, flavor, and texture. You can refresh steamed vegetables in the same way as boiled vegetables—by plunging in ice water or rinsing under cold running tap water—but if you're steaming for fear of leaching out nutrients, you probably won't want to do this.

Last, don't burn yourself. Steam is surprisingly hot and because it's almost invisible, it can surprise you and quickly cause painful burns. When checking the vegetables in a steamer, carefully lift the lid at an angle so that it opens away from you. Let the steam dissipate for a few seconds before reaching or looking into the steamer.

Chinese steamer.
Couscous steamer (couscousière).
Steaming green leafy vegetables.

✎ REHEATING BOILED AND STEAMED VEGETABLES ✍

Many cooks, especially restaurant cooks, take infinite care in preparing their vegetables and then they ruin them by reheating them incorrectly.

Root vegetables, as long as they haven't been overcooked in the first place, are easy to reheat in the oven or on the stove with a little unsalted butter or a tablespoon or two of water to keep them from drying out.

Reheating green vegetables poses greater problems. In most restaurants, green vegetables are boiled or steamed ahead of time, quickly refreshed, and kept cold until just before serving. This is fine as long as the vegetables aren't cooked more than a few hours before serving—if kept much longer, they begin to lose their color. When it's time to reheat the vegetables, most cooks plunge the vegetables back into a pot of boiling water to reheat them, so the vegetables end up being boiled twice and all their flavor ends up leached out into the water. A far better technique is to reheat the cooked and chilled green vegetables by tossing them in a sauté pan with a couple of tablespoons of water over high heat until they are heated through, removing them from the heat, and quickly adding unsalted butter or a little olive oil. Don't reheat green vegetables by sautéing them in unsalted butter, oil, or other fats because they'll become greasy.

A lot of us get hung up on having just the right equipment when in fact we can sauté in just about any pot or pan if we know a little about how heat and food work together.

When sautéing, it's helpful to have a heavy pan that heats evenly and doesn't burn the vegetables in the spot right over the heat source. On the other hand, don't buy a pan that's so heavy you can hardly lift it. You'll also want a pan that has sides that flare out at about a 45° angle to make it easy to flip vegetables by giving the pan a quick pull (a technique that takes some practice to learn). Avoid sauté pans that stick. Tin-lined copper pans, as beautiful as they are, love to stick to sautéed foods. Cast-iron skillets are cheap, heavy (for some, too heavy), and, if taken care of, develop their own nonstick surface. French-style cast-iron skillets (called *poëles*) are a tad lighter than American skillets and have the important flaring sides. But the safest bet for sautéing vegetables is a heavy-bottomed—most of the good ones are aluminum—nonstick pan.

For some vegetable dishes, such as glazed vegetables, or for pan-frying, a straight-sided pan works best. There are many styles on the market. Heavy stainless steel–lined copper is my favorite, but these pans are heavy and cost a mint. All-Clad brand makes pans out of several layers of metal for optimum conductivity. These pans are lighter than copper but almost as expensive. Whatever pan you do buy, I recommend one with a shiny inner surface. Should something start to burn, you'll be able to see the darkening juices immediately on the bottom of the pan.

The traditional vessel for stir-frying is, of course, the wok, but a heavy-bottom sauté pan will also work. It's important that the pan be heavy so that it will retain heat during the stir-frying.

Sautéing and Stir-Frying

The usual way to sauté is to heat a small amount of fat in a heavy-bottomed pan over high heat and then add the food to be sautéed. The fat keeps the food from sticking to the pan—you'll always need a little fat even if you're using a nonstick pan—and provides flavor Depending on what it is you're sautéing, you can toss, shake, or turn with tongs the contents of the sauté pan.

The purpose of sautéing vegetables is to bring out their flavor with high heat and, for some vegetables, to lightly brown them. Vegetables such as mushrooms, cucumbers, tomatoes, and leafy green vegetables—vegetables that contain a lot of water—may release water into the pan, so they actually stew in their own juices instead of sauté. For some vegetables, especially leafy green vegetables, this is of no great consequence, but mushrooms, for example, should be added to the pan in small batches so their moisture has a chance to evaporate instead of accumulating in the pan and defeating the browning process.

Most of us think of sautéing and stir-frying as different techniques, but in fact they're almost the same. The only difference is that the vegetables in a stir-fry, as the name implies, are stirred—usually in a wok—while sautéed vegetables are tossed (*sauter* means "to jump"), usually in a sauté pan or skillet. But whatever approach you decide on, don't worry—you can stir sautéed vegetables in a skillet and toss vegetables in a wok.

Some green vegetables, such as green beans, asparagus, and artichokes, can be boiled or steamed until virtually done before they are sautéed or stir-fried so they'll need to spend less time in the skillet or wok, where they would lose their color. Other green vegetables, such as spinach or zucchini, are tender enough that they can be sautéed or stir-fried directly in a little oil or butter over high heat until they "melt." Because leafy green vegetables, such as spinach or chard, release liquid into the pan, the vegetables actually stew instead of sauté. Quickly drain the vegetables in a colander—to get rid of the water—or continue cooking them over high heat until the water evaporates. Serve immediately.

Sautéing is sometimes called pan-frying. While the techniques are very similar, I usually reserve the term "pan-frying" for cooking in a relatively large amount of fat, but not enough to submerge what's being fried.

Some green vegetables—such as broccoli, broccoli rabe, fern shoots, and tougher leafy greens such as chard and kale, take especially well to sautéing without necessarily having been precooked. Because these vegetables don't release much water into the pan, you can sauté or stir-fry them directly without having to drain them when they're done. They're also firm and hearty, so they're less likely to overcook if you need to quickly boil down any liquid they've released in the pan.

❧ SWEATING VS. SAUTÉING ❧

Many cooks are confused by instructions for sweating vegetables. To "sweat" means to cook slowly in a small amount of fat in a heavy-bottomed pot or pan, sometimes covered, sometimes not, so the vegetables gradually release their own moisture (they sweat) without browning. The sweating is controlled by adjusting the heat (which is usually on the low side) and by covering, or not, the pan. Covering contains moisture and inhibits browning. The one downside to covering the pan, however, is that it's easy to forget and let the vegetables burn. Sweating differs from sautéing because when you sauté a vegetable, you use high heat to get the vegetable to brown, lightly caramelize, or just cook quickly without losing crunch. Sweating is most often used for chopped root vegetables—especially onions, carrots, celery, and garlic—to get the vegetables to release their flavor before other ingredients, especially liquids, are added.

Broccoli Rabe with Olive Oil and Garlic

This is a great standby method for almost any green leafy vegetable, not just broccoli rabe. I keep the cooking time relatively short so the broccoli rabe stays crunchy, but you may want to experiment a little with the cooking times to get the texture to suit you.

MAKES 6 SIDE-DISH SERVINGS

Cut the broccoli rabe flowers and leaves away from the larger stems. Discard the stems. Rinse and drain the leaves and flowers in a colander.

Heat the olive oil over medium heat in a wide skillet or sauté pan. Stir in the garlic and cook it while stirring for about 3 minutes, until lightly golden but not brown. Turn the heat to high and immediately add the broccoli rabe and stir the mixture around in the pan for about 5 minutes or until the broccoli rabe softens. If the garlic starts to turn dark brown, turn down the heat. Bite into a piece of the broccoli rabe to see if it's the way you like it. If it's too crunchy, cook it for a couple minutes more. Season with salt and pepper and serve immediately.

VARIATIONS:

Try finishing the broccoli rabe with some finely chopped garlic, olives, and anchovies crushed to a paste. Another combination: coarsely chopped toasted walnuts and diced dried apricots.

2 to 3 bunches broccoli rabe (about 3 pounds total)

3 tablespoons pure olive oil

4 cloves garlic, thinly sliced

Salt and freshly ground black pepper

Sautéing in olive oil.

◞ AN OPINIONATED NOTE ABOUT VEGETABLE OILS AND MARGARINE ◟

Vegetable oils, such as corn oil, canola oil, and safflower oil, are low in saturated fats, contain no cholesterol, and are inexpensive. I don't care for them because they have very little taste, and what taste they do have is vaguely chemical and they leave a peculiar slippery feeling in the mouth. Occasionally we may need to use something with as little taste as possible—when making a mayonnaise, for example—but most of the time it makes more sense to use less of something tastier, especially when it comes to fats.

If you're going to eat fat, eat flavorful fat—butter, olive oil, and pork, duck, and goose fats. These fats have so much flavor and are so satisfying that you'll get by eating less.

Keep in mind that olive oil comes in two basic varieties—so-called pure olive oil (oil that's been chemically stripped of its flavor components) and extra virgin olive oil. "Pure" oil is best in situations in which it's going to be heated quite hot—such as when deep-frying—and during which the flavor of extra-virgin olive oil would be lost.

As for margarine, I have nothing nice to say. There was a day when margarine made an inexpensive substitute for butter, but margarine is no longer cheap. It's only conceivable advantage over butter is that it contains no cholesterol, but it's still mostly fat and saturated fat at that—and the saturated fat isn't even naturally occurring but is made by hydrogenating vegetable oil. I don't believe that anything made this way—and with such a vile taste—could possibly be better for our health than butter.

Pan-Frying

The best implement for pan-frying is an electric frying pan. Electric frying pans have built in thermostats, which help control the temperature. In lieu of an electric frying pan, use a heavy skillet or pot. Larger pieces of vegetables or fragile cakes (such as the Pan-Fried, Sage-Scented Zucchini Pancakes on page 319), which would fall apart when plunged in hot oil, are sometimes better pan-fried than deep-fried. Whereas sautéing requires only enough oil to prevent the vegetables from sticking to the pan, pan-frying is used when more fat or oil is required to flavor the vegetables or get them to brown evenly. And unlike deep-fried vegetables, which are cooked completely submerged in hot oil, pan-fried vegetables are cooked in only enough oil to come halfway up their sides. For this reason, pan-fried vegetables must be turned over, usually halfway through the cooking.

Deep-Frying

Deep-frying is cooking foods completely submerged in extremely hot oil; it is the quickest way to cook a vegetable. Deep-frying seals in the flavor of most vegetables, better than any other method. When done well, the vegetables absorb very little oil and remain light and crispy. Some vegetables, such as potatoes, are best fried without any coating, while other vegetables, especially leafy greens, are best coated with a light batter before they are plunged into the hot oil.

Frying has been so maligned in recent years that it has become almost synonymous with unhealthy eating. It's easy to understand how frying got this reputation—just walk outside a restaurant that deep-fries and smell the rancid oil, or try a plateful of cheap fish and chips. But careful frying, with fresh olive oil and a feather-light batter that crackles under your teeth as you nibble gingerly at the almost-too-hot vegetables, is too wonderful to give up. And it's a surprise to discover that fried vegetables keep their flavor better than vegetables cooked using any other technique and that they absorb very little oil.

EQUIPMENT FOR DEEP-FRYING

Deep-frying can be dangerous if done in a flimsy or too-shallow pot. Working with the hot oil can also be risky if you have only a regular spoon to scoop out the hot vegetables. So if you deep-fry with any regularity, you may find it worthwhile to invest in a few simple implements.

DEEP-FRY THERMOMETER. If you deep-fry a lot, you'll learn to judge the temperature of the oil by how the vegetables behave when they're dropped in, but if you're frying for the first time, you'll feel more comfortable if you arm yourself with a deep-fry thermometer.

ELECTRIC DEEP-FRYERS, ELECTRIC FRYING PANS. Both of these make frying easier because they have their own thermostats so you're not constantly adjusting the heat of the stove to keep the oil at the right temperature.

FRYING BASKETS. A frying basket makes it easy to lower and raise a batch of vegetables into and out of the oil all at once. A frying basket is especially handy for making french fries, which have to be dipped twice into the oil.

POTS. Choose a pot that is heavy enough so it won't slide around easily if you happen to bump it and that will retain heat. A large pot helps keep the temperature of the oil constant so you're not constantly fiddling with the heat to adjust the temperature. Whatever size pot you do choose, to prevent spattering and overflow, don't fill it more than half full with oil.

SLOTTED SPOONS. These will work for frying small amounts of vegetables but have the disadvantage of bringing up too much oil when you spoon out the vegetables. You're better off using a spider (see below).

SPIDERS. These gadgets are well named because they look like spider webs with long handles attached to one side. A spider is a great alternative to a frying basket if you're working with small amounts of vegetables or are deep-frying in something relatively shallow, such as a skillet, electric frying pan, or wok.

TOWELS. Deep-fried vegetables should be drained on a plate or sheet pan covered with cloth towels to absorb excess oil before they are transferred to a plate or serving platter. Paper towels should be avoided, as they disintegrate easily and cling to the food.

WOKS. Chinese cooks prefer woks to any other vessels for almost any kind of cooking, including deep-frying. A wok is perfect if you're frying small amounts of vegetables because the vegetables can be stirred around in the oil so they brown evenly and you won't have to use much oil. Don't fill a wok more than one-quarter full with oil—the oil spills too easily. Always use a wok stand so the wok doesn't sit precariously on the stove.

OILS AND FATS FOR DEEP-FRYING

Vegetable oils, such as corn, peanut, canola, or safflower oils, are the most commonly used oils for deep-frying because they are inexpensive, relatively unsaturated, and can sustain high temperatures without burning or smoking. But your deep-fried vegetables will taste a lot better if you deep-fry in pure olive oil. While no olive oil is cheap, olive oil labeled as "pure" has been stripped of most of its flavor and is only a little more expensive than vegetable oil. Rendered animal fats, such as beef suet (the rendered white fat that surrounds the steer's kidneys), lard, and duck fat, aren't as popular as they once were, but they'll give your fried vegetables—especially french fries—superlative texture and flavor.

Any time you deep-fry you'll want to get by using as little oil or fat as possible—oils and fats are expensive and can be a nuisance to store—but keep in mind that the more oil or fat you use, the easier it is to control the temperature. If a large number of sliced vegetables are added to a small amount of oil, the temperature of the oil will drop and you'll end up frying at too low a temperature; your vegetables will absorb too much oil and will end up greasy. Don't fry too many vegetables at a time, and fry in at least 3 inches of oil.

FRYING TEMPERATURES

Most vegetables are fried at a relatively high temperature—around 360°F. Because the vegetables are cut into manageable-size pieces, they cook very quickly. If the oil or fat isn't hot enough, the vegetables will absorb too much oil and end up greasy; if the oil is too hot, the vegetables will brown unevenly and the insides will be raw. Larger pieces of vegetables and the first stage of cooking french fries are started at a lower temperature, 320° to 350°F. Pieces of vegetables for frying should be allowed to come up to room temperature (if they've been in the refrigerator) so they don't further lower the temperature of the oil.

If you don't have a deep-fry thermometer, you'll need to judge the temperature of the oil by sight and smell. To do this, just put one of the coated pieces of vegetable into the oil and see what happens. If the vegetable sinks and doesn't rise to the top within a second or two, the oil isn't hot enough. If the vegetable floats and is immediately surrounded by bubbles, the oil or fat is probably near the right temperature. Watch the vegetable and see how long it takes for the coating to turn to the right color. (This will depend on the coating: flour, or flour and water batter, should turn ever so slightly brown—ivory—while leavened batters and batters containing egg should turn a pale golden brown.) Most vegetables, if thinly sliced, should be done in just a few minutes, but check the individual recipes.

STORING AND REUSING OILS AND FATS

Oil usually can be reused at least once or twice, but if it turns dark or smells burnt, throw it out. (Don't pour it down the sink. Let it cool, put it in a tightly closed bottle, and put it in the garbage or recycle it.)

To store oil or fat that's been used for frying but that still smells and looks good, let it cool and strain it through a fine-mesh strainer—or a nylon stocking—into a clean bottle or jar to eliminate minute particles that burn and spoil the oil's flavor and color. Store the used oil, tightly sealed, in the refrigerator.

COATINGS AND BATTERS FOR DEEP-FRYING

While some vegetables (especially potatoes and root vegetables) can be deep-fried with no coating at all, other vegetables (such as zucchini, eggplant, mushrooms) will absorb too much oil unless coated with an impermeable batter or coating. The batter also gives the vegetable a pleasant crispy crunch and helps seal in the vegetable's flavor.

Coatings for deep-fried vegetables can be very simple—seasonings and flour alone make one of the best—or more involved, containing eggs, various seasonings, and sometimes bread crumbs. Some of the lightest coatings for deep-frying are made by incorporating air or carbon dioxide into the batter. Beaten egg whites, baking powder, club soda, beer, and yeast can all be used to produce this effect. While all of these batters can be used in the same way, they each produce a subtly different effect—you'll probably want to experiment and find which one you prefer.

FLOUR. One of the best and easiest ways to coat vegetables for deep-frying is to season them with salt and pepper and then roll them in all-purpose flour, patting off any excess. A good way to get rid of the extra flour is to toss the floured vegetables in a large medium-mesh strainer—or even better on a drum sieve—over a bowl so you shake off the extra flour without wasting it.

Properly deep-fried flour-coated vegetables have an almost imperceptible crispiness, and because the outer coating is so thin, they absorb very little oil. Deep-fry flour-coated vegetables until they take on a pale golden color—never let them turn dark brown.

FLOUR AND WATER BATTER. Deep-fried sliced vegetables coated with a batter of flour and water stay light and crispy and absorb very little oil. The vegetables should be deep-fried only until they turn a pale ivory color, not distinctly brown.

To prepare 2 cups of batter, slowly work $1^1/_2$ cups of water into 1 cup all-purpose flour with a whisk. Initially add only enough water to form a smooth medium-thick paste. This allows you to eliminate lumps before you add the rest of the liquid. If you add all the liquid at once, the lumps will remain. If, after all this, there are still lumps in the batter, strain it. Let the batter rest at room temperature for at least 30 minutes so the gluten in the flour has a chance to relax. Otherwise the batter may shrink and break during frying and leave pieces of the vegetables exposed.

Batter for frying.

FLUFFY EGG WHITE BATTER. Prepare a light flour and water batter by combining $^3/_4$ cup all-purpose flour with 1 cup cold water. Work the water into the flour slowly with a whisk to eliminate lumps. Let the mixture rest for 30 minutes. Shortly before you're ready to deep-fry, beat 3 egg whites with 1 teaspoon of salt in a copper bowl or in an electric mixer. If you're not using a copper bowl, add a pinch of cream of tartar to the egg whites before beating. Fold the egg whites into the flour batter with a rubber spatula.

CLUB SODA OR BEER BATTER. This batter is very light and the crispiest of all. Because the carbon dioxide in the club soda dissipates quickly, this batter needs to be made at the last minute. Starting out with $1^1/_2$ cups of club soda, use a whisk to stir just enough club soda (or beer) into 1 cup all-purpose flour to make a smooth paste. Work the mixture as little as possible. Gently stir in the rest of the club soda. Use immediately.

BAKING POWDER BATTER. This crispy batter is similar to a club soda batter because the baking powder produces carbon dioxide as soon as it comes in contact with water.

Sift 1 cup all-purpose flour with 2 teaspoons baking powder. Stir the mixture thoroughly until the baking powder is distributed throughout the flour. Just before deep-frying, use a whisk to quickly stir $^1/_2$ cup water into the flour to obtain a paste. Gently stir in another $^1/_2$ cup water and use immediately.

YEAST BATTER. This is a slightly thicker batter than the club soda or baking powder batter, but it's also extremely light and crispy because of the carbon dioxide produced by the yeast. Slowly stir $^3/_4$ cup warm (not hot) water into $^1/_2$ cup all-purpose flour in a 2-quart mixing bowl to make a smooth paste. Stir in 1 teaspoon active dried yeast and let rise, covered with plastic wrap, in a warm place for about 1 hour, until the batter has doubled in size.

BEATEN EGG AND BREAD CRUMBS. Some vegetables, such as tomatoes, need an especially impermeable coating to prevent them from absorbing too much oil. To coat vegetables with eggs and bread crumbs, roll the vegetable pieces in all-purpose flour, pat off the excess, and then dip the vegetables in beaten egg well seasoned with salt and pepper. Coat the vegetables with bread crumbs, preferably homemade (see below). You

---

⚬ MAKING YOUR OWN BREAD CRUMBS ⚬

Bread crumbs sold in boxes are often stale and are so coarse that they absorb too much oil. The best bread crumb coatings are made with fresh homemade bread crumbs. To make your own bread crumbs, cut the crusts off several slices of slightly stale, dense-crumbed white bread. (I use Pepperidge Farm white bread.) If the bread isn't stale, heat the slices for about 20 minutes in a 250°F oven to dry them out slightly but not completely. Zap the bread in a food processor and work the crumbs through a strainer or, better yet, through a drum sieve.

✺ FRITTO MISTO ∞

Among the delights of eating in Italy are platefuls of deep-fried food—*fritto misto*—so light that it's hard to imagine the vegetables ever touched a drop of oil. Almost any vegetable can be fried and turned into a light and elegant first course or hors d'oeuvre. You can fry a single type of vegetable, but frying two or three is no harder than frying one and makes a more dramatic impression. Once fried, the vegetables immediately should be passed around on a tray (as an hors d'oeuvre) or arranged on hot plates as a first course.

Vegetables for frying should be cut small enough so they cook quickly and don't have a chance to absorb much oil, but not so small that you can't recognize their shape. It doesn't make a lot of difference what shape you settle on—slices, sticks, or wedges—as long as all the pieces are about the same size so they cook evenly. If you're cooking more than one type of vegetable at a time, time the vegetables so you can fish them out of the oil at the same time. You will need 4 cups of cut vegetables to serve four as a first-course or six for hors d'oeuvres.

For most vegetables, any of the batters suggested on pages 15–16 will make an excellent coating, but some vegetables—such as tomatoes—will absorb too much oil if they're not coated in a relatively thick batter, such as beaten egg and bread crumbs.

Fritto Misto.

can also use packaged Japanese bread crumbs, called panko, which make a very light and crunchy coating and don't have the stale flavor I associate with most breadcrumbs in a jar.

SAUCES AND CONDIMENTS FOR FRIED VEGETABLES

The easiest and often best condiment for fried vegetables—or fried anything—is a squeeze of fresh lemon. But good vinegar is also interesting, especially on french fries (think of malt vinegar on fish and chips), and homemade mayonnaise, a Belgian favorite, is really great. Try some different homemade flavored mayonnaises, butters, and sauces (see pages 365–371).

DEEP-FRYING SAFETY TIPS

1. Use a heavy pot, wok, skillet, deep-fryer, or electric frying pan for deep-frying. It's important that the pot sit firmly on the stove or work surface so that if you bump it, it won't move around.

2. Never fill the pot for deep-frying more than half full of oil. Woks should never be more than one-quarter filled.

3. Keep the deep-frying pot set back, such as on one of the back burners of the stove, so you don't bump into it.

4. Make sure the deep-fryer or deep-frying pot is completely dry before you put in the oil. Any traces of liquid cause the oil to spatter.

5. Add vegetables to the oil with a spoon or spider, never with your fingers. Oil could splash up and burn you.

6. Add the vegetables slowly, especially at the beginning. Don't add too many pieces of vegetable at once or the oil could overflow. Test a few pieces at a time to get a sense of how much the oil froths up.

7. Have a box of baking soda handy in case the oil spills over and starts a grease fire. Water will only spread the fire. If a fire starts, pour over a lot of baking soda—don't skimp.

DEEP-FRYING VEGETABLES

The amounts suggested are to serve four to six. If you're serving more than one vegetable, adjust the amount of each vegetable you use (e.g., for two vegetables, halve the amounts; for four, quarter the amounts). The batters are found on pages 19–20.

ARTICHOKES. You can use 3 or 4 medium or 2 or 3 large turned artichokes with the chokes removed and cut into wedges, about a dozen baby artichokes (leaves trimmed off, halved lengthwise), or a 9-ounce package of frozen artichoke hearts, thawed and patted dry. Dip the pieces of artichoke in one of the suggested batters and fry at 360°F for about 3 1/2 minutes.

ASPARAGUS. Cut off the bottom inch or two of 1 pound of asparagus. Unless very thin, peel. Dip the asparagus in any of the suggested batters and fry at 360°F for 1 to 3 minutes, depending on thickness.

BROCCOLI. Cut a large bunch of broccoli into florets about 1 inch wide at the widest part. You can peel the larger stalk—the central trunk—and cut it into 1/8-inch-thick slices, but this is optional. Dip in the club soda batter—or other batter—and fry at 360°F for about 3 minutes.

CARDOONS. If the cardoons weigh more than 3 pounds, pull off and discard the outermost stalks. Pull off the inner, tender stalks and peel them with a paring knife or vegetable peeler. Cut them into 3-inch lengths and toss in fresh lemon juice. Dip in any of the suggested batters and fry at 360°F for about 3 minutes.

CAULIFLOWER. Cut a large head of cauliflower into florets about 1 inch wide at the widest part. Dip in any of the suggested batters and fry at 360°F for 3 minutes.

CELERIAC. Peel the celeriac with a paring knife (a vegetable peeler doesn't cut deeply enough) and slice it thinly as you would for potato chips with a vegetable slicer. If the celeriac is too large, cut it in half before slicing. Fry the chips in 350°F oil—you don't need batter—for about 1¹/₂ minutes.

EGGPLANT. Peel 1¹/₂ pounds eggplant and cut it into strips about ³/₈ inch thick and anywhere between 2 and 5 inches long. Dip in the club soda batter or flour and water batter and fry about a dozen at a time in 360°F oil until pale golden brown, about 4 minutes.

FENNEL. Fennel can be somewhat tough if it isn't cut into fairly small pieces. But be careful; if you don't cut fennel just right, it can fall apart. Peel the fennel and cut it into thin wedges about ¹/₄ inch wide at the thickest end. Dip the wedges in any of the suggested batters and fry in 360°F oil for 3 minutes.

KALE. Kale leaves, stems and all, become surprisingly delicate when deep-fried. If the leaves are large, cut them into 2-inch-wide strips. Coat the leaves with batter and fry in 370°F oil for about 1 minute.

MUSHROOMS. Cut the mushrooms into ¹/₄-inch-thick slices, coat in batter, and fry in 360°F oil for about 2 minutes.

ONIONS. For those of us who have encountered onion rings only in restaurants, homemade rings made with sweet onions and cooked in fresh oil are a highly addictive revelation. Onion rings are best when made with sweet onions, such as Maui or Vidalia, but red onions are also excellent. Peel and cut the onions into ¹/₄-inch-thick slices. Separate the slices into rings, dip the onion rings in any of the suggested batters, and fry in 360°F oil for 3 minutes.

PARSLEY. Amazing, but true, you can fry small sprigs of curly parsley in 370°F oil for 5 to 10 seconds and the parsley comes out bright green and crisp. Make sure the parsley is perfectly dry (don't use batter)—pat it with paper towels—and put a small handful at a time in the oil. As soon as it stops crackling, take it out of the oil and drain on paper towels. (Paper towels stick to some vegetables, but not to parsley.)

PARSNIPS. Peel 1 pound of parsnips and use a vegetable slicer to slice them to the same thickness as potato chips. Fry, without batter, for 1 to 1¹/₂ minutes in 350°F oil.

PLANTAINS. These chips are a good substitute for bread, rice, or potatoes when serving a bowl of spicy soup. Cut the ends off 2 green plantains and peel the plantains with a sharp paring knife. Keep the peeled plantains in a bowl of cold water, to keep them from turning dark, until you're ready to fry. Heat the oil to 360°F. Slice the plantains into paper-thin disks with a vegetable slicer and fry them—don't use any batter—about one-quarter of them at a time, until they turn golden brown, about 3 minutes.

POTATOES. See pages 275–277 for making french fries and potato chips.

SORREL. Your guests will be delighted to bite into a crispy and surprisingly tangy sorrel leaf. Leave the stems on the leaves so guests will have something to hold onto. Dip the leaves in any of the suggested batters, and fry for 15 seconds in 370°F oil.

SPINACH. Leave the stems on, dip the leaves in any of the suggested batters, and fry for 15 seconds in 370°F oil.

SWEET POTATOES. Peel the sweet potatoes and slice them into paper-thin chips with a vegetables slicer. Dip the chips in a flour and water batter and fry for 3 minutes in 360°F oil.

SWISS CHARD. Both the stems and leaves of Swiss chard are delicious deep-fried. Cut the leaves away from the stems of 1 bunch chard with a sharp paring knife. Wash and dry the leaves and cut the stems into 3-inch-long pieces. If the leaves are larger than a couple of inches at any point, tear them into strips about 2 inches wide. Dip both the leaves and stems in any of the suggested batters. Deep-fry the leaves and stems at 360°F for about 2 minutes.

TOMATOES. Cut firm ripe tomatoes into $1/4$-inch-thick slices. Pat with flour, dip in seasoned beaten egg, and coat with bread crumbs. Fry in 360°F oil for about 3 minutes.

TURNIPS. Peel turnips and thinly slice them (like potato chips) with a vegetable cutter. Fry for 1 to $1^1/2$ minutes in 350°F oil. Don't use batter.

ZUCCHINI AND SUMMER SQUASH. Slice 2 medium zucchini or yellow squash (about 1 pound total) into $1/8$-inch-thick rounds or cut into french-fry shapes. Heat the oil to 360°F, dip the slices in a club soda batter or one of the other batters, and fry the slices for about $2^1/2$ minutes, until they turn a pale golden brown.

ZUCCHINI FLOWERS. See page 318.

Grilling

Grilling is cooking over a heat source, traditionally a bed of coals. Even when a gas grill is used, grilled vegetables take on a light smoky flavor.

Grilling over a bed of coals is one of the easiest ways to cook vegetables during the hot summer months when you don't want to hover over a hot stove. Grilled vegetables go beautifully with other grilled foods, and they let you cook an entire meal outside on the barbecue without cooking anything in the kitchen.

Few cooking methods are simpler than grilling, nor are there many other methods that provide us with the primal satisfaction of cooking with real fire. The only problem that you may encounter when grilling vegetables, especially for a crowd, is that they take up a lot of room on the grill. A couple of zucchini, for example, cut lengthwise into thin strips, will cover a large barbecue and leave you with no room for cooking your main course. To avoid this problem you can just buy another grill—nothing fancy, the simple hibachis sold at most hardware stores are perfectly fine—or rig up a system for keeping the rest of your food warm while you're grilling the vegetables. My own little grill sits on the ground, so I set a metal patio table next to the grill—actually somewhat over it—to keep foods set on the table warm while I'm grilling other things.

Grilled vegetables don't require anything more than a good, hot fire from wood coals or a gas grill (or even a broiler or grill pan, if you're "grilling" vegetables inside) and a little oil to coat the vegetables to keep them from sticking. But you can work wonders with a few herbs. Try marinating the vegetables for a few minutes by tossing them in extra-virgin olive oil and chopped fresh herbs, such as marjoram, thyme, savory, rosemary, sage, oregano, hyssop leaves or flowers, or lavender flowers. If you're grilling more than one type of vegetable—or for that matter, just one vegetable—experiment with separating the sliced vegetables and marinating them with different herbs so that even though the vegetables may look the same, they'll all be flavored differently.

Grilling endive and radicchio.

Other more delicate herbs, such as basil, parsley, mint, chervil, and tarragon, can be sprinkled on the vegetables or combined with a little oil and brushed on just before the vegetables are served. The delicate herbs lose their flavor quickly, especially if they're exposed to heat, so they are best added as soon as the vegetables come off the grill.

Most vegetables can be sliced or cut into pieces and grilled directly, but some vegetables—such as artichokes and fennel—won't cook through on the grill and have to be boiled for a few minutes and drained before they are ready for grilling. Smaller vegetables should be threaded onto skewers and grilled as kebabs or the vegetables might fall through the spaces in the grill. If you're using wooden skewers, arrange the vegetables on the skewer with none of the wood exposed so the skewer doesn't burn where it's not covered by vegetables.

GRILLING WITH WOOD OR CHARCOAL

While many of us avoid the rites of fire building in favor of instant-light briquettes, electric fire starters, or gas-powered grills, the careful tending of a fire is among the most satisfying of cooking rituals. Cooking with wood or charcoal also gives foods an inimitable and satisfying outdoor flavor.

Many of us are stumped by how to light a fire in the first place. There are a number of gadgets sold to solve the problem how to light a fire, but the most elegant in its simplicity (and low cost) is a chimney—a gadget shaped like an oversized tin can with a handle on the side. You just fill the top three-quarters of the cylinder with charcoal, stuff newspaper in the bottom, set the whole contrivance on the bottom of the grill, and light the newspaper. It takes 30 to 45 minutes for the coals to heat completely and start to glow. You then you just dump them out into the barbecue.

The easiest and least expensive way to scent foods with the taste of wood smoke (unless you have access to a lot of wood) is to build the fire with charcoal briquettes (not the self-lighting kind, which smell like kerosene). Then add a couple of handfuls of wood chips (soaked in water for 30 minutes) when the briquettes are all lit. When you add the chips, you're ready to start grilling. The best woods are hardwoods, such as maple or hickory, or fruit woods, such as apple, cherry, or pear, or mesquite, which imparts a somewhat stronger flavor. Avoid resinous woods, such as pine or eucalyptus, which will flare up and give an acrid taste to foods.

When your fire is ready—the coals are glowing bright red—adjust the grill rack so it's about 4 inches above the coals. Put the vegetables on the grill and start grilling. If the vegetables are taking too long to cook, or if they're browning too quickly, adjust the height of the grill accordingly. If you're cooking slow-cooking vegetables such as relatively large pieces of root vegetables, you may want to partially cover the barbecue.

GRILLING WITH A GRILL PAN

When the urge to grill strikes us at midnight or the day after Christmas when there's snow on the ground, we may not feel like going out and building a fire. A grill pan offers a quick solution. When buying a grill pan, buy the heaviest one you can find. The weight of the metal is important so that it will retain and transmit heat. When using the grill pan, put it over high heat for about 5 minutes before adding the vegetables.

Meat and vegetable kebabs on a grill pan.

❧ TERIYAKI SAUCE ☙

One of the most versatile and useful sauces for grilling is teriyaki sauce. You can buy teriyaki sauce in little bottles at the supermarket, or you can make your own by combining mirin—a sweet rice wine for cooking—and soy sauce. If you're in a bind, just add a little sugar to soy sauce for a makeshift but perfectly acceptable teriyaki sauce. To make enough teriyaki sauce for four servings of grilled vegetables, combine in a small mixing bowl 3 tablespoons Japanese dark soy sauce and 2 tablespoons mirin (sweet rice wine) or 2 teaspoons sugar (instead of the mirin), dissolved in 1 tablespoon water. Brush your vegetables with teriyaki sauce during grilling. The sauce can also be used as a marinade.

Grilled Mixed Vegetable Kebabs

One of the easiest and prettiest ways to grill vegetables is to cut an assortment of vegetables into same-size pieces or slices and thread them onto skewers. Some vegetables may need to be precooked but most can just be slid on skewers raw. This recipe is an example of just one combination—make up your own according to what you find in the market or have growing in your garden. You can thread each type of vegetable onto separate skewers, which allows you to control the cooking of the individual vegetables, or, for a more colorful effect, mix the vegetables on each skewer.

MAKES 8 SIDE-DISH SERVINGS

8 baby artichokes, or 2 large artichokes, or 1 (9-ounce) package frozen artichoke hearts

3 tablespoons extra-virgin olive oil

Salt

8 small cultivated or wild mushrooms

8 (walnut-size) white boiling onions, peeled and halved vertically

1 medium zucchini or summer squash, halved lengthwise, each half cut crosswise into 8 pieces

1 medium red bell pepper, halved crosswise, stemmed, seeded, and each half cut into 8 equal pieces

1 tablespoon chopped fresh marjoram, or 2 teaspoons chopped fresh thyme

Freshly ground black pepper

Trim the tops and leaves off the baby artichokes; if you're using large artichokes, trim them as shown on page 97. Simmer the baby artichokes or artichoke bottoms in water for about 15 minutes, or until they soften slightly. Cut baby artichokes in half from top to bottom and the large artichoke bottoms in quarters. If you're using frozen artichokes, let them thaw. Toss the artichokes in 1 tablespoon of the olive oil and sprinkle with salt.

Thread the artichokes, mushrooms, onions, zucchini, and bell peppers onto wooden or metal skewers. If you're using wooden skewers, make sure the vegetables are right next to each other so the skewers don't burn. You can also wrap the ends of the wooden skewers—what's not covered by vegetables—in a little piece of aluminum foil to prevent them from burning.

Put the skewers on a baking dish or plate, brush them with the remaining 2 tablespoons olive oil, and sprinkle with the fresh herbs. Sprinkle with salt and pepper.

Grill the kebabs over a hot fire—you'll need to regulate the cooking by moving the kebabs farther away from or closer to the heat, but 4 to 6 inches above the heat is usually about right. Grill the vegetables for about 7 minutes, turning every couple of minutes so they cook evenly and brushing with the herbs and olive oil left in the pan. Serve hot, either alone or with one of the flavored mayonnaises suggested on page 368.

VARIATION:

Toss the grilled vegetables with a little olive oil and vinegar to make a delightful salad.

Vegetable Kebabs.

Mixed Vegetable Grill

This recipe is more a series of suggestions than anything else. The fun is deciding which vegetables to grill, depending on what you find at the market or have growing. Remember, too, that a mixed vegetable grill can be a simple affair with two or three vegetables—maybe designed to accompany meat or fish at a barbecue. Or, it can take center stage and become the main course in a summer meal with various sauces. If you're using small vegetables, such as mushrooms and pearl onions, thread them onto skewers so they don't fall through the spaces in the grill. One or more of the mayonnaises suggested on page 368 can be served at the table with the vegetables.

MAKES 6 MAIN-COURSE OR 12 SIDE-DISH SERVINGS

If you are using large artichokes, simmer for 15 minutes in a large pot of water. Then drain and remove the choke. Toss the artichokes in 1 tablespoon of olive oil, sprinkle with 1 teaspoon of the herbs and salt and pepper, and let marinate for 30 minutes to 2 hours.

Spread the zucchini slices in a baking dish and toss them with 1 tablespoon of the olive oil, 1 teaspoon of the chopped herbs, and salt and pepper. Let marinate for 30 minutes to 2 hours.

If the mushrooms are larger than 1 inch across at the widest part, cut them into halves. Toss the mushrooms with 1 tablespoon of the olive oil, 1 teaspoon of the chopped herbs and salt and pepper. Let marinate for 30 minutes to 2 hours.

Rub the garlic into the flat side of the tomatoes. Sprinkle each tomato with 1 teaspoon of the herbs and salt and pepper. Let marinate for 30 minutes to 2 hours.

Arrange the onion slices in a baking dish and rub them with 1 tablespoon of olive oil. Sprinkle with 1 teaspoon of the herbs and salt and pepper, and let marinate for 30 minutes to 2 hours.

Grill the vegetables on a hot grill for 5 to 10 minutes for the most part (tomatoes take longer)—take each vegetable off as it browns and softens and looks ready. Brush the vegetables with the chopped basil and serve immediately on a hot platter.

6 baby artichokes, trimmed and cut in half, or 2 large artichokes, prepared as shown on page 97 and each cut into 6 pieces, or 1 (9-ounce) package frozen artichoke hearts, thawed, patted dry

4 to 6 tablespoons extra-virgin olive oil

5 teaspoons chopped fresh herbs, such as thyme, marjoram, rosemary, lavender flowers, savory, and hyssop (use as few or as many as you like) chopped with 1 tablespoon olive oil (the oil prevents blackening)

Salt and freshly ground black pepper

1 medium zucchini, trimmed and cut lengthwise into 1/8-inch-thick slices

12 medium cultivated or wild mushrooms

2 cloves garlic, minced and crushed to a paste

6 ripe medium tomatoes, halved and seeded

2 medium red onions, cut into 1/3-inch-thick slices

1 medium red bell pepper, halved lengthwise, stemmed, seeded, each half cut into 3 strips

1 medium yellow bell pepper, halved lengthwise, stemmed, seeded, and each half cut into 3 strips

20 fresh basil leaves, finely chopped

Broiling

For lovers of grilled vegetables who may not feel like lighting their grill in a rainstorm or in the dead of winter, there is always the broiler. To broil vegetables, line a baking sheet with aluminum foil, brush the foil with olive oil, and spread the vegetables on top.

Broiling indoors produces some of the same effects as grilling outdoors on a barbecue. The main difference is that a grill provides heat from below and a broiler provides heat from above. Experiment with different positions and different distances between the food and the heat source.

Roasting

Vegetables are roasted in the oven without any liquid except for a small amount of oil or butter to coat them and seal in their moisture. The oven's dry heat concentrates the flavor of the vegetables and seals in the vegetables' natural juices.

Roasted vegetables are especially savory when roasted in the same pan as a nice meat roast. To roast vegetables with meat, just put the vegetables in the roasting pan with a leg of lamb, a chicken, or a roast beef. The vegetables roast at the same time as the meat and absorb the meat's flavorful juices. You need only to coordinate the timing, adding vegetables at different stages during the roasting so that everything is done at the same time.

While vegetables can be roasted whole (they need only be peeled and coated with oil or melted butter to prevent drying out), most of the time they are cut into manageable pieces. Carrots and parsnips can be cut into cylinders an inch or two long or they can be cut into wedges as shown on pages 3 and 259. Turnips, celeriac, and rutabaga can be cut into wedges or sticks and, if you're being meticulous, the sharp edges trimmed off by turning.

When roasting vegetables with meat, move the vegetables around in the pan every 20 minutes or so with a long spoon so they're coated with juices and roast evenly. If you have a nice looking roasting pan, you can bring the roast, surrounded with vegetables, straight into the dining room, where it will make an impressive sight.

If you're roasting vegetables alone, without meat, be sure to coat them with a light layer of melted butter or olive oil to prevent them from drying out in the oven. Make sure that no part of the surface of the pan is visible— if it is, juices can run onto this exposed section and burn.

While the recipes given here are for more than one vegetable, more often than not we're likely to only want to roast one or two vegetables.

TIPS FOR ROASTING VEGETABLES

1. Always use a heavy roasting pan. Vegetables release juices as they roast. If the roasting pan is thin, it will be too hot in spots and the vegetable juices will burn.

2. Use a roasting pan just large enough to hold the vegetables in a single layer. If there aren't enough vegetables in the pan, the pan will get too hot and may cause the vegetables to burn. If too many vegetables are heaped into the pan, some of the vegetables won't brown properly—they'll steam instead of roast.

3. Make sure the vegetables are lightly coated with fat. You don't need much, but a little olive oil or melted butter will seal in their moisture and keep them from drying out. The fat also helps the vegetables to brown evenly.

4. If you notice the vegetables or their juices in the roasting pan becoming too brown or if they're threatening to burn, add a little liquid—just enough to barely cover the bottom of the pan. Technically this turns the roast vegetables into glazed vegetables (see Glazing, page 35), but the liquid—a little water or broth—will prevent burning.

5. Most vegetables should be peeled, but the peels of very tender baby vegetables, such as turnips, carrots, and beets can be left on. Vegetables with soft peels, such as zucchini or summer squash, do not need to be peeled.

WHAT'S THE DIFFERENCE BETWEEN ROASTING AND BAKING?

We often see recipes using the terms "baking" and "roasting" interchangeably. Other than the fact that baking often applies to desserts (we never talk about roasting a cake), and roasting applies to meats and vegetables, what is the difference?

Traditionally roasting meant cooking on a spit in the open air in front of a roaring fire. Nowadays we almost always roast in the oven, but we try to duplicate as best as possible the conditions of spit roasting—high heat and no moisture so that the outer surface of food browns and seals in flavors.

Baking is much the same, but it implies a gentler process of using lower heat to penetrate foods without browning them, at least not right away. Most gratins are baked, as are larger vegetables or stuffed vegetables that require more time for the heat of the oven to penetrate.

Roasted Assorted Fall and Winter Vegetables

Almost any vegetable can be roasted as long as you peel and cut the vegetable so it cooks evenly and looks attractive on the plate or platter. Root vegetables are the most obvious fall and winter vegetables, and many of the vegetables that you may want to roast in the spring are the same as in the winter, only larger. Large whole winter root vegetables, such as turnips, celeriac, carrots, parsnips, beets, and onions can be awkward to cook and hard to serve. Because of this, root vegetables are usually cut into pieces so they cook more quickly and evenly and look presentable at the table.

The simplest way to prepare root vegetables for roasting is just to peel them and then cut them into pieces—usually wedges or cylinders—all about the same size. Professional cooks like to turn the vegetables to get rid of sharp edges and to make the vegetables easier to stir around in the pan so they cook evenly.

The recipe given here will make 10 side-dish servings if you use all the vegetables. If you can't find all the vegetables or don't want to bother, just use fewer and either increase the amounts of the other vegetables or count on serving fewer guests.

MAKES 10 SIDE-DISH SERVINGS

Cut the carrot pieces lengthwise into wedges all the same size.

Cut the turnip, celeriac, and parsnips into thick sticks about the same size as the carrot pieces. You can leave the sticks with square edges, but they'll be easier to move around in the roasting pan if you trim the edges slightly so the vegetables have an elongated cylindrical shape with rounded edges.

Preheat the oven to 400°F.

Trim any brown spots off the mushrooms and toss the mushrooms with 2 tablespoons of the oil. Put the carrots, turnip, celeriac, parsnips, mushrooms, onions, chestnuts, and garlic, and remaining 3 tablespoons oil in a heavy-bottomed roasting pan (or a couple of cast-iron skillets) just large enough to hold the vegetables in a single layer. Sprinkle the vegetables with salt and stir them around in the pan(s) so they're all coated with fat.

Roast the vegetables for 1 to 1½ hours. (The exact time will depend on the size of your roasting pan.) Gently stir the vegetables around twice during the cooking so they brown evenly. Take the vegetables out of the oven when they're all easily penetrated with a knife, but not mushy. Sprinkle with salt, pepper, and the chopped parsley. Serve immediately in the roasting pan or on a platter.

2 medium carrots, peeled and cut into 1½-inch pieces

1 medium turnip, peeled

1 medium celeriac, peeled

2 medium parsnips, peeled

10 medium mushrooms, preferably cremini or shiitake

5 tablespoons extra-virgin olive oil, clarified butter or ghee (see page 149), or goose or duck fat

10 (walnut-size) white boiling onions, peeled

10 fresh chestnuts, shelled and peeled (see pages 151–152), or 20 bottled chestnuts

10 large cloves garlic (don't use elephant garlic)

Salt and freshly ground black pepper

2 tablespoons finely chopped fresh parsley

Roasted root vegetables.

I use pork in several forms. Bacon, which is actually smoked breast of pork, can be gently rendered and the fat used as a replacement for butter, olive oil, or other cooking fats. The bacon itself can be cut into thin strips or little cubes, gently cooked, and sprinkled on vegetables to give the vegetables a savory note of salty smokiness.

Sometimes bacon's smokiness is overpowering, and something gentler is called for. Pancetta is Italian-style bacon—again, fatty cuts of pork—that is simply cured with salt and sometimes various spice or herb mixtures.

Prosciutto is another important pork product that can be used in several ways. One of the easiest is to cut thin slices into 1-inch strips and then toss these with hot vegetables a minute before serving. The fat on the outside of the prosciutto is also useful stuff. You can cut it off the edges of sliced prosciutto or have the store trim off the rind and then slice you a strip of fat. Finely chop the fat and cook gently until it renders liquid fat, which you can then use for sautéing vegetables or gently sweating aromatic vegetables for soups or stews. When cooking with prosciutto fat or pancetta fat, don't let the fat get too hot—it should never begin to smoke—or you'll destroy its delicate flavor.

Preserved duck—duck confit—and duck fat can be used to give a special, delicate flavor to vegetables. The duck fat that's released when you slowly cook duck will keep in the refrigerator for months. You can use it to sauté vegetables (and for that matter, just about anything) as a substitute for less flavorful fats.

Braising

Nowadays there's such an emphasis on the freshness, crunchiness, and bright colors of most vegetables that we've forgotten the slow, gentle cooking of the past. True, some vegetables are easily ruined if overcooked, but other vegetables, especially older vegetables, dried vegetables, and cabbage, are better if they're braised slowly in a covered pot so their flavors release and their textures soften.

To braise is to cook over low heat, in a small amount of liquid, for a relatively long time. Unlike boiling, which requires a large amount of water and cooks very quickly, and unlike steaming, which cooks the vegetables as they are suspended over the boiling water, braising concentrates the flavors of the vegetables in a very small amount of liquid; this savory and nutritious liquid then becomes a natural sauce for the vegetables. Braising and stewing are much the same thing, except that vegetable stews often contain more than one vegetable—and sometimes meats—and more elaborate vegetable stews may combine vegetables that have been cooked using a variety of techniques (see Making Stews, page 56, for more about these dishes).

Almost any vegetable can be braised, but vegetables that are somewhat tough and have a full flavor work best. Older green vegetables, dried beans and lentils, cabbage, and root vegetables all benefit from braising. Root vegetables are best when glazed, a method of braising partially covered so the vegetable's natural juices coat the vegetable in a savory glaze (see page 35).

BRAISING GREEN VEGETABLES

Most of us like to cook green vegetables quickly so they stay bright green and slightly crunchy. But there are advantages to slow cooking in a covered pot. The flavors of strong-tasting greens, such as collard greens, are softened and the textures of some green vegetables, such as kale, leeks, broccoli, and cabbage end up being more palatable. And there are those who claim that slow-cooked vegetables release their nutrients so they're more easily digested and absorbed.

The best way to braise green vegetables is to heat them gently in a covered pot on the stove or in the oven in a very small amount of liquid or, occasionally, no liquid at all—since some green vegetables release liquid of their own. Most recipes for braised vegetables include a small amount of fat: smoked pork products, such as bacon, are popular, but olive oil, butter, or goose fat can enhance the flavor of the vegetables and give them a melting suavity and savor. Cooking times for slow-cooked vegetables range from 20 minutes to 3 hours (for Southern-style collard greens).

Your braised vegetables will be most successful if you prepare a flavorful mixture of aromatic vegetables before adding the green vegetables. A mixture of chopped garlic and onion gently sweated in a little olive oil—perhaps with a pinch of thyme or marjoram—makes a delicious base for the green vegetables. You can also use more complicated mixtures of finely chopped celery, onion, carrots, garlic, and tiny cubes of bacon, prosciutto, or pancetta gently cooked in olive oil, butter, or duck fat until soft before adding the green vegetable. You can then add the green vegetables and immediately cover the pot so they cook only in their own juices, or you can add a little wine or broth. When the vegetables are cooked, you need only to stir them with a little salt and pepper and, if you like, a little butter. Chopped fresh herbs such as parsley, basil, mint, chives, tarragon, or chervil tossed with the vegetables just a few minutes before serving also give them a lovely freshness. And braised vegetables can be turned into a soup just by pouring over broth or water.

Braised Broccoli with Garlic and Olive Oil

Broccoli takes especially well to slow cooking and reveals a depth of flavor that the usual quick boiling or steaming does not. You can also use this recipe for broccoli rabe and Chinese broccoli.

MAKES 4 SIDE-DISH SERVINGS

Cut the broccoli florets away from the large central stem. The size of the florets is up to you, but I usually cut them so the flower part is about 2 inches in diameter. If you want smaller florets, cut the smaller stems just beneath each flower. If you want to use the large stems, peel them with a paring knife and slice them about the thickness of a quarter.

Heat the olive oil in a skillet with a tight-fitting lid over medium heat. Stir in the garlic and keep stirring until the garlic sizzles and smells fragrant, about 3 minutes. Stir in the sliced broccoli stems and cook for 2 minutes more. By this time the garlic should barely begin to turn brown. Add the broccoli florets and water and cover the pan. Cook covered for about 15 minutes, uncover the pan, turn the heat up to high, and cook just long enough to evaporate any liquid left in the bottom of the pan.

Sprinkle with lemon juice, salt, and pepper and serve immediately or let cool and serve as an antipasto.

VARIATIONS:

Pine nuts or slivered almonds provide a crunch that contrast well with the soft texture of the broccoli. Simply stir 2 tablespoons of pine nuts or slivered almonds into the pan at the same time as the garlic. The nuts will have a better flavor if they brown slightly before you add the broccoli.

Anchovies also give a delightful savory zest to broccoli, but not everyone likes them. Soak 6 anchovy fillets for 5 minutes in cold water—or skip the soaking if you like them strongly flavored—dry them on paper towels, and chop them coarsely. Stir them into the oil at the same time as the broccoli stems.

You can also add one or two seeded and minced jalapeños to the hot oil at the same time as the broccoli stems, or you can simply sprinkle the broccoli with dried red pepper flakes a minute or two before serving.

Raisins or dried currants are another nice touch and can be added at the same time as the broccoli florets. And, of course, you can incorporate any combination—even all—of these variations in the same dish.

I (1^1/$_2$-pound) head broccoli

2 tablespoons extra-virgin olive oil

3 cloves garlic, minced

^{1}/$_2$ cup water

I tablespoon fresh lemon juice

Salt and freshly ground black pepper

Glazing

To cook root vegetables and some nonroot vegetables so they're coated with a savory and appetizing glaze, simmer them in a sauté pan or skillet, on the stove, in just enough broth or water to come halfway up their sides. Cover the vegetables loosely with a sheet of aluminum foil or parchment paper and cook them uncovered, or forget the foil or paper and just cook the vegetables partially covered. As the vegetables cook, they release flavors into the surrounding liquid; as the liquid evaporates, it concentrates and coats the vegetables with a glaze of their own flavors. The vegetables can then be served immediately or they can be cooked slightly more so the glaze caramelizes. Glazed vegetables also can be finished with a little bit of cream, which converts the glaze into a small amount of delicious sauce, and the glazed vegetables can be sprinkled with finely chopped herbs, such as parsley, chervil, basil, or mint to give them color and a fresh flavor.

Most of the time, vegetables for glazing are cut into manageable pieces, unless they are baby vegetables, in which case they're already the right size. Ideally, root vegetables should be turned so they roll around in the pan when you give it a shake and thus glaze evenly.

The trick to glazing carrots and other root vegetables is to regulate the heat so the surrounding liquid is completely evaporated at the same time the vegetables are done. If the heat is too low, the vegetables will cook before the surrounding liquid has evaporated and formed the necessary glaze; if the heat is too high, the vegetables will remain undercooked, the surrounding liquid will evaporate, and the vegetables may even burn. Glazed vegetables can be served in dishes at the table, but they're especially dramatic when arranged on a platter with a roast.

❧ TO COVER OR NOT TO COVER ❧

The logic is simple. When simmering slow-cooking ingredients (braising)—dried beans for example—cooking with the lid on keeps the liquid from evaporating so you're not always adding liquid to keep the pot from running dry. On the other hand, it's best to cook uncovered when what you're cooking—broth, for example—requires frequent skimming and when you want to encourage evaporation to concentrate the flavors in the pot.

Cooking partially covered is a good compromise for liquids that tend to boil over in a covered pot—if your pot of beans keeps boiling over, pull the lid back an inch or two to release steam.

Recipes for glazed vegetables often suggest loosely covering the vegetables with a sheet of aluminum foil or parchment paper. The foil or paper allows liquid to evaporate into a glaze, but it also holds enough heat next to the

continued

Top to bottom: Cut out a circle of parchment paper to cover.
To glaze carrots, combine with butter and seasoning and enough water or broth to come about halfway up the sides of the pan. Place the parchment overt the carrots, leaving a small hole for escaping steam.

vegetables so those parts of the vegetables not submerged in hot liquid cook at the same rate as those that are. Glazing vegetables can be carefully controlled by moving a lid partially on and off or over the pot. When completely covered, the vegetables will continue to cook with very little evaporation. When partially covered, the vegetables will continue to cook as the glazing liquid evaporates and concentrates. When uncovered, the liquid evaporates and concentrates without the vegetables cooking.

Glazed Celeriac or Turnips

While you can glaze these vegetables in slices (see Port-Glazed Turnips with Hot Foie Gras, page 352) it's more common to cut them into smaller pieces, which should be turned into football shapes. They can also be cut into elongated strips and the edges rounded off.

1 large celeriac or 2 large turnips, peeled

2 tablespoons unsalted butter

$^1/_2$ teaspoon sugar

MAKES 4 SIDE-DISH SERVINGS

Peel and cut the vegetables into cubes as shown on page 351, adjusting the size according to your taste. Carefully trim the edges of the pieces to round them off.

Put the vegetables in a pan just large enough to hold the pieces in a single layer. Add the butter and sprinkle over the sugar. Add enough water to come halfway up the sides of the vegetables. Partially cover the pan and simmer over medium heat, rapidly moving the pan back and forth every few minutes so the vegetables cook evenly. The idea is to get the glazing liquid (the water) to evaporate at the same time the vegetables cook. After about 15 minutes, start poking the vegetables with a paring knife to judge doneness (they should be just slightly resistant). If they're underdone and there's still a lot of water in pan, turn the heat up and uncover the pan. If the water runs out before the vegetables are done, add a couple of tablespoons and turn down the heat and/or cover the pan.

When the vegetables are done and all the water has evaporated, they should be covered with a light, clear glaze. If you want a brown and deeper-flavored glaze, keep the pan over medium heat until a brown crust forms on the bottom. Add a couple of tablespoons of water to the glaze to dissolve it and get it to coat the vegetables. Boil it down slightly if necessary to get it to coat the vegetables. Serve as an accompaniment to roast meats or seafood.

Glazing root vegetables.

Making Salads

WHEN MOST OF US THINK of salads, we imagine green salads with the occasional vegetable or crouton sprinkled over for color and crunch. It often comes as a surprise to my cooking students to see salads made out of an almost infinite combination of raw or cooked vegetables. And while a certain few combinations don't work (such as beets and tomatoes), it's hard to make something bad with two or three vegetables lovingly combined.

I hesitate to give exact recipes for vegetable salads because inventing your own salads on the spur of the moment is at least half the fun. But I can't resist including a few favorite combinations, many of which have come about by accident over the years, to provide starting places for your own inventions.

When setting out to make a salad, your best bet is to wander around a farmers' market or good supermarket. I get funny looks in supermarkets as I dreamily push around an empty cart gazing at the vegetables, thinking about dinner. Usually something pops out—something especially bright, green, and fresh—and I start building from there. You can use this same technique in your own refrigerator, which, if it is like mine, will be considerably less inspiring but can offer the satisfying challenge of making something good out of a limited number of less-than-perfect ingredients.

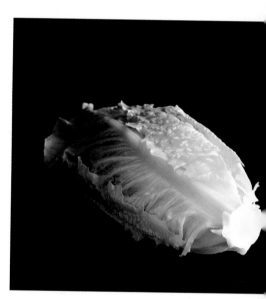

Romaine lettuce.

When making a mixed salad, it's sometimes helpful to let one ingredient—usually a mildly flavored one—form the base of the salad so that you can then add other ingredients to it. In the summer, my base vegetable is almost always tomatoes or green beans (especially the little French haricots verts) or both. Or sometimes it's a combination of equal parts basil and arugula leaves. During other times of the year, beans, potatoes, fennel, pasta, bitter lettuces, or rice are often the starting points.

Salad Dressings

Most of the time my own salad dressing is a combination of extra-virgin olive oil, sherry vinegar, salt, and pepper. Many cooks end up with less than wonderful salads simply because they don't use good oil and vinegar.

Extra-virgin olive oil is much less expensive than it once was (true, the best Tuscan oil can still break the bank), and while good wine vinegar isn't cheap, you don't need much. Distilled white vinegar is a disaster and will ruin any salad.

When dressing a salad, don't bother mixing the ingredients to make a vinaigrette; just pour everything over the salad, in front of your guests or family, at the table. In this way, the salad doesn't sit in the vinegar and wilt—and, if you've carefully arranged the salad, you can show it off at the table before tossing everything together. I usually just pour over the oil and vinegar straight out of their bottles (sprinkle over about 1 tablespoon of vinegar and 3 tablespoons of olive oil for 6 people), but if you don't trust your eye, you can measure them out until you get the knack.

Occasionally you may want to use more exotic ingredients to make a salad dressing. Nut oils made from toasted nuts—especially walnut and hazelnut—can be delicious, especially with slightly bitter greens, green beans, and artichokes. Heavy cream can replace oil and is great in the winter with cool fennel, cucumber, Belgian endive, or mushrooms, or other green vegetables in various combinations. In the summer, I sometimes use yogurt to replace the olive oil. Yogurt is light and gives a tangy acidity to spicy salads in which I've included some hot chiles and perhaps some cilantro. One problem with yogurt is that it is often too thin and will make a salad watery, but you can thicken the yogurt by draining it in a coffee filter for 2 to 3 hours.

I've never been a fan of blue cheese dressings. The salad is a lot tastier if you toss the blue cheese in little chunks right in the salad. Your salad will be best with authentic French Roquefort (although I sometimes buy a sheep's milk blue cheese from upstate New York that's every bit as good), Gorgonzola, Stilton, or Fourme d'Ambert. Avoid Danish blue, which has an aggressive sour aroma and flavor.

⚜ TIPS ABOUT NUT OILS ⚜

Natural nut oils from walnuts, hazelnuts, and almonds give a delicious accent to salads, especially those that include bitter greens. Nut oils, however, turn rancid very quickly and should always be stored in the refrigerator. Unfortunately most nut oil is starting to turn rancid while still in the jar or can—especially upsetting since nut oils are never cheap. The only sure way I know to avoid rancid nut oils is to buy nut oils made from toasted nuts. The toasting not only brings out the nuts' flavor—in the same way as toasting nuts in the oven—but also makes the oil much less vulnerable to rancidity. Le Blanc brand has long been the only brand in which the nuts are toasted, but other brands of toasted nut oils are beginning to appear on the market. Be sure to check the label before buying.

Green Salads

There are a couple of secrets to a successful green salad. The mistake that most people make is handling the green roughly, which causes minute cracks to form, which in turn absorb the vinaigrette and turn the greens soggy. Wash greens gently and don't overwork them in a salad spinner. Also, make sure the greens are perfectly dry before tossing them with dressing.

Butter lettuce.

Dandelion greens.

Romain lettuce.

Galisse lettuce.

Oskard lettuce.

Green leaf lettuce.

Green leaf lettuce.

Red leaf lettuce.

Frisee lettuce.

Salads with Nuts

You can make an otherwise ordinary salad a study in crunch by adding a handful of toasted nuts. I recommend that you toast your nuts—15 minutes on a sheet pan in a 350°F oven will do the trick (except for pine nuts, which should be toasted for 10 minutes)—because the toasting helps firm up the nuts and gives them a more intense flavor. I toast all my nuts as soon as I get them home and then keep them in the freezer. Don't hesitate to substitute different nuts from those suggested in recipes—almost any nut will do and each one will produce a slightly different effect.

Single Vegetable Salads and French-Style Crudités

Most of the salads listed below can be served on their own as simple first courses or side dishes, or you can make several salads and serve them together on the plate in the style of French crudités.

The French have a completely different idea of crudités than we Americans, who think of crudités as carrot sticks at a cocktail party. The French version is an assortment of individual vegetable salads arranged, separately but on the same plate, in little mounds and served as a first course. The individual plates can be arranged in the kitchen, but it's more fun and convivial to pass the individual salads in decorative bowls at the table.

When serving crudités, you're best off with at least five different salads, although you can sneak by with three or have as many as nine. Here are some salads that are especially good for crudités:

Baby Artichoke and Pecan Salad (page 100)

Beet and Walnut Salad (page 112)

Celeriac Rémoulade (page 151)

Cucumber and Yogurt Salad (page 189)

Fennel Salad with Shaved Parmesan (page 199) (omit the cheese)

Grated Carrot Salad (page 142)

Marinated Bell Peppers (page 114)

Marinated Mushrooms with Fresh Tarragon (page 239)

Red Cabbage Salad with Pecans (page 131)

A few small radishes also make a nice addition to a plate of crudités.

Mixed Vegetable Salads

You can mix a surprising variety of vegetables, sprinkle over a little vinegar and oil, and almost always come up with a delicious salad. I find it helpful when setting out to make a salad—even a completely improvised one— to base the salad on combinations of ingredients that remind me of specific countries from my travels. Following the basic recipe are variations inspired by my trips to Italy and Mexico.

Spring or Summer Vegetable Salad

While the version of the salad given here is unbeatable, don't feel compelled to follow this recipe exactly; certain foods may not be available, especially the morels which can be replaced with more easily obtained mushrooms. Shiitakes, stems removed, are especially good.

MAKES 4 FIRST-COURSE OR LIGHT MAIN-COURSE SERVINGS

Melt the butter over medium heat in a skillet just large enough to hold the morels in a single layer. Add the morels and sauté until for 5 minutes.

Boil the green beans, uncovered, in about 8 quarts of boiling water containing 2 tablespoons of salt for about 4 minutes. Fish the green beans out of the water with a spider or skimmer and , then plunge in ice water or rinse with cold running water until completely cool. Drain and spin or pat dry.

If using fresh peas, boil for 1 minute in the water you used for the peas. Take out the peas with a skimmer or spider , then plunge in ice water or rinse with cold running water until completely cool. Drain and spin or pat dry. If using frozen peas, simply thaw them.

Boil the corn for 1 minute in the water used for boiling the peas. Take the corn out with a skimmer or spider, then plunge in ice water or rinse with cold running water until completely cool. Drain and spin or pat dry.

Boil the asparagus for 1 to 2 minutes in the water used for boiling the other vegetables. Drain immediately in a colander, then plunge in ice water or rinse with cold running water until completely cool. Drain and spin or pat dry.

Combine the mushrooms, green beans, peas, corn, asparagus, tomatoes, and cherry tomatoes. Sprinkle over the herbs. Pour over the oil, add the vinegar to taste, and season with salt and pepper. Toss and serve.

Spring or Summer Vegetable Salad.

2 tablespoons unsalted butter

12 large morels

8 ounces green beans, preferably haricots verts, trimmed

3/4 cup fresh or frozen peas

Kernels from 1 ear corn

Tips from 1 bunch asparagus

3 tomatoes, peeled, seeded, and cut into wedges

12 cherry tomatoes, peeled (peeling optional) and left whole

Fresh herbs such as hyssop, lavender, and thyme flowers

1/4 cup extra-virgin olive oil

1 to 2 tablespoons sherry vinegar

Salt and freshly ground black pepper

Italian-Style Summer Vegetable Salad

You can make this salad as simple or as elaborate as you like. If you can't find or don't want to bother with all the ingredients listed here, just use more of those you do use. The tomatoes and onions, however, are essential.

MAKES 8 SIDE-DISH SERVINGS

Cut the tomatoes vertically into 8 wedges each. Slide your thumb and forefinger along the sides of the wedges to take out the seeds. (Seeding isn't essential, but it helps keep the salad from getting watery.) If the tomatoes are hard and underripe, thoroughly rub or toss the tomato wedges with 2 teaspoons of the coarse salt and drain in a colander for 30 minutes.

Slice the onion as thinly as you can—a vegetable slicer will make this easy—and rub the slices thoroughly with 2 teaspoons of coarse salt. Drain the slices for 30 minutes in a strainer or colander.

Use a spoon to scoop the seeds out of the cucumber halves. Slice the halves into 1/8-inch-thick crescent-shaped slices. Thoroughly rub the slices with the remaining 2 teaspoons of the coarse salt—until you can't feel the salt under your fingers—and let drain for 30 minutes in a colander.

If your green beans are thick, you may want to french them by cutting them in quarters lengthwise. Boil the beans, uncovered, in about 3 quarts of water containing 1 tablespoon of salt until they retain only the slightest crunch, 5 to 10 minutes. Drain immediately in a colander, then plunge in ice water or rinse with cold running water until completely cool. Drain and spin or pat dry.

Slice the mushrooms into 1/8-inch-thick slices and toss with 1/4 cup of the olive oil, 1 tablespoon of the vinegar, the thyme, and salt and pepper. Let sit for 30 minutes to 5 hours in a covered mixing bowl.

Toss the bread cubes with 1/2 cup of the olive oil in a wide skillet over medium heat until the cubes are crispy and brown on all sides, about 10 minutes. Reserve. (If you're worried about the oil, toast the bread cubes instead—but serve the salad right away or the cubes will get soggy.)

Cut the bell peppers lengthwise into 1/8-inch-wide strips and set aside.

Squeeze the cucumbers and onion, in small bunches, in your hands to get rid of as much of their liquid as you can.

No more than 30 minutes before serving, arrange the salad ingredients decoratively in a large salad bowl so that each ingredient is visible. Be sure the bowl is large enough to allow you room to toss. In front of your guests, sprinkle over the basil leaves—if they're big, tear them in pieces, otherwise leave them whole—and pour over the remaining 1/2 cup olive oil and 2 tablespoons vinegar. Toss gently but thoroughly, and serve.

VARIATIONS:

It's easy to turn this salad into a main course by tossing in pieces of cooked chicken, strips of meat, shrimp, mussels, or even lobster.

Italian-Style Mixed Vegetable Salad.

4 ripe medium tomatoes

6 teaspoons coarse salt

1 medium (8-ounce) red onion

1 long hothouse cucumber or 2 regular cucumbers, peeled and halved lengthwise

12 ounces green beans, preferably haricots verts, trimmed

8 ounces cremini mushrooms

1 cup extra-virgin olive oil

3 tablespoons sherry vinegar, balsamic vinegar, or good-quality white wine vinegar

1 teaspoon chopped fresh thyme leaves, or 1/2 teaspoon dried

Salt and freshly ground black pepper

3 (1/2-inch-thick) slices French bread, 6 inches in diameter, crusts removed, cut into 1/2-inch cubes

2 red or 1 red and 1 yellow bell pepper, charred, peeled, and seeded

30 fresh basil leaves

Mexican Salad

More than any real recipe from Mexico, this salad is inspired by typically Mexican ingredients and typically Mexican traditions of combining them.

MAKES 6 SERVINGS

Rub the onion slices with the coarse salt until you no longer feel the salt under your fingers, a minute or so. Put the onion slices in a colander to drain for 30 minutes.

Boil the corn for 5 minutes in salted water. Drain immediately in a colander, then plunge in ice water or rinse with cold running water until completely cool. Drain and pat dry.

Squeeze the onion in small bunches in your fists to extract as much water and salt as possible.

Combine the onion, corn, tomatoes, avocados, poblano chiles, chipotle, fresh lime juice, and cilantro. Season with salt and pepper and serve.

1 large onion, peeled, very thinly sliced

1 tablespoon coarse salt

Kernels from 2 ears corn

3 tomatoes, peeled, seeded, and cut into wedges

2 avocados, peeled and cut into 6 wedges each

2 poblano chiles, charred, peeled, seeded, and cut lengthwise into strips

1 chipotle chile in adobo sauce, rinsed, stemmed, seeded, and very finely chopped

2 tablespoons fresh lime juice, or more to taste

2 tablespoons chopped fresh cilantro

Salt and freshly ground black pepper

Mexican Salad.

À la Grecque Salads

À la grecque is French for "Greek style" and means cooking covered, with a small amount of white wine, olive oil, and coriander seeds. The French like to name foods after foreign countries and cities, but because these dishes are more French in character than the places they're named for, you're much more likely to run into a salade grecque in Paris than in Athens. There are all sorts of variations on the basic salade grecque recipe, some with lemon juice, others with saffron, others with different herbs—either included in a bouquet garni or sprinkled over the salad near the end of cooking. You can make salades grecque with individual vegetables, such as fennel or mushrooms, but the most popular salades grecques are made with an assortment of vegetables. Salade grecque is best served slightly cool as a first course or as a side dish at an informal dinner.

Mixed Salad Grecque.

Mixed Salade Grecque

If you can't find one or two of the ingredients for this salad, leave them out and add more of the others.

MAKES 8 SIDE-DISH SERVINGS

Peel the pearl or boiling onions by first plunging them in a couple of quarts of rapidly boiling water for 30 seconds and then quickly draining and rinsing. Green onions, not to be confused with scallions (see page 255), may not need to be peeled, but if their peels seem slightly dull or thick, go ahead and peel them.

Trim the tops and leaves off the baby artichokes (see page 99). If you're using frozen artichokes, pat them thoroughly dry with paper towels. Toss the artichokes in a bowl with the lemon juice to keep them from turning dark.

Cut off the ends of the zucchini and cut the zucchini into 1-inch long pieces. If you like, you can bevel the edges of the zucchini pieces with a sharp paring knife.

Trim any dark ends off the bottoms of the mushroom stems. If you're using medium mushrooms, quarter them from top to bottom.

Rinse the leek halves under cold running water. Hold the root ends up and flip through the layers, rubbing each one between your thumb and forefinger, to get rid of dirt. Shake out the excess water.

Select a wide nonaluminum pot that will hold the vegetables in no more than three layers. Put the onions, garlic, leeks, and fennel in the pot first (because there's more heat on the bottom of the pot and these vegetables are slower cooking). Sprinkle over the fresh artichokes, mushrooms, and carrots. Pour the white wine and olive oil over the vegetables, and sprinkle in the coriander seeds and salt.

Bring to a gentle simmer on top of the stove, cover the pot, and turn the heat down to low. Cook gently over low to medium heat for 20 minutes. Add the frozen artichokes, if using, and cook for 5 more minutes. Remove the lid and poke the vegetables with a paring knife. They should offer a gentle resistance

20 pearl onions

16 fresh baby artichokes, or 2 (9-ounce) packages frozen baby artichokes, thawed

1 tablespoon fresh lemon juice

2 medium zucchini

16 small or 8 medium cultivated or cremini mushrooms

4 small to medium leeks, whites with about 1 inch of the palest green part left attached, halved lengthwise

8 cloves garlic

1 medium fennel bulb, trimmed and cut into 8 wedges

1 medium carrot, peeled and sliced into $1/8$-inch-thick rounds

1 cup dry white wine

$1/4$ cup extra-virgin olive oil

1 heaping teaspoon coriander seeds

Salt

1 tablespoon finely chopped fresh parsley, chervil, or chives

but should be neither crunchy nor soft—if they're still undercooked, give them another 10 minutes. When the vegetables are done, scoop them into a serving bowl with a slotted spoon, sprinkle over the parsley, and pour the cooked white wine and olive mixture left in the pan over the vegetables. Let the salad cool at room temperature and then refrigerate it for about 15 minutes before you're ready to serve so it ends up slightly cool.

VARIATIONS:

Most recipes for salade grecque don't include delicate green vegetables because most green vegetables will turn a sad olive green when cooked covered with white wine. You can, however, boil green vegetables separately and sprinkle them over your salad just before serving to make the salade grecque look even fresher and more festive. Try boiling a couple of handfuls of green beans, peas, or broccoli florets, and sprinkle them over the salad just before serving. You can also garnish the salad with strips of grilled and peeled peppers .

Bean and Lentil Salads

The closest you're likely to get to a bean salad in the United States are the little bowls of canned red kidney beans and chickpeas that show up in salad bars.

Italians are the real masters at making bean salads in ingenious combinations by combining cooked beans with seafood, flavorful vegetables (especially fennel), fresh herbs, and plenty of extra-virgin olive oil.

To make a bean salad, just soak and simmer dried beans or boil fresh shell beans and then toss the beans with olive oil, herbs, and other ingredients as whim and inspiration dictate. A more sophisticated approach, used for seafood bean salads, is to simmer dried beans in the cooking liquid from seafood so the flavor of the seafood actually makes its way into the beans.

Dried Bean and Mussel Salad

Although we usually associate beans with meaty dishes, the combination of beans and shellfish is surprisingly good. The Italians are the masters of this combination (the seafood equivalent of France's meaty cassoulet), and they incorporate various combinations of fish and shellfish, the simplest and most common being canned tuna. In this version, mussels are steamed open and the briny liquid they release is then used to cook the beans. You can also just toss cooked beans with plenty of extra-virgin olive oil, lemon juice, some parsley, and whatever cooked seafood you have left over from the dinner the night before or what looks tempting at the fish store. Shrimp, lobster, clams, and chunks of cooked swordfish or barely cooked fresh tuna are a few of my favorites.

When buying mussels, look for cultivated mussels, which usually have less sand and a more delicate briny flavor than the larger wild mussels. Make sure the mussels are tightly closed—or close up if you tap a couple together. When you get the mussels home, brush them under cold running water and press sideways against their shells in opposite directions so that any dead ones will break apart in your hand (toss them out). Store the mussels in a bowl covered with a wet towel—never submerge mussels in water—for up to 24 hours.

MAKES 8 SIDE-DISH SERVINGS

Spread the beans on a sheet pan and pick through them to eliminate any debris. In a large bowl, soak the beans in enough warm water to cover by 3 inches for about 3 hours, or overnight, until the skins wrinkle. Drain and reserve.

Combine the garlic and half the shallots with 1 cup of water in a pot large enough to hold the mussels. Bring to a rapid boil, add the mussels, and cover the pot. Steam the mussels for about 5 minutes, or until they've all completely opened. Turn off the heat, remove the lid, and let the mussels cool slightly. Take the mussels out of the pot with a slotted spoon or skimmer. Reserve the cooking liquid in the bottom of the pot.

Drain the beans and put them in a heavy-bottomed pot large enough so that the beans don't come more than two-thirds of the way up the sides (the beans expand as they cook). Slowly pour in the liquid from the the mussel pot, leaving any grit or sand in the bottom of the pot. If there isn't enough liquid to come about an inch over the top of the beans, add more water. Bring the beans to a simmer, partially cover the pot (leave about an inch opening), and simmer very gently until the beans have completely softened, $1^1/2$ to 2 hours. If the beans start to run dry, add $^1/4$ cup of water from time to time; if they seem too liquid, remove the lid.

While the beans are cooking, take the mussels out of their shells. Discard the shells and reserve the meats, covered in the refrigerator.

When the beans are cooked and have absorbed all their cooking liquid—ideally they shouldn't need to be drained—toss them with the reserved mussels, olive oil, and the remaining chopped shallots, lemon juice, and parsley. Season to taste with salt and pepper. Serve slightly warm or at room temperature.

$1^1/2$ cups dried beans, such as cranberry, cannellini, great Northern, or navy beans

1 clove garlic, minced

4 shallots, minced

4 pounds cultivated mussels or clams in the shell, rinsed and drained

$^3/4$ cup extra-virgin olive oil

3 tablespoons fresh lemon juice

3 tablespoons finely chopped fresh parsley or basil

Salt and freshly ground black pepper

Add mussels to garlic and shallots.

Steam the mussels to open.

Dried Bean and Mussel Salad.

Lentil Salad

A few spoonfuls of these vinegary lentils along with a few cornichons, and maybe a spot of mustard, make the perfect accompaniment to a slice of pâté or leftover cooked meats.

MAKES 6 SIDE-DISH SERVINGS OR ENOUGH TO ACCOMPANY
10 SLICES OF PÂTÉ OR LEFTOVER COOKED ROASTED MEATS

20 pearl onions or 1 medium white onion, sliced

3/4 cup de puy (tiny green) or brown lentils

2 cups cold water, plus more as needed

4 sprigs of fresh thyme, or 1/2 teaspoon dried thyme

1/2 imported bay leaf

2 tablespoons tarragon wine vinegar or good-quality white wine vinegar, or more to taste

5 tablespoons extra-virgin olive oil

Salt and freshly ground black pepper

2 tablespoons finely chopped fresh parsley

Plunge the pearl onions into boiling water and blanch for 1 minute, and rinse under cold running water. Peel.

Rinse and drain the lentils and put them in a heavy-bottomed pot with the water and the onions. Tie the thyme and bay leaf into a bouquet garni with string—or if you're using dried thyme, in a piece of cheesecloth—and add the bundle to the lentils. Bring to a slow simmer over medium heat, decrease the heat to low, and simmer, covered, for 30 to 40 minutes or until the lentils are tender.

After 20 minutes of cooking, scrape along the bottom of the pot with a wooden spoon to keep the lentils from sticking, but don't stir them too much or they'll turn mushy. If the lentils dry out during the cooking, add 1/4 cup of water. If there is liquid left after cooking, remove the lid and simmer the lentils until they are dry.

Stir the vinegar and olive oil into the still-hot lentils and let cool. Remove the bouquet garni and season to taste with salt and pepper. When the lentils are cooled, stir in the chopped parsley. Serve at room temperature.

Pasta Salads

Most of the pasta salads we encounter at cocktail parties and potluck suppers aren't very exciting because they have too much pasta and not enough of the flavorful ingredients. Another cardinal and common sin is cheap oil—only extra-virgin olive oil or occasionally cream will do. Other vegetable oils or pure olive oil will make the cold pasta end up slippery and unappetizing.

A pasta salad doesn't have to be complicated to be good. One of my favorites is cooked macaroni tossed with coarsely chopped tomatoes, a few basil leaves, and extra-virgin olive oil. You can, of course, get more complicated and cook various vegetables and then toss the vegetables with cooked pasta just before serving—pasta salads are incomparable when made with grilled vegetables (onions, fennel, mushrooms, tomatoes).

There are so many exotic shapes of pasta that you don't have to limit yourself to one kind—almost any pasta will do, although I avoid stringy pastas, such as fettuccine or spaghetti, at stand-up or eat-on-your-lap parties because they can be hard to eat. I sometimes use rigatoni (shaped like giant macaroni with grooves), penne (little pointed macaronilike quills), or *orecchiette* (literally "little ears").

Tomato, Basil, and Macaroni Salad

The trick to this salad is to use a lot of the best tomatoes you can find. Another tip is to salt the tomatoes to drain off much of their water before stirring them with the pasta to avoid making the salad soggy. I make this salad in late summer and early fall, during peak tomato season. You can prepare the tomatoes earlier the same day and toss together the salad just before serving.

MAKES 6 SIDE-DISH OR FIRST-COURSE SERVINGS

Cut the tomatoes in half crosswise and squeeze the seeds out of each half. Coarsely chop the tomatoes and toss with the coarse salt. Put the mixture in a colander to drain. Allow to drain until you're ready to toss the salad, at least 30 minutes.

Bring about 4 quarts of water to a rapid boil in a large pot. Add salt and pour the pasta into the pot. Check the pasta after about 5 minutes—just bite into a piece—to see if it has softened without losing all of its texture. Keep checking every couple of minutes until the pasta is al dente (cooked through but retaining a slight resistance under the tooth). Drain in a colander.

Immediately transfer the hot pasta to a mixing bowl and toss with the olive oil. Let cool for at least 20 minutes.

Just before serving, stir in the drained tomatoes, basil, and vinegar. Season to taste with salt and pepper.

8 ripe tomatoes, peeled

1 tablespoon coarse salt

1 pound pasta, such as elbow macaroni, penne, or orecchiette

1/3 cup extra-virgin olive oil

30 fresh basil leaves

3 tablespoons good-quality balsamic vinegar, red wine vinegar, or white wine vinegar

Salt and freshly ground black pepper

Tossed Diced Vegetables: The Macédoine Salad

I once taught cooking in a French cooking school in New York, where one of the beginning lessons was to make a macédoine salad of precisely cut cubes of turnips, carrots, green beans, and peas all tossed together with mayonnaise. One afternoon I got so bored with the salad that I decided to liven it up with capers and a few sour gherkins cut into cubes along with everything else. When the French chef discovered the remains of the salad the next morning in the refrigerator, I was tracked down and reprimanded. Such deviations were not permitted.

But the discovery that traditional and sometimes stodgy recipes can be updated with a little imagination was worth the trouble, and I've since played around with various combinations of vegetables, cut into cubes (never as precise as at the school—I'm too impatient) and tossed with various sauces. In these updated recipes, I replace the plain mayonnaise with a homemade mayonnaise flavored with plenty of fresh herbs, or I use a simple and light vinaigrette.

You can improvise your own salads by cutting leftover cooked vegetables into cubes or small pieces and tossing them together in a sauce as simple as a little olive oil and lemon juice. I usually include a starch, such as cooked beans or rice; sometimes something savory, such as cubes of cooked chicken, shrimp, ham, prosciutto, or anchovies; occasionally something sweet, such as raisins or dried currants; and almost always some freshly chopped herbs, usually parsley, but sometimes tarragon, basil, chervil, or even cilantro.

Mushroom, Artichoke, Rice, Raisin, and Chicken Salad

I was skeptical the first time I saw a recipe similar to this one in an old French cookbook, but one afternoon I gathered all the ingredients and decided to give it a try. It's a fantastic and unusual salad. This salad is interesting enough to serve as a first course, but you can also serve it as a side dish.

MAKES 6 FIRST-COURSE SERVINGS

Soak the raisins in $1/2$ cup cold water for 30 minutes, tossing occasionally. Drain.

If you're using fresh baby artichokes, simmer them in a nonaluminum pot with the lemon juice and enough water to cover by 2 inches until tender, about 15 minutes. Drain, let cool, and cut in half from top to bottom.

Chop the basil leaves.

Combine the raisins, artichokes, rice, ham, peas, mushrooms, basil, oil, and vinegar in a large mixing bowl. Season with salt and pepper. Decorate with the sprigs of herbs. Pass at the table or serve in mounds on individual plates.

$1/2$ cup raisins or dried currants

12 baby artichokes, trimmed, or 1 (9-ounce) package frozen artichoke hearts, thawed and drained, or 1 (8-ounce) jar artichoke hearts

1 tablespoon lemon juice (only if using fresh artichokes)

1 cup cooked long-grain rice, preferably basmati

1 ($1/8$-inch-thick) slice cooked ham, cut into $1/8$-inch cubes, or 2 cooked boneless chicken breasts, cut into $1/2$-inch cubes

$1/2$ cup cooked fresh baby peas or thawed and drained frozen peas

8 ounces small mushrooms, thinly sliced

20 fresh basil leaves

$1/2$ cup extra-virgin olive oil

$1/4$ cup sherry vinegar, good-quality balsamic vinegar, or white wine vinegar

Salt and freshly ground black pepper

Sprigs of fresh basil or other herbs

Mushroom, Artichoke, Rice, Raisin, and Chicken Salad.

Japanese Salads

I tasted my first Japanese salad at a small village inn on Japan's northernmost island, Hokkaido. The kitchen staff, obviously flustered by the presence of a Westerner, asked as best they could what I wanted for dinner. Through a combination of grunts and sign language, it was decided that a salad was in order. The salad arrived, a heap of shredded lettuce covered with mayonnaise (squeezed out of a tube in decorative patterns) and strawberries. I showed as much delight as I could as other diners looked on, obviously perplexed about Western tastes in food.

Most Japanese vegetable salads are similar to Western versions, except for the dressing. Japanese cooks rarely use salad oil or olive oil in their salads and almost never cream.

JAPANESE SALAD DRESSINGS

Because Japanese salad dressings contain little or no oil, they're perfect for low-fat diets. They are usually made with savory combinations of rice vinegar, soy sauce, dashi (a smoky broth), sesame paste or oil, and mirin (a very sweet rice wine used for cooking) or sugar. Most Japanese salad dressings have a thin consistency, but some include thickeners such as egg yolks (the dressing is cooked in a double boiler), cornstarch (again, the sauce is cooked), tofu (the mixture is pureed in a blender), or miso.

The Japanese have strict traditions governing which sauces are used when, but I've never figured it all out and instead just add ingredients here and there to taste.

Basic Japanese Salad Dressing

MAKES 6 TABLESPOONS

1/2 tablespoon sugar dissolved in 1 tablespoon of hot water, or 1 1/2 tablespoons mirin, or more or less of either to taste

2 tablespoons rice wine vinegar

1 tablespoon Japanese dark soy sauce

1/2 teaspoon toasted sesame oil

2 tablespoons Dashi (page 77) or water

In a bowl, stir together the dissolved sugar, vinegar, soy sauce, oil, and dashi.

Miso Salad Dressing

MAKES 2 TABLESPOONS

1 tablespoon white or brown miso (white miso is sweeter and less salty than brown)

1 tablespoon water

Basic Japanese Salad Dressing

Work the miso into a paste with the water. Stir into the Basic Japanese Salad Dressing.

Tofu Dressing

MAKES I SCANT CUP

4 ounces soft tofu, drained

1 tablespoon Japanese dark soy sauce

2 tablespoons red wine vinegar

3 tablespoons water

1 teaspoon sugar, or 1 tablespoon mirin

1/2 teaspoon toasted sesame oil

Combine all the ingredients in a blender and puree for 1 minute.

Making Gratins
and Casseroles

GRATINS AND CASSEROLES ARE REALLY the same thing, except that a gratin is usually made with a thinner layer of vegetables and is usually served in an oval dish. Vegetable gratins and vegetable casseroles are made by layering partially cooked or raw vegetables with sauce (usually béchamel sauce), sometimes cream, and often cheese in a baking dish and then baking slowly, uncovered, so a crust forms on top of the dish. Bread crumbs and grated cheese are sometimes sprinkled over the top of gratins to enhance the crust.

Most vegetables are easy to convert into gratins: arrange whole or sliced vegetables in a gratin dish or baking dish, pour over liquid, sprinkle with cheese or bread crumbs, and bake. There are a number of choices for the best liquid for pouring over the vegetables. You can use a savory sauce, cream, milk, cheese (baked macaroni and cheese is a gratin), tomato sauce, milk or cream simmered with smoked meats such as bacon, coconut milk, and even hollandaise sauce. The possibilities are almost limitless. The vegetables—which may or may not be precooked—release their flavors into the sauce as the sauce thickens and its flavor concentrates in the oven. Gratins are usually ready when everything is bubbling—usually after about an hour in the oven—and the vegetables are easily penetrated with a knife.

If you're not used to making casseroles or inventing things in the kitchen (the fun of gratins and casseroles is making them up), a good way to start is to surround root vegetables with Béchamel Sauce (page 53) or similar sauce. You can also make delicious and very simple gratins by just pouring cream over sliced vegetables and then baking until the vegetables are cooked and the cream has cooked down to a thick sauce. (The Leek Gratin on page 255 is an example of this method.) But béchamel sauce is less rich than cream and, if well made, every bit as savory. Cream, however, does work better for starchy vegetables, such as potatoes—béchamel, being a starchy sauce, somehow seems redundant.

Some vegetables—those that take a long time to cook or are strongly flavored, such as turnips or rutabagas—are sometimes precooked before they're arranged in a gratin dish or baking dish.

GRATIN DISHES AND BAKING DISHES

The best dishes for baking gratins and casseroles are heavy-bottomed oval dishes with handles on each end to make them easy to get in and out of the oven. Oval dishes also look great on the table, so once you've put a trivet in place, you can bring the gratin straight from the oven to the dining room. Square or rectangular glass or porcelain baking dishes are also great for gratins, even if they don't look as elegant as oval dishes. If you're making a big gratin, you can also use a roasting pan or even a sheet pan if it has sides that come up at least an inch.

If you're inventing a gratin or following a recipe for the first time, you may be confused about what size gratin dish or baking dish to use. My own collection of gratin and baking dishes is a mishmash of French porcelain and copper, all in sizes that make sense in the metric system but are odd at best when converted to American measurements.

TO BUTTER OR NOT TO BUTTER

Most of the time a gratin dish should be buttered to make the dish easier to wash. Very rich gratins—those containing a lot of cream and butter—don't need to be baked in a buttered dish because the cream or butter keeps the food from sticking.

CHEESE FOR GRATINS

Usually the best cheese for gratins is dry and strong so you can add flavor without adding too much cheese, which makes the gratin gloppy. The best all-purpose cheese is authentic Italian Parmesan, called *Parmigiano-Reggiano* or a close second, *grana padano*. The price of these cheeses may shock you, but once you start grating, you'll see that a little chunk fluffs up to a lot of cheese. Don't buy grated cheese—it just doesn't have the same flavor.

There are, of course, plenty of other cheeses you can use instead of Parmesan. I never hesitate to try local cheeses that I encounter at the farmers' market, but I always taste them to make sure they're hard (hardness also makes them easier to grate finely) and sharp tasting. Other than Parmesan, some of my favorite cheeses for gratins are Swiss Gruyère, French Comté, sharp English or American cheddar (avoid cheddar that has been colored orange—the dye is harmless but makes the gratin look weird), aged Gouda, Fontina Valle d'Aosta, fairly hard and dry goat cheeses, such as Chavignol or Tome de Chèvre from France, and aged American goat cheeses. I've never tried using blue cheeses, but I imagine a gratin made with Roquefort, Gorgonzola, or Stilton—perhaps combined with other milder cheeses—would be wonderful. One word of warning: Don't use

⚜ BÉCHAMEL SAUCE ⚜

Béchamel sauce is the longtime favorite for making gratins and casseroles, and it works especially well in wintry gratins made with root vegetables. Most root vegetable gratins are made in exactly the same way except that some stronger-tasting or slower-cooking vegetables, such as turnips, need to be precooked for a few minutes to mellow their flavor and get the cooking started.

Many gratin or casserole recipes that call for béchamel sauce can also be made with plain cream or milk. Plain cream or milk makes sense in gratins made with starchy vegetables, such as potatoes or winter squash, when a starchy sauce (béchamel) would just be too much. Leeks are also magnificent with cream. But béchamel remains the gratin sauce par excellence because of its relative neutrality, its tendency to bubble up and form a crust, and its stability—it won't break unless desperately overcooked.

At its simplest, béchamel sauce is made by adding milk to a simple roux of cooked flour and butter, and then simmering the sauce until it thickens. This is a good method in a pinch—the sauce takes about 10 minutes—but béchamel has a complicated history and over the centuries has been made in many different ways, all of them better than the contemporary, stripped-down version called for in most cookbooks. The recipe given here borrows from the recipes of the past.

One easy way to enhance a béchamel sauce is to cook a little chopped onion with the butter and flour mixture before adding the milk. You can also add a little chopped carrot and celery, or follow Escoffier's advice and include a few chunks of meat (he used veal, but unsmoked prosciutto or pancetta is even better) and a little nutmeg. Here is my version; it makes a medium-thick sauce.

MAKES 2 CUPS

Melt the butter in a heavy-bottomed 2-quart saucepan over medium heat. Add the prosciutto, onion, carrot, and celery and stir for about 10 minutes, until the vegetables smell fragrant. Stir in the flour (if you're not using the optional ingredients, stir in the flour as soon as the butter is melted) and continue to cook, stirring with a wooden spoon, until the flour smells toasty, about 5 minutes.

Pour in 1 cup of the milk and bring to a simmer while whisking. When the milk has reached a boil and the sauce is smooth, add the remaining 1 cup milk, the nutmeg, and the bay leaf, and bring to a gentle simmer. Reduce the heat to low, and simmer for 15 minutes. Season to taste with salt and pepper and strain.

3 tablespoons unsalted butter

1 heaping tablespoon finely chopped unsmoked prosciutto or pancetta (optional)

1 small onion, or 2 shallots, minced (optional)

1 (1-inch) piece carrot, peeled and minced (optional)

1 (1-inch) piece celery, minced (optional)

2 1/2 tablespoons all-purpose flour

2 cups milk

Very small pinch of ground nutmeg, or 1 small grating of whole nutmeg

1 imported bay leaf, torn in two

Salt and ground white pepper

domestic "Swiss" cheese, which has a vague, rather dull flavor compared to an authentic Swiss cheese.

There are times when softer cheeses are more appropriate in gratins, such as lasagna or eggplant Parmesan. If you live near an Italian neighborhood, you'll probably be able to find fresh mozzarella and smoked mozzarella, which are excellent in gratins. (Don't bother with supermarket mozzarella, which is hard and rubbery.) Buffalo milk mozzarella is imported from Italy and can be a real treat, but it's expensive and very perishable. When buying buffalo milk mozzarella, taste it or at least smell it before leaving the store so you can be sure it isn't sour—it should have a fresh milky smell.

When buying cheese, remember that 3 ounces of medium-hard cheese such as Gruyère makes about 1 cup coarsely grated. For harder cheeses, such as Parmesan, count on about 2 ounces per cup of finely grated cheese.

Gratins and Casseroles Made with Tomatoes or Tomato Sauce

Most traditional gratins—those made with béchamel sauce or cream—are too rich to serve in the summer or in places where it's warm all the time. Good hot-weather alternatives are gratins made with a simple tomato sauce—or a layer of tomato slices or cubes—and fresh herbs. These gratins can be sprinkled with grated cheese or layered with a soft cheese such as goat cheese, mozzarella, or ricotta. Eggplant Parmesan (pages 194–195) and lasagna are examples of gratins made with tomato sauce, but lighter versions are popular in Provence.

Think of tomato gratins as similar to pizzas (without crusts, of course), and it will be easy to come up with ideas for flavoring the gratins by imagining your favorite pizza toppings. It's hard to go wrong with a tomato gratin, but because tomatoes contain a lot of water that they release during baking, the gratin will end up more like soup if you're not careful. To avoid this, just bake the gratin in a 300° F oven long enough—usually an hour to an hour and a half—until all the moisture evaporates. Another trick is to include pieces of crusty bread in the gratin so the bread soaks up any liquid. A third method is to pour the liquid off the hot gratin, boil it down until syrupy, and pour it back over the gratin.

While most gratins can be turned into tarts by baking in a prebaked pastry shell instead of in a gratin or baking dish, tomatoes release too much liquid, which makes the pastry shell soggy. If you want to make a tomato tart, make the gratin, spoon the cooked tomatoes into the prebaked tart shell, and heat in the oven.

Tomato and Herb Gratin

MAKES 4 SIDE-DISH SERVINGS

Cut the tomatoes in half from top to bottom and cut each of the halves into 4 wedges. Use your thumb and forefinger to push the seeds out of each of the wedges. Toss the tomato wedges with the coarse salt and drain in a colander for 30 minutes.

Preheat the oven to 350°F.

Sprinkle the basil leaves with 2 teaspoons of the olive oil and coarsely chop. (The oil helps keep the leaves from turning black.) Immediately combine the basil with the remaining olive oil in a small bowl.

Spread a third of the basil mixture in an oval gratin dish or square baking dish just large enough to hold the tomatoes in a single layer. Arrange the tomatoes in the dish, overlapping them slightly if necessary. Spoon a second third of the basil mixture over the tomatoes and sprinkle over the Parmesan cheese. If you're using any of the other toppings, arrange them on top.

Bake for 1 to 1¹/₂ hours, until there is no liquid left in the baking dish and a light crust has formed on top. If the cheese or toppings start to become too brown before the liquid has evaporated, turn down the oven and bake somewhat longer. Brush with the remaining basil mixture and serve immediately.

VARIATION:

Try cutting peeled and seeded tomatoes into large chunks and baking with some cream and rendered bacon. Include herbs such as thyme or marjoram.

6 ripe tomatoes, peeled

I teaspoon coarse salt

30 fresh basil leaves

3 tablespoons extra-virgin olive oil

¹/₄ cup finely grated Parmigiano-Reggiano cheese

OPTIONAL TOPPINGS

8 anchovy fillets, soaked for 5 minutes in cold water and drained on paper towels (soaking optional)

¹/₄ cup pitted and chopped olives (don't use canned olives)

2 red or green bell peppers, charred, peeled, seeded, and cut into ¹/₄-inch strips

2 tablespoons capers, drained

Tomato Gratin with Anchovies.

Making Stews

A VEGETABLE STEW IS almost the same as a soup except that in a stew the vegetables are left in larger pieces and a stew contains less liquid. Making a vegetable stew can be as simple as putting vegetables in a pot with a little butter or olive oil and gently cooking, covered, so the vegetables steam in their own moisture, although occasionally you may want to add a tiny bit of broth or water so the pot doesn't dry and the whole thing burn. A slightly more sophisticated approach is to add vegetables to the pot at different times—depending on the vegetable's own cooking time. More sophisticated yet is to cook the vegetables separately, especially those that don't take well to slow cooking in a covered pot or whose flavor is so strong it might dominate the whole concoction. Despite all the little tricks that can enter into its preparation, a well-made vegetable stew is well worth the effort, melding the flavors of the vegetables into something that often exceeds the sum of their parts.

You can serve a vegetable stew lightly coated or surrounded by its own juices—sometimes there's just enough liquid to coat the vegetables and give them an appealing sheen—but often you'll want to add other liquids, such as broth or cream, at the end of cooking to extend the flavor or to give the cooking liquid a velvety richness. Vegetable stews that contain a fair amount of liquid are best shown off when served as first courses in wide soup plates. Vegetable stews with little or no extra liquid can be served as side dishes, even on the same plate with other foods.

When setting out to make a vegetable stew, use your intuition to select those vegetables that make the best combinations. I usually wait until I'm at a farmers' market or good supermarket to make the final decision so I can buy what looks best. Once you've chosen which vegetables to include, you need to decide how best to cook them and for how long.

Start root vegetables, such as onions , carrots, and turnips, in the pot first because they take longer to cook and don't lose their color in a covered pot. Add slow-cooking green vegetables, such as leeks and fennel, at the same time as root vegetables, but add more fragile green vegetables, such as broccoli, green beans, and leafy greens later because they cook quickly and can turn an unappealing gray if cooked for too long in a covered pot. You may also boil green vegetables—so they stay green—and add them to the stew just a few minutes before serving. Some vegetables, such as spinach, beet greens, and Swiss chard, release strongly flavored juices as they cook. You may want to quickly boil or steam these vegetables and add them to the stew at the end so they don't release their juices into the stewing liquid and take over the flavor of the whole thing.

While most of the time small amounts of water or broth are best for starting a vegetable stew, some cooks like to include wine (especially fortified wines such as madeira or port) or a light tomato sauce. Both wine and tomato sauce give a delicious tang to a vegetable stew, but because of their acidity they can slow down the cooking so you'll need to cook the vegetables about 10 minutes longer.

French-Style Vegetable Stew.

French-Style Vegetable Stew

French cooks are experts at making rich and luxurious vegetable stews. While the cream and butter in such concoctions make some of us nervous, you can get by using surprisingly little. There are a couple of tricks for getting the most out of the cream and/or butter you do add. Don't add cream until near the end of cooking—especially if the vegetables are being cooked in a covered pot—because the acidity in the vegetables may cause the cream to separate. The same is true for butter; if too much is added to a vegetable stew at the beginning, the butter will separate and the vegetables will turn oily. Butter is best swirled into a vegetable stew—over a very low heat or completely off the heat—minutes before serving.

Almost any vegetable can be combined into a stew. I've made this recipe purposely complicated—it contains nine vegetables—in order to show how the vegetables are best combined, but the stew is just as good (and may even be better) with as few as three vegetables. Just simplify accordingly and combine those vegetables you like. Increase the amounts of each vegetable if you use fewer varieties than called for here.

One of my favorite combinations starts out with pearl onions and a root vegetable, such as carrots, turnips, or parsnips. While these vegetables are slowly cooking in a covered pot, I prepare other vegetables that take less well to slow covered cooking using various methods—usually sautéing, boiling, or steaming—and then add them to the root vegetables at different stages depending on their cooking times.

This is such a dramatic tasting and looking dish that I usually serve it as a first course, but a simplified version can also be used as a garnish for meat stews or as an elegant addition to pasta . This stew should be finished just before serving, but most of the vegetables can be peeled or trimmed—and some cooked—earlier the same day so you only need to do the last-minute cooking before serving.

MAKES 6 FIRST-COURSE SERVINGS

If you're using fresh baby artichokes, trim off their outer leaves (see photos, page 99). Bring 4 cups water to a boil with the olive oil in a nonaluminum pot. Add the artichokes and simmer for about 15 minutes, or until easily penetrated with a skewer, but not soft. Drain, let cool, and cut in half from top to bottom. If you're using frozen artichokes, thaw and pat them dry with paper towels.

Bring 5 quarts of salted water to a rapid boil. Cut the fennel bulb in half vertically, then cut each half into three wedges, leaving a section of the core along one side of each of the wedges to keep them from falling apart. Boil the fennel wedges for about 10 minutes, until they've softened but still retain some texture. Remove the fennel with a slotted spoon or spider and let cool on a plate. If you're not finishing the stew right away, rinse the fennel in a colander under cold running water.

In the same pot, boil the green beans until tender, about 5 minutes, remove with a slotted spoon or a spider, and let cool on a plate. If you're not finishing the stew right away, rinse the beans under cold running water.

6 fresh baby artichokes or 12 frozen baby artichoke halves

1 tablespoon extra-virgin olive oil (if using fresh artichokes)

1 small fennel bulb

4 ounces green beans, preferably haricots verts, trimmed and cut into 1-inch lengths

24 small or 12 large asparagus tips

12 ounces fresh fava beans, shelled and peeled, or 8 ounces fresh baby peas, shelled, or 1 cup frozen peas, thawed

12 medium spinach or sorrel leaves, stemmed, stacked, rolled up, and sliced into $1/8$-inch shreds

6 cloves garlic

18 pearl onions

12 baby carrots, scraped, $1/4$ inch of green left attached, or 2 medium carrots, trimmed, peeled, and cut into 1-inch pieces

1 tablespoon unsalted butter

3 tablespoons water

4 ounces cremini mushrooms, quartered vertically

1 cup heavy cream

1 tablespoon finely chopped fresh chives

1 tablespoon finely chopped fresh parsley

1 tablespoon finely chopped fresh chervil or tarragon (optional)

Salt and freshly ground pepper

In the same pot, boil the asparagus for 3 to 5 minutes and remove with a slotted spoon or spider. If you're not serving the stew right away, rinse the asparagus under cold running water.

In the same pot, boil the fava beans or fresh peas (there's no need to boil frozen peas) and the spinach for 1 minute, scoop out with a spider, and rinse under cold running water and reserve.

In the same pot, boil the garlic for 15 minutes, or until they're easily penetrated with a knife; scoop out with a slotted spoon and let cool.

While the garlic is cooking, put the onions and carrots in a heavy-bottomed 4-quart pot with the butter and water over medium heat. When the water starts to steam, cover the pot, and decrease the heat to low. Cook until the vegetables soften but still have some texture when you poke them with a paring knife, about 20 minutes.

While the onions and carrots are cooking, simmer the mushrooms with the cream in a medium pot over medium heat until the cream starts to thicken slightly, about 10 minutes. Stir in the chives, parsley, and chervil and season to taste with salt and pepper.

Just before serving, combine the vegetables in a large, wide pot. Pour over the mushroom-cream mixture and gently reheat all the vegetables. Season to taste with salt and pepper and serve on hot plates.

Indian-Style Vegetable Stew

Indian cooks have a special talent for vegetable stews. Whereas a French cook might use cream or butter to finish and give body to a stew, and a Mediterranean cook might use a light tomato sauce, Indian cooks thicken vegetable stews with pureed beans or lentils. Instead of cream, they use coconut milk and occasionally ghee (clarified butter) or yogurt. And while European cooks flavor their vegetable stews with a scattering of herbs, Indian cooks use spices.

This recipe is a hybrid derived from several recipes in Julie Sahni's wonderful book, *Classic Indian Vegetarian and Grain Cooking*. Ms. Sahni uses broccoli, cabbage, and eggplant in an assortment of stews, each with subtle differences in seasoning. She mostly uses cooked and pureed lentils or mung beans as thickeners and also calls for combinations of coconut milk and ghee to give a velvety richness to her interpretations of these traditional dishes.

Fresh turmeric.

Once you make a flavorful Indian-style souplike base for the stew, almost any vegetable can be precooked or simmered directly in the mixture to make a satisfying main course or side dish. The stew given here calls for seven vegetables (plus those used for seasoning)—mainly to show how each can be cooked and added to the stew—but the stew is perfectly satisfying with as few as three of those vegetables. If you cut down the number of vegetables, just increase the amounts of the others accordingly. The spicy lentil sauce can be prepared a day or two in advance and kept covered in the refrigerator. I like to serve this dish with plenty of basmati rice.

MAKES 4 MAIN-COURSE OR 6 SIDE-DISH SERVINGS

continued

To make the liquid base, spread the lentils on a baking sheet and pick out anything that doesn't look like a lentil. Put the lentils in a fine-mesh strainer and rinse thoroughly under cold running water.

Combine the lentils with the onion, turmeric, and water in a heavy-bottomed, nonaluminum pot and simmer gently, partially covered, over medium-low heat until puree-tender, about 30 minutes. Add the tomatoes and coconut milk and simmer, uncovered, until the mixture thickens, about 15 minutes, stirring every few minutes so the lentils don't stick or burn. Let cool for 15 minutes. Puree by working through a food mill or strainer or by processing in a food processor for about 1 minute.

While the lentil mixture is cooking, bring about 6 quarts water with 2 tablespoons salt to a boil in a large pot for the vegetables.

Heat the butter in a small saucepan over medium heat and stir in the garam masala. Stir over the heat for about 30 seconds, or until you smell the fragrance of the spices. Stir half the spice mixture into the lentil mixture. Taste the lentils—if they need more spice, add the rest of the spice mixture. Season to taste with salt. Cover the lentil mixture and reserve.

To prepare the vegetables, boil the cauliflower florets for 6 minutes, transfer with a slotted spoon or spider to a colander, and rinse with cold water. Reserve. In the same pot, boil the green beans until they retain only the slightest crunch, 5 to 8 minutes, then remove with a slotted spoon or spider, rinse, and reserve. If you're using fresh peas, boil for 1 minute, remove with a slotted spoon or spider, rinse, and reserve. (Just defrost frozen peas.) Add the garlic to the water and simmer for about 30 minutes, or until the cloves are completely soft when pierced with a knife. Remove with a slotted spoon or spider, rinse, and reserve. Lastly, boil the spinach for 30 seconds and drain in a colander. Rinse with cold water, gently squeeze the water out of the spinach, and reserve.

Cut each of the cucumber halves lengthwise into thirds. Cut the cucumber strips into inch-long pices. If you like, you can trim the edges of the cucumber pieces to give them a more rounded look.

About 30 minutes before you're ready to serve the stew, start adding the vegetables to the hot lentil mixture. Add the pearl onions and sweet potato, and simmer over low heat, covered, for about 10 minutes. Add the cucumber and cauliflower and simmer for 5 minutes more. Gently stir in the green beans, peas, garlic cloves, spinach, cashews, and cilantro and simmer for 5 minutes—just long enough to reheat the boiled vegetables. Add more salt if needed and serve immediately.

NOTE: This recipe calls for peeled tomatoes, but if you're working the sauce through a strainer or food mill—instead of pureeing it in a food processor—you don't need to bother with the peeling.

LIQUID BASE

1 cup yellow, red, or pink lentils, sorted and rinsed

1 medium onion, chopped

1/2 teaspoon ground turmeric

2 1/2 cups water

3 ripe medium tomatoes, peeled, seeded, and coarsely chopped, or 2 cups drained and seeded canned tomatoes (one 28-ounce can), coarsely chopped

1 cup unsweetened coconut milk

2 tablespoons salt

1 1/2 tablespoons unsalted butter or vegetable oil

1 1/2 tablespoons garam masala or curry powder

Salt

VEGETABLES AND FINISHES

Florets from 1 small head cauliflower

8 ounces green beans, preferably haricots verts, trimmed and cut into 1-inch lengths

1 cup fresh peas, or 1 (10-ounce) package frozen peas

12 whole cloves garlic, peeled

Leaves from 1 (10-ounce) bunch spinach

1 cucumber, peeled, halved lengthwise, and seeded

12 pearl onions

1 medium sweet potato, peeled and cut into 1/2-inch cubes

1/2 cup toasted, salted, cashew nuts

2 tablespoons finely chopped fresh cilantro

Combining Pasta with Vegetable Stews

One of the loveliest ways to make a simple meal or an elegant pasta course is to cook several vegetables—as though making a vegetable stew—and then toss them with the cooked pasta immediately before serving. The vegetables can be cooked ahead of time and then reheated while you're cooking the pasta, so there's very little last-minute work in the kitchen.

When preparing vegetables to toss with pasta, you need to give a little thought to the character of the final dish. For a typically southern Italian dish, use plenty of tomatoes, olive oil, and garlic; to cook like a northern Italian, simmer the vegetables with cream and/or butter so they make their own velvety sauce. Whichever approach you take, remember to have fun and improvise freely because almost any vegetable or combination will work—just be sure to get everything ready before you start cooking the pasta.

Northern Italian-Style Pasta with Mixed Vegetables

Northern Italian pasta and vegetable dishes are different from their southern cousins because cream and/or butter are more likely to be used in the north instead of olive oil. Northern versions are also more likely to contain mushrooms—or even truffles—and delicately flavored spring vegetables bound together in a delicate cream sauce. I cook northern Italian versions in the winter and spring when the cool weather leaves me craving something creamy, and I make southern Italian versions during the hot summer months. If you prepare more or fewer than four of the vegetables suggested below, adjust the amounts of the others accordingly. You can prepare the vegetables up to 3 hours in advance.

MAKES 6 PASTA-COURSE OR 4 MAIN-COURSE SERVINGS

To prepare the vegetables, bring 6 quarts of salted water to a boil. Add the green beans and cook for 5 to 10 minutes or until they retain only the slightest resistance when you bite into one. Remove with a slotted spoon or spider, rinse with cold water, and reserve. (If you are using thin beans, leave them whole; if the beans are fat, cut into 1-inch lengths.)

To cook the fresh peas, boil for 1 minute. Remove with a slotted spoon or spider, rinse with cold water, and reserve. If you are using frozen baby peas, just defrost.

To cook the fresh fava beans, boil for 2 minutes. Remove with a slotted spoon or spider, rinse with cold water, and reserve.

To cook the spinach, boil for 30 seconds. Remove with a slotted spoon or spider, rinse with cold water, squeeze out any excess water, and chop very coarsely.

To cook the mushrooms, combine with 1 tablespoons of the butter or heavy cream in a small sauté pan over medium heat and cook until any water they release evaporates, about 10 minutes. Remove from the pan with a slotted spoon and reserve.

4 ounces green beans, trimmed

1 pound fresh peas, shelled, or 1 (10-ounce) package frozen baby peas, thawed

1 pound fresh fava beans, shelled and peeled

1 (10-ounce) bunch spinach, leaves coarsely chopped

5 ounces cultivated white or cremini mushrooms, quartered

1 to 2 tablespoons unsalted butter, or 2 tablespoons heavy cream

16 baby carrots, scraped

SAUCE

1 1/2 cups heavy cream

2 tablespoons finely chopped fresh parsley, chives, or basil

Salt and freshly ground black pepper

PASTA

2 pounds fresh or 1 pound dried pasta, such as fettuccine or linguine

Salt and freshly ground black pepper

Freshly grated Parmigiano-Reggiano cheese, for serving

continued

To cook the carrots, combine the carrots, remaining 1 tablespoon butter, and water in a small pot over medium heat. Cover and cook until slightly soft, about 15 minutes. Reserve.

To prepare the sauce, shortly before you're ready to serve, boil the cream in a small saucepan while stirring until it thickens slightly, about 10 minutes. Stir in the parsley and season to taste with salt and pepper.

Cook the pasta in a large pot of boiling salted water. To check for desired doneness, remove a piece of pasta out with a spoon and bite into it. Drain the cooked pasta, put it back in the empty pot, pour over the cream and the vegetables, and toss quickly. Season to taste with salt and pepper and serve immediately on wide hot plates or pasta bowls. Pass the Parmesan cheese.

NOTE: If you are using basil, sprinkle it with a teaspoon of olive oil before chopping so it doesn't turn black

Making Soups

A FRESHLY MADE VEGETABLE SOUP is such a delight and so easy to make that anyone willing to experiment will soon give up soup out of a can. You can make the simplest soups in minutes by combining a few chopped vegetables in a pot with water, broth, or milk and simmering until the vegetables soften and release their flavor into the surrounding liquid.

While most soups are based on this simple simmering in liquid, cooks sometimes enhance the flavor of vegetables soups with special techniques or ingredients. Some recipes suggest sweating or roasting (see page 14) some or all of the vegetables in a small amount of fat before liquid is added, other recipes suggest thickeners such as all-purpose flour to give the soup body; others add pungent garlicky mixtures just before serving to give the soup a final burst of flavor.

While some soups are based on broth, many soups get their flavor and bulk from vegetables alone, accented at times with cheese, hot chiles, Southeast Asian herbs, or miso paste. Each of these soups can be used as a stepping-off point for dozens of improvisations using different vegetables and flavorings.

VEGETABLE CREAMED SOUPS

Nowadays people are put off by creamed soups because they contain cream. But surprisingly, most creamed soups, especially when made with milk, are creamy enough without the cream. You can also make a richly, silky cream soup by using very little cream—as little as a teaspoon and a half per serving.

There are certain basic techniques that apply to all vegetable creamed soups so that once you've made one you can make all the others. Traditionally, vegetable creamed soups are started out by gently cooking aromatic vegetables, such as onions, leeks, carrots, and celery, in a little butter and then, when the vegetables soften, adding flour to come up with a flavorful roux, or thickener, before liquid is added. Nowadays, we're less likely to use flour to thicken our soups and may instead add starchy ingredients, such as potato or rice, along with milk, broth, or water, and then simmer the whole thing until the potato or rice softens. The vegetable to be creamed—the one that gives its title to the soup—is added at any stage depending on how long it takes to cook. Chopped celery, for example, can be added at the same time as the potato, but very quick-cooking vegetables, such as spinach, are best added when the soup is all but ready.

Occasionally cream soups are thickened with egg yolks which gives them a silky consistency unlike any other thickener. Such soups are typically finished with a fair amount of cream. Rich combinations such as this are off-putting to some people, but the results are inimitable.

Basic Creamed Soup

Once you've made this simple base—essentially milk or broth thickened with a cooked potato—you can make almost any cream of vegetable soup by adding the vegetable to the simmering potato mixture. When to add the vegetable depends on the cooking time for that particular vegetable.

MAKES 8 TO 12 CUPS SOUP, DEPENDING ON THE VEGETABLE

Heat the butter in a 4-quart nonaluminum pot over medium heat. Add the leeks and cook, stirring, until they turn translucent, about 8 minutes. Add the potato, milk, vegetable of choice (if it's slow cooking, otherwise it should be added nearer the end of cooking) and bring to a gentle simmer. Simmer for about 20 minutes, or until the potato and vegetable have completely softened and are easy to crush against the side of the pot with the back of a fork.

Most of the time, vegetable creamed soups are best when quickly pureed in a blender and then worked through a food mill or through a medium-mesh strainer with the back of a ladle. If the mixture is thicker than you like your soup, thin it with a little milk or broth before adding the cream.

Heat the soup, add as much cream as you like, and season with salt and pepper.

3 tablespoons unsalted butter

4 medium leeks, white parts only

1 large (12-ounce) Yukon Gold or Idaho potato, peeled and cut into 1-inch-thick slices

6 cups milk, Basic White Chicken Broth (page 374), or a combination

1 to 2 cups chosen vegetable

1/4 to 1 cup heavy cream (optional)

Salt and freshly ground black pepper

VARIATIONS THAT USE THE BASIC RECIPE FOR CREAMED SOUP AS A BASE:

CREAM OF ASPARAGUS SOUP. Trim 2 pounds of asparagus by cutting off and discarding 2 inches from the base of each spear. Cut off the asparagus tips and boil them for 3 minutes in boiling salted water. Drain in a colander, rinse with cold water, and reserve. Cut the remaining stalks into 1-inch pieces and reserve.

Prepare the soup base, adding the cut-up asparagus stalks at the same time as the potato. Puree the soup in a blender and work it through a food mill or a medium-mesh strainer with the back of a ladle.

Cream of Asparagus Soup.

Reheat the soup and add as much cream as you like. Thin if necessary with additional broth, milk, or water. Season with salt and pepper (preferably white). You can add the reserved asparagus tips directly to the soup or heat them at the last minute in a little water and arrange them on top of the soup. Makes 8 servings.

CREAM OF BEET SOUP. Prepare the soup base. Roast or boil 2 pounds of beets—about 6 medium—until fully cooked (see page 111). Peel, slice thinly, and add them to the soup base when the potato has softened; simmer for 2 minutes. Puree the soup in a blender and strain through a food mill or strainer with the back of a ladle. Add as much cream as you like. Thin if necessary with extra liquid such as broth, milk, or water. Season to taste with salt and pepper (preferably white). Serve each bowl with a dollop of sour cream or crème fraîche or pass the sour cream or crème fraîche at the table. Makes 8 to 9 servings.

～ FLAVORINGS FOR CREAMED SOUPS ～

Creamed soups should capture the flavor of a vegetable without additional ingredients. Certain herbs and spices, however, can be used to enhance flavor.

Add hearty herbs, such as thyme, sage, and bay leaf, near the beginning, or tie them into a bundle (a bouquet garni) if fresh or in a packet of cheesecloth if dried, and add at the same time as the liquid.

Chop delicate herbs, such as parsley, chervil, basil, tarragon, and marjoram, at the last minute and simmer in the soup for a minute before serving so their flavor isn't cooked off by the heat.

When used sparingly, spices make the perfect accents. Add a tiny pinch of nutmeg to cream of mushroom or spinach soup. Curry powder or ground coriander provide a savory backdrop for corn, carrot, winter squash, or fennel soup. Grated fresh ginger simmered will wake up carrot or fennel soup. A pinch of saffron added to cream of cauliflower a few minutes before pureeing tints the soup a lovely yellow and gives it a mysterious exotic flavor.

CREAM OF BROCCOLI SOUP. Remove the florets from two ($1^1/_2$-pound) bunches of broccoli and reserve 8 small florets for decorating the soup. Boil the 8 small florets for 4 minutesin 6 quarts of water. Drain and rinse with cold water. Slice the broccoli stalks about $1/_4$- inch thick. Prepare the soup base. When the potato has softened, stir in the uncooked florets and the sliced stalks and simmer gently for 7 minutes. Puree in a blender and work through a food mill or through a strainer with the back of a ladle. Thin if necessary with additional broth, water, or milk. Finish the soup with the cream, and the salt and pepper (preferably white). Decorate each bowl of soup with a reserved floret. Makes 8 servings without the cream.

To puree most creamed soups, just put them in the blender—but be careful when pureeing hot liquids. Never fill the blender more than half full, hold the lid down firmly with a towel wrapped around your hand, and start with very quick short pulses, gradually building up the length of the pulses. If you turn the blender on high right away, the hot soup causes the air in the blender to expand quickly, and hot liquid may shoot out the top. You may also use an immersion blender.

CREAM OF CARROT SOUP. Prepare the soup base. Peel and slice 5 medium carrots and add when you add the potato. Simmer until the potato and carrots are easily crushed against the inside of the pot. Puree in a blender and work the soup through a food mill or through a strainer with the back of a ladle. Finish with as much cream as you like. Thin if necessary with additional broth, milk, or water. Season to taste with salt and pepper. Makes 8 servingss without cream.

CREAM OF CAULIFLOWER SOUP. Cut one 2-pound head of cauliflower into florets, discarding the core. Cook 2 tablespoons unsalted butter and 2 tablespoons all-purpose flour in a heavy-bottomed 4-quart pot over medium heat, stirring until the flour smells toasty, about 3 minutes. Whisk in 2 cups milk or chicken broth, bring to a slow simmer, and whisk until smooth. Whisk in 2 more cups milk or broth and the cauliflower florets. Cover the pot and simmer gently over low heat until the florets fall apart when you crush them against the inside of the pot with the back of a spoon, about 25 minutes. Puree the soup in a blender and then work it through a food mill or strainer with the back of a ladle, into a clean pot. If you want it perfectly smooth, work it again through a fine-mesh strainer. If you wish, add $1/4$ to 1 cup heavy cream and bring back to the simmer. Thin if necessary with extra milk or broth. Season to taste with salt and white pepper. Serve immediately in hot bowls. Makes 6 to 8 servings.

CREAM OF CELERY SOUP. You can make cream of celery soup with celery that has lost its crunch or been frozen. Thinly slice 8 celery stalks. Prepare the soup base and add the celery at the same time as the potato. Puree the soup in a blender and work the soup through a food mill with the finest attachment or through a strainer with the back of a ladle, into a clean pot. Bring the soup to a simmer, stir in as much cream as you like, and thin the soup with more broth or milk. Season to taste with salt and pepper (preferably white). Makes 8 to 10 servings.

CREAM OF CORN SOUP. You'll need the kernels from about 15 ears of corn or five (10-ounce) packages of frozen kernels to make 6 cups. Prepare the soup base. About 10 minutes after you've added the potato, add the corn, and simmer, covered, for until the potato has completely softened, 10 minutes more. Puree the soup in a blender. If you want the soup to have a smooth texture, work it through a food mill or a medium-mesh strainer with the back of a ladle. Thin if necessary with more milk or broth. Finish the soup with as much cream as you like. Season with salt and pepper (preferably white). Makes 10 to 12 servings.

CREAM OF FENNEL SOUP. Coarsely chop 1 tablespoon of the green leafy fennel fronds and reserve for decorating the soup. Chop 2 medium fennel bulbs and add them along with the potato and milk (or other liquid) to the soup base. Simmer until the potato and fennel are easily crushed against the inside of the pot with the back of a fork. Puree in a blender and strain through a medium-mesh strainer with the back of a ladle or through a food mill. If the soup is too thick, thin it with additional milk, broth, or water until it has the consistency you like. Finish the soup with as much cream as you like, and salt and pepper (preferably white). Makes 10 to 12 servings.

CREAM OF MUSHROOM SOUP. Coarsely chop $1^{1}/_{4}$ pounds mushrooms and add to the soup base. Simmer until the potato is easily crushed against the inside of the pot with the back of a fork. Puree the soup in a blender. If you want a fine consistency, strain it through a food mill or a strainer with the back of a ladle. Finish the soup with as much cream as you like. Thin if necessary with additional milk, broth, or water, and season to taste with salt and pepper (either white or black). Makes 10 servings.

CREAM OF PARSNIP SOUP WITH APPLE AND BACON. Peel and core 3 large tart apples (such as Granny Smith or a local heirloom variety). Coarsely chop 2 of the apples and put them in a heavy-bottomed non-aluminum pot with 3 peeled and sliced medium parsnips (about 1 pound total); 1 peeled and sliced small Idaho potato; 3 cups chicken broth (preferably brown) or water; and 1 cup apple juice. Cover the pot and simmer gently until the potatoes and parsnips are both easy to crush with the back of a fork against the inside of the pot, about 25 minutes. Cut the third apple into $^{1}/_{4}$-inch cubes and toss the cubes in a mixing bowl with 1 teaspoon of cider vinegar.

Cut 4 thick-cut bacon slices into $^{1}/_{4}$-inch cubes and cook in a skillet over medium heat until they release fat and barely begin to turn crispy, about 8 minutes. Remove the cubes with a slotted spoon and drain on paper towels. The bacon fat can be saved for another recipe.

Puree the soup in a blender or food mill with the finest attachment and transfer it to a clean pot. If you want the soup to be slightly thinner or to have a very smooth texture, work it through a fine-mesh strainer with the back of a ladle. Stir in $1/2$ to 1 cup cream, 2 tablespoons cider vinegar, the bacon cubes, and 2 tablespoons Calvados (optional), and simmer for 1 minute. Thin if necessary with extra broth or water, and season to taste with salt and pepper (either white or black pepper).

Distribute the reserved apple cubes in small mounds in the middle of six hot bowls. Ladle the soup into each bowl and serve. Makes 6 servings.

CREAM OF PEA SOUP. Prepare the soup base but don't puree it. Add 2 cups freshly shelled baby peas or one 10-ounce package frozen baby peas (petits pois) and simmer for 5 minutes. Puree and strain. Thin if necessary with milk, broth or water and add cream to taste. Makes 8 to 10 servings.

CREAM OF SORREL SOUP (I). Unlike most cream soups, which start out with a leek and potato base or a béchamel sauce base (with flour the thickener instead of potato), this classic soup is thickened with egg yolks and finished with heavy cream. The result is a smooth, silky, and very luxurious soup is wonderful served cold. It thickens as you chill it, so you may want to thin it with a little vegetable broth, milk, or water.

Cream of Sorrel Soup.

I sometimes reinforce the tanginess of the sorrel by adding the juice of a lemon, but some people find it too sour, so use your judgment.

To make six servings of soup, remove the stems from 1 pound fresh sorrel. Combine the sorrel, 4 cups chicken or vegetable broth, and $1^1/_2$ cups of the cream in a small pot. Bring to the simmer and puree with an immersion blender. Whisk 6 egg yolks for about 2 minutes until they turn slightly pale and ladle in about 1 cup of the hot soup while whisking. Take the pot off the heat and add the egg yolk mixture. Put the pot over low to medium heat and stir constantly until the soup has a silky consistency. Don't let it boil or the egg yolks will curdle. Reach into the corners of the pot while stirring, or the egg yolk will stick there and curdle.

As soon as you notice the soup thickening (at 176°F), turn off the heat, add $^1/_4$ cup ($^1/_2$ stick) unsalted butter, and stir for a minute to melt the butter. Strain the soup through a fine-mesh strainer. Season to taste with salt and white pepper.

Lightly whip the another $^1/_4$ cup heavy cream. Decorate each serving of soup with a spoonful of the whipped cream and 6 chervil leaves or 2 sorrel leaves, finely shredded.

CREAM OF SORREL SOUP (II). Prepare the soup base, but use $1^1/_4$ pounds of potatoes. When the potatoes are completely cooked, stir 1 pound sorrel into the soup and simmer for 5 minutes. Puree in a blender and strain through a food mill or medium-mesh strainer with the back of a ladle. If you want the soup very smooth, strain it again through a fine-mesh strainer. Finish the soup with as much cream as you like and salt and white pepper. Thin if necessary with extra broth or milk. Serve hot or ice cold. Makes 8 to 10 servings.

CREAM OF SPINACH SOUP. Prepare the soup base. Before pureeing, add the leaves from one 10-ounce bunch spinach. Simmer for 2 minutes, puree, and, if desired, strain. Thin if necessary with milk, broth or water and add cream to taste. Season with salt and pepper. Serves 8 to 10.

∽ KEEPING THE COLOR ∾

Soups made with green vegetables can turn a dingy gray if kept hot too long before serving. If you're making a soup in advance, add the green vegetables just a few minutes before serving or immediately chill the finished soup by putting the whole pot in a bowl of ice water. If you're making a pureed creamed soup in advance, you can also puree the cooked green vegetables in a blender with just enough water to get them to turn around and immediately chill this mixture. Stir the chilled puree into the hot soup base just before serving.

CREAM OF TOMATO SOUP. The best cream of tomato soup is the simplest, made with the best and most ripe tomatoes you can find. Peel, seed, and chop 5 pounds (about 15 medium) of very ripe tomatoes. Heat the chopped tomatoes in a pot over medium-low heat and when they come to a simmer, stir in $1/2$ to 2 cups heavy cream. Bring back to a simmer and season to taste with salt and either white or black pepper. Makes 8 servings.

CREAM OF WATERCRESS SOUP. Prepare the soup base, but use $1^1/_4$ pounds of potatoes. Cut off and discard the bottom third of 3 bunches of watercress. Boil the watercress for about 1 minute in salted water, drain, and rinse with cold water. When the potatoes are cooked, add the watercress, puree in a blender, and strain through a food mill or medium strainer with the back of a ladle. Add as much cream as you like, and thin if necessary with additional milk or broth. Season to taste with salt and either white or black pepper. Serve or chill immediately. Serve hot or cold. Makes 8 to 10 servings.

Miniature Croutons

Miniature croutons provide the perfect crunchy accent to the smooth texture of most creamed soups. The easiest way to make croutons is to cut dense-crumbed white bread into cubes and bake the cubes in a 300°F oven until they dry out and lightly brown, but I like to cook the bread cubes in butter until brown and crispy so they won't get soggy in the soup. I sprinkle a few croutons on each bowl of soup and pass the rest at the table.

MAKES 8 SERVINGS

Cut the crusts off the bread and cut the bread into $1/_4$-inch cubes. Heat the butter in a wide skillet over medium-low heat—be sure not to let the butter burn—and toss in the bread cubes. Cook gently until the cubes start to brown; then start tossing or gently stirring until they are evenly browned on all sides, about 10 minutes.

4 slices white bread with a tight crumb (such as thin-sliced Pepperidge Farm white bread)

6 tablespoons ($3/_4$ stick) unsalted butter

MIXED VEGETABLE SOUPS

While creamed soups are usually made with one starring vegetable (aromatic vegetables, such as onions, may be included in the background, but there's usually only one star), some of the best soups are made with an assortment of vegetables. The simplest and often the best approach is just to add the sliced or chopped vegetables to a pot of simmering liquid, usually water or broth. Another method is to gently cook some or all of the vegetables in a little olive oil, butter, or some kind of rendered fat to get the vegetables to release their flavor before you add liquid.

INGREDIENTS IN A MIXED VEGETABLE SOUP

When making a mixed vegetable soup, keep in mind that the various ingredients will cook differently and should thus be added at different moments during the cooking. Some vegetables respond better to cooking in fat than others (aromatic and root vegetables especially benefit from a preliminary sweating in oil or butter) while other vegetables, especially green vegetables are usually best added near the end of cooking.

THE LIQUID. Some of the best vegetable soups are made with only water so that the pure flavor of the vegetables is prominent in the soup. Some vegetable soups, however, especially those containing only one or a couple of vegetables (onion soup comes to mind), need a full-flavored broth to function as a backdrop (see pages 372–377 for broth recipes).

OIL, BUTTER, OR ANIMAL FATS. Many lovely vegetable soups are made by simmering the vegetables directly in liquid, but some vegetables—especially so-called aromatic vegetables, such as onions, garlic, carrots, and celery—release their flavor best when they're chopped or sliced and cooked with a small amount of oil or fat before any liquid is added. Many a recipe—and not just soup recipes—starts out with this preliminary cooking of aromatic vegetables. The kind of fat to use depends on what was (and is) available in the place where the soup first evolved. Italian soups are often made with olive oil or the rendered fat from prosciutto or pancetta; French recipes often call for butter or rendered pork fat and occasionally goose or duck fat; American recipes may use bacon fat (avoid vegetable oil). Some cooks get nervous when they read a recipe that says to first cook vegetables in butter or oil—or, worse, bacon fat or lard. But the good news is that virtually all this fat can be skimmed off once the liquid has been added and the soup is brought to a gentle simmer. To skim the fat off a hot soup or broth, swirl the soup ever so slightly with the bottom of a medium ladle and, while holding the ladle flat, quickly catch the fat that moves up to the edge of the pot. If this just all seems like too much, let the soup cool, refrigerate it overnight, and spoon off the congealed fat in the morning.

FLAVORFUL MEATS. You can give a lot of extra flavor to some vegetable soups by cooking a small amount of meat with the aromatic vegetables. Small cubes of pork, veal, prosciutto, pancetta, bacon, or duck or goose confit can be gently cooked in fat with the aromatic vegetables to give body and flavor to the soup. A good trick is to gently cook the meats and vegetables while stirring until the meats brown and their juices caramelize on the bottom of the pan. This brings out their flavor before you add liquid.

TEXTURE ENHANCERS AND THICKENERS. There are times when cream will give a vegetable soup just the needed body or velvety texture to make it satisfy, or when a cup of coconut milk added to a Southeast Asian–style soup will round out the flavors and make disparate tastes seem as one. Another way to give body to a mixed vegetable soup is to puree a cup or two of the cooked vegetables in a blender and return them to the soup. If the soup contains starchy ingredients, especially beans, all or some of them can be pureed in the blender and stirred into the soup.

STARCHY INGREDIENTS. It's easy to round out a vegetable soup and make it more substantial by adding starchy ingredients, such as beans, potatoes, rice, pasta, or croutons, or by serving the soup over slices of crusty bread. Leftover cooked beans can be added to a vegetable soup minutes before serving or fresh shell beans can be added to the soup 15 minutes or so before the soup is ready. Cubes of potato can be simmered in the soup for about 20 minutes (depending on the size of the cubes), and leftover rice or pasta can be reheated in the soup at the last minute. If the rice or pasta is uncooked, add it to the soup so it has time to cook— about 20 minutes for rice and 2 to 10 minutes for most pasta. Adding Miniture Croutons (page 70) is a great trick for making a vegetable soup more substantial, and if you cook the cubes of bread in butter or olive oil, they'll stay crunchy when you sprinkle them over the individual bowls of soup. An old European trick is to put a slice or two of crusty French bread—you can rub it with a clove of garlic first—on the bottom of each soup bowl before ladling over the soup.

FLAVORFUL FINISHES FOR VEGETABLE SOUPS. To give vegetable soup a burst of flavor, add Aïoli (page 369), Picada (page 208), or Pesto (page 206) to the soup immediately before serving.

Mediterranean Mixed Vegetable Soup

Rather than closely follow a recipe for a particular Mediterranean vegetable soup—every region seems to have its own version—it's more fun to follow a few guidelines and come up with a soup based on what you have on hand or what inspires you at the market. Once you understand a few basic principles, you'll be able to make dozens of vegetable soups, all based on the same techniques but each very different in flavor.

This "recipe" makes a lot of soup because it's as easy to make a large pot as it is a small one, and if you're making too little soup, you'll find yourself buying ridiculously small quantities of each vegetable. Besides, vegetable soups are easy to reheat over the days that follow or freeze for future use. I give recommendations for how much of each of the following ingredients, but you can include as many or as few as you like—just use a greater or lesser amount of those that you do use.

The secret to Mediterranean-style soups—what takes them out of the realm of everyday vegetable soups into the celestial—is the use of flavorful pastes whisked into the soup pot just before serving and then passed around at the table for guests to help themselves to more.

You can start this soup the day before and add the herbs and green vegetables only a few minutes before serving.

MAKES AT LEAST 12 FIRST-COURSE OR 8 MAIN-COURSE SERVINGS

SLOWER-COOKING VEGETABLES (CHOOSE THREE)

1 pound celeriac, peeled and cut into 1/4-inch cubes (15 minutes)

1 medium fennel bulb, chopped (15 minutes)

2 medium parsnips, peeled and chopped or thinly sliced (15 to 20 minutes)

3 medium waxy, Yukon Gold, or Yellow Finn potatoes, peeled and cut into 1/4-inch cubes (15 to 20 minutes)

1 medium turnip, peeled and cut into 1/4-inch cubes (15 to 20 minutes)

1 pound fresh shell beans, shelled, or about 1 cup after shelling (about 15 minutes)

FASTER-COOKING VEGETABLES (CHOOSE 4)

8 ounces green beans, trimmed and cut into 1-inch lengths (5 to 10 minutes)

Fava beans (about 2 minutes)

1 pound baby peas, shelled, or about 1 cup after shelling (2 to 5 minutes)

Leaves from 2 (10-ounce) bunches spinach, coarsely chopped (1 minute)

Leaves from 1-pound bunch Swiss chard, coarsely chopped (5 minutes)

6 medium tomatoes, peeled, seeded, and coarsely chopped, or 4 cups drained, seeded, and chopped canned tomatoes (two 28-ounce cans) (2 minutes)

STARCHY INGREDIENTS (CHOOSE ONE, OPTIONAL)

1 cup dried pasta, such as elbow, orzo, orrechiette (5 to 10 minutes), or 2 cups cooked pasta (2 minutes)

3/4 cup uncooked rice (20 minutes), or 3 cups cooked rice (1 minute)

1 1/2 cups cooked or canned beans, such as cranberry, fava, lima, borlotti, or great Northern (1 minute), canned beans drained

To prepare the aromatics, stir the onion, carrots, garlic, and meat cubes in the oil or fat in a large heavy-bottomed soup pot over medium heat. If you're using pancetta or bacon, you can use 1 tablespoon oil or fat because the meat cubes will render fat of their own. Stir the mixture until the vegetables smell fragrant and the onions turn translucent, about 10 minutes.

continued

Add the broth to the soup, turn the heat to high, and bring the soup to a simmer. Decrease the heat to maintain the soup at a steady but very slow simmer. Add the slower-cooking vegetables—using the cooking times as shown—and uncooked rice if you're using it, and simmer for 20 minutes. Then, 5 to 10 minutes before you're ready to serve the soup, slide in the faster-cooking vegetables—again, follow the cooking times given. Several minutes later, add any quick-cooking starchy ingredients, if you haven't already added rice.

Within a minute or two of serving, take the bouquet garni out of the soup and stir in any chopped herbs you've reserved for finishing the soup. At this point, depending on which vegetables you used, you may find the soup too thick. If so, add more broth or water to thin it.

If you're using one of the flavorful pastes or sauces, put 1 cup of the paste or sauce in a large mixing bowl and whisk in 2 to 3 cups of the hot soup. Return the sauce-soup mixture to the soup pot and heat gently while stirring for about 30 seconds. If you're using Aïoli, don't let the soup boil at any point or the Aïoli will curdle. If you're using the garlic paste, just stir it into the soup a minute before serving. Ladle the soup immediately into hot bowls. Pass the remaining sauce and any accompaniments, such as croutons, toasted bread, or grated cheese for guests or family to help themselves.

CHOPPED HERBS

1/4 cup finely chopped fresh parsley, basil, or chervil, or 2 teaspoons finely chopped fresh marjoram or oregano

FLAVORFUL PASTES AND SAUCES

2 cups Aïoli (page 369), or 2 1/2 cups Picada (page 208), or 1 1/2 cups Pesto (page 206), or 2 tablespoons minced garlic, crushed to a paste

FINAL SEASONINGS, GARNISHES, AND FLAVORINGS

Salt and freshly ground black pepper

Freshly grated Parmigiano-Reggiano cheese

Slices of French bread (1 per serving), toasted, or Miniature Croutons (page 70)

Vegetable Soup Gratin

Long an Italian staple and a great way to use leftover soup, vegetable soup gratin is essentially made by ladling the soup over stale bread, sprinkling it with cheese, and baking.

MAKES 6 FIRST-COURSE SERVINGS

Preheat the oven to 350°F. Bring the soup to the simmer. Tear the bread into large chunks—vaguely an inch on each side—and arrange them on the bottom of a gratin dish or baking dish. Ladle over the soup, sprinkle with the cheese, and bake until bubbling, about 20 minutes. Let cool for 10 minutes and serve.

VARIATION:

Obvious variations can be prepared by simply altering the cheese. Replacing the Parmesan with Emmental, for example, will make the cheese stringy and the gratin dramatic as you serve it.

4 1/2 cups leftover vegetable soup

3 to 4 slices country bread, about 1 inch thick, toasted

1 cup freshly grated Parmigiano-Reggiano cheese

SOUPS MADE WITH LENTILS, BEANS, AND DRIED PEAS

Beans and lentils are great in soups because they absorb the flavors of meats and aromatic vegetables and have a subtle savor of their own that melds with the flavors of the other ingredients.

Lentils and beans can be simmered in water or broth with the vegetables and herbs to make a satisfying soup, but there are a couple of tricks for giving the soup extra pizzazz. Pork works wonders, and inexpensive cuts such as pork shoulder work the best. Smoked pork products, such as ham hocks and bacon, also give a certain magic to soups, but in some recipes they should be used sparingly or they'll take over the flavor of the other ingredients. Bean and lentil soups also can be made with no meat at all, but I find that these soups require other fats, such as cream, butter, or coconut milk, to improve their texture and give them a silky creaminess.

Indian Curried Split Pea Soup

This dish sounds a bit prosaic, especially if you just say to your assembled guests that you're serving split pea soup with a little curry in it. But as soon as you set down the bowls, you will hear gasps of delight.

Different approaches are used for cooking this soup depending on the cook and where in India he or she is from. In southern India, coconut milk is more often used than the cream, and the nutty-tasting ghee (clarified butter) is used in northern India. The spices also seem to vary from place to place, with some recipes calling for cumin and mustard seeds and others for more elaborate homemade curry powders.

My own approach to this soup is somewhat free-form. If I have coconut milk on hand, I use it; if I'm feeling lazy, I use bottled curry powder (heresy to an Indian cook) instead of homemade.

MAKES 8 FIRST-COURSE SERVINGS

Thoroughly rinse the split peas in a strainer and let drain.

Cook the onion, celery, and jalapeños in 2 tablespoons of the butter in a heavy-bottomed 4-quart pot over medium-high heat until the onion smells good and turns translucent, about 10 minutes. Add the split peas and the water to vegetables and bring the mixture to a simmer. Reduce the heat to medium and simmer gently, covered, for 10 minutes. Stir in the tomatoes and simmer, covered, for 20 minutes more, until the split peas are easily crushed between thumb and forefinger.

Melt the remaining 2 tablespoons butter in a small saucepan over medium-low heat and stir in the garam masala and turmeric. Stir the spices for about 1 minute, or until you smell their fragrance. Immediately remove them from the heat and reserve.

continued

Ingredients

1 medium onion, minced

1 stalk celery, halved lengthwise and thinly sliced

2 jalapeños, seeded and minced

$1/4$ cup ($1/2$ stick) unsalted butter

$1^1/2$ cups yellow split peas or channa dal

3 cups water

4 medium tomatoes, peeled, seeded, and chopped, or 2 cups drained and seeded canned tomatoes (one 28-ounce can), chopped

1 tablespoon garam masala or curry powder

$1/2$ teaspoon ground turmeric

1 (14-ounce) can unsweetened coconut milk, or 2 cups heavy cream

2 tablespoons finely chopped fresh cilantro

Salt

Pinch of paprika, for garnish

Stir the coconut milk into the soup and bring the soup quickly to a simmer. Stir the spice mixture into the soup, a teaspoon at a time, tasting as you go until you've added the amount you like. Stir in the cilantro and salt to taste. Serve immediately in hot bowls. Decorate the center of each bowl with a tiny pinch of paprika.

JAPANESE SOUPS

Because some of the ingredients are unfamiliar, Japanese soups may sound exotic or difficult. In fact, they are among the easiest of soups because they are almost all based on dashi, a delicately flavored smoky and savory broth, the heart and soul of many Japanese dishes.

You can buy packets of instant dashi—called *dashi-no-moto*—but the best dashi is made by gently infusing dried seaweed (kombu) and bonito flakes in water.

The Japanese dry and smoke bonito, a fish similar to a small tuna, until the bonito shrinks and hardens to the texture of wood. A finished smoked bonito looks like a dark brown banana. The tasty dried bonito is finely shaved and the shavings used as the basic flavoring for dashi. Traditional cooks shave the bonito themselves, but it's easier to buy the bonito, already shaved, in cellophane bags. Bonito flakes, called *katsuobushi*, look like wood shavings.

Once in hand, dashi is flavored with soy sauce, mirin (a sweet rice wine especially for cooking), regular sake, or miso. Miso—a nutritious salty paste of fermented soybeans—is one of the most popular ingredients used for adding zip to a basic dashi. Miso comes in various strengths and colors ranging from pale brown to dark reddish brown. Darker miso is stronger flavored and saltier and is used mostly in winter soups, while so-called white miso (which is really pale brown), because of its more delicate flavor, is used to make soups in the summer. Most Japanese chefs use more than one miso and blend various combinations of white and brown until they get a mix they like. Most of us, however, can get by perfectly well by keeping on hand only one jar (or bag) of medium-brown miso. Miso keeps for at least a year in the refrigerator.

Allow kombu to steep in hot water.

Remove kombu.

Add shaved bonito.

Dashi

Dashi, the basic Japanese broth, only requires bonito flakes and kombu—dried seaweed—and a little hot water. And unlike Western broths, it takes about 15 minutes to make.

MAKES 6 CUPS (1¹/₂ QUARTS)

2 (12-inch) lengths kombu

6¹/₂ cups cold water

1¹/₂ ounces shaved bonito

Wipe the kombu with a moist towel and fold the kombu over on itself. Put it in a 2-quart saucepan and pour over the water. Put the saucepan over low heat so that it takes about 15 minutes to come to a simmer. Remove the kombu as soon as the water comes to the simmer (some cooks use kombu twice, but it won't have as much flavor the second time around).

Increase the heat so the broth comes to a full boil. Pour in the bonito flakes and immediately take the saucepan off the heat. Let the bonito flakes sit in the broth for 1 minute, then immediately strain the soup through a fine-mesh strainer— push on the bonito with the back of a ladle—or through an ordinary strainer lined with a single layer of cheesecloth.

The dashi can now be served as is or as a base for other clear soups and Japanese dishes. Dashi keeps for 5 days in the refrigerator and for several months in the freezer.

Miso Soup with Vegetables

Everyone I know likes miso soup, but most of us don't bother to make it at home because we're intimidated by the ingredients. But once you track down a couple of them—nowadays available in most supermarkets—making miso soup takes about 15 minutes.

This miso soup broth is so flavorful that you can serve it alone, but it also makes a perfect backdrop for assorted vegetables and other ingredients. Japanese cooks sometimes convert miso soup into a full meal by adding noodles, tofu, vegetables, and perhaps some seafood, such as shrimp. This version includes julienned carrots and leeks, watercress, and cubes of tofu, but once you make the basic soup you can add almost any vegetables you like.

MAKES 6 FIRST-COURSE SERVINGS

Cut the leek in half lengthwise and rinse each half thoroughly to eliminate grit. Cut it into fine julienne and reserve (see photos, page 253).

Cut the carrot into 3-inch-long pieces and julienne.

Bring 4 cups water to a boil in a small saucepan, add the julienned leeks and carrots, and simmer over low heat for about 8 minutes. Remove the leeks and carrots with a slotted spoon, rinse them with cold water, and reserve. Repeat with the watercress leaves, but boil for only 1 minute.

In a small pot, bring the dashi to a simmer. In a small mixing bowl, whisk 3 tablespoons of the miso with 2 tablespoons of the hot dashi until smooth; whisk this mixture into the simmering dashi. Taste the broth and, if you like, make more miso paste and add it to the soup. (Miso is very salty, so if the soup tastes too salty don't add more miso.)

Arrange some of each of the vegetables and tofu in individual bowls—preferably dark Japanese-style bowls with lids—and ladle over the miso soup. Serve immediately.

I large leek, white part only

I medium carrot, peeled

I bunch watercress, leaves only

6 cups Dashi (page 77)

3 to 5 tablespoons brown, white, or red miso

I (7-ounce) package soft or silken tofu, cut into 1/2-inch cubes

SOUTHEAST ASIAN VEGETABLE SOUPS AND INGREDIENTS

Much like Japanese soups, Southeast Asian-style soups can be made without long-simmered meat or poultry broth and with very few special ingredients. Those that you do need to track down will keep almost indefinitely.

COCONUT MILK. Coconut milk is not the liquid contained in a fresh coconut but rather is extracted by soaking grated coconut pulp in hot water. While you can make your own coconut milk, canned coconut milk is so inexpensive and of such good quality that I rarely bother. The best brands come from Thailand, but there are also some acceptable Spanish brands. Avoid sweetened coconut milk, containing sugar or stabilizers, which is meant for piña coladas.

FISH SAUCE. Fish sauce is made by salting anchovies and sometimes squid or shrimp in barrels and capturing the liquid that runs out over several months. Don't let this put you off—fish sauce is surprisingly delicate when combined with other ingredients. Because the strength of fish sauce differs among brands, you may have to adjust the quantities given in a particular recipe. Add a little bit at a time, tasting as you go along. Think of fish sauce as salt and when the saltiness of the dish is right, you've added just enough. Tiparos brand, Flying Lion brand, Phu Quoc, and Ruang Tong brand are particularly good and available in most parts of the country.

Kaffir lime leaves.

GALANGAL. Galangal looks a little like ginger but has a completely different taste—a pleasant pine resin flavor. Southeast Asian cooks use slices of galangal in soups and sauces or grind it into their curries. Most Asian markets sell frozen whole galangal or fresh galangal that you can store indefinitely in your freezer at home. Galangal is also sold in powder form under the Indonesian name, *laos*.

KAFFIR LIME LEAVES. Kaffir lime trees are closely related to our common lime, but the flavor of kaffir lime is more pungent and aromatic. Kaffir lime leaves are used throughout Southeast Asia and are added whole or shredded to soups and sauces or finely ground as an ingredient in Thai curry pastes. Strips of lime zest can be substituted.

Thai Hot and Sour Soup

This soup takes only minutes to make once you have gathered the ingredients.

MAKES 6 FIRST-COURSE SERVINGS

Heat the water in a medium pot over high heat until it comes to the boil. Turn down to maintain at a gentle simmer. Add the chiles, garlic, shallots, galangal, lime leaves, lemon grass, lime juice, fish sauce, and pepper. Simmer gently, uncovered, for 20 minutes to infuse the flavors of the ingredients. Add the scallions and cilantro and simmer for 2 minutes more. Serve immediately.

7 cups water

3 small Thai or serrano chiles, stemmed, seeded, and finely chopped

3 cloves garlic, minced

2 shallots, minced

1 (1/4-inch-thick) slice galangal

4 kaffir lime leaves, or 4 strips lime zest, finely shredded

1 (6-inch) length lemon grass, white part only, very thinly sliced

Juice of 2 limes

1/4 cup fish sauce, or more to taste

Freshly ground black pepper

1 scallion, white and green parts, thinly sliced

2 tablespoons chopped fresh cilantro

Making Pasta, Gnocchi, and Risottos

MANY CLASSIC ITALIAN PASTA DISHES are made by gently stewing vegetables in a little butter or olive oil and tossing them over the pasta just before serving. To convert almost any vegetable dish into a main course or elegant first course, just toss the cooked vegetables with pasta or stir them into a creamy risotto. Sometimes you'll need to cut the vegetables into small pieces, but otherwise there's nothing to do except maybe add a little extra olive oil or butter to keep the pasta from sticking to itself. Gnocchi—handmade Italian dumplings—involve a somewhat different approach, but they make a great medium for finely chopped green vegetables (spinach is the classic) worked into the dough itself.

Pasta with Green Vegetables

You can coarsely chop or shred almost any green vegetables, sauté it in a little olive oil or butter, and then toss it with pasta. Italians are more likely to serve these vegetable pasta dishes as first or second courses (an antipasto often makes up the first course at an Italian meal) to be followed by a main course of meat or fish. This Italian style is a great way to serve pasta—it makes it more special when it's its own course—but a dish of pasta with vegetables can also be served as a main course.

Italians have firm traditions about what kind of pasta should be served with what sauce, with each region having both its favorite pasta and its favorite vegetable. A thin or slippery strand pasta, such as fettuccine or linguine, is best with a richer sauce because less of the rich sauce will cling to the slippery noodles. Pasta with nooks and crannies, such as conchiglie (shells), fusilli (spirals), or orecchhiette (little ears), or hollow pasta, such as elbow macaroni, rigatoni (large ridged tubes), or penne (little quills), are best with chopped vegetables or with sauces that are less rich—more of the sauce sticks to the pasta.

Stuffed Pasta

If you make your own pasta—a surprisingly simple and pleasant process—then going a step further and improvising your own stuffings becomes a gratifying way to use up leftover cooked vegetables.

To make stuffed pasta using either of the two basic methods, you need first to roll the pasta out into sheets. I use a simple and inexpensive crank-type pasta maker that clamps onto the side of the kitchen table, but there are electric models that may be worthwhile if you find yourself addicted to fresh pasta. Once you get the pasta rolled out into thin sheets, you must keep it from drying out by covering it tightly with plastic wrap (if you're not using it right away) and keeping it loosely covered with a very slightly dampened towel as you're working with it. You can stack sheets of pasta, but you must sprinkle them liberally with flour and use them right away or they'll stick to each other.

Even though you can stuff pasta with almost anything, Italians use certain standby ingredients that provide a reliable starting point for improvisation. Bread crumbs are usually included in stuffing mixtures to absorb excess liquid and help hold the stuffing together. It's essential that you make the bread crumbs yourself with fresh or only slightly stale white bread—bread crumbs bought in a box or made from stale bread will remain hard in the stuffing and give it a peculiar grainy texture. Some kind of cheese almost always enters into pasta stuffings to give them flavor. The two most useful cheeses for stuffing are authentic Italian Parmesan cheese, which has such an intense flavor that you don't have to use much, and ricotta, which is delicately flavored but helps provide body. Eggs are usually added to help the stuffings hold together once they're cooked. In addition to these standard ingredients, you'll probably want to add finely chopped herbs, such as sage, marjoram, parsley, or oregano. I sometimes add finely chopped stewed meats and a little of the concentrated broth from the stew.

If you keep these standard ingredients in mind, it's easy to improvise stuffings by chopping or pureeing cooked vegetables and combining them with the standard ingredients to give the stuffing body and flavor.

⤸ WONTONS: A QUICK RAVIOLI TRICK ⤷

If you don't have the energy or time to roll out your own pasta, a good work-around is to use wonton wrappers. Buy square or round wonton wrappers, wet the edges after piping in the filling and press a second wonton wrapper on top. Be sure to keep the wontons covered with a damp towel while you're working so they don't dry out.

SAUCES FOR STUFFED PASTA

Once you've cooked your stuffed pasta by gently simmering (don't cook stuffed pastas at a hard boil or they will burst open), you'll need to add a sauce. Keep in mind the flavor of the filling so the sauce and filling flavors will go together. You don't want a sauce that is so strong that it masks the flavor of the filling.

The easiest of all sauces is a little extra-virgin olive oil and a sprinkling of grated Parmesan. One alternative is to serve the noodles in typical Italian fashion, surrounded by a simple chicken broth. Because a plain chicken broth is relatively bland, it will better show off the flavor of your stuffing.

SAGE BUTTER SAUCE. Butter and sage also make a marvelous and simple pasta sauce. For four first-course pasta servings, cook a stick of unsalted butter ($1/2$ cup), 2 thinly sliced garlic cloves, and 8 fresh sage leaves in a saucepan until the butter very lightly browns. Spoon the hot sage-scented butter over the pasta, making sure that each serving gets 2 sage leaves.

TYPES OF STUFFED PASTA

Pasta provides plenty of opportunity to use vegetables. Try making stuffings by sweating a little onion in butter and adding leftover chopped vegetables. Sprinkle in plenty of parmigiano reggiano. Mushrooms make an especially exciting stuffing and are best just chopped and sweated until they lose all their moisture. They should then be finished with a little heavy cream.

When serving stuffed pasta, don't try to make the outside flavors match the inside. In other words, the flavor of the inside filling should come as a little surprise, not as a continuation of a theme announced when the dish is served. For example, don't serve mushroom-stuffed ravioli topped with additional mushrooms or mushroom sauce. You're better off in these situations just surrounding the pasta with a light broth.

AGNOLINI. To prepare these "little rings," cut a sheet of pasta into 2-inch squares (or use wonton wrappers), and brush each square with cold water. Place a rounded $1/2$ teaspoon of stuffing in the middle of each square. Fold each square in half diagonally—to form a triangle—and pinch around the sides of the triangles to form a seal. Wet one corner of the triangle with your finger and bring it around so that it touches the opposite corner. Pinch the two corners together to form a little ring.

CANNELLONI. You can buy these large tubes of pasta in dried form or stuff the pasta yourself by cutting a sheet of fresh pasta into 4-inch squares, cooking it for 1 minute in boiling water, and then rolling the pasta around $1/4$ cup of stuffing in each square.

RAVIOLI. Brush a 1^1/$_2$- to 2-foot sheet of pasta with water (or use wonton wrappers). Place teaspoon-size mounds of stuffing in 2 rows on the pasta sheet, keeping each mound about 2 inches from the next. Lay a second sheet of pasta over the first—easiest if you roll up the pasta on a rolling pin and unroll it over the first sheet. Press around the mounds with your fingers to seal in the stuffing and cut the sheet into individual squares with a fluted pasta cutter or a sharp knife. If you make ravioli a lot, you may want to buy a ravioli mold. Ravioli molds are rectangular metal grids over which you roll out the sheets of pasta. Squares in the grid allow the pasta to droop and form indentations for filling with stuffing. There's also a gadget that fits onto the end of a pasta machine—just feed in the stuffing and the two sheets of pasta—have a friend help with the feeding—and the raviolis come out the other end.

TORTELLINI. Tortellini are made in the same way as agnolini except the dough is cut into circles, while the dough for agnolini is cut into squares. Cut a sheet of pasta into 2-inch diameter rounds with a cookie cutter. Brush each round with cold water and place a mounded 1 teaspoon of stuffing in the center of each round. Fold the rounds in half and press around the edges to seal in the stuffing. Wet one corner of the stuffed half-moons, bring it around to the other corner, and pinch the two together.

A FEW COOKED VEGETABLE STUFFINGS

In addition to the suggestions I give above, keep in mind that ricotta makes an excellent and versatile filling. You can flavor it with virtually any herb, give it more pizazz with Parmigiano Reggiano, and add chopped vegetables, cooked first in a little butter or olive oil.

SPINACH, SWISS CHARD, OR BEET GREENS. Because leafy green vegetables have a delicate flavor that can be lost easily in a highly seasoned stuffing, I usually combine them with ricotta to give the stuffing body without masking their flavor. Cook the leaves from 2 pounds spinach, Swiss chard, or beet greens. Thoroughly wring dry. Finely chop 1^1/$_2$ cups by hand or in a food processor and combine with ^{3}/$_4$ cup ricotta cheese, ^{1}/$_2$ cup freshly grated Parmigiano-Reggiano cheese, ^{1}/$_2$ cup fresh bread crumbs, 2 garlic cloves, minced and crushed to a paste, and 1 teaspoon finely chopped fresh marjoram or thyme, or ^{1}/$_2$ teaspoon dried. Season to taste with salt, pepper, and freshly grated nutmeg. You can also add Concentrated Broth (page 377) made from beef or the cooking juices from a good stew or roast to give the stuffing a fuller flavor, but this isn't essential. Ravioli or other stuffed pastas made with this stuffing are best served with lightly browned Sage Butter Sauce (opposite). Makes 3 cups; enough for about 90 ravioli, 12 cannelloni, or 200 agnolini or tortellini.

MUSHROOMS. You can use the Mushrooms "Truffle Style" (page 236), but you'll need to chop it up for agnolini or tortellini or the Mushroom Duxelles mixture (below) as a stuffing for pasta. A triple recipe of duxelles—2 cups—will make about 60 ravioli, 8 cannelloni, and 100 agnolini or tortellini; one recipe of the Mushrooms "Truffle Style" mixture will make 40 ravioli, 6 cannelloni, and 80 agnolini or tortellini.

⁓ MUSHROOM DUXELLES ⁓

Named after a long-forgotten marquis, this versatile stuffing lives on. A duxelles is made by chopping mushrooms and then cooking them down until they are dry. The classic flavoring is onion or shallot, but garlic or chopped herbs can also be used. I sometimes finish my duxelles with a little cream to give it a smoother texture and a delicate flavor and to help hold it together.

A duxelles can be used to stuff poultry, fish, other mushrooms, or as a filling for omelets or pasta. I sometimes make duxelles out of mushroom stems and then freeze it until I encounter a use for it. Duxelles made fom wild mushrooms stems is especially marvelous. If I'm eager to impress, I sometimes chop and add a handful of dried porcini or morels, first softened in warm water, to the rest of the mushrooms before chopping.

MAKES 2/3 CUP

Chop the mushrooms to the consistency of hamburger relish either by hand or in a food processor. If you're using a food processor, use the pulse mechanism so you don't end up with too fine a puree.

Cook the shallots gently in butter in a 12-inch sauté pan over medium-low heat until they turn translucent, about 5 minutes. Stir in the mushrooms and turn the heat up to high. The chopped mushrooms will immediately release liquid, which should be boiled away until the mixture is completely dry, about 10 minutes. As the mushrooms begin to dry, stir them with a wooden spoon to keep them from sticking to the pan. Stir in the cream and parsley, cook for a minute or two more—until the mixture stiffens—and season to taste with salt and pepper.

2 cups mushrooms or mushroom stems

2 small shallots or 1 small onion, minced

1 tablespoon butter

2 tablespoons heavy cream (optional)

1 tablespoon finely chopped parsley

Salt and freshly ground black pepper

WINTER SQUASH. A puree of sweet winter squash, flavored with nutmeg and authentic Italian Parmesan cheese, is a classic pasta stuffing in Italy's Emilia-Romagna region. Bake 3 pounds winter squash, such as acorn or butternut (see page 355), scoop out and discard the seeds, and spoon out the pulp. Puree the pulp in a food processor or blender. (If the pulp seems runny, cook it for about 20 minutes in a saucepan over medium heat to dry it out.) You should end up with about 2 1/4 cups of puree. Combine the puree with 3/4 cup freshly grated Parmigiano-Reggiano cheese and 3/4 cup fresh bread crumbs. Season to taste with salt, pepper, freshly grated nutmeg, and, if you like, a little sugar. Sage

Butter Sauce is the classic sauce for squash pasta (page 82). Makes 3 cups, enough for about 90 ravioli, 12 cannelloni, or 200 agnolini or tortellini.

Gnocchi

Most gnocchi, which in Italian simply means "dumplings," are made by combining mashed potatoes with a little flour and seasonings and sometimes eggs and/or cheese. Occasionally, however, a recipe may contain no potatoes and instead be made with flour, Parmesan and ricotta cheeses, and another vegetable, usually spinach. Gnocchi can be served very simply with a little extra-virgin olive oil or melted butter, pesto sauce, the Sage-Butter Sauce on page 82, the Black Truffle Cream Sauce on page 347, a little reduced cream with some Gorgonzola stirred in, or even a tomato sauce. You can also convert gnocchi into a gratin by cooking, draining, and drizzling the gnocchi with cream, sprinkling them liberally with grated cheese, and baking them for about 30 minutes, or until a crust forms on the surface.

To form the gnocchi, roll the dough with your fingers into $^3/_4$-inch-thick rolls and cut the rolls into $^3/_4$-inch-long pellets. Use plenty of flour during the shaping to keep the gnocchi from sticking to the work surface. Traditionalists gently press against the rounds of dough, flattening them slightly, with the back of a fork dipped in cold water to make the characteristic shape, but this is a lot of work and isn't really necessary. Spread the gnocchi on a sheet pan well dusted with flour. When it comes time to cook the gnocchi, simmer them in a large skillet of boiling water (a skillet helps the gnocchi spread apart) for about 7 minutes. You can also poach the gnocchi ahead of time, toss them with a little butter or olive oil to keep them from sticking, and then heat them in a hot sauce (or bake them in a gratin) just before serving.

POTATO GNOCCHI

These are a snap if you have extra mashed potatoes. The potatoes must be perfectly smooth (riced or worked through a drum sieve), and you can't use mashed potatoes that contain liquids, such as cream, milk, or butter, or the gnocchi will be too wet. The next time you make mashed potatoes, make extra and set some aside (they freeze well) before you add liquids.

If you're starting from scratch, you'll need $2^1/_4$ pounds of russet potatoes to make 3 cups mashed potatoes. Work the 3 cups mashed potatoes in a mixing bowl with a wooden spoon, with 3 extra-large eggs, 1 tablespoon salt, and about 2 cups all-purpose flour—just enough to keep the dough from sticking. The dough should have the consistency of bread dough.

Season to taste with pepper and freshly grated nutmeg. Chill the dough, covered, for at least an hour before forming the gnocchi. Makes 100 gnocchi; 6 side-dish or first-course servings, or 4 main-course servings.

SPINACH GNOCCHI

Cook about $1^1/_2$ pounds of spinach to get 1 cup. Firmly squeeze the cooked spinach in your hands to wring out any water. Put the spinach in a food processor with $^1/_2$ cup ricotta, 3 extra-large eggs, 1 cup all-purpose flour, and $1^1/_2$ cups freshly grated Parmigiano-Reggiano cheese. Puree for about 1 minute. Transfer the dough to a large bowl and work in 2 cups flour, 1 teaspoon finely chopped fresh sage, 1 tablespoon salt, a big pinch of pepper, and a small pinch of freshly grated nutmeg. Add a little more flour if necessary to keep the dough from sticking to your fingers.

Roll the dough out into five rolls, each about 15 inches long and $^3/_4$-inch thick. Cut the dough into $^3/_4$-inch pellets (you should get about twenty pellets per roll). Poach the pellets in a large skillet filled with simmering water for about 7 minutes. Lift the gnocchi out with a slotted spoon or skimmer and transfer them to a bowl with 3 tablespoons of butter or extra-virgin

Gnocchi with Sage Butter.

Cut the dough into 5 equal mounds.

Roll the mounds into ropes.

Cut the ropes into pellets.

Finished cut gnocchi.

Cut gnocchi, ready to cook.

Sauté gnocchi in butter or olive oil.

olive oil in it. Toss them in the bowl to keep them from sticking. (Gnocchi can be cooked ahead and kept in the refrigerator for several days.) Simmer and toss the cooked gnocchi in hot sauce or bake them in a gratin. Makes 100 gnocchi; 6 side-dish or first-course servings or 4 main-course servings.

Spinach Gnocchi with Sage Butter

You can easily substitute olive oil for the butter called for in this Tuscan classic, but don't expect it to froth up in the same way.

MAKES 6 FIRST-COURSE SERVINGS

Prepare and drain the gnocchi. Melt the butter with the sage over medium heat in a pan ideally large enough to hold the gnocchi in a single layer. When the butter froths up and then subsides slightly, indicating that it is browning, add the gnocchi. Shake the pan to heat the gnocchi through. Spoon the gnocchi onto heated plates with some of the frothy butter and a sage leaf on each serving.

Spinach Gnocchi (opposite)

$3/4$ cup ($1^{1}/_{2}$ sticks) unsalted butter

6 sprigs fresh sage

Salt and pepper

MAKING PASTA, GNOCCHI, AND RISOTTOS

Risotto

This wonderful dish of creamy rice, so long ignored by Americans, has finally caught on in the United States. Risotto is an understated dish that may not look like much on the plate, but it has an almost uncanny ability to give substance and accent to delicate herbs and spices and, of course, vegetables.

I suspect that another reason for risotto's limited popularity is that most people assume it has to be cooked just before serving, the whole time stirring ever so gently over a hot stove. But it is possible to start the risotto earlier in the day, cooking it for only about 10 minutes and using only half of the flavorful liquid called for in the recipe. Then, shortly before serving, the risotto can be reheated and finished with the rest of the liquid. This last stage takes only about 10 minutes.

You can add almost any vegetable to a risotto—little cubes of sautéed zucchini, asparagus, green beans, even beets (the risotto will end up blood red), but mushrooms— except for that occasional holiday folly, truffles— are my favorite.

Risotto with Spring Vegetables.

Don't use long-grain rice when making risotto. Italian short-grain rice is essential to give the finished risotto its characteristic creamy texture. Of the Italian varieties, Arborio, Vialone Nano, and Carnaroli are the best.

Risotto with Spring Vegetables

This dish is really made out of two recipes: a simple risotto and the Spring or Summer Vegetable Salad on page 41, minus the vinaigrette.

MAKES 4 FIRST-COURSE OR LIGHT MAIN-COURSE SERVINGS

Heat $1/4$ cup of the butter in a medium to large skillet over medium heat. Add the onion and stir the onion around until translucent, about 5 minutes. Add the rice and the remaining $1/4$ cup of butter. Stir over medium heat for 5 minutes. Add 1 cup of the broth and stir until the broth is absorbed. Add another 1 cup of broth. Continue in this way, adding broth as it's absorbed until you've used it all, and the rice is soft, but with a slightly resistant core, about 20 minutes. You can adjust the consistency of the risotto to whatever you like by adding more or less liquid (use water if you run out of broth); the risotto can range from stiff to almost soupy. Stir in the cheese and season with salt and pepper.

Spoon the risotto into heated bowls and arrange the salad ingredients on top. (Or, if you want the vegetables to be hot, stir them into the risotto just before serving.)

$1/2$ cup (1 stick) unsalted butter

1 medium onion, finely chopped

$1^{1}/2$ cups Italian short-grain rice, such as Vialone Nano, Carnaroli, or Arborio

5 cups Basic Brown Chicken Broth (372), Basic White Chicken Broth (page 393), or water

1 cup freshly grated Parmigiano-Reggiano cheese

Salt and freshly ground pepper

Spring or Summer Vegetable Salad (page 41), without the oil and vinegar dressing

Making Pureed Vegetables

DESPITE BOTTLED BABY FOOD and school cafeterias that have left many of us with unpleasant and indelible associations, one of the best ways to prepare a vegetable is to puree it. No other technique so thoroughly brings out the natural flavor of vegetables or allows us to enjoy vegetables so effortlessly. Pureeing also makes it easy to flavor vegetables with ingredients, especially herbs and spices.

To make purees that dispel associations with baby food, use plenty of seasoning. Undersalted purees or purees with no pepper will indeed be bland. I add plenty of butter and cream to my purees (both glaringly absent in cafeterias), which give the purees a luxurious texture and richness. While you don't have to use as much of these ingredients as I do, you have to use some. I'm also fond of adding herbs and spices that accent the particular vegetable's flavor.

When making purees, you're sacrificing the vegetable's natural texture in favor of something silky smooth, so don't go halfway and make lumpy puree. The easiest way to make most purees is to zap them in a blender or food processor and then work them through a drum sieve, ricer, or food mill. But it's best to avoid the blender or food processor when making starchy vegetable purees containing a lot of potato, especially waxy potatoes, because the violent movement may cause the puree to turn gluey.

Some vegetables take better to pureeing than others. Starchy vegetables work best—potatoes are the very best—but green vegetables make flat-tasting purees that tend to be runny because there's not enough starch to provide bulk. If you want to make a green vegetable puree—such as with peas—combine the puree with mashed potatoes. One word of advice: green vegetables turn gray if they're kept hot for more than 15 or 20 minutes, so you're best off making the green vegetable puree separately and keeping it cool until just before serving when you can then fold it into the starchy puree.

Unlike some cooked vegetables, purees keep well in the freezer for several months. Here is an example of carrot puree.

Drum sieve.

Carrot Puree

Carrot puree is risky stuff because, of any puree, it's the most likely to remind people of baby food. Plain carrot puree has a monotonous texture and can be cloyingly sweet, so you'll almost always want to jazz it up. I combine carrot puree with mashed potatoes—I just cook the carrots in the pot with the potatoes before pureeing—and then add a good amount of butter, salt, and pepper to the finished mixture. You can also season the finished puree with spices, such as ginger or ground coriander, or combine other vegetables such as fennel with the carrots while they are cooking.

It's easiest to puree carrots in a food processor or blender, but if your puree contains potatoes—as does the recipe given here—be careful not to overwork the puree or the potatoes may turn gummy.

MAKES 6 SIDE-DISH SERVINGS

I pound carrots, peeled and sliced into $^1/_4$-inch-thick rounds

I medium (12-ounce) russet or Yukon Gold potato, peeled and sliced

$^1/_2$ cup (1 stick) unsalted butter, cut into chunks

Salt and ground white pepper

Combine the carrot and potato slices in a heavy-bottomed 4-quart pot with only enough water to barely cover the vegetables. Cover the pot and bring to a boil. Decrease the heat and maintain a gentle simmer for 25 minutes. Stir from time to time to make sure the vegetables aren't sticking.

Drain, reserving the liquid, and puree the mixture by working it through a drum sieve, food mill, or ricer, or by pureeing it in a food processor or blender. If you're using a food processor or blender, you may have to add some of the reserved liquid to get the mixture to turn around.

Put the puree into a 2-quart saucepan with the butter and stir gently over medium heat until the butter is melted. If the mixture seems too thick, thin it with some of the reserved cooking liquid. Season to taste with salt and pepper. Serve immediately.

VARIATIONS:

Carrot Puree with Fennel and Coriander or Ginger. Cook a coarsely chopped fennel bulb with the carrots and potato. Add 1 teaspoon ground coriander (or more to taste) or 2 teaspoons grated fresh ginger to the carrots 10 minutes before the end of cooking. Puree. If there's liquid left in the pan after cooking the vegetables, boil it down until only about 2 tablespoons are left and stir it into the puree.

PART II

The Vegetables:
A to Z

AMARANTH

Identifying amaranth is complicated by the fact that there are many species and many of the them don't look alike. On page 92 we show purple amaranth, but green amaranth is actually more common. The leaves are cooked and eaten much like spinach, while the seeds, once popular with the Incas, can be popped or simply toasted. Amaranth comes in varying textures—from as thick as collard greens to as delicate as baby spinach. Baby amaranth can be used in salads, again just like spinach.

Amaranth has been around practically forever. It seems to have first been domesticated in what is now Mexico around 4000 BC although there have been similar findings in South America and even Arizona.

Steamed Amaranth with Lemon and Olive Oil

This is the easiest way to cook amaranth. You can also blanch it for a minute in boiling water and quickly drain and refresh it.

MAKES 4 SIDE-DISH SERVINGS

Stem the amaranth as though it were spinach (peel away any thick stems). Steam the leaves until they wilt, 5 to 15 minutes, depending on the thickness of the amaranth. Sprinkle with lemon juice and olive oil and season with salt and pepper.

I large bunch (about I pound) amaranth

I to 2 tablespoons fresh lemon juice

2 tablespoons extra-virgin olive oil

Salt and freshly ground black pepper

ARRACACHA (APIO, PERUVIAN PARSNIP)

This bizarre-looking tuber, also known as apio and Peruvian parsnip), is usually found only in South American or Caribbean markets, but like so many exotic foodstuffs, it's gradually working its way into the mainstream. Peeling arracacha presents a bit of a challenge because the shape is so irregular—a single trunk is covered with large protrusions. But getting at the pale yellow flesh is worth the effort. While its flavor is usually more complex, arracacha can be used much like potatoes and will work in all sorts of creamy gratins or soups made in the same way as leek and potato soup, substituting arracacha for the potatoes. Use about $1\frac{1}{2}$ pounds arracacha for 4 cups broth.

Simmered Arracacha with Butter or Olive Oil

The hardest part of this project is peeling the arracacha. You'll have to accept the fact that there's going to be a certain amount of waste because arracacha aren't nice and smooth like potatoes. But once you get your arracacha peeled, there's a lot you can do with it, including this simple dish and myriad soups and salads.

MAKES 4 SIDE-DISH SERVINGS

Steam or simmer the arracacha for about 20 minutes, until easily penetrated with a skewer. Drain, mash, and work in the butter or olive oil. Season to taste with salt and pepper.

4 pounds arracacha (anticipating a fair amount of waste), peeled

Unsalted butter or extra virgin olive oil

Salt and freshly ground black pepper

ARTICHOKES

The first brave and inventive person to eat an artichoke not only had to figure out how to scrape the pulp off the leaves but also how carefully to eat around the choke and arrive at the meaty heart—techniques that fortunately for us have been passed down through the centuries.

Artichokes range in color from dark violet to pale green and from walnut size to the size of a softball. Large and medium artichokes are best served with a simple sauce as an appetizer, while baby artichokes, which also make delicious hot or cold appetizers, are best served as an accompaniment to meat or fish.

Whatever size artichoke you buy, make sure the leaves cling tightly to the body of the artichoke and aren't unfolding and sticking out. Turn over the artichoke and check the stem where the artichoke has been cut off—if the stem is dark brown or black, the artichoke is probably old. Press against the bottom of the artichoke with your thumb—where the bottom leaves join the stem—and make sure the artichoke is firm and that there are no brown or soft spots—signs that the inside may be rotten.

You can store artichokes loosely in the vegetable drawer for a couple of days, but don't store them in plastic bags, which trap moisture and may cause them to rot.

Artichokes are simple to cook, but if overcooked they'll be mushy; if undercooked, they'll be hard and the flesh will be impossible to scrape off the leaves with your teeth. They should be cooked just until they can be penetrated with a paring knife but should still offer resistance. The other thing to watch for is color. If the simmering artichokes are exposed to too much air or are cooked in an aluminum pot, they'll turn an unappetizing dark gray. Cook artichokes in enough water so they're thoroughly immersed. Don't cover the pot, which will cause the artichokes to darken.

BASIC BOILED LARGE ARTICHOKES

Select large artichokes, one per person. Slice off the stem where it joins the base of the artichoke with a straight cut, so the artichoke will rest upright on the plate. Remove the fibrous peel from the stem with a paring knife and boil it along with the artichoke. Pull off and discard any small leaves clinging around the bottom of the artichoke. If there are any thorns on the ends of the leaves (some artichokes can give you a good poke), you can cut them off with scissors, but I never bother since they soften once the artichokes are cooked.

Put the artichokes in a nonaluminum pot and add enough cold water to cover completely. (The artichokes will bob up in the water so you'll have to push down on them to know when you've added enough.) Add a tablespoon of olive oil to the water and put a plate or nonaluminum pan lid on top of the artichokes to push them down into the water. Put the pot over high heat until the water comes to a simmer, and then turn the heat down just enough to keep the artichokes simmering gently. Simmer for 20 to 25 minutes, until you can smell the artichokes and a paring knife slides into the base of the artichoke with somewhat less ease than it would a baked potato.

Artichoke.

ꬠ HOW TO EAT AN ARTICHOKE ꬔ

If you've never had anyone show you how to eat an artichoke, here's how: Pull the leaves off the cooked artichoke, one by one, starting at the outside and near the base of the artichoke. Dip each leaf as you go in whatever sauce is being served and scrape the pulp off the fat end of the leaf by sticking the leaf halfway into your mouth and pulling it out while biting down with your top teeth—so your teeth scrape off the pulp.

When you've eaten most of the leaves—they'll start to get thin and flimsy—the artichoke will begin to look like an inverted cone set on a base. Pull the cone off with your fingers and put it in the bowl with the used leaves. You've now arrived at the notorious choke, circular and made up of tiny bristles. Find where the bristles end on the bottom and join the artichoke heart, and scrape and pull gently on the bristles with a spoon. The choke should gradually pull away. Remove and discard all the choke, being careful not to cut into the heart. You've now earned your final artichoke reward—the heart. Eat it with a knife and fork, dipping each bite in the sauce.

SAUCES FOR ARTICHOKES

Half the pleasure of eating an artichoke is deconstructing it and dipping each leaf into a delicious sauce. Mayonnaise is probably the popular sauce for artichokes—try the Aïoli on page 369, the Saffron Aïoli or the Morel Mayonnaise on page 368—but a simple olive oil vinaigrette is just as delicate and a little less rich. Hollandaise Sauce (page 370) or Beurre Blanc (page 371) are all great. You can also use the Greek garlic and potato dip, Basil Skordalia (page 205). Count on 1 cup of sauce for four artichokes. You can put a bowl of sauce in the center of the table, but it's neater and more convenient if each guest has an individual container. Frozen artichokes have already been cooked, so don't bother cooking them as you would fresh artichokes—just defrost them.

TURNING ARTICHOKES

When I was working in fancy Parisian restaurants, I was often called on to trim the leaves off artichokes—an extravagant process called turning— so that diners had only to eat the meaty heart. To turn an artichoke, cut the thick stem off the bottom, level with the base of the artichoke, so the artichoke will rest flat on the plate. (You can also peel the artichoke stem and cook the meaty interior with the artichoke bottoms.) If you're right-handed, hold the artichoke in your left hand. With a very sharp knife in your right hand, rotate the artichoke against the blade while holding the knife perpendicular to the base of the artichoke. Continue rotating until you see the white flesh of the artichoke bottom appear where the leaves have fallen off. When you've exposed the artichoke bottom on all sides, switch the angle of the knife and, again, while rotating the artichoke,

Rotate each artichoke against a sharp paring knife to remove outer leaves.

Switch the angle so you're cutting on a diagonal.

Cut away the bottom.

Rub the bottom of the artichoke with lemon juice.

Trim the edges of the artichoke bottom.

Simmer the artichoke bottoms in water with lemon juice.

Scoop the choke out of the bottom.

Cut the bottoms into wedges or leave them whole.

Artichoke wedges.

trim off any patches of green on the bottom of the artichoke. Trim off any dark green spots or leaves on the top side of the artichoke bottom. Rub the artichoke bottoms with half a lemon. If you're simmering the artichoke bottoms—artichoke bottoms are cooked in the same way as whole artichokes but for only 15 to 20 minutes—gently scoop the choke out of the cooked artichokes with a spoon after cooking. For some recipes—for example fried artichoke bottoms—you'll need to remove the choke before cooking the artichokes. To do this, cut the artichoke bottom in half vertically and, with a sharp paring knife, carefully cut between the choke and the meat of the artichoke while rotating.

Artichoke and Morel Salad with Hazelnut Mayonnaise

I serve this salad whenever artichokes are in season, and I can find really giant impressive ones. The morels are less of a problem since dried morels work as well or even better than fresh morels. If you're using fresh morels, sauté them for about 5 minutes in olive oil before incorporating them into the salad.

MAKES 4 FIRST-COURSE SERVINGS

Cut the artichoke bottoms into wedges.

If you're using fresh morels, sauté them for about 5 minutes in olive oil over high heat until fragrant. If you're using dried morels, soak them in just enough water to come up halfway up their sides for 30 minutes. Squeeze out the water.

Put the mayonnaise into a small bowls and stir in the hazelnut oil. Toss the artichokes and morels with the mayonnaise. Season to taste with salt and pepper. Serve on chilled plates.

4 large artichoke bottoms, cooked as shown on page 97

1 pound fresh morels, or 1 ounce dried

3 tablespoons pure olive oil (if using fresh morels)

$1/4$ cup plain mayonnaise

1 tablespoon hazelnut oil added to 4 tablespoons Basic Mayonnaise (page 367)

Salt and freshly ground black pepper

❧ FROZEN ARTICHOKES ❧

It's sometimes hard to find baby artichokes, and trimming the leaves off of large artichokes can take a lot of time, especially if you've never done it before. Artichoke hearts are available in jars, but often they have a strong briny taste that makes them good served alone or more appropriate for stronger-flavored dishes where their own flavor won't interfere. Frozen artichokes are the best substitute for fresh. Most frozen artichokes are baby artichokes that have been trimmed and halved. Thaw frozen artichokes thoroughly at room temperature, then press on them with paper towels to absorb some of the moisture—they tend to be very wet.

BABY ARTICHOKES

While "baby" artichokes require individual trimming, the trimming goes quickly because there's no choke to remove. Abundantly cover the baby artichokes in water, add 1 tablespoon of lemon juice and 1 tablespoon of olive oil to the water to prevent oxidation. Simmer until they offer only slight resistance when poked with a skewer, about 15 minutes.

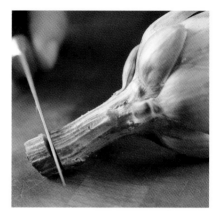

Cut off the end of the stem if it is dark or cracked.

Use a vegetable peeler to expose the stem.

Trim off the outermost leaves.

Give the artichoke a final trimming with a vegetable peeler.

Toss the artichokes in lemon juice.

Simmer in water containing lemon juice and olive oil.

Baby Artichoke and Pecan Salad

The texture and flavor of the pecans makes a lovely complement to the somewhat nutlike texture of the artichokes. I serve this salad as a first course and either spoon it out onto individual plates in the kitchen or pass it in a big bowl in the dining room.

MAKES 6 FIRST-COURSE SERVINGS

Preheat the oven to 350°F. Spread out the nuts in a cake pan and toast for 15 minutes or until lightly browned.

In a bowl, toss the whole cooked baby artichokes with the vinegar, olive oil, toasted nuts, salt and pepper and serve. This salad can be made a day in advance, except for the nuts which should be added just before serving or they'll get soggy.

⤳ TOASTING NUTS AND SEEDS ⤳

To toast nuts or seeds, put them on a sheet pan in a 350° oven for about 15 minutes (start checking at 12 minutes or when they smell fragrant). This brings out their flavor and ensures that they are crunchy. Toasted nuts and seeds have more flavor and have a better shelf-life than raw. For this reason, I toast all nuts and seeds as soon as I buy them and then I store them in the freezer.

¹/₂ cup shelled pecans or walnut halves

16 baby artichokes, cooked (see page 99)

2 tablespoons sherry vinegar or balsamic vinegar, or more to taste

¹/₄ cup extra-virgin olive oil, toasted walnut oil, or toasted hazelnut oil

Salt and freshly ground black pepper

Baby Artichoke and Pecan Salad.

Baby Artichoke, Asparagus, Fava Bean, and Walnut Salad

This elegant salad may be somewhat time consuming to prepare (the favas have to be peeled), but it can be made ahead of time (the artichokes benefit by sitting in a little lemon juice) and then dressed at the last minute.

MAKES 4 FIRST-COURSE SERVINGS

Toss together the artichokes, asparagus, fava beans, walnuts, olive oil, and vinegar. Season with salt and pepper. Serve immediately.

12 baby artichokes, cooked (see page 99), and tossed with lemon juice

12 large asparagus tips, boiled, drained, and cut into 2-inch-lengths

1 pound fava beans, peeled twice and boiled for 1 minute in salted water

¹/₂ cup toasted walnuts, coarsely chopped

3 tablespoons extra-virgin olive oil

1 tablespoon sherry vinegar or fresh lemon juice

Salt and freshly ground black pepper

ARUGULA

Sometimes called by its English name "rocket," arugula was hardly known in the United States until a decade or two ago. In Italy, arugula (there called *rucula*) is only used in its baby form. American farmers are catching on and now marketing rucula under the name "baby arugula."

Arugula has a distinct spicy flavor that makes it good alone but also a perfect match in a summer salad for basil. The two combined make a heavenly base on which to build a more elaborate mixed salad.

Arugula Salad with Flowers and Eggs

Giving a recipe for this sort of salad goes a little bit against the spirit of the thing since its origin had more to do with collecting wild herbs and flowers from the surrounding hillside and making a salad with whatever is found. But this version is so spectacular (largely because of the flowers) that it's worth duplicating.

MAKES 4 FIRST-COURSE SERVINGS

Combine the arugula and basil leaves in a large salad bowl and sprinkle over the flowers. Arrange the eggs and tomatoes in the salad bowl in a pleasing pattern. Sprinkle over the oil, vinegar, salt, and pepper and toss. Serve immediately.

2 bunches arugula, leaves with small stems attached

Leaves from 1 bunch basil

1 small (1/2-pint) box or medium handful of nasturtium flowers

3 hard-boiled eggs, cut into wedges

2 to 3 tomatoes, cut into wedges

3 tablespoons extra-virgin olive oil

1 tablespoon sherry vinegar

Salt and freshly ground black pepper

Arugula Salad with Flowers and Eggs.

ASPARAGUS

No vegetable, except perhaps the heart of a big artichoke, is as satisfying or as full of flavor as a thick stalk of asparagus. Cooks are forever debating which is better—thick or thin asparagus—but for me thick asparagus has it hands down over thin. Thin asparagus may look pretty on the plate, but it has none of the meaty texture of thick asparagus. In the market, I search for the thickest asparagus I can find.

Unless it is very thin indeed, asparagus must be peeled. This not a rarefied affectation perpetuated by the French (like peeling mushrooms), but rather helps the asparagus cook evenly and makes almost the entire stalk as tender and as delightful to eat as the tip. Peeled asparagus couldn't be easier to cook—just lower it into a big pot of boiling salted water or steam it. You can forget the elaborate tying with string and plunging into boiling water in batches found in many cookbooks.

The green versus white debate is less vehement than the thickness argument, probably because most of us don't have access to white asparagus and may have tasted it only out of a can or during foreign travel. I first tasted white asparagus in Paris, where it was sold during April and May for the price of filet mignon. The stalks were an inch thick with a deep, rich flavor and a meaty texture I'll never forget. But the French must hoard their asparagus, since the only white asparagus I've been able to find in the United States—at four times the price of green—is thin, woody, and bitter and rarely worth bothering with. Purple asparagus is sometimes available in the spring at about twice the price of green, and though purple asparagus is fun to look at, it turns green when cooked and tastes the same as green.

When buying asparagus, make sure that all the spears in the bunch have the same diameter so they'll cook evenly. Avoid spears whose bases appear woody, cracked, or dried out, or spears with tips that seem on the verge of flowering or that are moist or slimy. Give the asparagus a sniff—it should have a clean vegetable smell with no odor of rot. When you get the asparagus home, don't leave it in a plastic bag, which may cause it to rot, but rather undo the bunches, loosely wrap the asparagus in a paper bag, and store it in the vegetable bin of the refrigerator. If you need to store the asparagus for more than a day or two, set it, tips up, in a container of water.

Asparagus is usually served as a side dish, but dramatically fat spears are special enough to serve as a first course.

Asparagus.

Cut the bottom inch or two off the stalks and discard.

Peel the stalks.

Basic Boiled or Steamed Asparagus

Asparagus is easy to cook by steaming or by just plunging it into boiling salted water. Once it's cooked, you'll need only to drain it (if you boiled it), arrange it on hot plates, and either anoint it with sauce in the kitchen or pass a sauce at the table. If you're serving it cold, drain it in a colander and rinse it immediately with cold water to stop it from overcooking. Once the asparagus is cool, drain it immediately—so it doesn't soak up too much water—and pat it dry with paper towels.

MAKES 4 FIRST-COURSE OR SIDE-DISH SERVINGS

To prepare the asparagus, cut the woody bottom—usually about 1 to 2 inches—off the asparagus stalks with a sharp knife. Peel the asparagus by laying them flat, one at a time, on a cutting board. If the asparagus are very thin, use a vegetable peeler and peel each asparagus starting at the base of the tip and peeling all the way down to the base of the stalk, eliminating the fibrous peel and revealing the pale green flesh. If the asparagus are very thick or woody—common with white asparagus—use a paring knife and start peeling from the base upward toward the flower.

To boil the asparagus, bring about 6 quarts of salted water to a rapid boil in a covered pot large enough to hold the asparagus.

To steam the asparagus, set up a steamer with about 2 cups of water and bring the water to a rapid boil.

If you're boiling the asparagus, carefully lower the asparagus into the water. Turn the heat to low and simmer the asparagus, uncovered, until the spears are easily penetrated with a knife, usually about 5 minutes, but from 1 minute for very thin asparagus to 12 minutes for the very thickest. If you're steaming the asparagus, count on a couple of minutes longer for the asparagus to be done.

Drain the boiled asparagus in a colander. If you're serving the asparagus hot, toss it with the butter and arrange it immediately on hot plates. Season with salt and pepper. Spoon over any melted butter left in the bottom of the bowl. If you're serving it cold, rinse it off under cold water and pat the stalks dry. At this point you can toss it with olive oil or vinaigrette or just pass those at the table.

2 pounds asparagus, the thicker the better

2 to 4 tablespoons unsalted butter, extra-virgin olive oil, or Vinaigrette (page 370), to serve

Salt and pepper

Peeled asparagus with olive oil and lemon.

❧ SAUCES AND ACCOMPANIMENTS FOR ASPARAGUS ❧

FOR HOT ASPARAGUS:

Sprinkle with Parmigiano-Reggiano cheese

Hollandaise Sauce (page 370)

Maltaise Sauce (page 371)

Mousseline Sauce (page 371)

FOR COLD ASPARAGUS:

Vinaigrette (page 370)

Morel Mayonnaise (page 368)

Truffle Mayonnaise (page 368)

Asparagus and Morel Salad

I try to serve this salad during the spring when both asparagus and morels are at the height of their season. If you can't find fresh morels—or they're just too expensive—-dried morels work surprisingly well.

MAKES 6 FIRST-COURSE SERVINGS

Unless it is very thin, peel the asparagus. Plunge the asparagus into a large pot of rapidly boiling salted water. Simmer for 5 to 10 minutes, or until the asparagus is easily penetrated with a fork but still has a little crunch. (If you're unsure, just bite into an end, but don't burn yourself.) Drain in a colander and plunge into a bowl of ice water or quickly rinse with cold tap water.

Asparagus and Morel Salad.

If you're using fresh morels, quickly rinse them, pat dry, and sauté over high heat in 2 tablespoons of the olive oil until they soften and smell fragrant, 5 to 7 minutes, shaking the pan every minute or so to prevent sticking and so they cook evenly. Let cool.

If you're using dried morels, quickly rinse them under cold running water and then soak them for 30 minutes in the Madeira until they have softened. Squeeze out the excess liquid and sauté the mushrooms in the same way as fresh.

Cut the asparagus tips away from the peeled stalks on a diagonal. Cut the stalks, again on a diagonal, into 1-inch pieces.

Just before serving, gently toss the asparagus and mushrooms with the remaining 6 tablespoons olive oil and vinegar (don't do this in advance or the vinegar will cause the asparagus to lose its color) while sprinkling over salt and pepper to taste. Arrange in mounds on individual plates. Garnish each serving with a chervil sprig. Serve at room temperature or slightly cool.

18 thick stalks green, white, or purple asparagus

8 ounces medium to large fresh morels, or 1/2 ounce dried

1/2 cup extra-virgin olive oil

3 tablespoons Madeira or sherry (if using dried morels)

2 tablespoons sherry vinegar or balsamic vinegar

Salt and freshly ground black pepper

Chervil sprigs or chopped fresh parsley, for garnish

Roasted Asparagus

Roasting is a great technique for cooking asparagus, especially if it is watery or bland. Roasting does, however, cause the asparagus to lose a little of its color.

MAKES 4 FIRST-COURSE OR SIDE-DISH SERVINGS

Preheat the oven to 400°F. Trim and peel the asparagus, toss it in the olive oil, and arrange it in a baking dish just large enough to hold it in a single layer. Sprinkle with salt and pepper and roast for 15 minutes, gently tossing or pushing the asparagus around with a spoon every 5 minutes to help the asparagus cook evenly. Serve immediately or serve when cool.

2 pounds medium asparagus

2 tablespoons extra-virgin olive oil

Salt and freshly ground black pepper

AVOCADOS

Though avocados are a fruit, we usually eat them as though they were a vegetable.

You're most likely to encounter one of two varieties of avocados. The smaller, rough-skinned Haas avocados, usually from California and in season in the spring and summer, are the richest and most buttery, but you'll also find the smoother and paler Fuerte avocados, usually from Florida. If you're fortunate enough to live in Hawaii, you'll find the large spherical and delicious Hawaiian avocados.

Ripe avocados can be difficult to find, so if you have the foresight, buy underripe avocados 2 or 3 days before you need them and leave them out at room temperature. When fully ripe, avocados should yield when pressed firmly with your thumb but should by no means feel soft. Don't buy overripe avocados—they'll feel too soft—or avocados with soft spots. Never refrigerate avocados.

To prepare avocados, cut them in half lengthwise with a chef's knife—rotate the avocado so you cut up to and all around the pit—and pull the two halves apart. To remove the pit, carefully give it a whack with a knife blade so the blade embeds itself about $1/2$ inch into the pit. Then twist the knife to get the pit to pop right out. The avocados will be easiest to peel if you cut each half again lengthwise and then peel the skin off each quarter with your fingers.

Once peeled, avocados should be used right away, or they'll turn dark. I've read that keeping the pit in contact with the avocado halves or with the chopped avocado helps prevent the avocado from darkening; but when I tried this, it didn't make any difference. Tossing the avocado with lemon or lime juice does slow down the darkening somewhat and makes sense, since most avocado dishes include lemon or lime juice anyway.

Avocado on Toast

One of the best and simplest ways to eat an avocado is to just slice the peeled avocado pieces, crush them onto slices of toasted and buttered French bread (or, in a pinch, on toasted white sandwich bread), and sprinkle with a little fresh lemon or lime juice, salt, and pepper for a light lunch or afternoon snack. (See photos, below.)

Halve the avocado, hack into the pit with a chef's knife, and twist to remove.

Slice the avocado before smearing it on the toast.

Smear the avocado on buttered toast.

Guacamole

Given a good supply of ripe avocados, I could eat guacamole every day of the week. Most of us encounter guacamole only as a start to a meal in Mexican restaurants but, unfortunately, in all but the best places, the guacamole is a gloppy, underseasoned mixture of pureed avocado made with too much mayonnaise or sour cream.

The trick to making the best guacamole is not to crush the avocados but instead to chop them so they don't lose their buttery texture. Other essentials include something tangy (lime juice is best, but lemon juice will work), something spicy hot (finely chopped chipotle chiles are best, but serrano or jalapeño chiles will work; even a few good dashes of Tabasco sauce will do in a pinch), something to lighten the rich mixture (I usually use tomatoes but tomatillos are even better), and seasonings, including freshly minced onion, cilantro, and garlic.

Guacamole is best made within a couple of hours of serving it so the avocados don't turn dark or the tomatoes watery. Guacamole is great in the usual way with corn chips and margaritas. Try making your own chips by baking wedges of tortillas until crispy in a 375°F oven. Guacamole is also delicious rolled up—guests helping themselves—in warmed tortillas. You can also serve it as a salsa atop grilled chicken or fish.

MAKES 8 TO 10 HORS D'OEUVRE SERVINGS

Toss the tomatoes with the salt and pour into a strainer. Let the tomatoes drain for 30 minutes.

Peel the avocados and chop them into chunks roughly 1/4 inch on each side. Toss the chopped avocados with the lime juice and the chiles. Stir the garlic, onion, drained tomatoes, and cilantro into the avocados. Season to taste with salt and pepper. Serve at room temperature.

3 medium tomatoes, peeled (optional), seeded, and coarsely chopped

2 teaspoons salt, plus more to taste

4 ripe avocados, preferably Haas

Juice of 1 lime

2 chipotle chiles in adobo sauce, rinsed, or 2 jalapeños, stemmed, seeded, and minced

2 cloves garlic, minced and crushed to a paste

1 medium red onion, minced

2 tablespoons finely chopped fresh cilantro

Freshly ground black pepper

Chopping an avocado.

Guacamole.

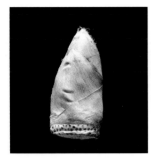

Fresh bamboo shoot.

Trim away the base and the sides of the bamboo shoot to reveal the tender flesh beneath.

Bamboo Shoot and Pineapple Salad.

BAMBOO SHOOTS

Fresh bamboo shoots are bullet shaped with leaf-like membranes that are trimmed away. While fresh bamboo shoots are a little rarified, you can find them in Chinese markets in the spring. Canned bamboo shoots are more common and have little flavor although they do have an interesting texture and absorb other flavors well.

Trim the bamboo shoots by cutting away the outer membranes until you come to a solid cone-shaped mass. Once you have your bamboo shoots trimmed, boil them immediately (they turn bitter if they sit out for more than 10 minutes) for about an hour. Cut the bamboo shoots into any shape you like. Add bamboo shoots to stir-fries.

Bamboo Shoot and Pineapple Salad

Because even fresh bamboo shoots don't have a lot of taste, this recipe is a study in textures as much as anything else. The bamboo contrasts with the somewhat similar texture of the pineapple and the crunch of pumpkin seeds. The flavor is brought out with cilantro, lime juice, shallots, and chiles.

MAKES 4 FIRST-COURSE SERVINGS

Toss together all the ingredients and chill before serving.

1 cup vertically sliced bamboo shoots

2 cups fresh pineapple wedges

2 Thai chiles or 4 jalapeños, seeded and minced

2 tablespoons chopped fresh cilantro

3 tablespoons toasted unsalted pumpkin seeds (see page 100)

Juice of 1 lime

1 tablespoon minced shallot

Salt

BEETS

Because of their strong earthy flavor and fearsome, impossible-to-ignore color, most of us either love beets or hate them. I was an ardent beet hater until my first bite of cold beets in a salad with plenty of mustardy vinaigrette. The beet's appeal has since crept up on me, and now I can't get enough of them, regardless of how they're prepared.

Beets come in many different varieties and colors. The common beet is slightly smaller than a baseball and deep crimson, but there are golden beets, white beets, and multicolored beets, such as the Chiogga variety, which is candy-striped with red rings when sliced. Beets range from baseball size down to the size of marbles. Some beets are grown for their greens, with the beet itself resembling a slender root.

Except for the occasional raw beet salad, beets are either roasted, boiled, or steamed before they are sliced, diced, or julienned and finished using other methods. There are really no subtle tricks for selecting beets. If they still have their greens attached you'll be sure of their freshness, but you can make plenty of delicious beet dishes with everyday supermarket beets without greens. When buying beets without their greens, just make sure they're heavy and firm and not wrinkled or sprouting. If you're storing the beets for more than 2 days, remove their greens—leave about an inch of green attached—and store the beets loose in the refrigerator. They'll keep for about a week.

Beets.

TO BOIL, ROAST, OR STEAM WHOLE BEETS

I roast beets if I have a lot and it's a cool day, but I boil, steam, or microwave beets if I have only a few, or when the weather's hot and I don't want to turn on the oven.

To prepare beets, cut off the greens but leave about an inch of the stems attached at the top of the beet. Don't cut the stems off where they join the beet or the beet will "bleed" and lose flavor and color during cooking. If the beet has a slender "string" still attached to its base, leave this attached or it will leave a wound from which, again, flavor and color will leach out. When the beets are finished cooking, let them cool just long enough so you can handle them. Then peel them while they're still warm by just pulling the peel away with your fingers or with a paring knife. Cold or raw beets are harder to peel and may require a vegetable peeler. "Peel" baby beets by scrubbing them with a rough sponge before cooking.

I can't give exact times for cooking whole beets because beets sold in bunches are never the same size, and older beets take longer to cook than younger beets. Fresh beets, with their greens still attached, cook faster than

Peel roasted or boiled beets while they're still warm.

Cut beets into sticks for some salads.

beets that have been sitting around for a while, but none of this is terribly important—you just have to know how to judge when the beets are done. Whether boiled, roasted, or steamed, small and very young beets take at least 30 minutes but usually closer to an hour to cook. Large old beets may take as long as 2 hours. The best way to determine when beets are done is to poke them with a skewer or sharp paring knife. The skewer should go all the way through but the beets should still offer some resistance—if they feel like baked potatoes, they're overdone. Avoid poking the beets too many times during cooking or their inky juices will run out of the holes and they'll lose flavor.

Cooked beets will keep for up to three days in the refrigerator.

MICROWAVING BEETS

Because beets—especially if they're large or old—take so long to cook, it makes good sense to cook small numbers of beets in the microwave. To microwave four medium (6-ounce) beets or the equivalent weight of large beets, arrange the unpeeled beets in a microwavable dish with a lid or cover the dish with plastic wrap. Microwave on high for 8 minutes and let rest, without taking off the lid or plastic wrap, for 5 minutes. Turn the beets over, cover again, and microwave for 3 minutes more. Let sit without removing the cover or plastic for 10 more minutes. Poke the beets with a small knife. If they're easy to penetrate, they're done. If they still offer resistance, cover them again and microwave for 3 minutes more. Let cool slightly and peel with a small paring knife.

Basic Boiled or Steamed Beets

Because of their full flavor, beets go best with rich and flavorful red meat, duck, or chicken dishes. Boiled or steamed beets can be sliced and tossed with a little butter or olive oil, or they can be sautéed.

MAKES 4 SIDE-DISH SERVINGS

Put the beets in a pot or steamer. To boil the beets, add enough cold water to cover by 1 inch, bring to a boil, and turn down the heat to maintain at a gentle simmer. To steam the beets, put enough water in the steamer so it doesn't run dry and bring to a rolling boil. Cover the pot or steamer and simmer or steam for 20 minutes (for baby beets) to an hour or more (for large beets), or until the beets can be penetrated (but not too easily) with a skewer or paring knife. You may have to add water from time to time to keep the beets covered or the steamer from running dry. Drain and let cool just long enough so you can handle them. Most of the peel will just slip off, but stubborn patches can be peeled off with a paring knife. Cut off the root and, if you like, the greens.

If you're using larger beets, cut them into $1/4$-inch-thick slices; if you're using small beets, leave them whole. Toss the sliced or whole beets with the butter and season to taste with salt and pepper.

4 (6-ounce) beets, or 16 baby beets (about 1 inch in diameter) with root and 1 inch of greens attached, if possible

$1/4$ cup unsalted butter, or 3 tablespoons extra-virgin olive oil

Salt and freshly ground black pepper

Basic Roasted Beets

Much of the time I opt for boiling beets instead of roasting them because, unless I'm cooking for a crowd, I don't want to leave the oven on for 1 to 2 hours it takes to roast beets. On the other hand, roasted beets have an even more intense, and to my mind are more satisfying, flavor than boiled beets.

Wrap beets in aluminum foil before roasting, or just rub with a little oil before sliding them into the oven. Beets that are just rubbed with oil and roasted will leak juices and mess up the roasting pan. If you roast beets with neither oil nor foil, they'll take forever to cook and will dry out.

Like boiled or steamed beets, roasted beets are best with full-flavored foods, such as red meats. Roasting is also a first step for making other recipes, such as Sautéed Beets with Olive Oil, Garlic, and Parsley on page 112).

MAKES 4 SIDE-DISH SERVINGS

Preheat the oven to 400°F.

Rub the beets with the 1 tablespoon oil and either place them in a small lightly oiled casserole or wrap them tightly in aluminum foil. Even foil-wrapped beets should be put on some kind of pan so if any juices leak out—especially when you're poking them to see if they're done—they won't mess up the oven. If you're roasting a lot of beets, you may want to wrap the smaller beets in a separate packet from the larger beets so you can take the smaller ones out of the oven when they're done. Bake for $1^1/4$ to $1^1/2$ hours. The beets are ready when they can be easily penetrated with a skewer or paring knife. Don't bother unwrapping the beets to check them, just poke right through the foil.

4 (6-ounce) beets with root and 1 inch of greens attached, if possible

1 tablespoon olive oil or canola oil

$1/4$ cup ($1/2$ stick) unsalted butter, or 3 tablespoons extra-virgin olive oil

continued

Let the beets cool until you can handle them—but not more, or they'll be hard to peel. Cut off the root and the greens and slip off the peel with your fingers, cutting off any stubborn patches with a paring knife. Slice the beets and toss them with butter or olive oil while they're still hot.

Beet and Walnut Salad

If you don't like beets or find their flavor overpowering, this salad may change your mind. The sherry vinegar provides the right accent, but balsamic vinegar will also work. If you're using an inexpensive brand of balsamic vinegar, you can improve it by boiling it down by half and keeping it on hand. The walnuts give this salad a welcome crunch, but other nuts, such as pine nuts, pecans, or slivered almonds, will also work.

I serve this salad at a casual lunch at the same time as everything else, but at dinner I serve it as a first course, either alone or with other small salads.

MAKES 4 FIRST-COURSE SERVINGS

Preheat the oven to 350°F.

Roast the nuts on a baking sheet for 15 minutes, until very lightly browned and fragrant. Let the nuts cool slightly and chop coarsely.

Slice the beets between $1/8$ and $1/4$ inch thick. Toss gently with the vinegar. At this stage the beets can sit in the refrigerator for up to a couple of days.

Just before serving, toss the beets with the nuts, olive oil, and parsley. Season with salt and pepper. If you're not serving this salad right away, toss in the nuts just before serving so they don't turn soggy.

VARIATION:

Try combining the cooked beets with the Horseradish Cream Sauce on page 217 instead of the butter.

$1/4$ cup walnuts or other nuts

4 medium cooked beets, peeled

$1 1/2$ tablespoons sherry vinegar or 2 tablespoons balsamic vinegar that's been boiled down by half

3 tablespoons extra-virgin olive oil

1 tablespoon finely chopped fresh parsley

Salt and freshly ground black pepper

Sauteed Beets with Olive Oil, Garlic, and Parsley

This is one of the easiest ways to serve beets. I especially like this method because the flavor of the garlic keeps up with the flavor of the beets without overpowering them.

MAKES 4 SIDE-DISH SERVINGS

Slice the beets between $1/8$ inch and $1/4$ inch thick. Heat the olive oil in a nonstick or well-seasoned sauté pan over medium heat. Add the garlic. When the garlic begins to sizzle, slide in the beets and toss or gently stir for about 5 minutes, just long enough to heat the beets through. Sprinkle the parsley and salt over the beets, grind over some fresh pepper, and sauté for 1 minute more. Serve immediately.

4 medium cooked beets, peeled

2 tablespoons extra-virgin olive oil or unsalted butter

1 large clove garlic, minced

1 tablespoon finely chopped fresh parsley

Salt and freshly ground black pepper

BELL PEPPERS

Nowadays bell peppers come in all sorts of bright colors—the brighter the color, it seems, the more expensive the pepper. Red, yellow, and orange peppers are riper and sweeter than green peppers, but I buy different colored peppers because they're pretty to look at more than because of very subtle differences in taste.

When shopping for bell peppers, make sure they don't have any soft or dark spots and avoid peppers with wrinkled skins. Try to find peppers with flat sides so they'll be easier to roast and peel. Raw bell peppers can be kept for up to 3 days in the refrigerator in a plastic bag with holes poked in it. Cooked peppers can be kept, covered, for up to 2 days in the refrigerator.

Some people like to add raw bell peppers to salads, but I prefer to roast or grill them and then scrape off their skins. Roasted peppers have a gentler (and to my mind, immensely better) flavor than raw peppers.

Though bell peppers are actually chiles—neither chiles nor bell peppers have any relationship to the ground pepper we sprinkle on food—bell peppers are completely without heat, so much of the time we use them differently than we use hot chiles. Because of their lack of heat, bell peppers are often called sweet peppers.

Miniature bell peppers.

Marinated Bell Peppers

These are an Italian favorite to serve as an antipasto or to include in various concoctions, including mixed salads and bruschette. The bell peppers are grilled or roasted, the charred skin is peeled off, and the pepper cut into thin strips and sprinkled with olive oil. I like to add chopped fresh herbs, especially if I have any marjoram around. Marinated bell peppers can also be added to a mixed crudité plate, used on pizza, or included in sandwiches. I sometimes serve marinated pepper strips with small slices of toasted bread for guests to help themselves. Marinated peppers will keep for 2 days in the refrigerator; if kept much longer, they sour.

MAKES 1 CUP, ENOUGH FOR 4 ANTIPASTI SERVINGS
OR 6 SERVINGS ON A CRUDITÉ PLATE

2 medium red or yellow bell peppers, or one of each

2 tablespoons extra-virgin olive oil

1 teaspoon salt

2 teaspoons chopped fresh marjoram leaves, or 1 teaspoon chopped fresh thyme leaves (optional)

Char, peel, and seed the peppers. Cut the peppers lengthwise into $1/4$-inch-wide strips. Toss the strips with olive oil, salt, and marjoram. Serve cool or at room temperature.

Bell Pepper and Anchovy Bruschette

I sometimes pass around these crunchy little toasts during the cocktail hour or put a plate of them on the table to start a simple meal. The peppers can be peeled and cut into strips ahead of time, but the bruschette must be assembled just before serving or they'll get soggy. You can garnish these bruschette with capers and pitted olives.

MAKES 8 HORS D'OEUVRE OR ANTIPASTI SERVINGS

16 slices French bread, 2 to 3 inches in diameter and $1/2$ inch thick

2 cloves garlic

2 tablespoons extra-virgin olive oil

32 anchovy fillets, soaked for 5 minutes in cold water and patted dry (soaking optional)

Marinated Bell Peppers (above)

Toast the French bread slices on both sides—it's easiest to do this under the broiler—and rub each slice on one side with a clove garlic and brush with the olive oil.

Place 2 anchovy fillets in an X on each slice and arrange the pepper strips, in rows, on top. Serve slightly warm.

Bell Pepper and Anchovy Bruschette.

BITTER MELON

While we may tolerate the occasional endive leaf or bite of bittersweet chocolate, we Americans aren't big on bitter. This isn't true for people in other parts of the world where children are as likely to anticipate a bitter snack as they are a sweet one.

Bitter melons look a bit like cucumbers, except some varieties are deeply ridged while others look like they have the skin of a crocodile. In any case, rarely is there any need to peel them. As any cursory appraisal of a typical Asian food stall will attest, bitter melons are wildly popular. They're appreciated all over Southeast Asia, in China, and especially in the Philippines, where they're used in the traditional stew, *pinakbet*. They can also be served cold, in the manner of cucumbers, with a little sugar and rice wine vinegar. They're enhanced with a sprinkling of chopped chiles and at times, perhaps, a little cilantro. Try adding them to Asian soups and stews and letting them simmer for 10 minutes or so.

Thai Bitter Melon and Chicken Soup

I don't know if they really have an exact version of this soup in Thailand, but the flavors are so consistent with things Thai that it seems they should. The soup calls for Thai curry paste, either red or green, which is made by grinding aromatic ingredients (lemon grass and kaffir lime leaves to name a few) until smooth. This is impossible to pull off with a food processor, which fails to achieve the proper smoothness. If the paste isn't smooth, the mixture will release its flavor more slowly and less efficiently than if an authentic Thai curry ground perfectly smooth is used.

MAKES 6 SIDE-DISH SERVINGS

Cut the bitter melons in half lengthwise and scoop out the pulp. Slice the two halves into 1/4-inch thick crescents.

Heat the peanut oil in a large wok or sauté pan over the highest heat. When the oil begins to ripple, stir in the chiles, let them sizzle for about 30 seconds, and add the Thai curry. Turn the heat up to high and stir the mixture around until you smell the aroma. Be careful sniffing—all those chiles heated up can knock your head back. Add the chicken and stir about 2 minutes more, still over high heat. Add the bitter melon, chicken, broth, coconut milk, cilantro, and fish sauce. Simmer gently for 10 minutes. Taste the soup for salt. If it needs salt, add fish sauce unless you find it intolerably strong. Serve immediately.

2 bitter melons

3 tablespoons peanut oil

2 to 5 Thai or serrano chiles, stemmed, seeded, and thinly sliced

3 tablespoons Thai Red Curry, (page 176)

2 boneless, skinless chicken breasts, cut into 1/2- by 3-inch strips

6 cups Basic BrownChicken Broth (page 373), Basic White Chicken Broth (page 374), or pork broth

1 (14-ounce) can unsweetened coconut milk

2 tablespoons chopped fresh cilantro

3 tablespoons fish sauce, or more to taste

BOK CHOY

Unless you live in a Chinese neighborhood, if you shop at the local supermarket or greengrocer, you'll probably only encounter only one kind of bok choy. But if you venture into a Chinese market, you may run into as many as four, as well as closely related mustards and cabbages. The most common bok choy—what you see at the supermarket—has beautiful, pure white stalks and dark green leaves that hold loosely together in elongated bunches.

In a Chinese market, things get a bit more complicated. One popular winter variety of bok choy is Shanghai bok choy, which is more squat than common bok choy and has pale green spoon-shaped stalks. Shanghai bok choy is usually sold in relatively small bunches, 6 to 8 inches long. You may also run into a small variety of bok choy that looks like Shanghai bok choy except that it has white stalks instead of green—or you may spot smallish bunches of bok choy sum with little yellow flowers and irregularly shaped leaves. Bok choy sum, also called choy sum, or "flowering cabbage," has much the same flavor as regular bok choy, but the little edible yellow flowers look so good in stir-fries that given the choice, you may want to buy bok choy sum when you see it.

Don't worry if you can't figure out which is which because all the varieties are cooked the same way. Even though you can cook bok choy as you would broccoli, broccoli raab, and other Western greens, most of us associate it so inextricably with Chinese cooking that there's something disorienting about cooking it in a European way. Because of this, I almost always stir-fry bok choy and include typically Chinese flavors and ingredients. Stir-fried bok choy is a great addition to a Chinese meal, but most of the time I serve it as a vegetable to go with simple roasted or grilled meat or fish.

To prepare bok choy for cooking, cut an inch off the bottom of the stalk and gently fold back and separate the branches, as you would celery. After washing, you can then just slice across the bok choy leaves, but I usually cut the leaves off the white stalks so I can cook the stalks for a few minutes before adding the greens. Once you get everything separated, all you need to do is slice the stalks and cut the leaves into strips.

Bok choy.

A FEW OTHER GREENS LIKE BOK CHOY

I'm always amazed when I walk through Chinatown in New York City and discover produce and other foods I've never seen before. A few Chinese vegetables have become special favorites.

CHINESE BROCCOLI (*gai lan*). It has the full flavor of broccoli raab but without the bitterness. A bunch of Chinese broccoli has more leaves than both broccoli and broccoli raab and the leaves are larger. It often has the familiar dark green buds that we see on broccoli raab, but much of the time the buds have blossomed into pretty little white flowers. Chinese broccoli has dark green stalks, so it's easy to distinguish it from bok choy, which has white or pale green stalks. Cook every part of the Chinese broccoli, except for the thick central stem (which I don't eat), as you would broccoli raab.

OIL SEED RAPE (*yau choy*). This variety is easy to recognize by its yellow flowers, oval leaves, and diminutive stalks. It's usually sold in 6- to 8-inch long bunches and is completely edible except for the largest central stalk at the base. Sauté or stir-fry oil seed rape as you would beet or turnip greens, broccoli raab, or chard. And if you like, flavor it in typical Chinese fashion with a few drops of toasted sesame oil. Oil seed rape is also delicious simmered for about 10 minutes in mixed vegetable or miso soups.

BAMBOO MUSTARD CABBAGE (*juk gai choy*). While it looks similar to other mustard greens, it's nothing like what we usually think of as cabbage. It's easy to recognize because its leaves have saw-toothed edges. It's usually sold in small bunches of about 8 inches long with thin, very pale green stalks. Bamboo mustard cabbage can be added to soups or stir-fried or sautéed like other greens, but it should be boiled for a couple of minutes first.

WRAPPED HEART MUSTARD CABBAGE (*dai gai choy*). This variety looks like an elongated cabbage—slightly bulbous at one end but with dark green leaves opening at the other. Mustard cabbage is most often pickled, but it can also be shredded and added to soups in the same way as regular cabbage.

TATSOI. Related to bok choy and cabbage, it fans out in a series of lollipop-shaped leaves. This tendency to spread open may be one reason it is sometimes called flat cabbage. It's rarely found alone but you're likely to encounter it as a component in mesclun mixes.

TAH CHOY. It looks a little like spinach except that it has thicker, whitish, stems. Fortunately the stems are fine to eat. Tah choy is best included in stir-fries with other vegetables or meat.

Totsoi. (top)
Tah choy. (middle)
Yu choy sum. (bottom)

YU CHOY SUM. Similar in appearance to mustard greens—it has little yellow flowers—except that it has broad green leaves and long white stems. It's delicious in stir-fries.

BOTTLED FLAVORINGS FOR CHINESE VEGETABLES

Many Chinese green vegetable recipes are simply recommendations for stir-frying or steaming and then tossing the vegetables in a sauce—often bottled—just before serving.

CHINESE BLACK VINEGAR. Chinese black vinegars have a deep flavor and are much less expensive than other fine vinegars, such as Italian balsamic vinegar. (Good quality, albeit not authentic, Italian balsamic vinegar makes an acceptable substitute.) Buy the best black vinegar you can. Bruce Cost, in his excellent book *Bruce Cost's Asian Ingredients*, recommends Gold Plum brand Chinkiang vinegar from China.

CHINESE CHILE PASTE. While chili pastes come from throughout Asia, Chinese brands seem to be the best. They are delicious added to stir-fries when heat is desirable. But be careful—they're very hot. Bruce Cost in his book *Bruce Cost's Asian Ingredients* says that Lan Chi Brand "Chilli (sic) paste with garlic" or Chilli (sic) with Soybean", both which come in 8-ounce jars.

HOISIN SAUCE. This soy-based, garlicky, and rather sweet sauce is delicious when stirred into a bowl of hot Chinese vegetables. Use it sparingly—a tablespoon or two for four servings—because it's very sweet. I sometimes add a teaspoon of toasted sesame oil to the vegetables when I'm using hoisin sauce. Bruce Cost's first choice is Ma Ling hoisin sauce from China, followed by Koon Chun Sauce Factory and Wei-Chuan brands.

OYSTER SAUCE. Not everyone is fond of oyster sauce, but there are those who like to sprinkle it on just about anything. Cheap brands may smell like low tide, but better brands have a clean oyster smell and flavor. Bruce Cost recommends Sa Cheng Oyster Flavored Sauce from China. If you can't find this brand, buy the most expensive.

SOY SAUCE. I prefer the flavor of Japanese dark soy sauce, even for Chinese dishes. A tablespoon or two of soy sauce in a stir-fry or as a seasoning for steamed green vegetables makes an interesting alternative to salt. Soy sauce is especially good when combined with finely chopped ginger, garlic, and sesame oil. A good brand is Kikkoman.

TOASTED SESAME OIL. This deep brown oil is so intensely flavored that you'll need only $1/2$ to a 1 teaspoon to flavor a dish. Be sure to buy toasted sesame oil, not the pale oils that sometimes show up in health food stores. Japanese brands seem to be the best.

Sauté-Steamed Bok Choy with Cashews

I gave "sauté-steaming" its hybrid name because the process is started out in a sauté pan with hot oil—the bok choy is sautéed—but as the bok choy releases moisture of its own, it steams rather than actually sautés. A little water is added to create extra steam. You can use this method for any green leafy vegetable.

MAKES 4 SIDE-DISH SERVINGS

Cut 1 inch off the bottom of the bok choy bunch and separate the stems and leaves. Cut the stems into 1-inch pieces and the leaves crosswise into 1-inch-wide strips.

In a wok or large pan, sauté the garlic and ginger in the peanut oil for about 1 minute over medium heat. Add the stems and the cashews and sauté over high heat for about 3 minutes more. Add the leaves and water and cook for 6 minutes, stirring occasionally. Season to taste with salt or soy sauce and pepper. Stir in the sesame oil.

VARIATIONS:

Try finishing the bok choy with $1/2$ teaspoon of Chinese chile paste, 2 teaspoons toasted sesame oil, a trace of sugar, and 3 tablespoons Chinese black vinegar. You can also finish this basic recipe with 3 tablespoons of oyster sauce. Another possibility is to add a little hoisin sauce to taste.

1 large bunch bok choy or bok choy sum, or 2 bunches of a smaller variety, such as Shanghai bok choy

1 clove garlic, minced

1 tablespoon grated fresh ginger (optional)

1 tablespoon peanut oil

$2/3$ cup roasted whole salted or unsalted cashews

2 tablespoons water

Salt or Japanese dark soy sauce

Freshly ground black pepper

1 teaspoon toasted sesame oil (optional)

Sauté-steaming the bok choy.

Sauté-Steamed Bok Choy with Cashews.

BROCCOLI

Because it's available year-round, inexpensive, and easy to cook, broccoli is one of America's favorite vegetables. Surprisingly broccoli is relatively new to American cooking. It wasn't marketed here until the late 1920s and didn't become firmly established until the 1950s.

Shop for broccoli with tightly closed, dark, evenly green florets (the little bunches of flowers are called florets). Avoid broccoli with flowers that have begun to yellow or unfold. Give the broccoli a sniff. If it smells strong and cabbagy, don't buy it. Broccoli is best eaten right away, but it can be stored for about 2 days in the vegetable bin in a plastic bag with a few holes poked in the plastic to allow excess moisture to escape.

Because broccoli is a flower, it's tender and cooks quickly and can even be eaten raw. Many cooks discard the broccoli stems, which are relatively tough, but the stems can be perfectly satisfying to eat—they just take longer to cook. If you want to use the stems, peel them with a paring knife and then slice or chop them. Whichever method you use for cooking the broccoli, put the stems in a few minutes ahead so they'll be done at the same time as the florets. You can cut the florets away from the stems so the florets range in width from 1 to 2 inches.

Most people cook broccoli by plunging the florets into a pot of rapidly boiling water, but broccoli also takes well to steaming since it cooks very quickly and won't lose its color. (Prolonged steaming can make green vegetables look drab.) You can serve steamed or boiled broccoli with a little lemon juice and/or butter. Cooked broccoli can also be sautéed in olive oil flavored with various ingredients, such as garlic and hot peppers.

Broccoli.

Basic Pan-Steamed or Boiled Broccoli
with Lemon and Parsley

Boiling and pan-steaming are the easiest and quickest ways to cook broccoli. Pan-steaming is a method of cooking vegetables directly in a pot or sauté pan with a small amount of water instead of in a steamer. Pan-steamed broccoli should be prepared at the last minute and served immediately—pan-steamed broccoli doesn't reheat well. If you want to cook broccoli ahead of time, it's better to boil it. Boiling is a good technique for a dinner party, when you want to cook the broccoli in advance and reheat it at the last minute. Restaurant cooks sometimes plunge precooked broccoli into boiling water for the final reheating, with the unfortunate result that the broccoli ends up with no flavor at all. A better reheating method is to gently sauté the cooked and refreshed broccoli in a little butter or olive oil—just long enough to reheat the broccoli—immediately before serving. This method also makes it easy to flavor the broccoli by cooking ingredients such as chopped garlic, chiles, or shallots in the butter or olive oil before adding the broccoli.

If you want a completely fat-free dish, leave out the butter. Broccoli goes with just about anything—meats, seafood, pasta, or other vegetables.

continued

Cut the stems off the broccoli.

Cut the florets into the size you like.

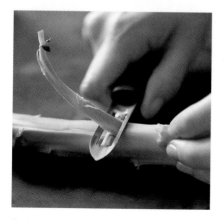

Peel the stems.

Cut the stems into bite-size rounds.

BROCCOLI

Cut the florets away from the large stem. The size of the florets is up to you, but I usually cut them so the flower part is about 2 inches in diameter. If you want smaller florets, cut the smaller stems just beneath each flower. If you want to use the large stems, peel them and slice them to about the thickness of a quarter.

TO STEAM: Put the thinly sliced stems (if you're using them) and florets in a wide pan or pot with a tight-fitting lid. Pour over 3/4 cup of cold water, cover the pan, and bring to a boil over high heat. Turn down the heat to low to maintain a slow simmer and steam the broccoli for 5 minutes, shaking the pan back and forth every minute or so—don't lift the lid even for a second—to help the broccoli cook evenly.

Remove the lid. Turn the heat up to high to evaporate any liquid left in the bottom of the pan. Stir in the parsley and butter and season to taste with salt and pepper. Sprinkle over the lemon juice just before serving—don't add it earlier or it will turn the broccoli gray. Serve at once.

TO BOIL: Bring about 3 quarts of salted water to a rapid boil in a large pot. Toss the stems and florets into the boiling water. Boil, uncovered, for 4 minutes. Drain immediately in a colander. Toss the broccoli with the parsley, butter, and lemon juice in a warmed dish and season with salt and pepper. Serve at once.

To prepare broccoli for later in the day, boil the broccoli as above for 4 minutes, drain it, rinse it in cold running water, and drain again. Just before you're ready to serve, heat the broccoli in butter in a sauté pan and sprinkle it with the parsley, lemon juice, salt, and pepper. Serve at once.

VARIATIONS:

One of the best ways to liven up a plate of broccoli is to toss the cooked broccoli with various herb-flavored butters. Garlic-Parsley Butter (page 366) is one of the best. Heat 3 tablespoons of garlic and parsley butter over medium heat in a wide skillet until it froths. Leave out the lemon and butter in the recipe for boiled broccoli and toss the cooked broccoli (either hot or cold) into the skillet. Toss for about 2 minutes—or a little longer if you started out with cold broccoli—season with salt and pepper, and serve immediately. I sometimes sprinkle about a teaspoon of Pernod into the hot butter just before adding the broccoli. Boiled broccoli is also delicious with hollandaise sauce: make the recipe above but leave out the butter and lemon juice. Serve the Hollandaise Sauce (page 370) at the table for guests to help themselves.

1 (1½-pound) head broccoli

1 tablespoon finely chopped fresh parsley

2 tablespoons unsalted butter (optional)

Salt and freshly ground black pepper

1 tablespoon fresh lemon juice

Refresh boiled and drained broccoli in cold water.

Sautéing broccoli.

BROCCOLINI

These slender stalks with flowers at one end are somewhat reminiscent of asparagus in appearance, but much less so in flavor—they taste like broccoli rabe without the bitterness. They can be quickly boiled or steamed, drained, and tossed with butter or olive oil. They are also delicious when grilled.

Broccolini with Pancetta, Anchovies, and Raisins

Most people don't hesitate to eat broccolini stems because they're more tender than, say, broccoli rabe stems. But if you just want to eat the flowers, cut off the stems and double the basic amounts of broccolini called for here.

MAKES 4 SIDE-DISH SERVINGS

Combine the pancetta and olive oil in a large sauté pan and cook the pancetta, uncovered, over low to medium heat until it barely begins to turn crispy, about 5 minutes. Add the broccolini, turn the heat to high, and stir for about 4 minutes, until the broccolini wilts slightly. Stir in the anchovies and raisins and season to taste with salt (go easy because of the anchovies) and pepper. Serve at once.

4 ounces pancetta, diced

2 tablespoons pure olive oil

1 pound broccolini (or 2 pounds if removing the stems)

10 anchovies, drained, finely chopped, and crushed to a paste

$1/2$ cup raisins or other diced dried fruit

Salt and freshly ground black pepper

❧ ANCHOVIES ❧

To soften the flavor of commercially packed anchovies and to get rid of the strong-flavored oil that surrounds them, you can soak them in cold water for 5 minutes and pat them dry with paper towels.

If you can get to an Italian or Spanish neighborhood, you'll find cans of salted anchovies, which are meatier and have a much deeper flavor than anchovies packed in oil. The problem is that once the can has been opened, the anchovies get very fishy, so you have to buy a whole can and pack the anchovies yourself in olive oil in small storage jars, preferably the European kind with clamp-down lids. The cans aren't small—they are at least 600 grams, about $1^{1}/_2$ pounds, so you'll end up with a lot of anchovies. I've had luck with a Sicilian brand, *Agostino Recca*.

Open the can and run cold water over the top of the anchovies. Gently pull the anchovies away from each other and put them in a large mixing bowl filled with cold water. Change the water in the bowl and let the anchovies soak for 20 minutes. Gently pull the two fillets away from the backbone—remember these are whole fish—with your thumb and forefinger. Work under gently running cold water, which will rinse away any viscera clinging to the head end of the fillets. Pull any obvious pin bones away from the fillets. (But don't get obsessive, a bone or two won't make any difference.) Pat the fillets dry with kitchen towels. Pack the fillets in jars and pour over enough extra-virgin olive oil to completely cover by at least a half inch. Push down on the fillets to make sure the oil gets down into the jar. Store in the refrigerator for up to several months. Unlike anchovies out of a jar or can, your own bottled anchovies don't need to be soaked before they are used.

BROCCOLI RABE

I discovered broccoli rabe about fifteen years ago, when I quickly grabbed a bunch mistaking it for broccoli. When I got it home I didn't quite know what to do, so I cooked it up in a little olive oil and have been addicted ever since. Broccoli rabe is not to everyone's taste because it is somewhat bitter, but I and most of my friends (who admittedly are more adventurous than most) must have broccoli rabe—often.

Italians call broccoli rabe *broccoli di rape,* which means, literally, "turnip sprouts," but broccoli rabe looks and tastes very little like turnip greens, and for that matter, not much like broccoli. Broccoli rabe has very much its own flavor with a particular gentle bitterness.

Broccoli rabe does look a bit like regular broccoli except that it has smaller flowers, more leaves, and thinner stems attached to one thick central stem. A bunch of broccoli rabe is made up of a bundle of long shoots, covered with flowers and leaves. When buying broccoli rabe, look for tightly closed flowers and avoid bunches with a lot of yellow flowers, especially if the flowers are faded or the leaves are wilted. Inspect the stems carefully and make sure there are no areas that have begun to rot or that look slimy. You can keep broccoli rabe in the refrigerator, loosely wrapped in a plastic bag with holes poked in it, for up to 2 days.

To prepare broccoli rabe, just break off and use the flowers and the leaves and discard the thick stems (these can also be peeled, sliced, and sautéed). Unlike regular broccoli, whose stems have a somewhat delicate flavor, broccoli rabe stems are tough and bitter. After washing and draining the broccoli rabe flowers and leaves, you can sauté the broccoli rabe in olive oil or in butter or, for some recipes, you can boil or steam them. Both methods take 5 to 10 minutes.

Broccoli rabe leaves.

Japanese-Style Cold Broccoli Rabe

Although I've never encountered broccoli rabe in Japanese restaurants, its full flavor makes it a natural with Japanese ingredients. I serve each guest his or her own little bowl of the broccoli rabe, each with a few tablespoons of the light brothy sauce.

MAKES 4 SIDE-DISH SERVINGS

Bring about 4 quarts of salted water to a rapid boil.

Cut the broccoli rabe flowers and leaves away from the larger stems. Discard the stems. Rinse and drain the leaves and flowers in a colander.

Bring the dashi, mirin, and soy sauce to a slow simmer in a small saucepan and let cool.

Boil the broccoli rabe leaves and flowers, uncovered, over high heat for about 5 minutes and drain in a colander. Rinse immediately with cold water and spin dry in a salad spinner. Distribute the broccoli rabe among four small bowls and spoon over the cool broth. Sprinkle with the sesame seeds and serve immediately.

NOTE: If you want to serve the broccoli rabe hot, don't rinse it. Transfer it to four warmed bowls, spoon over the hot broth in the small bowls, and sprinkle over the sesame seeds.

I (1-pound) bunch broccoli rabe or Chinese broccoli

I cup Dashi (page 77)

2 tablespoons mirin, or I tablespoon sugar dissolved in 2 tablespoons hot water

2 tablespoons Japanese dark soy sauce

2 teaspoons white sesame seeds (optional)

Orecchiette with Broccoli Rabe or Swiss Chard

Orecchiette are "little ears" made by pinching bean-size pieces of fresh pasta dough between thumb and forefinger into little concave circles. You can make your own orecchiette, but most people, even in Italy, buy orecchiette dried. If you can't find orecchiette at your local supermarket or gourmet store, substitute another pasta such as rigatoni, penne, elbow macaroni, or conchiglie.

MAKES 6 PASTA-COURSE OR 4 MAIN-COURSE SERVINGS

Bring about 4 quarts of salted water to a rapid boil in a large pot.

Cut the broccoli rabe flowers and leaves away from the large central stems. Chop the flowers, leaves, and smaller stems coarsely and discard the large stems, which are usually too bitter. If you are using Swiss chard, separate the leaves from the stems, discard the stems, and chop the leaves coarsely.

Heat 3 tablespoons of the olive oil in a wide skillet or sauté pan over medium heat. Add the garlic. Once it starts to sizzle, turn the heat up to high and stir in the chopped leaves, stems, and flowers, or the Swiss chard leaves. Stir for about 5 minutes, or until the greens have completely wilted.

While the greens are cooking, put the orecchiette in the pot of boiling water, 5 to 10 minutes for dried and about 2 minutes for fresh. Test the orecchiette for doneness by fishing a piece out with a spoon and biting into it.

Drain the pasta, return it to the empty pot, and pour over the greens, the remaining 5 tablespoons of the olive oil, and the cheese; toss quickly. Season with salt and pepper and serve immediately. Pass extra Parmesan cheese at the table.

2 pounds broccoli rabe or Swiss chard

1/2 cup extra-virgin olive oil

2 cloves garlic, minced

I pound dried or 1 1/2 pounds fresh pasta, such as penne or orecchiette

Salt

Freshly ground black pepper

1/2 cup freshly grated Parmigiano-Reggiano cheese, plus more to serve

BRUSSELS SPROUTS

Much of Brussels sprouts' reputation for strong flavor comes from their being overcooked until they end up soggy, gray, and odoriferous. While Brussels sprouts are never mild tasting, they're at their best when only lightly cooked and when cooked with savory or smoky ingredients (such as bacon) that balance their flavor.

Brussels sprouts look like tiny cabbages—in fact, the French call them *choux de bruxelles*, or "Brussels cabbages." If you've seen Brussels sprouts only in packages at the supermarket, it may come as a surprise to see them on their stalks, looking like toy models of DNA.

Brussels sprouts are best in the late fall and early winter and are among the few vegetables that aren't killed or severely stunted by the cold. You're most likely to find Brussels sprouts on the stalk in the fall, which is some guarantee of freshness and better flavor. If you can't find them on the stalk—your chances are best at a farmers' market—buy them loose or in those little cellophane-covered boxes they sell at the supermarket. If you're buying them loose, pick ones all the same size. I look for the smallest ones I can find, just because they look pretty—larger Brussels sprouts taste just as good. Inspect the leaves to make sure they aren't wilted or speckled with tiny worm holes and check the bottoms of the Brussels sprouts—where they've been cut away from the stalk—to make sure they're not dark brown or dried out—signs that the cutting was done a bit too long ago. Don't store Brussels sprouts in plastic bags. Brussels sprouts will keep for several days in a paper bag, but use them as soon as you can—when refrigerated for too long they start to become strong tasting.

Brussels sprouts.

Brussels sprouts don't need much trimming. If you're buying them already cut off the stalk, you'll have to shave off any traces of brown on the bottom of the sprouts. You should also peel off and discard the outermost, dark leaves. If you find small Brussels sprouts—a half inch wide or so—you can cook them whole, but larger sprouts are best cut in halves or even into quarters through the base so they'll cook more quickly and be easier to eat. Brussels sprouts should be boiled, uncovered, in salted water for 6 to 8 minutes before they are simply tossed with butter and served, or before they are cooked using other methods. You can also peel the leaves away from Brussels sprouts and quickly cook them with a little bacon or prosciutto into a warm wilted salad. Brussels sprouts can also be grilled or cooked in a gratin.

Because of their strong flavor, Brussels sprouts are best served with full-flavored foods, such as roasted meats.

Trim the tiny root end away from the sprouts.

Pull off the outer leaves.

If the sprouts are large, cut them in halves or quarters.

Brussels Sprouts with Bacon

The smoky flavor of bacon makes a perfect accent for root vegetables and anything even vaguely related to cabbage. Some cooks are frightened of bacon because of its fat, but because bacon has such a full flavor, you'll need very little.

I like to serve this dish in the late fall with roasted meats. It makes a great accompaniment to the Thanksgiving turkey.

MAKES 6 TO 8 SIDE-DISH SERVINGS

If the Brussels sprouts are $^3/_4$ inch wide or smaller, leave whole. If they are about 1 inch wide, cut in half through the base, and if larger, cut in quarters.

Bring about 6 quarts of salted water to a rapid boil in a large pot. Boil the Brussels sprouts for 7 minutes, uncovered, and drain in a colander. If you're serving the Brussels sprouts right away, don't rinse them. (If you're using them later or for a cold dish, rinse them with cold water so they don't overcook.

Heat the bacon in a wide skillet or sauté pan over medium heat until the bacon renders slightly and just begins to turn crispy, about 8 minutes. Toss or stir the Brussels sprouts with the bacon over medium heat for about 3 minutes or slightly longer if the sprouts are cold. Season to taste with salt and pepper, but be careful with the salt—the bacon is already salty. Serve immediately on individual plates or in a heated serving dish.

1$^1/_2$ pounds loose Brussels sprouts, or 2 (10-ounce) packages, trimmed

2 thin-cut slices bacon, finely chopped

Salt and freshly ground black pepper

Brussels Sprouts with Bacon.

Brussels Sprouts with Raisins and Pistachios

The juxtaposition of sweetness helps relieve Brussels sprouts' gentle bitterness. You can also add raisins and pistachios to Brussels Sprouts with Bacon (above).

MAKES 4 SIDE-DISH SERVINGS

Sauté the Brussels sprouts in the olive oil for about 8 minutes. Add the raisins and pistachios, sauté for 1 minute more and season to taste with salt and pepper.

12 ounces loose Brussels sprouts or 1 (10-ounce) package, trimmed

3 tablespoons pure olive oil

$^1/_2$ cup golden raisins

$^1/_2$ cup shelled and peeled pistachios (unroasted, unsalted)

Salt and freshly ground black pepper

BURDOCK

Burdock is a long, slender, cylindrical hairy root that looks a little like salsify. After peeling, keep burdock submerged in water with a little lemon juice in it to keep it from darkening. When shopping for burdock—in the fall or winter—make sure the roots are stiff and don't have any soft spots.

Japanese cooks are experts at burdock cookery. The orange pickled burdock encountered at sushi bars is a delicious version. I sometimes buy it canned or in jars in Japanese groceries under the name *gobo* and serve it with raw fish or rare-grilled tuna steaks. I cook burdock by loosely following a recipe in Shizuo Tsuji's *Japanese Cooking: A Simple Art*. Mr. Tsuji whittles a medium burdock into little slivers—as though sharpening a pencil with a paring knife—and then stir-fries the slivers in a tablespoon of vegetable oil for about 3 minutes. He then adds 2 tablespoons sake, 2 tablespoons Japanese dark soy sauce, and 2 to 3 teaspoons of sugar and stir-fries for about 5 minutes more, until the liquid reduced to almost nothing and leaves the burdock coated with a shiny glaze. He then sprinkles the burdock with 1/4 teaspoon red pepper flakes or Japanese seven-spice mixture (*shichimi*). Mr. Tsuji suggests serving this dish with rice or grilled seafood.

Peeling burdock.

Burdock.

CABBAGE

Perhaps because it grows well in winter and has become a staple in cold countries, cabbage is often thought of as a food for the poor. Many of us eschew it in favor of more trendy vegetables or hothouse greens, but because of its ability to foil richly flavored meats such as pork, squab, and foie gras, the modest cabbage has sneaked in through the backdoor of some of the world's most luxurious restaurants.

There are dozens of varieties of cabbage—including many Chinese varieties—but those we normally think of as cabbage usually come in ball-shaped pale green or dark red heads. The most familiar variety of cabbage, the common cabbage, comes in both red and green. Savoy cabbage, except for the outer leaves, is pale green and has somewhat looser leaves, which make it easier to use in dishes where the leaves must be peeled away one by one.

Buy cabbage that is heavy and that has shiny, tightly packed leaves with no signs of yellowing, dark patches, or insect holes.

You can keep common cabbage in the refrigerator in paper bags or in plastic bags with holes poked in them for up to 2 weeks.

Some dishes call for quartering and/or slicing the cabbage before cooking (or for eating raw). To keep the cabbage from falling apart, cut it so that some of the center core is left attached to the pieces (see photos, below and on page 130).

To separate the leaves from a whole cabbage, dip the head in boiling water for 1 minute, rinse with cold water, and peel off the leaves. Keep repeating the dipping and rinsing until you've removed all the leaves.

When cooked by itself, cabbage has a somewhat insipid flavor, but it comes into its own when combined with meats such as pork, duck, or goose in braised dishes and soups.

Purple cabbage.

Cutting the cabbage in half after removing the outer leaves.

Baked Red Cabbage with Apples and Bacon

The French are fond of sweet-and-sour flavors with red cabbage, the classic sweet-and-sour ingredients being apples and vinegar. I also include a smoky element like the bacon here. Bake the cabbage in an earthenware, glass, enameled iron, or stainless steel pot—cabbage, especially green cabbage, has a weird way of reacting and turning gray when baked in aluminum, cast-iron, or tinned copper.

MAKES ENOUGH FOR 8 SIDE-DISH SERVINGS

Thinly slice the cabbage with a chef's knife or vegetable slicer (see photos, below).

If you're using slab bacon, slice it into 1/4-inch-thick strips. If you're using presliced bacon, cut the bacon slices crosswise into 1-inch strips.

Cook the bacon strips in a heavy-bottomed pot over medium heat until they barely begin to turn crispy, about 8 minutes. There should be about 3 tablespoons of bacon fat in the pot, but if your bacon is very fatty, spoon out the excess. Scoop out the bacon strips with a slotted spoon and reserve.

Cook the onions in the bacon fat over medium heat until they become limp but not brown, about 10 minutes. Add the cabbage and the reserved bacon to the pot with the onions, and stir over medium heat for about 5 minutes, until the cabbage becomes limp.

Preheat the oven to 350°F.

Peel the apples and cut them into quarters. Cut the core out of each of the quarters, and thinly slice the quarters. Toss the slices with the sugar and vinegar and gently stir everything into the cabbage mixture. Season to taste with salt.

Transfer the cabbage mixture into a stainless steel, glass, or earthenware pot, cover, and bake for 1 hour. Grind over fresh pepper and serve.

1 medium (2 1/2-pound) red cabbage, quartered

4 ounces bacon

2 medium onions, thinly sliced

3 large tart apples, such as Granny Smith

1 tablespoon sugar

6 tablespoons cider vinegar or good-quality white wine vinegar

Salt and freshly ground black pepper

Quartering the cabbage.

Removing the cores from each quarter.

Slicing the cabbage into shreads.

Red Cabbage Salad with Pecans

The idea of a raw cabbage salad never appealed until it occurred to me to use walnut oil and toss in toasted pecans. I serve this salad with one or two others as part of a crudité plate, but you can also serve it with grilled fish and meats or cold leftover roasts, especially pork roast. It's best to make this salad for a crowd because a whole red cabbage, even a small one, makes about 10 servings. This recipe calls for toasted walnut oil, but toasted hazelnut oil is also delicious, and olive oil will do. Be sure to use toasted nut oils (see page 38) and always keep them in the refrigerator once opened.

MAKES 10 FIRST-COURSE SERVINGS

Preheat the oven to 350°F.

Spread the nuts in a shallow pan and toast for 15 minutes.

Thinly slice the cabbage crosswise, with a chef's knife or vegetable slicer.

Toss the cabbage with the salt in a mixing bowl and rub the salt into the cabbage for a minute or two, until you no longer feel the salt under your fingers. Drain the cabbage in a colander for 30 minutes. Squeeze the cabbage in small balls in your hands to get rid of liquid and excess salt.

Toss the cabbage with the vinegar, walnut oil, and the toasted nuts. Season to taste with pepper and more oil or vinegar as needed. If you're not serving right away, leave out the nuts until you're ready to serve—otherwise they get soggy.

1 cup whole pecans or coarsely chopped walnut halves

1 small (1½-pound) red cabbage, quartered

1 tablespoon coarse salt

⅓ cup sherry vinegar or balsamic vinegar, or more as needed

½ cup toasted walnut oil or toasted hazelnut oil or extra-virgin olive oil, or more as needed

Freshly ground black pepper

Coleslaw

I've never been a big fan of coleslaw, probably because I don't like mayonnaise out of a jar, and I've always found something insipid about the combination of raw cabbage and mayonnaise. But you can eliminate these problems by using home-made mayonnaise with plenty of Dijon mustard and then adding capers and little cornichons (French sour pickles) to give the whole thing some zing. At the risk of turning traditional American coleslaw into something French, I've also called for fresh tarragon, but this can be skipped or replaced with the same amount of fresh dill or half as much dried dill.

MAKES 10 SIDE-DISH SERVINGS

Thinly slice the quarters, crosswise, with a chef's knife or with a vegetable slicer.

In a mixing bowl, rub the cabbage with the coarse salt for a couple of minutes until you can no longer feel the salt under your fingers. Drain the cabbage in a colander for 30 minutes. Quickly rinse the cabbage under cold water and squeeze it dry.

Stir the vinegar and mustard into the mayonnaise and add it to the cabbage in a large mixing bowl. Chop the pickles and capers to the consistency of hamburger relish and stir into the cabbage along with the red onion and tarragon. Season to taste with salt and pepper.

Coleslaw is best lightly chilled and served the same day it is made.

1 medium (2½-pound) red or green cabbage, quartered

2 tablespoons coarse salt

2 tablespoons sherry vinegar or good-quality white wine vinegar

2 tablespoons Dijon mustard

1 cup Basic Mayonnaise (page 367)

15 cornichons

3 tablespoons capers, drained

1 red onion, minced

2 tablespoons coarsely chopped fresh tarragon or dill, or 1 tablespoon dried dill

Salt and freshly ground black pepper

CHINESE CABBAGE

Sometimes called celery cabbage or napa cabbage, Chinese cabbage comes in two basic types. The most common is a very large and pale elongated cabbage, called napa cabbage. Less common is a slender variety called *chihi* cabbage, which is sometimes confused with bok choy, especially in Chinese vegetable markets, where the problem of language compounds the already confusing botanical relationships of dozens of varieties of radishes, mustards, various choys, and, of course, cabbage. Fortunately both the long and squat Chinese cabbages can be used interchangeably, and even if you strayed further from the mark and were to use bok choy, the results would be fine.

Chinese cabbage has a more delicate texture and flavor than both our common cabbage and Savoy cabbage, which means that Chinese cabbage can be used as a substitute for those stronger-flavored varieties. This is a boon for those of us who find the flavor of our more common cabbages to be too strong.

Napa cabbage.

Napa Cabbage, Bok Choy, and Wild Mushroom Stir-Fry

If you don't have wild mushrooms, substitute quartered cremini mushrooms or shiitake mushrooms.

MAKES 4 MAIN-COURSE SERVINGS

Heat the oil in a wok or skillet over medium heat and add the ginger and garlic. Let the garlic and ginger sizzle for about 1 minute and add the sesame oil. Add the cabbage, bok choy, and mushrooms; turn the heat to high, and stir-fry about 2 minutes. Add the broth, cover the wok or skillet, and simmer over low heat for about 10 minutes. Season to taste with oyster sauce and soy sauce. Serve immediately.

3 tablespoons peanut oil

2 tablespoons chopped fresh ginger

2 cloves garlic, minced

2 teaspoons toasted sesame oil

1/2 napa cabbage, shredded

1 bunch bok choy, shredded

1 pound assorted wild mushrooms, trimmed

3/4 cup Basic Brown Chicken Broth (see page 373) or water

2 tablespoons oyster sauce, or to taste

3 tablespoons Japanese dark soy sauce

Slicing napa cabbage into shreds.

Napa Cabbage, Bok Choy, and Wild Mushroom Stir-Fry.

Kimchi

Chinese cabbage is delicious when shredded, preserved with salt, and steeped with strongly flavored ingredients. The result is similar to sauerkraut, except that Chinese cabbage doesn't taste as strong or smell as sulfury. Chinese cabbage also takes well to treatment with Asian ingredients, so it's easy to come up with various coleslaw-like variations, each with an Asian twist.

The most familiar of Asian preserved cabbage dishes is kimchi, which Koreans use to accompany almost everything they eat in much the same way that we Americans use (or at least used to use) ketchup or mustard. I make a simplified and less potent version of kimchi (traditional versions contain fermented fish) that I like to serve with sautéed or grilled meats, especially pork chops and steaks. But beware—you may find this stuff addictive and end up pulling it out of the fridge, Korean style, at every meal. This recipe makes about 2 quarts that, depending on your eating habits, may last you a few days or a few weeks. Kimchi gets stronger as it sits in the refrigerator, but you'll have a good 3 or 4 weeks before it gets out of hand.

Squeezing the cabbage to drain excess liquid.

MAKES 2 QUARTS

Trim off any tough or wilted outer leaves from the cabbage and cut the cabbage lengthwise into quarters. Cut out and discard the section of core in the center of each of the quarters. Cut the quarters crosswise into 1½-inch pieces. Wash the cabbage in a large bowl of cold water and spin it dry in a salad spinner.

In a mixing bowl, rub the cabbage with the salt until all the salt dissolves and you can no longer feel it under your fingers, about 5 minutes. Put the cabbage in a colander to drain for 4 hours. Squeeze the cabbage in small clumps in your hands to get rid of excess liquid—by this time the cabbage will be quite wet. Toss the drained and squeezed cabbage with the garlic, ginger, red pepper flakes, and sugar.

Clean a 2-quart mason jar (or two 1-quart mason jars) by filling it with boiling water and letting it sit with its lid on for 5 minutes. Empty out the water and turn the jar over onto a paper towel to cool. Fill with the kimchi and place the lid very loosely. It's important that the lid not be on too tight at this stage because the kimchi releases gas as it ferments. Leave the jar at room temperature for 3 days.

At this point, taste the kimchi to see if it's strong enough. Some people, especially neophytes, like kimchi fresh and crunchy, while others like a stronger, more fermented flavor. If the kimchi isn't strong enough, leave it another day and taste again. If it's ready, go ahead and secure the lid and store in the refrigerator.

1 (3-pound) napa or Chinese cabbage

2 tablespoons coarse salt

3 cloves garlic, minced

1½ tablespoons finely grated fresh ginger

1 tablespoon red pepper flakes

2 teaspoons sugar

Tossing the drained cabbage.

Kimchi, ready to store.

STUFFED CABBAGE

In Europe, there are recipes for stuffed cabbage wherever cabbage grows, which is almost everywhere. Regardless of where these recipes originated, they have certain characteristics in common. The stuffing usually contains pork or leftover braised meats, a little bit of smoked meat such as bacon, chopped vegetables (often leftovers), bread crumbs to lighten the mixture and help hold it together, and various spices and seasonings. Once you've experimented a little, you'll learn to make up your own mixtures using leftovers. In addition to these more traditional mixtures, cabbage has reappeared in fine restaurants—after a long period of disdain—combined with expensive and luxurious ingredients such as wild mushrooms, pheasant, foie gras, and squab.

You can stuff cabbage in several ways. First, you can remove the leaves one at a time, boil them for about 10 minutes, and then stuff each leaf individually. Depending on the stuffing and the style of the dish, you can gently reheat these packets or braise them in a little broth. Another method is to boil the whole cabbage. You carefully pull apart the leaves without tearing them, push the stuffing in between the leaves, and then tie the whole thing up with string and poach it in broth. You can also stuff cabbage by lining individual bowls with the boiled leaves and the stuffing and covering with additional leaves. Then you cover the individual bowls with aluminum foil and bake them.

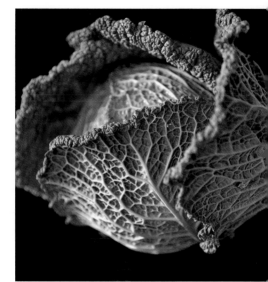

Savoy cabbage.

Potted Stuffed Cabbage

I learned this recipe from Robert Viret, the original French chef-owner of a restaurant I eventually owned in Greenwich Village in New York. This cabbage dish was so popular that people would come from miles around to taste it. As flattering as this was, it was frustrating because these lovers of stuffed cabbage would never try anything else on the menu. An attempt to take the cabbage off the menu during the hot summer months was met with angry indignation, so this filling dish was served all year.

Part of what makes this dish so lovely is that the vegetables are first cooked in olive oil and white wine and are then used as a topping for the cabbage itself. The mixture lightens the dish and makes it seem less filling. This dish is time consuming but amazingly satisfying and delicious.

MAKES 6 MAIN-COURSE SERVINGS

Select a cabbage with loosely packed leaves so the leaves will be easy to remove. Carefully pull away the leaves, discarding the dark green outer ones. If you can't peel away the leaves without breaking them, plunge the cabbage in a pot of boiling water for about 1 minute, rinse with cold water, peel off as many leaves as you can. Keep repeating this process until you've removed all the leaves. Discard the core or save it for soup. Simmer the cabbage leaves in a large pot of boiling salted water for 10 minutes—if you plunged the cabbage into boiling water, you can use the same water—drain in a colander, and rinse under cold running water. Cut any thick ribs or tough sections out of the leaves.

Slice the onions and carrots into rounds about $1/8$ inch thick and put in a wide pot or sauté pan with the olive oil. Cook the vegetables gently, uncovered, over medium-low heat for about 40 minutes or until they are tender but not brown. If the vegetables start to brown, lower the heat. Stir in the tomato paste, cover, and cook gently for 5 minutes more. Allow the mixture to cool.

Soak the bread in the milk for 15 minutes.

While the vegetables are cooking, prepare the stuffing. Finely chop the garlic, parsley, and juniper berries. (Crush the juniper berries, before chopping, under the bottom of a pot or with the side of a cleaver.) Work the soaked bread to a paste with your fingers and combine it with the juniper berry mixture, ground pork, diced bacon, egg, thyme, salt, and pepper. Work the mixture with your hands to evenly distribute all the ingredients, but don't work it any longer than necessary or the mixture will be tough after baking.

Preheat the oven 350°F.

To assemble and bake the stuffed cabbage, line six 10- to 12-ounce heatproof bowls—preferably bowls with lids—with the boiled and drained cabbage leaves. Leave enough extra cabbage hanging over the outside of the bowls to fold over and cover the stuffing. Divide the stuffing evenly among the bowls and fold over the overhanging cabbage leaves, sealing in the stuffing. Spread the vegetable mixture—including the oil—over the cabbage in each bowl and sprinkle over the white wine and the Calvados. Put the lids on the bowls or seal the tops with a double layer of aluminum foil.

Place the bowls on a sheet pan and bake for 1 hour. These potted stuffed cabbages may be served right away, but they are even better when allowed to cool, saved in the refrigerator for a day or two, and reheated for about 45 minutes, uncovered, in a 350°F oven.

1 medium (8-ounce) Savoy cabbage

2 medium onions

5 medium carrots, peeled

$1/2$ cup extra virgin olive oil

$1/4$ cup tomato paste

4 slices stale white bread, crusts removed

$1/2$ cup milk

4 large cloves garlic

1 bunch parsley, preferably Italian flat-leaf

20 juniper berries

$13/4$ pounds coarsely ground pork shoulder

4 ounces thick-cut bacon, cut into $1/4$-inch dice

1 large egg, lightly beaten

1 teaspoon chopped fresh thyme leaves, or $1/2$ teaspoon dried

1 teaspoon salt

1 teaspoon freshly ground black pepper

1 cup dry white wine

$1/3$ cup Calvados (optional)

While it is possible to make your own sauerkraut by rubbing shredded cabbage with coarse salt and allowing the cabbage to sour in a well-covered crock for 2 to 3 weeks, it's usually not worth the trouble. If you live in a big city, you can buy homemade sauerkraut in a German or Eastern European delicatessen; in smaller places, you'll have to rely on supermarket sauerkraut, sold in plastic bags, which isn't half bad.

Everyone has a strong opinion about sauerkraut, either hating or loving it. My father kept a crock of it in the back of the refrigerator, but its odor was so forbidding that I never ventured to try it. It wasn't until years later in France that I sampled *choucroute garnie*, a groaning platter heaped with sausages, pork chops, and sauerkraut. The sauerkraut, with its tangy crunch, was the perfect foil for the rich sausages and chops—the ultimate winter dish. Sauerkraut is also the perfect hot dog condiment.

Choucroute Garnie

Choucroute Garnie.

One of my favorite cold-weather French bistro dinners is a tray of oysters and a platter of choucroute garnie. A heaping platter of pork and sauerkraut, choucroute garnie can be simple or complicated depending on how many different sausages you can find and whether you include pork chops or even duck or goose. But once you've assembled the ingredients, the cooking method is the same regardless of what you include. Boiled small potatoes go especially well with choucroute and are the traditional accompaniment in Alsace, choucroute garnie's homeland.

MAKES 8 MAIN-COURSE SERVINGS

Drain the sauerkraut in a colander and squeeze in your hands to eliminate excess liquid.

Preheat the oven to 350°F.

Put the sauerkraut in a wide ovenproof stainless steel or earthenware pot and pour over the white wine. Crush the juniper berries by rocking over them with the bottom of a pot and wrap them in a small square of cheesecloth. Bury this little packet in the sauerkraut. Push the bacon down into the sauerkraut. Put the pot on the stove over high heat—if you're using earthenware, use a flame-tamer. When the white wine comes to the boil, cover the pot, and slide it into the oven.

After 1 hour of baking, slide the sausages into the sauerkraut, cover the pot, and return the pot to the oven.

Season the pork chops with salt and pepper and lightly brown them in the butter and oil in a skillet over medium-low heat for about 5 minutes on each side. Arrange the chops on top of the sauerkraut, cover the pot, and bake for 20 minutes more.

Serve by carefully reaching in and pulling out the bacon and sausages. Slice the bacon and sausages. Pile the sauerkraut on a platter or in mounds on individual hot plates and arrange the bacon slices, sliced sausages, and pork chops on top. Serve immediately with plenty of cool dry white wine or steins of cold beer.

3 pounds sauerkraut

2 cups dry white wine

10 juniper berries

8 ounces slab bacon, rind removed, left whole

1 pound sausage, such as garlic sausage (*saucisson à l'ail*) or other good-quality uncooked sausage

8 (8-ounce) center-cut pork chops

Salt and freshly ground black pepper

2 tablespoons unsalted butter

2 tablespoons pure olive oil or canola oil

CABBAGE SOUPS AND POTÉES

Cooked by itself cabbage is a bit of a bore, but when cooked with meats into hearty winter dishes, it's hard to beat. You can simmer cabbage with other vegetables and pieces of meat such as pork, lamb, duck, or goose to come up with rich and hearty soups. Sometimes these "soups" become so thick with so many ingredients added that they're really no longer soups but solid dishes of braised cabbage. The French call these *potées*.

Whether you set out to make a cabbage soup to serve as a winter first course or a thick and filling main-course potée, the steps are much the same, except that a potée will contain a higher proportion of meats, and the cabbage is cut into wide strips or pieces while in a soup the cabbage is usually shredded.

Cabbage Potée with Braised Duck Legs

If you ever serve duck breasts (one of my favorite dinner party foods because they're in between chicken and red meat), you'll probably find yourself with leftover duck legs. You can use duck legs to make confit or you can save them in the freezer and use them in this delicious winter potée. You can save leftover duck carcasses and make duck broth to use here by browning and simmering the carcasses as though you were making Basic Brown Chicken Broth (page 373), but if you don't want to bother, just use the chicken broth.

MAKES 4 MAIN-COURSE SERVINGS

Bring about 6 quarts of salted water to a rapid boil in a large pot.

Slice the cabbage into ¹/₂-inch-wide shreds with a chef's knife.

Add the cabbage to the boiling water. Cook, uncovered, over high heat for 10 minutes, then drain in a colander.

Cook the bacon in a wide heavy-bottomed pot or skillet over medium heat until the bacon barely begins to crisp, about 8 minutes. Scoop the bacon out off the fat with a slotted spoon and reserve, leaving the fat in the pan. Season the duck legs with salt and brown them on both sides in the bacon fat over high heat. Reserve the duck legs and discard the fat.

Preheat the oven to 350°F.

Wrap the juniper berries, bay leaf, clove, and thyme in a packet of cheesecloth to make a bouquet garni. Layer the cabbage, onion, carrots, turnip, garlic, reserved bacon, and duck legs in a flameproof casserole or ovenproof stainless steel pot with lid, sprinkling each layer with salt. Push the bouquet garni down into the pot, pour over the broth, and bring the mixture to a simmer on top of the stove.

Cover the pot, place it in the oven, and bake for 45 minutes. Pour over the wine and bake, covered, for 30 minutes more. Grind over fresh pepper and serve as a main course. Pass around plenty of French bread.

Cabbage Potée with Braised Duck Legs.

1 small (1¹/₂-pound) cabbage, preferably Savoy, quartered

8 ounces thick-cut bacon, sliced crosswise into 1-inch strips

4 duck legs, including the drumsticks

Salt

5 juniper berries, crushed

1 imported bay leaf

1 whole clove

2 sprigs fresh thyme, or 1 teaspoon dried

1 medium onion, minced

2 medium carrots, peeled and sliced

1 medium turnip, peeled, halved, and sliced

3 cloves garlic

8 cups duck broth or Basic Brown Chicken Broth (page 373)

¹/₂ cup dry white wine

Freshly ground black pepper

French bread, for serving

CACTUS PADS (NOPALES)

It took me a long time to try these since I assumed they were filled with needles that would be impossible to remove. You should know, before going any further, that cactus pads yield a viscous substance reminiscent of okra. If you don't like slippery foods, the best way to eat cactus pads is raw, cut into fine shreds. Otherwise, try cutting them into dice and sweating them for about 15 minutes in butter or olive oil or, as shown here, grill them. Cactus pads should be peeled with a swivel-bladed peeler before being cooked to eliminate needles. Be sure to peel the edges.

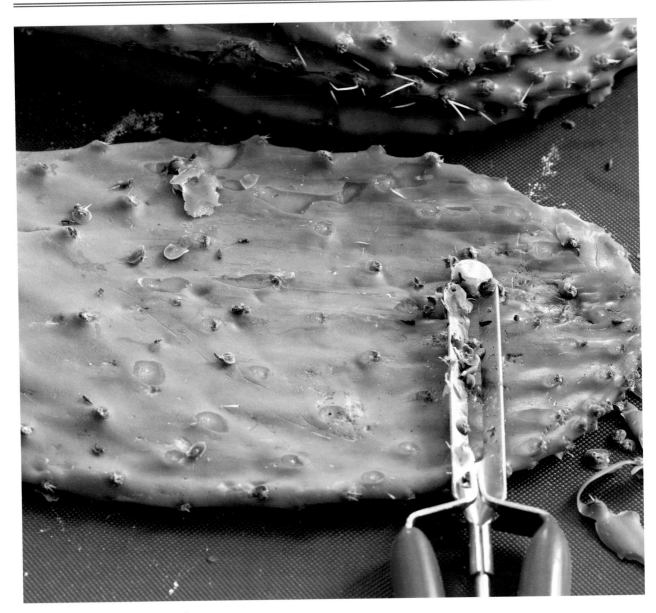

Removing the spines from cactus pads.

Grilled Cactus Pads

I got this idea from Elizabeth Schneider's incredibly thorough book, *Vegetables from Amaranth to Zucchini*. The only prep for the cactus pads is to peel and lightly score them lengthwise to let the flavors and tang of the lime juice penetrate the flesh.

MAKES 4 SIDE-DISH SERVINGS

Peel the pads with a vegetable slicer and score the pads lengthwise, making about 15 lines each about $1/8$ inch deep on each side. Grill over medium heat for about 7 minutes on each side. Brush with the lime and the olive oil. Serve immediately.

4 small to medium cactus pads

Juice of 1 lime

2 tablespoons extra-virgin olive oil

Salt

Grilling the cactus pads.

Slicing the grilled cactus pads into strips.

Grilled Cactus Pad Salad

This little salad makes a delicious first course or side dish. It contains a goodly amount of lime for acidity, cilantro and shallots for savor, Thai peppers for heat, and pumpkin seeds for texture. Serve it with other grilled foods such as meat, fish, or poultry.

MAKES 4 SIDE-DISH OR FIRST-COURSE SERVINGS

Slice the cactus pads into thin strips, between $1/8$ and $1/4$ inch thick. Toss with the cilantro, shallots, lime juice, Thai peppers, and pumpkin seeds. It's best if you can make this salad with the cactus pads straight off the grill. If you do, the salad will, of course, be warm.

Grilled Cactus Pads (above)

2 tablespoons chopped fresh cilantro

2 tablespoons minced shallot

$1/4$ cup fresh lime juice

2 Thai peppers, seeded and minced

2 tablespoons toasted pumpkin seeds

Salt

CARDOONS

I did a double-take the first time I saw cardoons in an Italian market in Manhattan. They looked like giant bunches of celery, except that they were hairy and wild looking. I grabbed one—it weighed six pounds—and dragged it home to experiment. After a little fooling around, I discovered that the outer-most stalks were tough and spongy and had to be thrown out and that only about half—the innermost tender stalks—could be used.

Cardoons are closely related to artichokes (both are members of the nettle family), and while some writers claim they have a similar flavor, I find that cardoons lack the artichoke's subtle complexity. I like cardoons mostly as a backdrop for other flavors in soups and gratins with plenty of garlic.

Don't buy cardoons that are sagging and limp or that have any brown patches. Cardoons can be stored for a day or two wrapped in a paper bag in a cool place—they're too big to fit into most refrigerators. Unless you find small bunches of cardoons weighing two pounds or less, you'll have to drag home a five- or six-pound bunch and pull off and discard the outermost stalks, leaving you with about half of what you started out with. Once you've removed the outermost stalks, cut off any leaves on the sides of the inner stalks and cut the stalks in half lengthwise. Cut away the thick membrane on the insides of the stalks and remove the fiber from the outside of the stalks by scraping with a paring knife or vegetable peeler. Cut the stalks into 3- to 4-inch pieces. When cutting or slicing cardoons, don't use a carbon steel knife, which will turn the cardoons black.

Once peeled, cardoons quickly turn brown in the same way as artichokes. Most cookbooks say to immediately rub the stalks with lemon, but I haven't found this to be of much help. It is helpful, however, to put the stalks immediately into a bowl of cold water and to cook them as soon as possible. Because cardoons are sometimes bitter, they should be boiled for 15 to 20 minutes in salted water with a little lemon juice before they are used in a recipe.

You may end up with more cardoons than you'll want to serve at a single meal. Once blanched for 5 minutes or so, extra cardoons can be sealed in plastic sandwich bags and frozen.

Cardoons are great in soups (they're great simmered with garlic, beans, and fennel) and gratins (topped with white sauce and baked).

Cardoons.

CARROTS

Carrots are a hard sell. My friends, who normally are curious about what I'm up to in the kitchen, politely change the subject when I tell them I'm experimenting with carrot recipes. While it's true that I never rush home eager to cook up a plate of carrots the way I might a basket of wild mushrooms, carrots are an essential presence (if a supporting one) in my everyday cooking. Carrots have the sweetness and delicate earthiness essential for making stews and various sauces, and I couldn't do without their color and sweetness in many a vegetable soup.

Besides the usual long, cylindrical, and orange variety, there are also tiny globe-shaped carrots, stubby cone-shaped carrots, white carrots, and yellow carrots. All these weirdly shaped and colored carrots are worth experimenting with—your best bet is to shop at a farmers' market—because they often have a fuller flavor.

While it's true there are carrots with little character or sweetness, much of the carrot's so-so reputation is undeserved and is the result of bad cooking. Cook carrots in as little liquid as possible—unless in a soup or stock—because the liquid draws out their natural sugars and flavors. Make sure that the liquid used for cooking the carrots ends up being served in the dish, as the liquid released by the carrots becomes their own sweet and savory glaze.

White carrots.

Of course, the problem is sometimes that the carrots, both large and small, simply don't have any sweetness. And it's usually not possible to judge sweetness and flavor without biting into one. While carrots store well in the refrigerator, they seem to lose their sweetness the longer they sit. Because of this, I always buy carrots with the greens still attached, which ensures they are reasonably fresh. The greens should be bright green with no wilting, and the carrots should never be limp. When buying carrots without the greens, avoid any that have tiny green sprouts forming where the green has been removed. Avoid carrots with cracks running along either side.

When you get your carrots home, cut off the greens about 2 inches above the carrot and store the carrots in the refrigerator, in tightly sealed plastic bags, for up to 3 days. Carrots that turn limp after a few days in the refrigerator can be used for cooking but will have lost their crispness for anything raw.

Most carrots are peeled before they are cooked or served raw, but baby carrots can be scraped—so you lose less of the carrot—with the back of a knife, a razor, or by rubbing them hard with a clean scrub pad. Large woody carrots can be quartered and their woody core cut out (see photos, page 3). The pieces can then be turned or cut into julienne. The peeled and rounded baby carrots sold in plastic bags in supermarkets aren't as tasty as some, but they're such a snap to cook that they're hard to resist.

Grated Carrot Salad

Freshly grated carrots make a simple beginning to a light and informal dinner. Instead of serving them alone, I serve them with at least two other simple salads as part of a crudité plate.

The simplest seasoning for grated carrots is just a little lemon juice, chopped parsley, and oil. The French usually use a tasteless vegetable oil while the Italians use extra-virgin olive oil. Olive oil lovers may want to follow the advice of the Italians, but some people (for example, the French) find that olive oil is too strong for the delicate carrots. More elaborate versions of grated carrots can include raisins (the sweetness makes them a natural), cubes of celery (a flavor accent and contrasting texture), spices (exotic and delicious), and herbs such as chervil or tarragon.

Grating a carrot shouldn't be a big deal, but I'm fussy about what kind of grater to use. If the carrots are too finely grated, they'll turn into a mushy pulp and if they're grated too coarsely their delicate flavor and texture will be lost, and everyone will have to work too hard to chew them. Because a food processor grates the carrots too finely, you'll have to grate them by hand. Be sure, also, to use a grater with tiny scoop-like teeth instead of the kind that looks like the metal has been punched out from the back. The punched-out kind will turn the carrots to mush. I use an old-fashioned four-sided grater that sits firmly on the cutting board.

MAKES 4 FIRST-COURSE SERVINGS

Grate the carrots by pushing them lengthwise along the grater teeth. Grate one side of the carrot pieces until you get down to the woody core. Rotate the carrot a half turn, grate again down to the core, give a quarter turn, and repeat until you've grated all four sides and are left with only the core. Discard the cores.

Toss the carrots with the oil, lemon juice, parsley, salt, and white pepper. Taste the carrots and toss them with the sugar if you think they need to be sweeter. Serve with other vegetables as part of a crudité platter.

VARIATIONS:

GRATED CARROTS WITH CELERY. Remove the string from 2 celery stalks with a vegetable peeler or paring knife and cut the stalk into $^1/_4$-inch cubes. Toss with the carrots as above.

GRATED CARROTS WITH RAISINS AND PINE NUTS. Soak 2 tablespoons golden raisins in 1 tablespoon water for 30 minutes. Toast 2 tablespoons pine nuts by tossing them in a sauté pan over medium heat until lightly browned, about 10 minutes, or by baking in a 350°F for about 10 minutes. Drain the raisins and toss them and the pine nuts with the carrots as above.

MOROCCAN SPICY CARROTS. Soak 2 tablespoons golden raisins in 1 tablespoon water for 30 minutes. Soak $^1/_8$ teaspoon saffron threads in a teaspoon of water for 30 minutes. Heat $^1/_2$ teaspoon ground cumin and 2 teaspoons ground coriander in 1 tablespoon vegetable or olive oil for about 1 minute in

4 large carrots, peeled and cut into 3-inch lengths

2 tablespoons canola oil, pure olive oil, or extra-virgin olive oil

1 tablespoon fresh lemon juice

2 tablespoons finely chopped fresh parsley

Salt and white pepper

$^1/_2$ teaspoon sugar (optional)

Grate carrots vertically against a box grater with small teeth.

a small saucepan until the spices turn fragrant. Prepare the salad as above and toss with the raisins and spices in a mixing bowl. Toss with 1 tablespoon finely chopped fresh cilantro, if desired.

GRATED CARROTS WITH DRIED CURRANTS AND BLACK OLIVES. Soak 2 tablespoons dried currants in barely enough warm water to cover for 30 minutes. Pit and coarsely chop 1 cup black olives. Prepare the salad as above and toss the carrots with the currants and olives.

Baked Carrots with Parsley (Carottes Vichy)

Vichy is a spa in eastern France famous for its curative waters. Vichy's mineral water is bottled and sold all over France, where its usual purpose is to cure a hangover. Vichy water has a strong mineral taste that gives the original version of this recipe an interesting subtle flavor. Fortunately this recipe is perfectly fine without it.

MAKES 4 SIDE-DISH SERVINGS

Preheat the oven to 400°F.

Spread the carrot slices in a metal baking dish, roasting pan, or straight-sided sauté pan just large enough to hold them in a layer about $1/2$ inch thick. Pour over just enough water to come one-third up the sides of the carrots. Dot the carrots with the butter and sprinkle with the sugar and salt. Put the baking dish over high heat on top of the stove and bring the water to a boil.

Loosely cover the carrots with a sheet of aluminum foil or parchment paper and slide them in the oven. Bake for 30 minutes. Poke the carrots with a knife—they are done when they're slightly soft and offer a gentle resistance to the knife. If there's water still left in the dish or pan, place the pan back on top of the stove with the carrots and boil over high heat until the liquid has evaporated down to a couple of tablespoons.

Sprinkle the carrots with the parsley and grind over some fresh pepper. Serve immediately.

4 medium to large carrots, peeled and sliced $1/8$ inch thick

1 ($1/2$-liter) bottle Vichy water, or 2 cups tap water

3 tablespoons unsalted butter, cut into cubes

1 teaspoon sugar

1 teaspoon salt

1 tablespoon finely chopped fresh parsley

Freshly ground black pepper

CASSAVA (YUCA AND MANIOC)

Originally from South America, cassava made its way to Africa, the Caribbean, and eventually to Southeast Asia, where it is an important food staple. Most Americans have encountered cassava without knowing it as tapioca pudding. This bland milky pudding with its soft curdlike pearls of starch is the perfect foil for rich or sweet ingredients, including butter and sugar.

Cassava is not a particularly attractive vegetable. It looks a little bit like wood and is typically cylindrical and about a foot long with a bark-like peel. The peel is usually covered with wax, which is added to help preserve the cassava. Much has been said about cassava's high cyanide content and the need for expert treatment before eating. In fact, those cassava that make it to American shores have little cyanide, so little that it's cooked off. This all being said, it's probably not a good idea to eat cassava raw.

Picking out cassava can be a little tricky since the best approach is to cut into a piece (often the vendor will have already sliced one for your inspection) and inspect it for any signs of darkening. The flesh should be perfectly white. If you can't see the inside of the cassava, at least make sure there are no cracks or moldy spots.

To prepare cassava, cut it into 4-inch lengths to make it easier to work with and peel away the bark with a vegetable peeler or sharp paring knife. Cut away any pinkish flesh. Check the interior of the cassava to see if it's fibrous; if it is, remove any fibrous pieces.

Simmer the cassava in boiling water for about 15 minutes, or until a toothpick stuck into it offers little resistance. The cassava should be tender and translucent but not mushy. Cassava can be served in this way as a side dish to go with rich meat stews. Cooked cassava is served with any number of sauces, often containing garlic and lime juice. If it's your first attempt at cooking cassava, I recommend preparing it just like mashed potatoes—you may find that it doesn't require the usual amount of butter. It can also be thinly sliced and fried like potato chips.

Cassava.

Yuca.

Baked and Mashed Cassava

Cassava can be baked and mashed just like potatoes. The trick is to start the baking with the peel on, continue baking wrapped in foil, and then slide off the peel. This system prevents the cassava from drying out. Once baked, the cassava is simply mashed and served in the same way as mashed potatoes.

MAKES 4 SIDE-DISH SERVINGS

3 pounds cassava

Butter

Sour cream

Crème fraîche

Preheat the oven to 350°F.

Bake the cassava for about 20 minutes, or until it begins to soften when you insert a knife or skewer. Wrap it in aluminum foil and continue baking until it's completely soft and has the consistency of a baked potato, about 30 minutes longer. Hold each cassava in a towel and slide off the peel. Cut each cassava in half lengthwise and pull out the center fibrous section. Mash the cassava with a potato masher and serve with butter, sour cream, or crème fraîche.

Lime-Flavored Coconut Tapioca Pudding

Tapioca for pudding comes in various forms. Two kinds are large pearl tapioca and small pearl tapioca. The problem with these traditional forms is their tendency to grow stale so that they no longer thicken, and unless you know your vendor, there's no way of determining the age of the tapioca on the shelf. A far easier approach is to use instant tapioca which in most places is the only kind available anyway. Most tapioca recipes are made with milk and eggs. This recipe replaces the milk with coconut milk and uses lime zest to give it the appropriate flavor.

MAKES 4 SERVINGS

1 (14-ounce) can unsweetened coconut milk

2 tablespoons sugar

1/4 cup pearl tapioca or instant tapioca

Pinch of salt

2 (2-inch-long) strips lime zest

1/2 teaspoon vanilla extract

Combine the coconut milk, sugar, tapioca, salt, and lime zest in a small saucepan over low heat. Simmer, uncovered, until the tapioca pearls double in size, about 40 minutes. (If you're using instant tapioca, follow the timing directions on the package.) Fish out the lime zest, stir in the vanilla, and pour into a bowl, or individual bowls, to set. Serve cold.

Large pearl tapioca.

CAULIFLOWER

While most cauliflower comes in large white heads surrounded by green leaves, small green or purple or orange cauliflower occasionally show up in farmers' markets. In addition to green broccoli, there's the pale green broccoflower, which looks like a cross between broccoli and cauliflower, but is really a type of cauliflower. Broccoflower probably got its name because of its color, but it isn't a broccoli-cauliflower cross as many think. Broccoflower tastes like white cauliflower and has the same shape.

Like Belgian endive, cauliflower is protected from the sun to keep it milky white and to prevent the development of green chlorophyll. With older varieties it was necessary for farmers to carefully tie the leaves over the cauliflower to keep the sun out, but modern cauliflower has been developed so the leaves wrap over the "flower" and do the work themselves.

Cauliflower.

It's hard to imagine that cauliflower, now taken somewhat for granted, was once the rage at the French court and served up in rich and elegant concoctions. Menon, one of the important food writers of the eighteenth century, suggests serving cauliflower in a rich sauce made with veal, ham, and cream and as part of a little stew of sweetbreads, mushrooms, and foie gras.

I find cauliflower a little bland and like it best baked with cheese and a little cream, or served up Indian style with plenty of spices, or Italian style with plenty of herbs and olive oil. Raw or barely cooked cauliflower is also good in salads.

When shopping, look for cauliflower with tightly packed heads and fresh-looking leaves with no signs of wilting. Avoid cauliflower with little brown specks on the heads, which form as the cauliflower ages. You can store cauliflower in the refrigerator in a plastic bag with holes poked in it for up to 2 days.

When you're ready to cook the cauliflower, cut it up into florets by first pulling away the leaves and then cutting around the large core on the underside of the cauliflower with a sharp paring knife. Once you take out the large core, you can separate the florets by cutting them apart from the inside of the cauliflower. The size of the florets—they can be cut into almost any size by cutting smaller and smaller branches—is largely up to you and depends on the final dish. For most cauliflower dishes, you will have to precook the cauliflower by boiling in salted water or by steaming to soften it; don't precook for more than 5 minutes, or it will develop a strong flavor and will fall apart.

Remove the green leaves at the base of the cauliflower. Cut in and around the base and remove it.

Cut from the underside, removing the florets as you go.

Trim each of the florets and cut smaller if desired.

Sicilian-Style Cauliflower Salad

This salad includes capers, olives, garlic, parsley, and anchovies (which you can leave out if you want)—all of which are designed to give the cauliflower a little zip. I sometimes serve it along with other salads or antipasti, such as thinly sliced salami, as a first course at an al fresco meal.

MAKES 4 FIRST-COURSE SERVINGS

To pit the olives, squeeze the two ends between your thumb and forefinger and the pit should pop right out. If it doesn't, you may have to use a small knife or even an olive pitter. Combine the olives with the capers and chop the two together, coarsely.

In a bowl, combine the garlic with the olive mixture. Add the anchovies. Chop the parsley and add. Stir in the olive oil and lemon juice and season to taste with salt and pepper.

Bring 8 quarts of salted water to a rapid boil. Cut the cauliflower into 1-inch-wide florets. Boil the florets for 5 minutes, drain (don't rinse), and return them to the empty pot. Put the pot over high heat and toss the cauliflower for a minute to dry it out.

Toss it the cauliflower gently in a salad bowl with the olive mixture. Let cool. Serve at room temperature.

1/2 cup large black imported olives (not canned)

2 tablespoons capers, drained

1 clove garlic, minced and crushed to a paste

8 anchovy fillets (optional), soaked for 5 minutes in cold water, patted dry, and coarsely chopped

1 small bunch parsley, preferably flat-leaf, leaves only

1/4 cup extra-virgin olive oil

2 tablespoons fresh lemon juice

Salt and freshly ground black pepper

1 (2-pound) head cauliflower

Basic Boiled or Steamed Cauliflower

MAKES 4 SIDE-DISH SERVINGS

In a large pot, bring 8 quarts of salted water to a rapid boil. Cut the cauliflower into 1-inch-wide florets. Add the florets to the pot and boil for 5 minutes, drain (don't rinse), and put return them to the empty pot. Put the pot over high heat and toss the cauliflower for a minute to dry it out. Remove the cauliflower to a serving bowl or dish and toss with the butter. Sprinkle with lemon juice, salt, and pepper and serve.

1 (2-pound) head cauliflower

3 tablespoons unsalted butter, sliced, or extra-virgin olive oil

2 tablespoons fresh lemon juice

Salt and freshly ground black pepper

Cauliflower Gratin

This crusty gratin made with plenty of cheese is my favorite winter cauliflower recipe. It's important to use a flavorful cheese. I use a combination of Swiss Gruyère and Italian Parmigiano-Reggiano, but most firm, full-flavored cheeses, such as a good American or English cheddar, will work. I like to include prosciutto in the béchamel, but it isn't essential. If you don't have any bread crumbs, break up a few slices of stale bread or lightly toast a little bread and work it through a strainer or drum sieve.

MAKES 4 TO 6 SIDE-DISH SERVINGS

Preheat the oven to 375°F.

Bring 6 quarts of salted water to a rapid boil. Cut the cauliflower into 1-inch-wide florets. Boil the florets for 4 minutes, drain without rinsing, and spread the cauliflower in a buttered, medium (about 8-cup) oval gratin dish or baking dish just large enough to hold the cauliflower in a single layer.

If the béchamel sauce is cold, bring it to a simmer on the stove while whisking. Stir in the Gruyère and add the salt and pepper to taste. Spoon the sauce over the cauliflower and sprinkle evenly with the Parmesan cheese and bread crumbs.

Bake until the gratin is bubbling and lightly browned on top, about 30 minutes. Serve immediately.

1 (1½-pound) head cauliflower

2 cups Béchamel Sauce (page 53)

1 cup finely grated Swiss Gruyère cheese

Salt and freshly ground black pepper

½ cup finely grated Parmigiano-Reggiano cheese or additional Gruyère

2 tablespoons bread crumbs, preferably fresh

Braised Cauliflower with Indian Spices

Because cauliflower has such a delicate flavor, I cook it using one of two fundamental approaches. The first approach is to treat it so carefully that nothing gets in the way of its own particular taste; the second approach—the one used here—is to use the cauliflower as an almost neutral backdrop for potent herbs and spices. This is one of the most interesting and brightest-tasting cauliflower dishes I've ever enjoyed and has come about after years of cooking from Julie Sahni's wonderful book *Classic Indian Cooking* and, more recently, Madhur Jaffrey's *A Taste of India*. Many Indian vegetable recipes call for vegetable oil, which is acceptable, but I prefer to use ghee (see below), which is more flavorful.

MAKES 6 SIDE-DISH SERVINGS

Remove and discard the leaves from the cauliflower, cut out the core, and separate the head into large florets about 2 inches across.

Heat the ghee in a wide skillet or sauté pan (have a lid handy for covering) over medium heat and toss in the coriander seeds. Stir the seeds in the hot ghee until you smell their fragrance and notice them browning very slightly, about 2 minutes. Stir in the jalapeños, onion, ginger, cumin, and turmeric and cook the mixture, stirring from time to time, until the onion starts to turn translucent, 5 to 10 minutes. Add the cauliflower and tomatoes and stir everything around so the cauliflower is well coated with the spice mixture. Cover the pan and braise over medium-low heat for 20 minutes, or until the cauliflower is tender but not falling apart. Check inside the pan from time to time to make sure the mixture is not running dry—if so, add a little water.

Sprinkle with lemon juice, cilantro, salt, and pepper and serve immediately.

- 1 large (2½-pound) head cauliflower
- ¼ cup ghee (see below) or canola oil
- 2 teaspoons coriander seeds
- 2 jalapeños, seeded and minced
- 1 small onion, minced
- 1 tablespoon grated fresh ginger
- ½ teaspoon ground cumin
- ½ teaspoon ground turmeric
- 3 medium tomatoes, peeled, seeded, and chopped, or 2 cups drained, seeded, and chopped canned tomatoes (one 28-ounce can)
- Juice of 1 lemon
- 3 tablespoons chopped fresh cilantro
- Salt and freshly ground black pepper

~ GHEE AND CLARIFIED BUTTER ~

Ghee is the Indian version of clarified butter made by slowly cooking whole unsalted butter until the water contained in the butter (usually about 25 percent) evaporates and the milk solids in the butter slowly caramelize and give the butter a delicious butterscotch flavor. The milk solids are then strained out and discarded. Because ghee and other forms of clarified butter contain no milk solids, they burn at a higher temperature than whole butter and therefore can be used to sauté over high heat.

To make 1¼ cups of ghee, gently cook 3 sticks (1½ cups) unsalted butter in a heavy-bottomed saucepan over medium heat for about 15 minutes. When the foam that floats to the top of the butter begins to subside and golden brown specks start to form in the butter, immediately remove it from the heat and strain the butter through a fine-mesh strainer, kitchen towel, or coffee filter. Ghee keeps for up to a year tightly covered in the refrigerator.

If you're clarifying more than a pound of butter, you may not want to bother making ghee because it takes awhile to boil down all the water contained in the butter. To make clarified butter in the classic way, simply melt the butter, skim off the milk solids that form on top (discard) and gently ladle off the middle layer of clarified butter, leaving the water and additional milk solids in a layer on the bottom.

CELERIAC (CELERY ROOT)

Celeriac's convoluted skin and stringy roots sticking out of a dull brown globe look like something out of a 1950s horror movie. Most people pass by celeriac at the market with queasy suspicion and never give it a try. But celeriac is one of the great underrated vegetables. It has a flavor similar to regular branch celery but is more subtle and intriguing. One of the best ways to eat celeriac is in celeriac rémoulade—julienned strips of raw celeriac coated with a homemade mayonnaise with plenty of mustard—but celeriac is also delicious when glazed (in the same way as turnips), when combined with mashed potatoes , cooked in soups, or baked in gratins. Cooked celeriac in almost any form is a natural companion to roast meats.

Celeriac is not the root from regular branch celery but is specially cultivated to enhance the root instead of the greens. The greens on a bulb of celeriac are darker, wilder tasting, and not as crispy as regular celery—they're great in soups.

When shopping for celeriac, try to find it with the greens still attached so that you can be sure it's reasonably fresh. But most of the time celeriac comes with the greens already removed, so you'll have to judge its quality by lifting it and feeling its weight—it should be heavy. Don't buy celeriac that feels light—it will be spongy and flavorless. Check it carefully for soft, brown, or moist spots, which show that it's starting to rot. You can store celeriac up to a week in the refrigerator, but leave it loose in the vegetable drawer or wrapped in a paper bag, not in plastic. If the celeriac has the greens still attached, cut them off about an inch above the root before storing. If there are small greens coming out of the celeriac, it means that the celeriac is getting old and sprouting.

Because of celeriac's rough and irregular surface, it must be peeled with a knife instead of a vegetable peeler; once peeled, it should be rinsed to get rid of dirt. Peeled celeriac should be rubbed with lemon to prevent browning, and slices or cubes should be tossed with lemon juice unless you are going to cook them right away.

Celeriac can be sliced (a vegetable slicer comes in handy here), chopped, or cut into elongated blocks and then "turned" into ovals in the same way as turnips.

Celeriac.

Peel celeriac with a knife.

Slice celeriac on a vegetable slicer.

Slice each of the slices into julienne.

Celeriac Rémoulade.

Celeriac Rémoulade

Celeriac rémoulade is celeriac cut into thin strips—julienned—and then tossed with a sauce dijonnaise (confusingly, not a sauce rémoulade) which is a home-made mayonnaise containing lots of mustard. I sometimes add other ingredients, such as finely chopped tarragon and chives, capers, chopped sour French pickles (cornichons), or even curry powder. You can serve celeriac rémoulade by itself as a first course or with two or more simple vegetable salads on a crudités plate.

It's easiest to slice the celeriac with a vegetable slicer and then slice stacks of the slices into a fine julienne with a chef's knife. Celeriac is too hard for the julienne attachment on the slicer.

MAKES 6 FIRST-COURSE SERVINGS

Cut the celeriac in half through the top and slice each half into $1/8$-inch slices, with the flat side of the half facing the blade—on a vegetable slicer. Cut the slices—stack two or three together—into $1/8$-inch-wide julienne.

In a mixing bowl, toss the celeriac with the lemon juice. Add the parsley.

Combine the mayonnaise with the mustard and season to taste with salt and pepper and, if you like, more mustard. Stir this sauce into the celeriac and parsley. Taste the celeriac rémoulade and add more salt and pepper, if needed. Serve alone or as part of an crudité plate.

1 large celeriac ($1^1/2$ to 2 pounds without greens), peeled

1 tablespoon fresh lemon juice

1 tablespoon finely chopped fresh parsley (optional)

$3/4$ cup Basic Mayonnaise (page 367)

1 tablespoon Dijon mustard, or more to taste

Salt and freshly ground black pepper (optional)

CELERY

Celery is best when served raw in salads, to which it contributes an essential crunch. I sometimes cut the stalks into cubes and combine them with cubes of other cooked or raw vegetables, meats, or seafood to lighten a dish and provide a contrasting texture. Celery cubes are delicious in salads made with beans because they contrast with the beans' softness. Another sublimely simple way to eat celery is just to munch away on a whole stalk while smearing it with some potent cheese, such as Roquefort or Gorgonzola.

Celery.

Almost all celery now sold in the United States is one of a so-called unblanched variety. At one time, celery required blanching, a method of protecting the celery from the sun by wrapping it in paper. The main thing to look for when buying celery is that it be stiff and crisp. Don't buy celery that sags or that has wilted leaves or leaves that are dark and semitranslucent (which means they've been frozen). Avoid celery with cracked outer stalks.

Celery wrapped tightly in a plastic bag will stay crisp in the refrigerator for a week or two. If you want to keep it longer, stick the base in a jar with enough water to come up a few inches, and cover the whole thing with a plastic bag fastened to the jar with a rubber band. One of the problems with celery is that it's sold in large bunches, and if you need only one stalk for a soup or stew, you're stuck with the whole bunch. A good trick is to seal the leftover celery in a plastic bag and freeze it. When you thaw the celery, it will have lost all its crunch and most of its bright color—you can't enjoy it uncooked, but you can use it as needed for dishes that cook the celery.

Celery is wonderful when braised—surround it with good concentrated broth and/or cream and bake it for about 25 minutes, until the liquid thicken(s)—a dish that is delicious with roast meats. But as a cooked vegetable, celery usually plays a supporting rather than a starring, role. Celery is often cut up into cubes and gently sautéed, along with onions and carrots, as the basic *mirepoix* used in French soups and sauces or in the Italian equivalent, the *soffritto*. Whole stalks of celery can also be tied up into the bouquet garni used for soups and stews.

I sometimes peel the stringy convex side of the outermost stalks with a vegetable peeler or a paring knife, but if you're cutting celery into small cubes or cooking it, you don't have to bother.

If you ever shop in an Asian market, you're likely to have encountered "Chinese celery," which has long rather scraggly and limp stalks and abundant leaves. It has none of the fat crunchy stalks we are used to. It does, however, have a pungency that our regular celery does not. So don't serve it raw—cook it in dishes that call for celery but that can handle the extra bite.

Celery, Walnut, and Apple Salad

Perhaps because I associate them with old-fashioned American restaurants and hotel dining rooms, where food is served with an agreeable and outdated formality, I've always had an affection for Waldorf salads. This is an almost classic Waldorf salad, except that it's made with homemade tarragon mayonnaise, a small change that makes all the difference. If you don't have fresh tarragon, you can substitute parsley, chervil, dill, or even grated horseradish. I serve this "study in crunch" as a refreshing first-course salad at a fall or winter dinner.

Celery apple salad.

MAKES 4 SIDE-DISH SERVINGS

Preheat the oven to 350°F.

Spread the nuts out in a shallow pan. Toast for about 15 minutes, until they start to smell good and brown very slightly. Let cool.

Peel the stringy fibers off the back of the celery stalks with a vegetable peeler and cut the stalks lengthwise into $1/4$-inch-wide strips. Slice the strips into $1/4$-inch cubes.

Prepare the mayonnaise by adding the egg yolk to the mayonnaise and then working in the oil(s). Chop the tarragon just before stirring it into the mayonnaise (save a few leaves for stirring in at the end).

Peel the apples, cut them into $1/4$-inch cubes, and toss in the lemon juice. Stir together the apples, mayonnaise, nuts, and celery. Season to taste with salt and white pepper. Serve slightly cooler than room temperature.

1 cup walnut halves or pecans, barely chopped
4 celery stalks
1 egg yolk
$1/2$ cup bottled mayonnaise
2 tablespoons argan oil
2 to 4 tablespoons toasted hazelnut oil (use 4 tablespoons if not using the argan oil)
1 tablespoon fresh tarragon leaves
2 tart apples, such as Granny Smith
1 tablespoon fresh lemon juice
Salt and white pepper

ARGAN OIL

Extracted from the kernels of the argan tree, argan oil is only recently being appreciated in the West for its delicious nuttiness. Traditionally argan oil is extracted from seeds found in the dung of goats. The goats digest the outer husk, making the inner nut easier to access. Argan oil is expensive, about twice the price of the best extra-virgin olive oil. This is easy to understand since making 1 quart of argan oil takes several days and 70 pounds of nuts, which are cracked open by hand. Use argan oil in vinaigrettes and homemade mayonnaise.

CHAYOTE

Chayote has long been popular in Mexico and Louisiana (where it is called mirliton) and little known any-where else. In recent years, however, it has become trendy and has made it to the shelves of most fancy food

stores and even supermarkets. Chayote has its devotees, but I've always found it a bit bland—much like zucchini, but at twice the price. Most of the recipes I use for chayote involve steaming it or boiling, techniques that do little to improve its flavor. I prefer to sauté chayote with plenty of garlic in the same way I would zucchini or summer squash. Chayote can also be baked in gratins as a substitute for root vegetables or zuc-chini. It is also often served raw in dishes that benefit from its cool and delightful crunch.

Smooth chayote (there is also a spiny variety, but I've never seen it) is easy to peel with a vegetable peeler. To prepare chayote for sautéing or for baking in a gratin, peel the chayote, cut it in half lengthwise, remove the central (pit unless the chayote are very young and the pit is tender), and slice the chayote into $1/8$- to $1/4$-inch pieces. Sauté the chayote as you would zucchini or bake it, sliced, as you would eggplant. Count on half a chayote per person.

Chayote.

CHESTNUTS

Technically chestnuts aren't a vegetable, but are rather a nut. But since they're served in a vegetable kind of way (glazed, mashed, and so on), I've included them here.

Chestnuts always remind me of holiday shopping and the smell of burning charcoal from the chestnut vend-ers selling them on cold city streets. A newspaper cone of hot chestnuts may not represent the chestnut at its most luxurious (*marrons glacés* prob-ably get that title), but there's something nostalgic and satisfying about pulling away the hot peels with mittened hands and blowing on the hot kernel before risking the first bite.

A lot of us don't cook chestnuts because of the work involved getting them out of their shells. True, chestnuts can be bought in jars, perfectly round and already peeled, but these are smaller, expensive, and somehow detract from the holiday camaraderie (it's best to get guests or family involved) of peeling and sorting. When buying chestnuts, pick out the largest chestnuts (you'll get more chestnut for the same amount of work) and avoid any chestnuts that are cracked or feel light. Buy about 10 per-cent extra—especially if it's late in the season (after November)—because some of the chestnuts may be moldy when you peel them. Chestnuts can be stored in a paper bag in the refrigerator for up to 2 weeks, but it's best

Chestnuts.

to use them as soon as possible because they may be developing mold that you can't see. Chestnuts can also be frozen, in or out of the shell, for up to 1 year.

To shell chestnuts, first make two large slits in an X along the full length of their flat sides, being careful not to cut into the chestnut meat. Don't skip this step or you may risk, as one of my French cookbooks puts it, a *grave accident*—the chestnuts will explode. Once you've made the slits, spread the chestnuts in a single layer on a baking sheet and bake in a 400°F oven for 20 minutes, shaking the pan to redistribute the chestnuts after 10 minutes (the slits will get wider). Wrap the hot chestnuts in a towel moistened with hot water and leave for 5 minutes to steam and loosen the peel. The peel comes off easier if the chestnuts are still hot (you may need to hold them in a towel), so if the chestnuts cool and peeling gets difficult, stick them back in the oven for 5 minutes. If you're lucky, the thin inner peel will come away at the same time as the outer peel, but if you end up with chestnuts with the inner peel still attached, boil them for 5 minutes and pick at the peel with the tips of your fingers and a paring knife—don't worry if you can't get all the peel off.

Chestnuts are delicious when glazed or pureed and when cooked in soups. Glazed or pureed, they are delicious accompaniments to roast meats, especially red meats and game.

Shelled chestnuts.

To remove the inner peel, plunge the chestnuts in boiling water.

Working chestnuts through a drum sieve to make puree.

❧ SWEET CHESTNUT CREAM (*CRÈME DE MARRONS*) ❧

Crème de marrons is a sweet, very smooth, delicious chestnut puree that's a favorite dessert in inexpensive Parisian bistros (now becoming oxymoronic). Nothing could be easier to cook and serve since crème de marrons comes in a can. It needs only be scooped out onto the plate and dolloped with a little crème fraîche. Sweetened chestnut puree also makes a delicious inside filling for a chocolate cake.

CHICKPEAS (GARBANZO BEANS)

My first encounter with the chickpea was in my student days when I had run out of money and food. The only thing left in the apartment was a bag of dried chickpeas, heaven knows how old. I cooked them up in boiling water for hours and served them, a watery soupy mess, with no olive oil or garlic or any of things that cooks use to make them palatable.

I didn't cook chickpeas again until many years later, after I had discovered them served in tasty salads in Italy and France, and I figured they were worth the effort after all. Chickpeas are used throughout the world but are most popular in Mediterranean countries, the Middle East, and in India. In India they are ground into flour and used to make dumplings; in the Middle East, they are made into a savory pastes such as hummus and spread on pita bread; and in Mediterranean countries, such as Spain and Italy, they are most popular in salads.

The easiest way to deal with chickpeas is to buy them already cooked, in a can. But if you have the same kind of blind aversion to canned foods that I do, you may want to cook your own starting with dried chickpeas. As is true when cooking most dried legumes, you're best off starting with those from the most recent harvest. I suppose there are experts who can somehow distinguish the age of dried legumes, but your best bet is just to buy them from a busy store—maybe one in an Indian or Italian neighborhood—that's unlikely to keep them in stock for too long. If you end up with a large supply, you can keep chickpeas in a jar for up to 6 months, but if you store them for much longer they'll begin to harden and will take longer to cook.

Chickpeas.

French cookbook writers make a big deal about not cooking chickpeas in regular tap water because the calcium in the water may keep them from ever losing their mealy texture. I've tried cooking chickpeas in tap water and in Evian bottled water (which contains no calcium), and the results have been identical. But it may depend on where you live. If your water is very hard and your chickpeas mealy, try cooking them in low-calcium bottled water.

✒ HUMMUS (CHICKPEA PASTE) ✒

Hummus, a Middle Eastern chickpea puree, is spread as an appetizer on pita bread and has worked its way onto the hors d'oeuvre trays of American cocktail parties. Middle Eastern cooks make a number of hummus variations, most flavored with garlic, sesame paste, and lemon juice, but I like to add herbs, such as parsley, cilantro, or mint to come up with variations of my own. You can find hummus in most food stores, but if you want your hummus to have a fresh flavor, you'll need to add ingredients such as fresh herbs, fresh garlic, and lemon juice.

Basic Cooked Chickpeas

You'll need to pass through this recipe on your way to making almost anything out of chickpeas. The recipe is simple, but the beans do require an overnight soaking.

MAKES 4 CUPS, ENOUGH FOR 8 FIRST-COURSE OR SIDE-DISH SERVINGS

Rinse the chickpeas and put them in a glass or stainless steel bowl with enough water to cover by about 3 inches. Soak overnight.

The next day drain the chickpeas and put in a pot with enough water to cover by about 2 inches. Tie the parsley and bay leaf together in a small bouquet garni with string and nestle the bouquet garni and the onion into the chickpeas. Bring to a gentle simmer, partially cover the pot, and cook until the chickpeas have completely softened. Skim off any froth that rises up during cooking. Depending on the age of the chickpeas, they'll cook in 45 minutes to $1^1/_2$ hours. Drain the chickpeas. The cooking liquid can be saved for making soups or boiled down and poured back over the chickpeas. Discard the onion and bouquet garni.

$1^3/_4$ cups dried chickpeas

1 bunch parsley

1 imported bay leaf

1 medium onion, peeled and left whole, poked with a whole clove

Mexican-Style Chickpea Salad

I don't know if they really serve a salad like this in Mexico, but it seems they should. Mexican cooks are fond of chickpeas and these ingredients are typically Mexican. I serve this salad as a side dish at outdoor barbecues.

MAKES 8 SIDE-DISH SERVINGS

Combine the chickpeas, onion, garlic, jalapeños, chipotles, tomatoes, olive oil, lime juice, cilantro, and salt and pepper. Let marinate for 2 hours. Adjust the salt and pepper and the lime juice to taste. Serve slightly cool.

4 cups cooked chickpeas (above), or 4 cups drained canned chickpeas (two 15-ounce cans), rinsed

1 medium onion, minced

2 cloves garlic, minced and crushed to a paste

3 jalapeños, seeded and minced

1 to 2 canned chipotle chiles in adobo sauce, rinsed, seeded, and minced

3 medium tomatoes, peeled, seeded, and chopped

$^1/_4$ cup extra-virgin olive oil

$^1/_4$ cup fresh lime juice, or more to taste

3 tablespoons chopped fresh cilantro

Salt and freshly ground black pepper

Mexican-Style Chickpea Salad.

CHICORIES: RADICCHIO, ESCAROLE, FRISÉE, AND BELGIAN ENDIVE

Most leafy greens are best tossed with a little vinaigrette in cool and crispy salads. Tender and baby greens don't cook well because they lose the crispiness that makes them such a delight in salads and end up tasting flat and uninteresting. On the other hand, firm-textured and stronger-flavored greens, such as radicchio, endive, frisée, and escarole, keep their flavor and texture when cooked. They can be braised, grilled, cooked in soups, or made into salads.

BELGIAN ENDIVE

The first time I saw endive—in a fancy supermarket in San Francisco—I was struck not only by its bizarre bullet-like appearance, but by how expensive it was—at least four times the price of any other salad green. Nowadays so many foods are imported and air freighted from around the world that endive has become a relatively inexpensive staple, even in ordinary supermarkets.

Belgian endive is sold as plump white shoots with smooth, tightly closed leaves. The leaves are white because the endive is grown in the dark, where no light reaches its leaves to turn them green. Belgian endive leaves have an appealing, gentle bittersweet flavor and cool crunch.

When buying Belgian endive, avoid any stalks that are turning green—this happens when endive has been sitting in a store exposed to light for too long. Avoid endive with outer leaves that are obviously wilted or feel slightly rough to the touch. Also avoid endive with brown or wet spots on its outer leaves. Endive keeps for a day or two, in a perforated plastic bag, in the refrigerator.

To prepare Belgian endive, discard the outermost leaves. To separate the rest of the leaves, cut a cone into the base of the endive and pull away any leaves that come loose. If the whole endive doesn't come apart, cut another slightly deeper cone. If you are going to cook the endive, just split it in half lengthwise.

Belgian endive is usually served in salads and is so clean that it needs very little washing. It also creates very little waste, unlike some lettuces that have tough outer leaves that have to be thrown out. Belgian endive can be baked as a gratin, with broth and/or cream. I like to include a little bacon, which provides a little smokiness, the perfect accent to the endive.

Grilled Endive and Radicchio.

Orange, Endive, and Walnut Salad

I make this simple and lovely salad at least several times a month during the winter. It's delicious both as a first course and after the main course. Buy nut oil, preferably toasted nut oil (see page 38), in the smallest containers you can find and keep it refrigerated at all times.

MAKES 4 FIRST-COURSE COURSE SERVINGS

Preheat the oven to 350°F.

If the outermost endive leaves show signs of wilting, pull them off and discard them. Separate all the leaves and add to a large bowl of cold water. Drain and dry on towels or spin dry in a salad spinner.

Spread the walnuts in a shallow pan and toast for 15 minutes, until they smell fragrant and brown very slightly. Set aside.

To make the vinaigrette, grate the zest off about half of the orange until you have about a teaspoon of grated zest. (Scrape along the inside of the grater with a small knife—this is where most of the zest will end up—and give the grater a good whack against the cutting board to get off any remaining zest.) Combine the zest with the vinegar and oil and season with salt and pepper. Cut the orange into wedges (below).

Toss the endive leaves in the vinaigrette just before serving. Arrange the endive in a salad bowl or on individual plates and sprinkle the orange wedges and nuts on top.

VARIATIONS:

Try adding boiled green beans (ideally the thin French haricot verts) and little pieces of Roquefort cheese. Beets also make an exciting addition.

4 Belgian endives

1/2 cup walnut halves or pecans

1 naval orange

1 tablespoon sherry vinegar or good-quality white wine vinegar

3 tablespoons toasted walnut oil, toasted hazelnut oil, or extra-virgin olive oil

Salt and freshly ground black pepper

↝ CUTTING AN ORANGE INTO SKINLESS WEDGES OR SLICES ↝

Slice off the top and bottom of the orange just deeply enough to expose the flesh. Set the orange flat on a cutting board and, with a very sharp knife, trim off the peel, following the contours of the orange so a minimum of flesh is left on the peel. Cut off any of the white membrane that still clings to the orange.

If you're serving the orange in slices, just cut the orange into rounds between 1/8 inch and 1/4 inch thick.

If you're serving the orange in wedges, hold the orange in your left hand (if you're right-handed) over a bowl and cut between each orange segment, along both sides of the thin membrane that separates each segment, with a very sharp stainless steel paring knife. Cut only to the center of the orange. Continue in this way, cutting on both sides of each membrane until all the orange segments fall into the bowl. Give the pulp left in your hand a good squeeze to get out all the juice.

ESCAROLE

I didn't appreciate escarole (it always seemed tough and bitter) until I traveled to Italy, where it shows up on menus grilled, sautéed, and in soups. Escarole has pale green outer leaves and very pale yellow, almost white, inner leaves. The leaves are firm and somewhat bitter—qualities that make escarole perfect for cooking.

Buy the palest and most delicate escarole you can find. If the heads are large, dark green, and tough-looking, check to see if they're being sold by the head or by the pound. If they're being sold by the head, then it's less important that they be small—you can just trim off the outer tough leaves and discard them (a compost heap or rabbit would be handy here). But if the escarole is sold by the pound, this approach can be expensive. Other than its obvious role in a salad, escarole can be gently sautéed, braised, or simmered in a soup.

Escarole.

Italian Escarole Soup with Garlic and Parmesan Cheese

You can make this soup with just about any tender green—Swiss chard and beet greens are great—but the gentle bitterness of escarole is beautifully matched by this soup's abundance of garlic.

If you've got some chicken broth on hand, this soup takes only about 25 minutes to make. If you want to make the soup more substantial, add pieces of cooked chicken peeled off the bones used for making the broth. I put a slice of toasted French bread in the bottom of each bowl before pouring over the soup. A half-cup of cream gives this soup a welcome richness on a cold night.

MAKES 4 FIRST-COURSE SERVINGS

Remove and discard the darkest, toughest outermost leaves from the escarole. Detach the smaller leaves at the base and cut out and discard any large, tough white sections near the bottom of the leaves. Wash in cold water and let drain. Cut the leaves crosswise into 1/2-inch-wide strips.

Heat the sliced garlic in the butter in a large, heavy-bottomed pot over medium heat until the garlic begins to brown slightly, about 5 minutes. Add the broth, saffron, and escarole. Reduce the heat to low and simmer gently until the escarole is tender, about 15 minutes. Stir in the vinegar, garlic paste, and cream and bring the soup back to a simmer. Season to taste with salt.

Put a slice of toasted French bread in the bottom of each of four heated, wide bowls. Ladle over the soup. Pass the pepper and the grated Parmesan cheese at the table.

1 (1-pound) head escarole or 2 smaller heads

6 cloves garlic, very thinly sliced, plus 4 cloves garlic, minced and crushed to a paste

1 tablespoon unsalted butter or extra-virgin olive oil

4 cups broth, preferably Basic Brown Chicken Broth (page 373), Basic Turkey Broth (page 374), or Basic Brown Beef Broth (page 375)

1/4 teaspoon saffron threads (optional)

1 tablespoon sherry vinegar, balsamic vinegar, or good-quality red wine vinegar, or more to taste

1/2 cup heavy cream (optional)

Salt

4 (3/4-inch-thick) slices crusty French bread, toasted

Freshly ground black pepper

6 tablespoons freshly grated Parmigiano-Reggiano cheese, or 1 1/2 cups Pesto (page 206)

Sautéed Escarole with Pine Nuts, Garlic, Raisins, Capers, and Anchovies

This typical southern Italian combination seems the perfect match for its bright sunshine and life-loving people. Each ingredient provides something essential to the dish—the pine nuts give crunch, the raisins some sweetness, and the capers and anchovies a salty tang—but you can also substitute ingredients freely and still end up with something delicious. I sometimes cook sliced onions in olive oil before adding the escarole, coarsely chopped green or black olives can replace or augment the capers, slivered almonds or even pecans can replace the pine nuts, and the anchovies can be left out completely.

I like to serve this escarole as a side dish with a plate of pasta or a bowl of soup.

MAKES 4 SIDE-DISH SERVINGS

Remove and discard the darkest, toughest outermost leaves from the escarole. Detach the smaller leaves at the base and cut out and discard any large, tough white sections near the bottom of the leaves. Wash in cold water and let drain. Cut the leaves crosswise into $^{1}/_{2}$-inch-wide strips.

Soak the raisins in a tablespoon of warm water for 20 minutes to soften them. Drain.

Finely chop the anchovies until you have a coarse paste.

Heat the olive oil in a skillet over medium heat and stir in the pine nuts. Stir until the pine nuts turn very pale brown and you can smell their aroma, about 5 minutes. Add the garlic and cook until the garlic turns pale brown, about 2 more minutes. Add the escarole—you may have to add it in batches to get it to fit into the pan—and turn the heat up to high. Stir until the escarole wilts and softens—you may want to reach in and taste a piece to see if it's how you like it—for about 5 minutes. Stir in the raisins, anchovies, capers, and vinegar and sauté for 1 minute more. Season to taste with salt and pepper and more vinegar, if the dish needs it. Serve immediately in a hot serving dish.

Sautéed Escarole with Pine Nuts, Garlic, Raisins, Capers, and Anchovies.

2 (12-ounce to 1-pound) heads escarole

2 tablespoon raisins, preferably golden

8 anchovy fillets, soaked for 5 minutes in cold water and patted dry (soaking optional)

3 tablespoons extra-virgin olive oil

2 tablespoons pine nuts

3 cloves garlic, minced

2 tablespoons capers, drained

1 teaspoon sherry vinegar or balsamic vinegar, or more to taste

Salt and freshly ground black pepper

FRISÉE

Taken from the French word for "curly," this chicory is distinctly bitter, but not so much so that it can't be served alone. It can be combined with other greens as part of a green or mixed salad, or it can be used as a foil for strongly flavored ingredients, such as bacon.

When shopping for frisée, look for those with the most yellow in the center. Carefully pull away the leaves from the base and wash them in plenty of cold water.

Frisée, Bacon, and Poached Egg Salad

This salad comes from Lyon and resembles the better-known *salade au lard* in which is frisée served with bacon. Croutons are included here to provide the requisite crunch, and a poached egg (you can also soft-boil the eggs) on each serving softens the strong flavors of smoky and bitter.

MAKES 4 FIRST-COURSE OR LIGHT MAIN-COURSE SERVINGS

Heat the bacon in a skillet over medium heat until it turns lightly crispy and renders its fat, about 8 minutes. Scoop out the bacon with a slotted spoon and add the bread cubes to the pan. Cook the bread cubes, while tossing or stirring every couple of minutes, until they brown evenly, about 5 minutes. Remove with a slotted spoon.

Toss the frisée with the vinegar and oil and arrange it on individual plates. Scatter over the bacon and the croutons. Place an egg on each serving. Season with pepper. Serve at once.

8 ounces thick-cut bacon, cut crosswise into 1-inch strips

4 slices white bread, cut into 1/4-inch cubes

1 large head frisée, yellow and bright green leaves discarded

2 tablespoons sherry vinegar

1/4 cup extra-virgin olive oil

4 poached or soft-boiled eggs

Freshly ground black pepper

Frisée, Bacon, and Poached Egg Salad.

RADICCHIO

Not too many years ago, radicchio was an exotic Italian "green" that never appeared in even the fanciest food stores in the United States. Today it's found in most supermarkets.

Two kinds of radicchio are sold in the United States. The most familiar, *radicchio di Verona* comes in tight, round, deep burgundy heads, usually about the size of a fist. *Radicchio di Treviso* is less common—it usually appears only in fancy food stores—and has long pointed leaves somewhat like Belgian endive, except the leaves are thinner, more separated, and deep purple. Because radicchio leaves are somewhat tough and can be quite bitter, I always mix them with other more delicate greens when making a green salad. But this same firmness makes radicchio especially well suited for cooking because it'll retain some of its texture after being exposed to heat.

Both kinds of radicchio keep well, especially if the heads are tightly wrapped in plastic wrap and kept in the refrigerator. I never cook radicchio di Treviso because it's expensive and the result is the same as radicchio di Verona. I save the beautiful spiky radicchio di Treviso to add drama to salads with raw greens.

Grilled Radicchio, Escarole, and Belgian Endive

It never occurred to me to grill something leafy until I encountered grilled radicchio and escarole in restaurants in Italy. To grill radicchio, buy rather large heads—4 to 5 inches in diameter. Remove any outer wilted leaves and cut the heads into quarters through the root end. It's important to cut through the root end so that the leaves stay together and the heads don't fall apart on the grill. Soak the radicchio in cold water for a few minutes to moisten it and to keep it from burning.

Grill the escarole by first removing the toughest and outermost dark green leaves and then cutting the center yellowish "heart" in half or in quarters through the base, again being careful to cut through the core so that the head doesn't fall apart on the grill. Like radicchio, escarole should be soaked for a minute or two in cold water so it's moist before it hits the hot grill.

Brush radicchio and escarole with extra-virgin olive oil just before they go on the grill and grill them over medium heat 4 to 6 inches from the top of the coals. Brush them every couple of minutes and turn them over several times to keep them from getting too dark. If they start to burn, move them to a cooler part of the grill. They are ready when the outer leaves are dark brown and begin to sag and feel soft to the touch, after about 10 minutes. Sprinkle with salt and pepper just before serving. Count on 2 heads of radicchio or 1 head of escarole for 4 servings.

Belgian endive is easy to grill—just cut the heads in half lengthwise, soak them in cold water for about 10 minutes, and toss them in olive oil. Season with salt and pepper, and chopped herbs if you like, and grill them. Turn them over every 2 to 3 minutes until they're lightly browned and slightly limp, about 15 minutes. Count on one endive (2 halves) per serving

Sautéed Radicchio, Orange, Bacon, and Pecan Salad

This salad makes a lovely start to a winter dinner. The sweet oranges and the smoky bacon are a perfect accent to the gentle bitterness of the radicchio, and the pecans give the whole thing a contrasting texture. I use double-smoked slab bacon, which is lean, has a good flavor, and is easy to cut into cubes, but thick-cut packaged bacon will also work. Just be sure to buy a brand that says "naturally smoked" and not "smoke flavored." Smoke-flavored bacon tastes like soap.

All the cooking for this salad can be done earlier the same day; only the final assembly has to be done at the last minute. This salad should be served at room temperature or slightly cool, not chilled.

MAKES 4 FIRST-COURSE SERVINGS

Preheat the oven to 350°F.

Spread the pecans in a shallow pan and toast for 15 minutes, until they brown very slightly and start to smell toasty. Set aside.

Pull any wilted leaves off the radicchio and cut the heads in half through their cores. Slice each half as thinly as you can—1/8-inch shreds are ideal—with a chef's knife or vegetable slicer.

Cook the bacon cubes in a heavy-bottomed skillet over medium heat until they render fat and barely start to turn crispy, about 8 minutes. Drain off the fat (you can save bacon fat for other recipes) by tilting the pan while holding the bacon back with a slotted spoon. Pour the olive oil into the pan. Turn the heat up to high and stir in the radicchio. Stir the radicchio until it has shrunk to about half and is completely wilted, about 5 minutes. Add the vinegar, stir for a minute more (you'll see the color of the radicchio brighten), and transfer to a mixing bowl. Toss the radicchio with the pecans and the bacon cubes and season to taste with salt and pepper and a little more vinegar, if needed. Let cool until no longer hot, but still warm.

Place the salad in mounds on individual plates. Arrange the orange segments in a circular pattern over each salad. Serve immediately.

1 cup shelled pecans

2 to 3 heads radicchio (12 ounces total)

4 thick-cut slices bacon, cut into 1/4-inch cubes

3 tablespoons extra-virgin olive oil

1/4 cup sherry vinegar or balsamic vinegar, or more to taste

Salt and freshly ground black pepper

4 navel oranges, peeled and cut into wedges

Sautéed Radicchio, Orange, Bacon, and Pecan Salad.

CHILES

At one of my first dinner parties, I made a cheese fondue and decided that it would be clever to pass around cut-up vegetables, instead of bread, for dipping into the bubbling cheese. Included in the vegetables were whole jalapeños. To get things started, I, a neophyte chile eater, jabbed one of the chiles with my long fork, rolled it around in the cheese, and plunged it whole into my mouth. The rest is easy to imagine. We picked out the jalapeños and saved them to use in discreet amounts in other dishes.

Most of us now know enough about chiles to approach them with a certain amount of caution, but we've also grown to love them as Mexican, Tex-Mex, and so-called border restaurants seem to be popping up in the most unlikely places. My students today enjoy hot foods and have a far higher tolerance for hot chiles than did students of twenty years ago, when most of us might have been familiar with bell peppers and one or two hot

Assorted chiles.

chile varieties. Today more chile varieties are showing up in markets and restaurants as we've begun to appreciate their subtle differences.

Chiles come in four forms: fresh, dried (smoked or unsmoked), canned, and powdered. Inspect fresh chiles for soft or dark spots—signs they're starting to rot—and avoid chiles that look wrinkled, meaning they're old. Dried chiles should feel flexible and leathery instead of crispy and very dry.

Fresh chiles keep in the refrigerator for 2 to 5 days, but keep in mind that larger chiles and red or orange chiles are more perishable than small chiles or green chiles. Roasted or grilled and peeled chiles will keep in the refrigerator, well covered with plastic wrap, for 2 days. Dried chiles should be tightly wrapped and can be kept in a cool, dry place for a couple of months. Both fresh and dried chiles can be frozen for up to 6 months.

Ajisito chiles.

Most of the time fresh chiles are cooked to soften their texture and to get them to release heat and flavor into a surrounding liquid. I start many a soup or sauce by gently cooking a mixture of chopped chiles, onion, and garlic in a little butter, olive oil, or bacon fat before adding liquid.

The best way to chop fresh chiles is to cut them in half lengthwise, pull the seeds and stem out of each half—you can also cut out the white pulp, which is responsible for a lot of the chiles' heat—and then just chop the halves. It's a good idea to wear gloves for this process because the oils contained in the chiles' seeds and membranes are very irritating to skin and eyes. I used to laugh at recommendations for wearing gloves while peeling chiles, but this was before I had encountered a Scotch bonnet. Scotch bonnets are so hot that it's important that you keep them off your hands and face. I suggest wearing thin disposable surgical gloves and never touching your face until you get the gloves off. Always stand back when heating Scotch bonnets or when pureeing them in a blender. Habaneros and rocatillos should also be approached with caution. They're as hot as Scotch bonnets. Whatever you do, don't touch your eyes or face until you've thoroughly washed your hands—and even then, wait a while.

Fresh chiles can be finely chopped and served raw as a condiment for soups and sauced dishes. This is a good approach if you're making a dish with chiles in it and you're unsure of your guests' tolerance for heat—just make the dish mild and pass some chopped chiles at the table. Some recipes call for roasting or grilling chiles and then peeling off the blackened skin. This roasting and peeling process softens the chiles and gives them a lovely smoky and toasty flavor (see page 8).

Dried chiles are a revelation to those of us who have used only fresh chiles. During the drying—and sometimes smoking—chiles develop subtle flavors that are reminiscent of dried fruit, tobacco, chocolate, leather, mushrooms, and other aromas that are hard to pinpoint. Dried chiles are easy to prepare—just cut them in half lengthwise, soak them, and pull out the stem and seeds. They can then be soaked again in a little warm water to soften them—then chopped or shredded in the same way as fresh chiles. Dried chiles can also be seeded and ground into a powder in a blender. The powder can be used as a last-minute seasoning for soups, stews, and salsas. Homemade chile powder made in this way will have a lot more flavor than anything you'll find in a jar and can be kept up to several months in the freezer (see page 169).

CHILE VARIETIES

ANAHEIM. Elongated, and usually about 6 inches long and 2 inches wide at the widest part Anaheim chilies are available both green (when under-ripe) and red (when ripe). As is true with most chiles, the red variety is the ripe version of the green and is sweeter and fruitier. Anaheim chiles are among the mildest of chiles (although unlike sweet bell peppers, they have some heat). They are best roasted and peeled, which brings out their flavor in the same way it does for bell peppers. They are also good for stuffing because of their size and the gentleness of their heat.

ANCHO. These are dried red poblano chiles and are the most popular and easiest-to-find dried chile. Anchos are shaped like flattened apples and are usually blackish-brownish red. In Mexico and, to a lesser extent, in the United States, an ancho's quality is related to its size—the biggest and thickest being the best. Ancho chiles are mildly hot—they're often hotter than fresh poblanos—and they have a lovely, vaguely smoky and fruity flavor. They're one of the most useful chiles to have around.

CHILHUACLE NEGRO. These dark, black chiles—they look somewhat like small bell peppers—never seem to show up fresh in the United States, but they are available dried in specialty stores or by mail order. Dried chilhuacles (there are also red and yellow varieties) are among the most delicious of chiles. Try them in moles and in the Dried Chile Cream Sauce on page 176.

CHIPOTLE. Chipotle chiles—jalapeños that have been smoked—are available dried or in (usually 7-ounce) cans, packed in adobo sauce. Chipotle chiles add a wonderful smoky complexity to almost any dish calling for chiles, but I like them best in soups and sauces. I usually use canned chipotles and rinse off the adobo sauce. Chipotles can be very hot, but you can attenuate their heat a little by scraping out the seeds.

GUAJILLO. These elongated orange-red chiles are one of the most common dried chiles. They're usually about 5 inches long and about an inch thick at the thickest end. They are often used with ancho chiles in salsas, soups, and moles.

HABANERO. These and Scotch bonnets, which look almost the same, are among the hottest chiles in the world. They're easy to spot because they look like caved-in little bells and come in all sorts of colors ranging from bright red to orange to almost burgundy. They're used mostly in Caribbean cooking where aficionados claim their fruit flavor is unsurpassed, but for most of us it's hard to get around the heat to the flavor. They're about 2 inches in diameter.

Habanero chiles.

HUNGARIAN WAX. These are another large and mild chile, usually red and about 5 inches long, that can be used for stuffing or in dishes that contain a large proportion of chiles where hot chiles would make the dish too hot.

JALAPEÑO. These are probably the best known of all chiles and are easy to find in almost any grocery store. Jalapeños come in both red and green, but green is the most common. There doesn't seem to be much difference in flavor or heat between the two. Jalapeños are cone-shaped and usually about 2 inches long and 3/4 inch wide at the widest part. In recent years, jalapeños have lost much of their heat, so on occasion it might be necessary to increase the amounts called for in a recipe. Smoked jalapeños are called chipotles (see above).

MULATO. These are dried underripe green poblanos—the kind we're more likely to find fresh—instead of the ripe red poblanos dried as anchos. Mulatos are darker than anchos, almost black. They can be used in the same way as, or in combination with, anchos.

NEW MEXICO. This is one of the most popular chiles in the Southwest and comes in green, red, and yellow and both fresh and dried. New Mexico chiles are fairly mild, although not as mild as Anaheim chiles. They are popular for stuffing because of their large size—6 to 8 inches long and 2 inches wide near the top—and are also used in a number of traditional New Mexican dishes, such as chile con carne.

PASILLA. This is a dried version of the dark chilaca chile, which according to Mark Miller in his *Great Chile Book*, is almost never found fresh in the United States. The dried version, called simply "pasilla," sometimes "pasilla negro," or simply "chile negro"—is easy to spot because of its distinctive elongated shape. It has shiny black skin and is usually about 5 inches long. It has medium heat. Pasillas are among the chiles that Mexican cooks most like to use for making moles. But to complicate matters, the word "pasilla" is also used for other chiles. Fresh poblanos and dried poblanos (anchos and mulatos) are called pasillas in parts of Mexico and California. This shouldn't be too hard to figure out though, because anchos are reddish and both mulatos and anchos are squat, and not elongated like the authentic pasilla negro.

PASILLA DE OAXACA. Like chipotles, these difficult-to-find chiles are smoked but have a lovely outdoor woody quality to their smokiness. About 4 inches long, orange-red, and quite hot, Pasillas de Oaxaca are named after the Mexican city of Oaxaca.

Jalapeño chiles.

Long peppers.

PEPPERONCINI. These little dried red chiles are sold in cellophane bags in Italy for flavoring pasta sauces. The chiles are usually so dry that you can crumble them into flakes easily and sprinkle them into sauces as you would red pepper flakes. They're usually between 2 and 3 inches long. Bottled red pepper flakes make a good substitute. Ocassionally pepperoncini are available fresh or pickled.

POBLANO. One of the most flavorful chiles, poblanos are usually dark green, although riper specimens may have splotches of deep red, and are shaped like elongated cones. They're typically about 5 inches long and about 3 inches across at the top. Poblanos are usually fairly mild, but occasionally you'll encounter a hot one. Cooked poblanos make a great starting point for flavorful soups and sauces. Dried red poblanos are called anchos; dried green poblanos are called mulatos.

Poblano.

ROCATILLO. These little chiles come in several colors—red, green, and yellow—and have the distinctive shape of their close relatives, habanero and Scotch bonnet. Rocatillos are popular in Caribbean cooking and can be used in the same way as habaneros. They're not quite as hot as habaneros, but still should be approached with caution.

SCOTCH BONNET. Because of their interesting shape and yellow or orange coloring, these are the prettiest of chiles, but caveat emptor—they're hot as hell. They're the same size, look similar to, and can be used in the same way as habaneros.

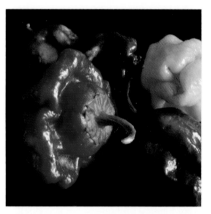
Scotch bonnet.

SERRANO. These are another of the more common chiles and, like jalapeños, they come in both green and red with very little difference in heat or flavor between the two. Serranos are hotter than jalapeños. I substitute one large serrano for two jalapeños. Serranos are usually about $1\frac{1}{2}$ to 3 inches long and are more bullet-shaped and elongated than jalapeños.

THAI CHILES. Sometimes called bird chiles, these chiles use heat to make up for their diminutive size. Thai chiles are the smallest chiles you're likely to encounter—they're usually only about an inch long (not including the stem) and $\frac{1}{4}$ inch thick at the stem end. They're usually sold in packages containing both red and green chiles with about twenty green chiles to one red—both have the same flavor and heat, although I sometimes pick out and use the red ones first because they look pretty. One Thai chile has about the same heat as two jalapeños.

Thai chiles.

❧ HOMEMADE CHILE POWDER ❧

Chile powder in a jar doesn't usually have much taste—just a generic hotness and a dusty flavor. Your own chile powder, made with any dried chiles you like will have a deep toasty flavor and character.

Cut the stems from 1 ounce dried chiles, cut the chiles in half lengthwise, and shake out the seeds. Put the chiles in an cast-iron skillet over high heat for about 5 minutes, tossing every few seconds until you smell a delightful toasty fragrance. (Be careful because some chiles will send you coughing out of the room—a price you must pay.) Let the chiles cool. They should feel dry and crispy; if they still feel leathery, toast them a few more minutes. Grind in a blender or food processor at high speed for 1 minute. Let the dust settle before removing the lid. Strain the mixture to eliminate any large pieces. You can keep homemade chile powder, tightly sealed in the freezer, for 6 months. Makes about 1/4 cup.

Beef Stew with Beer, Chiles, and Sometimes Beans (*Chili con Carne*)

Until I made it myself, I never had much of a liking for chili con carne, probably because I had tasted it only in little hole-in-the-wall chili parlors on busy city streets. This is not to say that such places aren't capable of making wonderful food, I just never lucked into a chili con carne that left me hankering for more.

But the idea of cooking meat with chiles has always held promise, so after a few experiments, I came up with the version here. I decided that instead of ground beef, I would use whole chunks of beef and prepare them in a flavorful stew made with beer, much like the Belgian carbonnade. The stewing liquid then forms the base and is used to cook an assortment of chiles—fresh, dried, and canned. If you like chili con carne with beans, you can stir in 6 cups of any variety of cooked beans (page 301) into the finished dish or you can add 2 1/2 cups rinsed and soaked dried beans to the stew at the beginning of cooking. Since this dish takes several hours from beginning to end, and it keeps well—even improves—for several days in the refrigerator, I usually make it for a crowd.

MAKES 10 TO 14 SERVINGS

Combine the beef, beer, orange juice, onion, and garlic in a nonaluminum mixing bowl. Tie together the thyme, bay leaves, and parsley with a piece of string (or with cheesecloth if you're using dried thyme), and nestle this bouquet garni in the marinating meat. Let the meat sit at room temperature for up to 2 hours, or overnight in the refrigerator.

Transfer the soaked beans and the contents of the mixing bowl into a large, preferably narrow pot (a narrow pot makes skimming easier). Cover the pot and place over medium heat until the liquids reach a slow simmer. If at any point the stew starts to boil, turn down the heat immediately. Cook over a very low heat so you just see a bubble or two floating up every few seconds. (If your stove won't go this low, use a flame tamer or put the pot in a 325°F oven.) Check the pot from time to time to make sure it hasn't accidentally reached the boil or that it isn't just sitting there doing nothing. If the liquid starts to run dry—a potential problem

8 pounds beef chuck, trimmed of fat and gristle, cut into 1-inch cubes

4 (12-ounce) bottles dark beer, preferably Negro Modelo or Dos Equis

1 cup orange juice

1 white onion, minced

3 cloves garlic, minced

4 sprigs fresh thyme, or 1 teaspoon dried thyme leaves

2 imported bay leaves

1 bunch parsley

2 1/2 cups dried beans, such as black beans, soaked for 3 hours or overnight and drained, or 6 cups cooked beans (optional, page 305)

8 ancho chiles

8 mulato chiles

8 large fresh chiles, such as poblano, Anaheim, or New Mexico

2 canned chipotle chiles in adobo sauce, seeded, rinsed, and minced

Salt

especially if you've included the beans—add enough beer, or water to keep the beans barely covered. Braise for 3 hours, until the meat is easily penetrated with a fork and beans are no longer mealy. If at any point the liquid seems to be running dry, add more water or beer.

While the meat is cooking, take the stems off the dried ancho and mulato chiles and cut the chiles in half lengthwise. Take out the seeds and, with a pair of scissors, cut the chiles crosswise into $^1/_4$-inch strips. Put the chiles in a bowl and pour over 1 cup of boiling water. Push the chiles down into the water so they're completely covered. Soak for 30 minutes. (Remember to be careful when working with chiles—wear gloves if possible and wash your hands well after.)

Roast and peel the fresh chiles. Carefully cut them open and remove and discard the stem and seeds. Cut the chiles crosswise into thin strips no longer than $^1/_4$ inch. Reserve.

When the meat is ready—bite into a piece; it should melt in your mouth—and the beans are soft, use a spoon or small ladle to carefully skim off and discard any fat and froth that have floated to the top. Place a large strainer over a clean pot and strain the stew, letting the liquid drip into the pot. Take out and discard the bouquet garni. Set the stew aside and bring the liquid to a gentle simmer over low to medium heat. Place the pot to one side of the heat so that fat and froth float to one side of the liquid where it's easier to skim off. Use a ladle to skim off any fat that floats to the surface and continue cooking down the liquid until only about 3 cups remain.

Drain the dried chiles and combine them with $^3/_4$ cup of the meat cooking liquid in a blender and puree for about 2 minutes until smooth. Strain this mixture into the rest of the reserved liquid from the stew. (Push it through the strainer with the back of a ladle.) Pour the reserved stewing liquid back over the meat in a clean pot and stir in the strips of fresh chiles and the minced chipotles. If you're adding cooked beans, add them now. Bring the stew to a gentle simmer, season to taste with salt, and serve.

⤳ HOW HOT IS HOT? ⤳

Chiles range in "temperature" from heatless (bell peppers, Hungarian sweet chiles) to incendiary (habaneros, Scotch bonnets). You can control the heat of a dish by adding more or less of a particular chile, but substituting one chile for another is a bit more complicated. Some authors have rated chiles using a hotness scale ranging from 0 to 10, but because this system doesn't take into account the size of the chiles, you can't just substitute according to hotness. Here is a reasonably accurate equivalent for the three most easy-to-find hot chiles—jalapeños, serranos, and Thai chiles:

4 jalapeños = 2 Thais chiles = 1 serrano.

(Even though jalapeños are much milder than Thai chiles, they are much larger).

Pan-Fried Cheese-Stuffed Chiles (*Chiles Rellenos*)

One of the best things I remember about living in San Francisco is the cheap Mexican food, served up in authentic, unpretentious places, where one could have a satisfying dinner for a couple of dollars. One of my favorite dishes was chiles rellenos. But in New York restaurants, chiles rellenos are expensive, so I've taken to making them at home.

One important trick is to use poblano chiles. Poblanos have an incomparable flavor and nowadays are fairly easy to find, even in a regular supermarket. When buying poblanos for this recipe, search through the pile until you find eight long ones, all the same length and preferably flat on all sides so they'll cook evenly and be easy to peel. Do keep in mind, however, that poblanos can be hot—if you're worried, use bell peppers, Anaheim chiles, or New Mexico chiles instead.

The chiles rellenos that most of us have encountered are the traditional ones stuffed with cheese, coated with a soufflé-like batter, and surrounded with a chile-flavored tomato sauce. I've also seen recipes that call for stuffing the chiles with a mixture of ground pork, raisins, and almonds (in Rick Bayless's *Authentic Mexican*), other recipes that suggest coating the chiles with cornmeal instead of the egg batter, one recipe that uses a sauce made exclusively with dried chiles, and another that calls for black bean sauce. My own preference is for the traditional version. I also like to fool around with different cheeses (goat cheese is wonderful), and instead of the usual deep-frying, I cook the chiles in a smaller amount of olive oil in a nonstick pan. The chiles can be roasted and peeled a day or two before you plan to serve them and kept covered in the refrigerator.

MAKES 4 MAIN-COURSE SERVINGS

Char and peel the chiles. Make a 2-inch slit in the side of each of the chiles; carefully reach in and pull out the seeds.

Cut the cheese into 16 strips slightly shorter than the chiles and about ⅓ inch thick on each side. Slip 2 strips into each chile.

To prepare the batter, combine the egg whites with the cream of tartar (leave this out if you're using a copper bowl) and salt and beat to medium stiffness—until they adhere to the end of the whisk, but don't stick straight out. Whisk together 1 tablespoon of the flour with the egg yolks until you have a smooth paste. Fold this mixture into the egg whites with a rubber spatula.

Dip the chiles in the remaining 4 tablespoons flour and pat them gently so they're very lightly coated with the flour.

Heat half the oil in a large nonstick or cast-iron skillet—or use 2 skillets and all the oil—over medium heat. Roll the chiles in the beaten egg mixture and carefully lower them into the hot pan(s). Cook them for about 6 minutes, or until golden brown on one side. Gently turn them over with a spatula and cook them on the second side for 6 minutes more.

Put two chiles each on hot plates and spoon over the heated sauce. Pass the remaining sauce and the sour cream at the table.

2 ounces firm cheese, such as cheddar, Monterey jack, Swiss Gruyère, manchego, or firm goat cheese

5 large eggs, separated

Pinch of cream of tartar (unless using a copper bowl)

Pinch of salt

5 tablespoons all-purpose flour

2 cups (or enough to come ½ inch up the sides of the pan) pure olive oil or canola oil

1½ cups Dried Chile Cream Sauce (page 176)

1 cup sour cream (optional)

8 large poblano chiles, preferably with flat sides

Chiles Rellenos with Chile Cream Sauce.

Mexican Chile and Tomato Soup

Many Mexican soups are based on a simple tomato broth flavored with chiles and garlic, but this soup is especially delightful because flavorful ingredients—cubes of avocado, strips of crispy fried tortillas, sour cream, lime wedges, and chiles—are passed at the table for guests to help themselves.

The tomato broth for this soup is simple to make, but it has its own special, robust character because the tomatoes, onions, and garlic are toasted on an cast-iron skillet and "fried" before they're combined with liquid.

I like to serve this soup as the first course at a festive—preferably outdoor—dinner. This recipe makes enough for twelve people each to have one bowl, but my experience is that everyone will want a second helping, so you may want to make this recipe for six or eight. You can prepare the basic soup a day or two in advance so you'll only need to prepare the garnishes on the day of serving.

You can use the same technique of roasting and frying tomatoes to make a delicious Mexican tomato sauce. Prepare the basic soup, but instead of adding 2 cups of broth, add only enough broth—maybe none at all—to give the soup base, now a sauce, the consistency you like. You'll end up with about 2 cups of sauce.

MAKES 12 FIRST-COURSE SERVINGS

To prepare the basic soup, heat a large cast-iron skillet over high heat for about 5 minutes. When the pan is hot—a drop of water instantly sizzles away—add the garlic and onions and stir every minute or two—the onions will separate into pieces—until the onions and garlic smell fragrant and begin to blacken, about 10 minutes. Remove from the pan and reserve. Add the tomatoes to the pan and keep rotating them around using tongs until their skin wrinkles on all sides, about 5 minutes. Turn off the heat and set aside to cool.

Pull the peels off the tomatoes, cut the tomatoes in half crosswise, and squeeze out their seeds. Put the garlic, onions, and tomatoes in a blender and puree to a smooth paste, about 2 minutes. If the mixture is too thick to turn around in the blender, add as little of the broth as you can—about $1/4$ cup—to get the mixture to turn around.

Heat the tablespoon of corn oil over high heat in the skillet used for cooking the vegetables, until the oil ripples. Quickly stir in the tomato mixture—stand back, it may spatter—and stir over high heat until the mixture comes together into a very stiff paste, about 10 minutes. Stir in 2 cups of the broth, bring to a simmer, remove from the heat, and reserve.

To prepare the garnishes, heat $1/4$ cup of the corn oil in a cast-iron skillet or other heavy-bottomed pot or pan over high heat. When the oil begins to ripple, add the chile strips and stir for about 30 seconds or until they sizzle and you feel their heat in your nose. Remove the strips with a slotted spoon and reserve on a towel.

Add the remaining $1^1/2$ cups of the oil to the skillet and heat until it ripples slightly. Slowly lower about one-quarter of the corn tortilla strips into the hot oil and fry for about 30 seconds. (Fry about a quarter of the tortilla strips at a time so you can judge how much the oil will bubble up—you don't want it to overflow.) Drain the fried tortilla strips on paper towels and reserve. Repeat with the remaining tortilla strips.

continued

BASIC TOMATO SOUP

10 cloves garlic, unpeeled

2 medium red onions, quartered

8 medium tomatoes

12 cups Basic Brown Chicken Broth (page 373)

1 tablespoon corn oil or canola oil

Salt

GARNISHES

2 cups corn oil or canola oil (for frying)

6 dried chiles, such as anchos, guajillos, mulatos, or pasillas, stemmed, seeded, cut into $1/8$-inch wide strips

12 (6-inch) corn tortillas, cut into $1/4$-inch wide strips

2 avocados, preferably Haas

2 tablespoons fresh lemon juice

2 cups grated Monterey jack or mozzarella cheese

3 limes, quartered

2 cups sour cream

1 bunch cilantro, leaves coarsely chopped

8 jalapeños, seeded and minced

Peel the avocados, cut them into $1/4$-inch cubes, and toss with the lemon juice.

To finish and serve the soup, bring the reserved tomato mixture to a simmer with the remaining $9\,3/4$ to 10 cups of the broth and season to taste with salt.

Put the chile strips, tortilla strips, avocado cubes, grated cheese, limes, sour cream, cilantro, and jalapeños in separate bowls on the table. Ladle the soup out into hot bowls and serve.

✿ PRESERVING CHILES ✿

If you're stuck with a large chile crop or there's a big sale at the green market, you may want to preserve chiles yourself by drying or pickling. Drying is the easiest method—just string the chiles and hang them in a dry place, preferably in the sun—but some chiles dry better than others. Most large chiles dry easily but some smaller chiles, such as Scotch bonnet, have trouble drying properly (perhaps because of their tightly packed seeds) and may turn moldy.

Chiles can be pickled by just stuffing them in a jar with enough vinegar, brine, or dry sherry to cover and then letting them sit for at least a week or as long as a year. If you use sherry or good wine vinegar, you can use the liquid from the jar as hot sauce for grilled fish or meats or add it to vinaigrettes to give them a little zing. (See Pickled Chiles, below.)

Pickled Chiles

You can pickle any kind of chile or a mixture of different varieties. My favorite chiles for pickling are poblanos and jalapeños.

MAKES I QUART

Rinse off the chiles and remove their stems. Cut large chiles in half lengthwise and, wearing rubber gloves, pull out their seeds. Leave small chiles whole. Fill a 1-quart mason jar with the chiles, distributing the onion, garlic, thyme, and salt evenly among the layers of chiles. Bring the vinegar to a boil and immediately pour it over the chiles. Be sure the chiles are completely covered with the hot vinegar. Immediately twist on the cap and let cool without opening. Refrigerate the chiles and serve within several weeks.

About I pound assorted large fresh chiles, such as poblano, Anaheim, or New Mexico, or $1\,1/4$ pounds small fresh chiles, such as jalapeños

I medium red onion, thinly sliced

4 cloves garlic

5 sprigs fresh thyme or marjoram

I tablespoon coarse salt

3 cups white wine vinegar or sherry vinegar

Pickled Chiles.

Chile, Anchovy, and Olive Pizza

A chile pizza is a delight for those of us who are used to the limited topping options at a regular pizza parlor. Here grilled chiles (New Mexico, Anaheim, or poblanos are best) are arranged in a crisscross pattern with anchovies and olives.

MAKES 1 13- x 17-INCH PIZZA

Combine the yeast with 1 tablespoon water, a good pinch of flour, and the sugar and allow to sit for 10 minutes.

Combine the remaining flour, remaining 1 cup of water, and the yeast mixture in a mixing bowl or the bowl to a stand mixer and stir to combine. Stir in the salt (the salt is never added directly with the yeast or it can kill it). Stir in the oil. Work the mixture by hand for about 20 minutes or with the paddle blade on medium speed for about 10 minutes. If the mixer starts to strain, switch to the dough hook. If you're using the dough hook, you can turn the mixer to high speed. When the dough can be stretched out so thin that it becomes translucent, put it in a bowl, cover with plastic wrap, and let rise, ideally at room temperature, but if you're in a hurry, in a slightly warm place, until doubled in size, 2 to 4 hours.

Preheat the oven to 500°F. Oil a 13 by 17-inch sheet pan.

Roll out the dough to the size of a sheet pan and transfer to the pan. Arrange the chiles and anchovies diagonally across the pizza in rows about 3 inches apart. Sprinkle over the olives and place a slice of mozzarella over each of the nine slices.

Bake for about 15 minutes, until the crust is crispy and brown. Cut into nine rectangles and serve.

DOUGH

3/4 teaspoon active dry yeast

1 cup plus 1 tablespoon barely warm water

4 cups all-purpose flour

Small pinch of sugar

1 teaspoon salt

1/2 cup extra-virgin olive oil

TOPPING

2 to 3 fresh chiles, such as poblano, Anaheim, or New Mexico, charred, peeled, seeded, and cut into long strips

30 anchovies, drained

About 50 brine- or oil-cured olives, pitted

1 pound fresh mozzarella, preferably buffalo milk mozzarella, sliced into 9 pieces

Chile, Anchovy, and Olive Pizza.

Dried Chile Cream Sauce

The very best chiles for this sauce are dried chilhuacle negros or dried pasillas de Oaxaca, but you can also use ancho, mulato, or guajillo chiles.

MAKES 1 CUP

Cut the stems off the chiles, cut the chiles in half lengthwise, and rinse out the seeds. Place in a pot and pour over enough boiling water to barely cover. Allow the chiles to soak for about 30 minutes, or until they feel soft and leathery. Drain, and discard the soaking liquid. Chop the chiles very fine to a paste-like consistency. Combine with the cream in a 2-quart saucepan.

Bring the chiles and cream to a slow simmer over medium heat, whisking continuously. Remove from the heat and let sit for about 5 minutes to allow the flavor of the chiles to infuse the cream. Return to the stove and simmer over medium heat, whisking continuously, for between 30 seconds and 2 minutes or until the sauce attains a consistency to your liking. Season with salt, and if additional heat is desired, a little cayenne pepper.

2 large dried chiles, such as ancho, guajillo, mulato, pasilla, pasilla de Oaxaca, or chihuacle negro

1 cup heavy cream

Salt

Cayenne pepper (optional)

Thai Red Curry

To use this curry to cook chicken or shrimp, combine 6 tablespoons of the curry with 2 (14-ounce) cans coconut milk. Simmer enough shrimp or chicken for four servings in the mixture.

MAKES 1/2 CUP

Combine the ginger, kaffir lime leaves, lemon grass, chiles, cilantro, shallots, coriander, cumin, black pepper, cloves, nutmeg, shrimp paste, and salt in a mortar and crush and work to a smooth paste, about 15 minutes. Work in the peanut oil. Keeps for up to a week in the refrigerator.

1 (1/2-inch) slice ginger, peeled and grated

2 kaffir lime leaves, finely chopped, or 1-inch strip lime zest, finely chopped

1 lemon grass stalk, bottom half only, thinly sliced and chopped

8 red Thai chiles, seeded and chopped

1/4 cup tightly packed fresh cilantro leaves

2 shallots, minced

2 teaspoons ground coriander

1 teaspoon ground cumin

1 tablespoon freshly ground black pepper

1/2 teaspoon ground cloves

1 teaspoon freshly grated nutmeg

1 teaspoon shrimp paste (optional)

1 teaspoon salt

1/4 cup peanut oil

⤳ THAI CURRIES ⤳

Many Thai stews and soups are flavored with Thai curry. Thai curry is unlike Indian curry in that it's really a moist paste, not a dried powder. You can make Thai curry by pureeing typically Thai ingredients (kaffir lime leaves, lemon grass, chiles, garlic, shallots, and so on) in a food processor, but the texture is never as smooth as an authentic Thai curry. You can also buy Thai curries in a can, but these lack the forthright flavor of homemade.

To make Thai curry in the old-fashioned way, you'll need a mortar and pestle. These are often sold in places where Thai ingredients are sold. When buying a mortar and pestle, buy the largest one you can possible manage or lift. The larger and heavier, the easier it is to crush the ingredients.

COLLARD GREENS

Collard greens make most of us think of Southern soul food. As a Northerner, I never tasted collard greens until I went as an adult to a restaurant specializing in Louisiana cooking. But for those who grew up with them, collard greens have irresistible associations with home-cooked meals, ham hocks and bacon, and corn bread. For some of us who have been initiated later in life, collard greens' full flavor is somewhat of an acquired taste.

Collard greens are large, paddle-shaped leaves with thick pale green stems. They are usually sold in rather large bunches. The leaves themselves have a waxy smoothness that's a lot like cabbage, but the leaves are flat instead of wrapped together into a head. Like most green things, the smaller, pale green leaves have a more delicate texture and flavor, but these aren't always easy to find. When buying collards, avoid any that are yellowing or wilting or that have wet spots on the stems or leaves. When you get your collards home, you can store them in the crisper drawer of the refrigerator for 1 day. If you want to store them for up to 3 days, wrap them in a damp towel.

Collard greens cooks are divided into two camps. Traditionalists insist on long cooking—a couple of hours or more—usually with pork or other meats and something smoked. Members of the modern school prefer to cook collard greens for only 15 or 20 minutes so the greens retain more of their color and crunch. I've tried both approaches and have found that the modern approach only works with the youngest, very tender greens. Older collard greens are best when long simmered with bacon or ham hocks. Regardless of your approach, cut out and discard the thick stems holding the collards together and wash the leaves in plenty of water. Some recipes suggest chopping the greens, but I roll up a few leaves at a time and cut them into 1/4-inch-wide strips.

Collard greens.

Curried Collard Greens

Indian cooks are experts at cooking greens, and while they have few recipes for cooking collard greens per se, many of their recipes for mustard greens and other hearty greens work beautifully with collards.

The exact ingredients and methods used for cooking greens depend on where in India they're being prepared. In Kashmir, mustard oil will probably be used for sautéing the greens, while in other parts of northern India, cooked and clarified butter (ghee) is used. In some of India's many sects, onion and garlic are forbidden so they use asafetida, a strongly flavored spice instead. In southern India, coconut milk, sometimes combined with yogurt, is often simmered with greens.

In this recipe, I've combined various Indian ingredients and techniques that, while perhaps not perfectly authentic, are guaranteed to satisfy.

MAKES 4 SIDE-DISH SERVINGS

Heat the ghee in a heavy-bottomed pot—large enough to hold the collard greens—over medium heat and stir in the onion, garlic, and jalapeños. Cook until the onion turns translucent, about 8 minutes. Add the ginger and garam masala, and stir until you can smell the fragrance of the spices, about 1 minute. Add the collard greens, coconut milk, and $^1/_2$ cup water, and bring to a boil over high heat. Turn the heat down to low, cover the pot, and simmer gently for about 1 hour, or until the greens are soft and tender. Check the pot from time to time to make sure the liquid isn't running dry. If so, add $^1/_2$ cup of water.

To toast the almonds, preheat the oven to 350°F. Spread the almonds in a shallow pan and toast for about 15 minutes, until pale brown.

If when the collards are done they seem soupy, remove the lid, turn the heat up to high, and boil down the liquid for 5 minutes or until the coconut sauce thickens slightly. Season to taste with salt and pepper and sprinkle with the toasted almonds.

3 tablespoons ghee (see page 149), or unsalted butter, or canola oil

1 small onion, minced

2 cloves garlic, minced

2 jalapeños, seeded and minced

1 tablespoon grated fresh ginger

2 teaspoons garam masala or curry powder

2 pounds collard greens, stemmed and leaves cut into $^1/_4$-inch strips

1 (14-ounce) can unsweetened coconut milk

$^1/_2$ to 1 cup water

$^1/_2$ cup sliced almonds

Salt and freshly ground black pepper

Curried Collard Greens.

Long-Cooked Collards with Ham Hocks

Like most members of the cabbage family, collards have a natural affinity for pork and the smoky flavor of ham hocks. Ham hocks take at least 2 hours to cook, a requirement that makes sense here because mature collard greens also take about 2 hours of cooking for their flavor to soften and meld with that of the ham hocks.

Most of us think of collard greens as an accompaniment to pork, but they're also great with red wine beef stew—the liquid from the stew mingles deliciously with the collard greens.

MAKES 8 SIDE-DISH SERVINGS

Put the ham hocks in a pot with just enough cold water to cover. Bring the water to a boil over high heat and boil the ham hocks for 2 minutes. Drain the ham hocks and rinse with cold water.

Put the ham hocks in a pot with the collard greens and 3 cups water. Bring to a boil over high heat, turn the heat down to low to keep the collards at a gentle simmer, cover the pot, and braise for $2^1/_2$ hours. Check the collards every 30 minutes to make sure the liquid hasn't run dry. If it has, add $^1/_2$ cup water.

After $2^1/_2$ hours, turn off the heat, reach in with a slotted spoon, pull out the ham hocks, and let them cool. Pull the meat and rind off the ham hocks, and pull the meat apart into little pieces with your fingers. Stir the ham hock meat into the collards. If you like ham hock rind (taste it and see), chop it and add it to the collards. At this stage, you can keep the collards, covered, in the refrigerator for a couple of days.

Just before you're ready to serve, reheat the collards and season to taste with salt and pepper.

1 (2-pound) or 2 (12-ounce) smoked ham hocks

4 pounds collard greens, stemmed, leaves cut into $^1/_4$-inch strips

Salt and freshly ground black pepper

CORN

Every season of the year one or two special vegetables take over and appear at almost all my dinners—squash in autumn, potatoes in winter, asparagus in springtime, and corn in the summer.

Corn is an all-American vegetable. I encountered it only once when studying cooking in France, in a restaurant in the Burgundy region. A special client had arrived—a famous chef—and the kitchen was in a tizzy about what to serve first. It was decided that a special salad was in order. I prepared the basic greens, but it was the chef who lovingly sprinkled the salad with sliced truffles, foie gras, and canned corn kernels! As far as I know, the French still don't appreciate corn at its best—freshly picked and still on the cob.

There are many varieties of corn. Some varieties mature more rapidly than others, some have almost pure white or golden or even blue kernels, and all have varying degrees of sweetness. Modern hybrids of sweet corn are often too sweet and lack flavor. Sweet corn is sold according to sugar content and breaks down into "sweet" (5 to 10 percent sugar), "sugar-enhanced" (15 to 18 percent), and "super-sweet" (up to 30 percent). Anything sweeter than "sweet" is usually too sweet. If you shop in farmers' markets, you're more likely to find more traditional corn varieties, which may not be as sweet as modern hybrids, but will have more corn flavor.

Corn that has to wait should be stored, with its husks left on, in the refrigerator for a day or two. Some super-sweet corn is designed for long storage and will keep for a week or more.

Corn on the cob is delightfully easy to cook and can be boiled, grilled, steamed, or cooked in the microwave. Those corn dishes that involve scraping the corn kernels off the ears are also more straightforward than they sound and usually involve only heating the kernels with flavorful ingredients on the stove. The key to success is to find good corn. This is easy if you live in the country and have a favorite vegetable stand or know reliable farmers; in a city supermarket, it helps to know what to look for. It is to be hoped that the greengrocer will have put out an ear of partially shucked corn from that batch so you can examine it without pulling back the husks to look at the kernels, a practice that causes the corn to dry out and the greengrocer to give you dirty looks. The husks should be tightly closed and the stem should be green and moist, not woody. There should be lots of golden brown corn silk coming out of the corn (the silk is essential to corn's fertilization) and the corn should feel plump through the husk. You can judge the ripeness of the corn by looking at the kernels. Underripe corn has smaller kernels with spaces between the rows. If you prick a kernel of underripe corn with your fingernail, the juice that runs out will be clear. The kernels of overripe corn or of corn that has been sitting around will be slightly wrinkled or look like they have dimples. Not much juice will come out when you poke a kernel with your fingernail. Perfectly ripe corn will have fat kernels with no spaces between the rows, and when you poke a kernel the juice that runs out will be milky. Corn is best when picked within a day (some say hours) of when you cook it because, once picked, the corn's natural sugars start turning into starch.

Corn on the Cob

Corn on the cob, like so many other naturally good things, is best cooked in the simplest way. The easiest way I know is to put about an inch of water in the bottom of a pot large enough to hold the corn, bring the water to a rapid boil—don't add salt—put the husked and silked corn in the pot, cover tightly, and steam for 7 minutes over high heat.

I've always been a fan of well-buttered corn on the cob that requires a stack of paper napkins for fingers and chins. I sometimes substitute flavored butters for plain butter.

TARRAGON BUTTER. This is a favorite and is easy to make by creaming a tablespoon of chopped fresh tarragon with a stick of butter. Other herb butters, such as thyme, marjoram, or chive, can be made in the same way. One of my favorite ways to serve corn-on-the-cob is to pass around a bowl of finely grated Italian Parmesan cheese so people can help themselves to a few spoonfuls and then roll the buttered corn in the cheese between bites.

✳ TO HUSK OR NOT TO HUSK BEFORE BOILING, STEAMING, OR GRILLING ✳

Everyone has his or her own opinion about whether the husks should be removed or left on before the corn is boiled or steamed. Boiling or steaming corn in the husk means that you'll need to pull the husk away when the corn is hot and hard to handle. While some people argue that a corn in the husk retains more flavor, it's a lot easier to remove the husk and silk ahead of time, and the flavor loss will be minimal. The husk is easy to peel off and the silk are easy to remove by rubbing the corn with a nylon brush or with a clean rough sponge.

Cooks are equally vehement about whether or not the husk should be removed before grilling. Either method works, but corn cooked in the husk takes on a grassy flavor from the husk, while corn without the husk takes on the scent of the grill. I usually remove the husk for the simple reason that corn without the husk cooks more quickly—in 8 to 12 minutes—and takes up less room on the grill than corn still in the husk. When I do cook corn with its husk attached—guests sometimes insist on this—I don't bother removing the silk or pouring water inside the husks despite the insistence of some cookbook authors. I just put the unopened corn on the grill and turn it around now and then for 25 minutes. The husk and silk are then peeled away when the corn is cooked.

✳ TAKING CORN OFF THE COB ✳

There are two ways to take corn off the cob, both of which are surprisingly easy. If you want whole intact kernels, hold the husked ear of corn on an angle over a large bowl and cut along the ear with a sharp chef's knife. Rotate the ear as you go until you've removed all the kernels. If you want a soupier and creamy mixture, grate each ear of corn, also working over a bowl.

Taking corn off the cob.

Mexican-Style Creamed Corn with Bacon, Chiles, Tomatoes, and Cilantro

Corn and chiles are such a natural combination that once you start associating one with the other, you'll find it hard to eat corn dishes without wanting to sneak in a chile or two. This is one of the best corn dishes I know.

MAKES 4 SIDE-DISH SERVINGS

If you're using the bacon, gently cook the cubes in a heavy-bottomed 4-quart pot over medium heat until the cubes just begin to turn crispy, about 8 minutes. Remove the bacon with a slotted spoon and reserve. If you're using the butter, simply melt it in the pot. Stir in the onion, garlic, and chiles and cook over medium heat, stirring every couple of minutes, until the onion has turned translucent but hasn't browned, about 8 minutes.

Add the tomatoes, cream, the reserved bacon, and the corn kernels. Simmer until the corn is heated through, about 10 minutes. Stir in the cilantro and cook for 2 minutes more. Season to taste with salt and pepper and serve immediately.

2 slices thick-cut bacon, or 3 thin-cut slices, cut into 1/4-inch cubes, or 1 tablespoon unsalted butter

1 medium onion, minced

2 cloves garlic, minced

2 poblano chiles, seeded and chopped

2 jalapeños, seeded and chopped

2 medium tomatoes, peeled, seeded, and chopped

1/2 cup heavy cream

2 cups corn (kernels from 5 plump ears)

2 tablespoons finely chopped fresh cilantro

Salt and freshly ground black pepper

Cold Succotash with Fava Beans

Using fava beans gives an old standby a luxurious touch. Most succotash recipes call for heavy cream, which converts them into rather elaborate versions of creamed corn. Here I serve the succotash cold and use vinaigrette instead of cream as a moistener, but feel free to serve this dish hot. The flavor comes from fresh tarragon.

MAKES 4 SIDE-DISH SERVINGS

Combine the fava beans and corn in a pot with the water and cover. Bring to a gentle simmer and steam, with the cover on the whole time, for about 10 minutes. Remove the lid. If there's any liquid left in the pot, boil it down until it evaporates. Let cool.

Just before serving, toss with the olive oil, vinegar, and tarragon. Season with salt and pepper.

2 pounds fava beans, shelled and peeled, or 1/2 cup peeled beans

1 cup corn kernels (fresh, canned, or frozen)

1/4 cup water

2 tablespoons pure olive oil

1 tablespoon sherry vinegar

1 teaspoon chopped fresh tarragon

Salt and freshly ground black pepper

Cold Succotash with Fava Beans.

Italian-Style Corn with Dried Porcini and Prosciutto

I can combine dried porcini mushrooms and prosciutto with just about anything and be happy with the results. This dish came about one evening when I had set out to make polenta with mushrooms but decided to use fresh corn instead.

MAKES 4 SIDE-DISH SERVINGS

Quickly rinse the porcini mushrooms, place in a small bowl with just enough warm water to come halfway up the mushrooms, and soak until soft, about 30 minutes. During soaking, turn the dried mushrooms around in their liquid every few minutes to get them to soften. Squeeze the water out of the mushrooms—save the water—and chop the mushrooms to the size of small peas.

Cut the fat off the edge of the prosciutto. Finely chop the prosciutto and the fat, keeping the two separate. If the prosciutto doesn't have any fat, use the 1 table-spoon butter instead.

Put the chopped prosciutto fat or butter in a heavy-bottomed 4-quart pot over medium-low heat. If you're using prosciutto fat, allow about 10 minutes for the fat to render and release into the pan. Stir in the chopped prosciutto, onion, and marjoram and cook gently over medium heat for about 5 minutes.

Stir the chopped porcini into the prosciutto mixture. Carefully pour in the porcini soaking liquid, leaving any grit behind in the bowl. Cook gently over medium heat until everything begins to caramelize and stick to the sides of the pan, 5 minutes. Stir in the corn and $1/4$ cup water. Cover the pan and simmer gently for 10 minutes. Check after 6 or 7 minutes. If the water has run dry, add a tablespoon or two more. Season to taste with salt and pepper and serve immediately.

$1/2$ cup (about $3/4$ ounce) dried porcini mushroom slices

1 ($1/8$-inch-thick) slice prosciutto, including the fat around the edges

1 tablespoon unsalted butter (optional)

1 small onion, minced

1 teaspoon finely chopped fresh marjoram or thyme, or $1/2$ teaspoon dried

2 cups corn (kernels from 5 plump ears)

$1/4$ cup water, plus more as needed

Salt and freshly ground black pepper

Creamed Corn

This simple dish is an irresistible revelation for those of us who have tasted creamed corn only out of a can. The corn kernels are left whole instead of being grated or pureed—the only other ingredients are heavy cream or half-and-half, salt, and pepper.

MAKES 4 SIDE-DISH SERVINGS

Bring the cream to a boil in a heavy-bottomed 4 quart pot over medium-high heat and pour in the corn kernels. Toss or gently stir the kernels with the cream over medium-low heat for about 10 minutes, until the kernels are cooked through and lightly coated with cream. Season to taste with salt and pepper and serve immediately.

1 cup heavy cream or half-and-half

2 cups corn (kernels from 5 plump ears)

Salt and freshly ground black pepper

HUITLACOCHE

Also called "corn smut," huitlacoche is a delicacy in Mexico. While it occurs naturally on corn in the United States, it is not really marketed here and can be hard to track down, except in a can or frozen.

Huitlacoche isn't particularly attractive. It looks like giant corn kernels that have become enlarged, blackened, and then partially wizened. Traditional cooks insist that it be chopped and cooked with aromatic vegetables, but its flavor is so subtle (it's been compared to that of the most delicate mushrooms) that I prefer it simply sautéed and served as a vegetable.

Sautéed Huitlacoche

Most recipes I read for cooking huitlacoche are relatively complex, with spices, chiles, lime juice, onions, tomatoes, and so on. This recipe captures the flavor of huitlacoche unadorned.

MAKES 4 SIDE-DISH SERVINGS

Thaw the huitlacoche if it's frozen. Rinse and pat dry.

Heat the butter or oil in a large sauté pan. When the butter froths or the oil ripples, add the huitlacoche. Toss or stir over medium heat for about 10 minutes. Season with salt and pepper and serve.

3 cups (about 12 ounces) frozen or fresh huitlacoche

3 tablespoons unsalted butter or corn oil

Salt and freshly ground black pepper

CROSNES

I hate to say it, but crosnes look to me like insect larvae or more specifically, maggots. That said, there's nothing off-putting about crosnes' flavor or texture, which is nutty and buttery. Some say that their texture and flavor is most reminiscent of Jerusalem artichokes.

Crosnes originally came from China but were introduced to the French in the late nineteenth century and soon after to Americans.

Crosnes are typically about an inch long. My earlier association aside, they look like little compact yet elongated coils. They should be crunchy, with nothing limp about them, and nut-like. They make a great component in vegetable stews or salads but can also be cooked on their own. I simply blanch them and sauté them in butter for about 5 minutes to attenuate their crunch.

Crosnes.

Sautéed Crosnes with Garlic and Chives

If you want to appreciate the subtleties of crosnes, leave the garlic out of this dish, but it does make a delicious accompaniment.

MAKES 4 SIDE-DISH SERVINGS

Put the crosnes in a small saucepan with just enough water to cover and bring to the simmer over high heat. Drain, transfer to a kitchen towel, and sprinkle liberally with coarse salt. Wrap them up in the towel and rub vigorously to eliminate peels. Don't worry if all the peels don't come off. Rinse the salt off the crosnes in a strainer.

Heat the butter in a medium sauté pan over high heat. As soon as the butter froths, add the crosnes and stir or toss over medium to high heat for about 3 minutes. Add the garlic, shake and toss thoroughly to distribute it, and sprinkle with chives and salt and pepper. Serve immediately

2 cups (about 1 pound) crosnes

Coarse salt

2 tablespoons unsalted butter

1 clove garlic, minced

1 tablespoon minced fresh chives

Salt and freshly ground black pepper

CUCUMBERS

Most of the time we eat cucumbers raw. This is easy to understand since raw cucumbers make a cool and refreshing summer treat. Cucumbers are also surprisingly good when cooked, provided they aren't overcooked.

Three kinds of cucumbers are commonly sold in the United States. Our familiar common cucumber—relatively short (about 8 inches long) and plump with a dark skin—is the easiest to find. European cucumbers, sometimes called "hothouse" or "gourmet" cucumbers, are larger (about 14 inches long), paler, and contain fewer seeds. The European cucumbers are usually twice the price of short cucumbers, but they're also about twice the size and probably a better value because they do in fact contain fewer seeds and less water. Firm and short (about 4 inches long) pickling cucumbers, called kirbys, can be used for most dishes calling for cucumbers, not just pickles.

The main thing to look out for when shopping for cucumbers is soft or dark spots, which indicate that the cucumber is starting to rot. Whether or not to peel cucumbers is up to you—you can also compromise and take off only half the peel by peeling the cucumber lengthwise into strips and leaving dark green stripes. Unless you're peeling the cucumbers completely, be sure to wash them with warm water. Common short cucumbers are usually coated with an "edible wax coating" similar to mineral oil to help preserve them. A little detergent in their washing water will do no harm. Cucumbers can be stored in the refrigerator, loosely wrapped in plastic bags with a few holes poked in them, for 2 to 3 days. Once cut open or cooked, cucumbers should be served right away.

Cucumbers are best served raw in salads with vinegar and oil or cream or yogurt. Cucumbers can also be sliced or cut into elongated rectangles or turned into large oval shapes and gently glazed with butter.

Cucumber halves.

SALTING CUCUMBERS

Guests who stroll into the kitchen are sometimes aghast to see me sprinkling a handful of coarse salt over a colander of sliced cucumbers—my hurried explanations are only met with polite skepticism.

But cucumbers are watery and if you toss them in a salty sauce, they release their water into the sauce and your lovely little salad is soon a soupy mess. The trick is to get rid of the water ahead of time by liberally sprinkling the cucumbers with salt and letting the cucumbers drain for about half an hour. You then need to rinse the cucumbers quickly to get rid of the salt and squeeze the cucumbers tightly in your fist, a bit at a time, to get rid of even more water. Your cucumbers will have shrunk because of the water loss but will be all the more flavorful.

Thai Cucumber Salad with Peanuts

This salad also makes a good relish because it provides a bright and refreshing counterpoint to grilled and spicy foods, especially kebabs and satays, but it goes well with practically any grilled meat or fish. You may find this salad surprisingly sweet, but because it contains so much vinegar, the sugar seems just right. Most authentic Thai recipes, and dishes you're likely to encounter in Thai restaurants, use distilled white vinegar. Distilled white vinegar has never been one of my favorite ingredients, so I use white wine vinegar, sherry vinegar, or rice wine vinegar instead.

MAKES 4 SIDE-DISH SERVINGS

Cut the cucumbers in half lengthwise and spoon out their seeds. Slice into crescent-shaped slices between $1/8$ and $1/4$ inch thick. Toss the slices with the coarse salt and drain in a colander for 30 minutes. Rinse the cucumbers under cold running water and squeeze the cucumber slices tightly in small bunches.

Stir together the sugar and vinegar until the sugar dissolves. Reserve this mixture in the refrigerator. Just before serving, combine the cucumbers, chiles, peanuts, and cilantro. Add the vinegar mixture and toss.

3 regular cucumbers or 2 long hothouse cucumbers, peeled (peeling optional)

1 tablespoon coarse salt

$1/2$ cup sugar

$1/2$ cup sherry vinegar

5 Thai chiles or jalapeños, seeded and finely chopped

$1/2$ cup dry-roasted, salted peanuts, coarsely chopped

3 tablespoons finely chopped fresh cilantro

Thai Cucumber Salad with Peanuts.

Japanese Cucumber Salad with Vinegar

Cucumbers with vinegar have long been an American staple, but Japanese cooks use a few tricks to make this salad especially good. One trick, shared by the French, is to seed and slice the cucumbers and then sprinkle them with salt and drain them to make the cucumbers less watery. I sprinkle the cucumbers with sugar, which balances the vinegar's tang—and I'm fussy about the vinegar. Distilled white vinegar is harsh and many brands of wine vinegar aren't much better, so I use either sherry vinegar or Japanese rice wine vinegar. Balsamic vinegar is also good, but it makes the cucumbers somewhat dark. If you want this salad to retain a distinct Japanese flavor, which makes it a delicious accompaniment to raw or cooked fish, use the bonito flakes (see page 76), which will give the cucumbers a delicate smoky flavor. Serve this salad in small mounds in individual Japanese bowls with a few tablespoons of the sauce surrounding the cucumbers.

MAKES 4 SIDE-DISH SERVINGS

Cut the cucumbers in half lengthwise and scoop out their seeds with a spoon. Slice each half into crescent-shape slices between $1/8$ and $1/2$ inch thick. Rub the slices with the coarse salt and drain in a colander for 30 minutes. Quickly rinse the cucumbers under cold running water and squeeze the cucumber slices tightly in small bunches.

If you're using the bonito flakes, combine them in a bowl with the vinegar, sugar, and soy sauce and let sit for at least an hour—or you can store the mixture indefinitely in the refrigerator. Shortly before serving, strain the bonito flakes out of the sauce. Toss the cucumbers in the sauce and add more sugar or soy sauce, if necessary, to taste.

If you're not using the bonito flakes, just toss the cucumbers with vinegar, sugar, and soy sauce.

To serve, arrange the cucumbers in mounds in individual bowls. (Little Japanese pottery or lacquer bowls look great.) Decorate the top of each mound with the slivers of nori.

4 regular cucumbers or 2 long hothouse cucumbers, peeled (peeling optional)

1 tablespoon coarse salt

3 heaping tablespoons bonito flakes (optional)

$1/4$ cup sherry vinegar, rice wine vinegar, or balsamic vinegar

1 tablespoon sugar, or slightly more to taste

1 tablespoon Japanese dark soy sauce, plus more to taste

1 (1- by 2-inch) rectangle nori, cut into 1- by $1/8$-inch strips (optional)

Cucumber and Yogurt Salad

A favorite dish in Indian restaurants is cucumber *raita*. Cucumber raita is both a salad and a condiment, and is almost always served as a refreshing accompaniment to hot and spicy foods. Most cucumber raitas are made by tossing seeded and sliced cucumbers with plain yogurt, sometimes combined with a little heavy cream and chopped fresh mint or cilantro. The French have their own cucumber salad variation—again flavored with mint—but with heavy cream (or more precisely, crème fraîche) instead of yogurt. Either approach is delicious, but I prefer to serve the richer French version as a first course at a simple meal and the Indian version at an Indian meal or at an outdoor summer barbecue where everyone is looking for something light and refreshing.

To avoid a salad that is too runny, the cucumbers must be salted, drained, and squeezed before they are combined with the yogurt, heavy cream, or crème fraîche—otherwise the cucumbers will release liquid into the yogurt. It's also important to use a very stiff yogurt. Laban yogurt sold at Middle Eastern grocers is best, but can be hard to find. Greek-style yogurt makes a nice substitute. I drain plain yogurt in a coffee filter or a cheesecloth-lined strainer in the refrigerator for about 4 hours to eliminate some excess liquid. If you're using cream, use either crème fraîche or buy the richest heavy cream you can find. When heavy cream is combined with lime juice, the acid in the lime juice causes the cream to thicken.

If you follow this recipe, you'll end up with a salad, but if you chop the seeded cucumbers—so you end up with chunks about 1/4 inch on each side—you'll have a salsa instead, which is delicious atop grilled chicken or fish. Remember to chop the mint or cilantro just before serving; if chopped too early, it will turn black.

MAKES 6 SIDE-DISH SERVINGS

Cut the cucumbers in half lengthwise and scoop out their seeds with a spoon. Slice into crescent-shaped slices between 1/8 and 1/4 inch thick. Rub the slices with the coarse salt and drain in a colander for 30 minutes. Rinse the cucumbers under cold running water and squeeze the cucumber slices tightly in small bunches.

In a bowl, whisk together the yogurt with the mint. Stir this mixture into the cucumber slices. Cover the bowl with a plate or plastic wrap and refrigerate for at least 30 minutes before serving. Season to taste with pepper.

VARIATIONS:

Raw fennel, shaved with a vegetable slicer and tossed with the cucumbers, gives the salad crunch and a subtle licorice flavor; thinly sliced red onions, shallots, or a minced clove garlic give the salad a little zing; and chopped serrano, jalapeño, or chipotle chiles give the salad a bit of heat, a trick that is especially good if you're chopping the cucumbers into cubes and serving the salad as a relish or raita. You can also make the Dried Chile Cream Sauce on page 176 (don't reduce it too much because it gets thick when cold) and use it, cold, as a sauce for cucumbers. Different herbs can be substituted for the mint—in addition to the cilantro used here, I especially like fresh marjoram—and spices can be used

4 regular cucumbers or 2 long hothouse cucumbers, peeled (peeling optional)

1 tablespoon coarse salt

1 cup plain yogurt, drained, 1/2 cup laban yogurt, 1/2 cup crème fraîche, or 1/2 cup heavy cream combined with 1 tablespoon lime juice

2 tablespoons coarsely chopped fresh mint or cilantro leaves

Freshly ground black pepper

Cucumber and Yogurt Salad.

in all sorts of subtle ways. A teaspoon or two of curry powder, gently cooked in oil just until fragrant, can be combined with the cream or yogurt, or individual ground spices, such as coriander seeds or cumin, as well walnuts and/or raisins, can be used to give the salad an exotic accent. Toasted sesame oil—use 1/4 teaspoon—combined with the cream is also delicious. All of these salads can also be made with cubed and chopped ingredients and used as relishes to accompany grilled foods.

Pickled Cucumbers

There aren't many of us who don't enjoy the sweet, tart, and salty crispness of a sour cucumber pickle or a pickled onion. While most of us don't bother pickling vegetables for long keeping—today we have access to most vegetables all year— traditional preserving techniques give pickled vegetables a flavor and texture all their own.

Even though pickling mixtures vary by country and according to individual taste, the methods are virtually the same everywhere. The easiest way to pickle vegetables is just to coat them with salt. Salt draws out the vegetable's moisture, concentrates its flavor, and helps preserve it. But more often, vegetables are marinated—pickled in mixtures of vinegar, salt, and usually sugar. Other ingredients, especially herbs and spices, are added according to the whim of the cook or the long-established habits of a traditional cuisine.

The recipe given here is not designed to be a traditional pickle that will keep for months on a pantry shelf. Keep this quickly made pickle in the refrigerator and eat within or 3 weeks but no sooner than two. The best cucumbers for pickling are the firm and squat kirbys available in the summer and early fall, but in a pinch use long and firm hothouse cucumbers or regular cucumbers.

Pickled Cucumbers.

MAKES I QUART

Cut the cucumbers in quarters lengthwise. Toss the cucumbers with 2 teaspoons of salt and let sit in a colander for 45 minutes to drain. Put the cucumbers in a 1-quart heatproof jar. Nestle the tarragon sprigs in between the cucumber spears.

Combine the remaining 2 teaspoons salt, vinegar, water, and sugar in a non-aluminum saucepan and bring to a boil. Pour the mixture over the cucumbers. Make sure the cucumbers are completely covered with the pickling liquid—if not, transfer everything to a smaller jar or other nonreactive container. Let cool for an hour at room temperature and refrigerate for at least 12 hours, but up to 3 weeks before serving.

3 regular, 2 long hothouse, or 5 kirby cucumbers

4 teaspoons coarse salt

5 sprigs fresh tarragon

I cup good-quality white wine vinegar or tarragon vinegar

I cup water

3 tablespoons sugar

DANDELION

While there are many varieties of dandelion, the two that appear most frequently are called simply "dandelion" or "wild dandelion." Wild dandelion is only available in the spring. I find most cultivated dandelion to be tough and bitter. Dandelion makes a great salad green for strong-tasting ingredients, such as the sardines suggested below.

Dandelion greens.

Wild Dandelion and Sardine Salad

When I first invented this salad, I was living in Paris and I was amazed by how good it made me feel soon after eating it. Whether it was simply the omega-3 fatty acids from the sardines or some magic combination, I don't know.

MAKES 4 FIRST-COURSE OR LIGHT MAIN-COURSE SERVINGS

Put the dandelion greens in a large salad bowl.

Filet the sardines by pulling the flesh away from their spines, and set aside.

Heat the pure olive oil in a nonstick pan until it ripples. Add the sardines and sauté over medium-high heat for about 3 minutes on each side or until the sardines are firm to the touch.

Arrange the fillets on top of the salad. Add the oil and vinegar, season with salt and pepper, toss, and serve.

2 bunches wild dandelion

12 plump fresh sardines

Pure olive oil, for sautéing

2 tablespoons extra-virgin olive oil

2 teaspoons red wine vinegar

Salt and freshly ground black pepper

EGGPLANT

Most cooks are so opinionated about this vegetable that when the subject comes up they either raise their eyebrows in distaste or carry on lovingly about their favorite eggplant dishes. The greatest source of contention among cooks revolves around its sometimes bitter seeds and juices and how to get rid of them. The most popular method is to slice or halve the eggplant, liberally coat the slices or halves with salt, and then weight or press them to extract the bitter liquid. I've tried everything: I've salted and weighted, frozen, and prebaked and haven't found that any of these methods makes any difference. Eggplant's bitterness has more to do with the eggplant itself than with anything you do to it.

There are dozens of varieties of eggplant, some less bitter than others. Except in farmers' markets in the late summer, most of us will probably run into only three or four kinds. The least bitter variety is the long, thin, pale purple variety usually called Chinese eggplant. A second delicately flavored variety is the Japanese eggplant. Japanese eggplant is shorter and generally smaller than the Chinese variety and has dark purple skin; it looks almost like American eggplant except it's about one-quarter the size. A third variety, Italian eggplant,

Thai eggplant.   Asian eggplant.   Assorted Western eggplants.

has the same dark purple color as the American, but is more streamlined, being only 2 to 3 inches in diameter and about 10 inches long. Some cooks insist that Italian eggplant is better than the easier-to-find bulbous eggplant we see at the supermarket, but once it has been cooked, I can't tell any difference. Our bulbous eggplant works well in any recipe, but buy smaller ones—they're less bitter and have smaller more palatable seeds. At a farmers' market in the summer, you'll run into eggplant of all shapes, sizes, and colors—large fat lavender eggplant, round and perfectly white eggplant (the white is especially mild tasting), and haphazard piles of other twisted and contorted and nameless varieties.

Look for eggplant with a firm but not hard texture and a smooth peel with no wrinkling. Avoid soft or brown spots. Store eggplant in a cool place somewhere in your house (not in the refrigerator) and cook within 2 days. Eggplant can be grilled, sautéed, and baked.

Peeling eggplant.

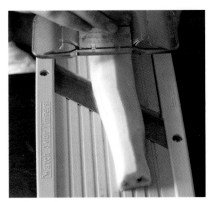

Slicing eggplant.

Basic Baked Eggplant

Baked eggplant slices look sautéed but absorb slightly less oil. Prepare the egg-plant slices in advance so you need only slide them in the oven about 20 minutes before serving.

MAKES 4 SIDE-DISH SERVINGS

Preheat the oven to 375°F. Brush a sheet pan with 1 tablespoon of the olive oil.

Peel the eggplant. Slice long and thin eggplants $3/8$ inch thick lengthwise; slice thick and bulbous eggplant $3/8$ inch thick crosswise. Toss the eggplant with the remaining 2 tablespoons of the olive oil. Arrange the slices in a single layer on the sheet pan and season with salt and pepper.

Bake for 20 minutes. Serve immediately or let cool if using in recipes calling for cooked eggplant slices.

3 tablespoons extra-virgin olive oil

$1^{1}/_{2}$ pounds large or small eggplant

Salt and freshly ground black pepper

Grilled Eggplant

Eggplant takes wonderfully to the grill and makes a quick and easy accent to an outdoor barbecue. I like to sprinkle the eggplant slices with one or more freshly chopped herbs. To make four side-dish servings of grilled eggplant, use $1^{1}/_{2}$ pounds. Slice crosswise into rounds if the eggplant is thick and bulbous or lengthwise if the eggplant is long and thin. Peeling is up to you—I don't bother when grilling. Toss the slices with 6 tablespoons extra-virgin olive oil and, if you wish, sprinkle the egg-plant with 1 tablespoon finely chopped fresh marjoram or thyme or 2 teaspoons dried oregano, and salt and pepper.

Grill on an outdoor grill—about 6 inches above the coals—for about 4 to 8 minutes on each side or until well browned.

Grilling eggplant.

Eggplant Parmesan

Even though this dish is served in so many restaurants and written about in dozens of cookbooks, I include it here because I can't resist the magical combination of cheese, tomatoes, and eggplant all stacked up in a melting casserole. Don't worry about following this recipe too carefully—I never cook it the same way twice and am always experimenting with various herbs (thyme, oregano, mint, basil), different vegetables (zucchini, mushrooms—regular cultivated and dried porcini), other cheeses (soft goat cheese, buffalo mozzarella) and meats (sausage, ground pork).

There are a couple of tricks. Baking the eggplant slices instead of frying or sautéing them makes the whole dish much less oily, and using authentic Parmigiano-Reggiano works wonders for the flavor.

MAKES 6 MAIN-COURSE OR 8 FIRST-COURSE SERVINGS

In a wide heavy-bottom pot or skillet, cook the onions and garlic in 2 tablespoons of the olive oil over medium heat until their aroma fills the room and they turn translucent, about 10 minutes. Don't let them brown. Add the tomatoes and bring to a boil over high heat. Decrease the heat to medium-high and simmer until the sauce is thick and stiff, 30 to 45 minutes. Stir every few minutes to prevent sticking. Stir in the vinegar and sugar and season to taste with salt and pepper.

Preheat the oven to 375°F. Rub the bottom of a large gratin or baking dish with the remaining $^1/_2$ cup olive oil.

Arrange half of the eggplant slices in a thin layer on the bottom. Then spread half the ricotta in a thin layer. Arrange half the mozarella on top of the ricotta. Spread over half of the tomato sauce. Sprinkle with half the marjoram and half of the Parmesan cheese; season with salt and pepper. Arrange the rest of the eggplant

2 medium onions, minced

5 cloves garlic, chopped

$^1/_2$ cup plus 2 tablespoons extra-virgin olive oil

12 medium tomatoes, peeled, seeded, and coarsely chopped, or 6 cups drained and seeded canned tomatoes (three 28-ounce cans), coarsely chopped

1 tablespoon good wine vinegar, such as sherry or balsamic, or more to taste

1 teaspoon sugar, or more to taste

Salt and freshly ground black pepper

Basic Baked Eggplant (opposite)

2 (15-ounce) tubs ricotta cheese

1 (12-ounce) ball mozzarella or 2 (6-ounce) balls buffalo milk mozzarella, sliced $^1/_4$ inch thick

1 tablespoon finely chopped fresh marjoram, or 2 teaspoons chopped fresh thyme, or 1 teaspoon chopped dried thyme

1 cup finely grated Parmigiano-Reggiano cheese

Brush eggplant slices with olive oil. Season with salt and pepper.

Arrange the baked slices in a baking dish.

Spread tomato sauce over the eggplant slices.

Spread a layer of ricotta.

Arrange slices of mozzarella on the ricotta.

Spread over a layer of grated Parmesan cheese.

slices on top, spread with the remaining ricotta and mozzarella, sprinkle with the rest of the marjoram, and spread over the remaining tomato sauce. Sprinkle with the remaining Parmesan cheese.

Bake the eggplant until the sauce starts to bubble up and the surface browns slightly, about 45 minutes. Let rest for 15 minutes before serving (if you serve right away there will be too much liquid) or better yet, let cool, refrigerate, and reheat and serve the next day.

Eggplant Parmesan.

Basic Sautéed Eggplant

Sautéed eggplant is great when simply coated with flour, but when coated with Parmesan cheese it takes on a crispy, savory taste that's hard to resist.

MAKES 4 SIDE-DISH SERVINGS

Peel the eggplant and slice it crosswise into $1/3$-inch-thick rounds. Grind the pepper over the slices.

Spread the Parmesan or flour on a large plate. Beat the egg with the salt and dip the eggplant slices in the mixture.

Heat 2 tablespoons of the olive oil in a large nonstick pan or heavy, well-seasoned cast-iron skillet over high heat. Turn the slices over in the cheese or flour and pat them to get rid of any excess. Slide the slices into the hot oil, in a single layer, and sauté gently for about 5 minutes on each side, until they soften and turn golden brown. If they brown too quickly, reduce the heat to medium. Add more oil and butter as needed to keep the slices from sticking. Drain on a kitchen towel. Repeat until you've used all the eggplant. About 1 tablespoon of oil is required per batch. Serve immediately.

$1^{1}/_{2}$ pounds large or small eggplant

Freshly ground black pepper

1 cup freshly grated Parmigiano-Reggiano cheese, or 1 cup all-purpose flour

2 large eggs (if using cheese)

1 teaspoon salt

3 to 5 tablespoons extra-virgin olive oil or unsalted butter

Eggplant Antipasti

One often-seen antipasto consists of sautéed eggplant slices topped with various cold vegetables. The first step in this dish is to prepare the sautéed eggplant slices (cheese-coated ones are best) and then arrange a tablespoon of one of the toppings, given below, on each of the slices. The amounts given here are enough for one batch of sautéed eggplant slices—about 12 large slices, to make four first-course servings. If you decide to prepare more than one topping, adjust the quantities accordingly. These antipasti are all served at room temperature or slightly cool.

Prepare the Basic Baked Eggplant or the Grilled Eggplant (both on page 193).

To top with sautéed onion slices, thinly slice 3 medium red onions and cook them gently in 2 tablespoons of olive oil over medium heat until completely soft, about 20 minutes. Don't let them brown. Season with salt and pepper. Arrange the onion mixture on top of each of the cooked eggplant slice. Sprinkle with chopped fresh parsley.

To top with grilled peppers, prepare Marinated Bell Peppers (page 114). Arrange a small mound of this colorful mixture on each eggplant slice. If you like, top each with an anchovy or two.

To top with marinated mushrooms, slice 8 ounces mushrooms and toss with 6 tablespoons extra-virgin olive oil, 2 tablespoons balsamic or sherry vinegar, or more to taste, and 1 tablespoon freshly chopped basil or tarragon. Season to taste with salt and pepper and let sit for 1 to 8 hours in the refrigerator before serving.

Grilled eggplant.

FENNEL

When I was growing up in California, fennel grew wild even along city streets and at certain times of the year would scent the air with its lovely fragrance. As kids we chewed on its woody stems as a free substitute for licorice sticks, but it wasn't until years later that I realized it could be eaten as a vegetable and in salads.

Fennel is cultivated in California and Europe and is sold in the United States mostly during the fall and winter. Only one basic variety, Florence fennel, is commonly seen, but it looks and tastes slightly different depending on where and how it is grown. It has fat bulbs, although young plants may have narrow somewhat elongated bulbs. Fennel also grows wild. Wild fennel is stronger tasting than cultivated fennel.

Fennel is underrated even by the French who, if they're not using the dried branches to grill a fish, cook it long enough to eliminate all its texture and most of its flavor. The Italians are more reverent and serve it raw in simple salads with olive oil and lemon juice. I like to use not only the fennel bulb but also the fine hairlike leaves, chopped and sprinkled on the finished fennel dish for decoration. The woody stems can be allowed to dry and tossed on the barbecue to scent grilled fish or chicken. Fresh fennel stems also work magic when combined with other aromatic vegetables in stews, stock, and soups, to which they give a subtle flavor. Fennel seeds are used to flavor breads and in spice mixtures.

Baby fennel.

Look for smallish bulbs when buying fennel and avoid fennel bulbs that are browning, cracked, or that have any moist patches. I prefer to buy fennel that has the stalks and the fuzzy fronds still attached. When you get the fennel home, cut off the greens and store the bulbs wrapped in a paper bag for up to 2 days in the refrigerator.

Unless the fennel is very small and delicate looking, you'll need to peel off the outer stringy membrane and root end with a vegetable peeler. When cutting fennel bulbs into pieces for cooking, be sure to leave the core of the bulb intact. The best way to cut up a fennel bulb is to lay it on its side and cut it in half, while looking at the bottom of the bulb to ensure you're cutting straight through the center of the core (see photos, opposite). The two halves can then be cut into two, three, or more wedges—always keeping a piece of core attached to each wedge—depending on the size of the bulb.

Fennel can be served raw, thinly sliced, in salads; it can also be gently braised in a small amount of liquid. It's also great in vegetable soups and surprisingly delicious when deep-fried.

Cutting off the fronds.

Peeling off the outer stringy membrane.

Slicing fennel with a plastic vegetable slicer.

FENNEL SALADS

Fennel is delicious in salads but must be shaved into very thin slices or it becomes difficult and monotonous to chew. A plastic vegetable slicer is usually essential, and the fennel should be sliced just before serving or it will turn brown and lose some of its aroma and crunch. The best flavoring for shaved fennel is extra-virgin olive oil and a little lemon juice, but you can also add shavings of authentic Parmigiano-Reggiano cheese. Fennel's subtle flavor and refreshing crunch make it easy to combine with other ingredients to come up with interesting improvised salads. It's great with potatoes, mushrooms, thinly sliced raw artichokes, baby leafy greens, and even truffles.

Fennel Salad with Shaved Parmesan

Even without the Parmesan cheese, this salad makes a crunchy and refreshing first course. Use the best olive oil you can find. Shave the cheese off a big chunk with a paring knife or vegetable slicer or vegetable peeler—you can even do this in the dining room for a bit of drama.

MAKES 4 FIRST-COURSE SERVINGS

Pull off a small handful of the green frizzy fennel fronds and reserve. Cut off the stalks where they join the bulbs. (You can save the stalks for making broth or for stews or dry them for barbecues.) Peel the outer fibers off the fennel bulbs with a vegetable peeler or paring knife.

Slice the fennel bulbs crosswise as thinly as you can with a vegetables slicer. Immediately toss the slices with the lemon juice, olive oil, and salt and pepper to taste. Coarsely chop the reserved fennel fronds and sprinkle them over the fennel. Arrange on plates—in the kitchen or in the dining room—and drop five or six 3-inch shavings of Parmesan cheese on each. Parmesan is easiest to shave with a vegetable peeler.

VARIATION:

Try combining the fennel with watercress and adding little chunks of authentic Roquefort (not Danish blue!). A few croutons are a nice addition too.

2 medium fennel bulbs

2 tablespoons fresh lemon juice

$1/4$ cup extra-virgin olive oil

Salt and freshly ground black pepper

Parmigiano-Reggiano cheese, for serving

Fennel, Orange, and Walnut Salad

In the south of France, a strip of dried orange zest often goes into meat and fish stews. Fennel is also popular—the dried twigs are used for grilling seafood and the bulbs are used as a flavoring in bouillabaisse and other seafood soups and stews. The combination of fennel and orange is a good one, and the texture of the walnuts (you can also use pecans) provides an intriguing crunch, similar to, yet contrasting with, that of the fennel.

MAKES 6 FIRST-COURSE SERVINGS

Preheat the oven to 350°F.

Toast the walnuts on a sheet pan in for about 15 minutes or until they darken slightly and smell fragrant.

Pull off a small handful of the green frizzy fennel fronds and reserve. Cut off the stalks where they join the bulbs and discard or reserve for broth or grilling. Peel the outer fibers off the fennel bulbs with a paring knife or peeler and trim a thin slice off the root ends.

Slice the fennel bulbs crosswise as thinly as you can with a vegetable slicer. Immediately toss the slices with the lemon juice, olive oil, and salt and pepper to taste.

Slice the onion as thinly as you can—a vegetable slicer is best for this—and rub the slices with 1 teaspoon salt. Drain the slices in a colander for 15 minutes and then grab them up in your hand and squeeze as much water out of them as you can. Put the onion in the bowl with the fennel.

Cut the oranges into rounds or wedges and very gently toss together the walnuts, orange slices, onion, fennel, salt, and pepper until everything is well coated with lemon juice and olive oil. Coarsely chop the reserved fennel fronds and sprinkle them over the salad. Serve at the table.

VARIATION:

I sometimes combine this salad with top halves of 2 bunches of watercress (which will make it enough for eight) and/or 8 ounces thinly sliced prosciutto, cut into strips and arranged around and over the salads on the plates.

1/2 cup shelled walnut halves or pecans

2 fennel bulbs

2 tablespoons fresh lemon juice

1/4 cup extra-virgin olive oil

Salt and freshly ground black pepper

1 small white onion

3 navel oranges

Fennel, Orange, and Walnut Salad

FIDDLEHEAD FERNS

Fiddlehead ferns appear in the markets for only about a month of the year—usually in April or May—so you have to grab them while you can. Fiddlehead ferns have a delightful crunch and a subtle, vaguely asparagus-like flavor, and their peculiar shape makes them look impressive on the plate.

The fiddleheads sold in the market are fern shoots from ostrich ferns and are so called because they are still curled up into tight little spirals. As the ferns mature, the shoots straighten out, harden, and become inedible lacy plants. Fern shoots are fairly easy to spot in the forest, so some people like to harvest their own, but since some varieties are poisonous I wouldn't recommend this unless you really know what you're doing.

You can boil or steam fern shoots, but I sauté them directly, usually in butter or olive oil with a lot of garlic and parsley. Purists sometimes object to using garlic—it obscures the delicate flavor of the fern shoots—but the combination is irresistible.

Fiddlehead ferns.

When shopping for fiddleheads, look for the smallest and most tightly wrapped ones you can find, and make sure they're not starting to unfold. Look for dark green fiddleheads that aren't dried out or yellowing. Check also to make sure they're not wet or mildewed. Fern shoots can be stored for a day or two in a paper bag in the refrigerator, but they're best used as soon as you buy them.

Before you're ready to cook, cut $1/8$ inch off the thick ends if they look brown and rinse the fern shoots thoroughly to get rid of the brown fuzzy chaff that clings to their sides. Dry the fern shoots thoroughly before cooking by spinning them in a salad spinner and then patting them with paper towels.

Try finishing sautéed fiddleheads with compound butters such as garlic and parsley butter (just knead together garlic that's been crushed to a paste, chopped fresh parsley, and butter) or with chopped fresh herbs, such as marjoram.

Sautéed Fiddleheads with Marjoram and Garlic Butter

If you don't have marjoram, feel free to experiment with other herbs, such as winter or summer savory, oregano, or parsley. Here the garlic is made subtle because it is worked with the butter before it is added to the fern shoots.

MAKES 4 FIRST-COURSE SERVINGS

Combine 4 tablespoons of the butter, the garlic, and marjoram on a cutting board and finely chop. (Chopping with the butter keeps the marjoram from turning black.)

Heat the remaining 2 tablespoons of butter in a large sauté pan over high heat. When the butter froths, add the fiddleheads and toss over high heat for about 5 minutes. If the butter burns—try to avoid this—drain it off. Add the marjoram butter off the heat and heat the pan until the butter froths. Toss thoroughly and serve.

6 tablespoons unsalted butter

1 small clove garlic, minced and crushed to a paste

1 tablespoon fresh marjoram leaves

1 pound fiddlehead ferns

Salt and freshly ground black pepper

FUZZY MELON

Most of the time these gourds aren't really fuzzy. They come in two basic shapes—a typical cylindrical squash and also in a stubby version that looks a little like a decorative candle. Because of its mild flavor, fuzzy melon can be used in stir-fries; it can also be steamed or used in soup.

Fuzzy melon.

Thai-Style Fuzzy Melon Soup

Because of its mild flavor, fuzzy melon takes on the surrounding flavors in a soup, including the Thai ingredients called for here. One of the nice things about this soup is that it doesn't require meat or chicken broth.

MAKES 8 FIRST-COURSE OR LIGHT MAIN-COURSE SERVINGS

In a pot large enough to hold the soup, cook the coriander, fennel, cumin, shallots, lemon grass, turmeric, and chiles in the peanut oil over medium heat, stirring, until the mixture becomes aromatic, about 5 minutes. Add the fuzzy melons, broth, coconut milk, and fish sauce. Simmer for 15 minutes. Add the cilantro and season to taste with pepper. Serve in heated bowls with the lime wedges and mint leaves.

2 teaspoons coriander seeds

1 teaspoon fennel seeds

1 teaspoon ground cumin

$^1/_2$ cup minced shallots

1 (6-inch length) lemon grass, sliced as thinly as possible

$^1/_2$ teaspoon ground turmeric

2 Thai, 2 serrano, or 4 jalapeño chiles, stemmed, seeded, and minced

2 tablespoons peanut oil

2 medium fuzzy melons, cut into thin rounds (no peeling necessary)

3 cups Basic Brown Chicken Broth (page 373), Basic White Chicken Broth (page 374), or water

1 (14-ounce) can coconut milk

2 tablespoons fish sauce, or more to taste

2 tablespoons chopped fresh cilantro

Freshly ground black pepper

Lime wedges

Mint leaves, torn, for garnish

Thai-Style Fuzzy Melon Soup.

GARLIC

I once read—in Elizabeth David, I think—that garlic was impossible to find in England before World War II and that even years later, it required a search through London's more bohemian neighborhoods (for example, Soho) to track it down. It's hard to imagine life without garlic, and although there are those who complain that it's difficult to digest, I rarely run into anyone who isn't crazy about it.

Garlic is usually cooked with other foods to give flavor to soups, sauces, pasta dishes, and stews. Raw garlic is amazingly powerful stuff, but when cooked, its flavor melds with that of the other ingredients and remains discreetly in the background.

If you live near a farmers' market, you'll run into the first shoots of baby garlic, usually called green garlic during the spring. Because green garlic has underdeveloped bulbs that haven't yet divided into papery cloves, they can be used in much the same way as leeks or green onions—gently simmered in a soup is best—and retain a delicacy that older garlic has lost (see Green Garlic Soup, page 204). In the spring and early summer it's possible to find fully developed fresh garlic with the long green shoots still attached, but most of the time we're stuck with garlic that has been out of the ground for a while. Buy garlic with large cloves—to make peeling easier— and check the bottoms and sides of the bulbs to make sure there are no soft spots or signs of browning. Never buy elephant garlic, which may tempt you with its giant cloves; the flavor is peculiar and unpleasant. You can store garlic, loose, unwrapped, in the refrigerator or in a cool, dry place for several weeks.

There are several ways you can use garlic to give subtle distinction to vegetable dishes. One of the most popular methods, especially in Italy, is to thinly slice or chop the garlic and cook it for a minute or two in a small amount of olive oil or butter before adding vegetables and sautéing. French cooks are fond of adding garlic at the end of sautéing, usually in the form of persillade—a mixture of garlic paste, finely chopped parsley, and sometimes bread crumbs—sprinkled over sautéing vegetables a minute before they come out of the pan. Garlic cloves can also be cooked whole and then worked and strained into a smooth puree that can be used for seasoning sauces, spreading on bread, or flavoring other purees, such as mashed potatoes.

Green garlic.

Young garlic.

SERVING WHOLE GARLIC

Though most of the time garlic flavors other foods, whole garlic cloves can be served as an accompaniment to roast meats or fish. Chicken with forty cloves of garlic, a southern French dish, is a simple oven-baked chicken with unpeeled cloves of garlic surrounding the chicken in the roasting pan. After about 30 minutes of cooking, the garlic cloves soften to the texture of mashed potatoes and at the same time delicately scent the chicken. The chicken is then served with the whole unpeeled cloves—guests crush the pulp out with the back of a fork or just pick up the cloves and suck on them—or the cook can force the cloves through a strainer or food mill (which will eliminate the peels) and use the pulp as a thickener and flavoring for a good gravy. This technique is also great with roast leg of lamb.

You can also peel the raw garlic cloves and simmer them in several changes of water for a total of 20 minutes until the cloves turn soft and surprisingly mild tasting. The cloves can then be spooned over fish and meats as a decorative and flavorful garnish.

GARLIC BREAD

A lot of recipes make garlic bread unnecessarily complicated by suggesting that chopped garlic be combined with melted butter and the mixture then brushed on the toasted bread. The easiest method is simply to toast the bread, rub each slice with a peeled garlic clove, and then just spread with butter or brush with olive oil. One medium garlic clove is enough for about six slices of bread. Garlic is easy to find year-round, but it's at its best in the late spring and summer.

GARLIC STEMS

Don't confuse garlic stems with garlic chives. Garlic stems are the actual stem of garlic bulbs and are solid, not hollow in the way of garlic chives. Cook garlic stems by blanching them for a couple of minutes in boiling water and then add them to salads or butter them and serve them as a vegetable. They are surprisingly mild once cooked. Used raw they tend to be aggressive. To spot them in Chinese markets in the summer or fall, look for foot-long green stems, usually with a small yellow flower on one end. They are very easy to confuse with flowering garlic chives.

Garlic.

Garlic Soup

To make this soup, simmer unpeeled garlic cloves in broth or water, then puree the soup and strain out the peels. The simplest version is lovely in itself, but I usually yield to the temptation of adding a sprig of fresh thyme or marjoram (or a pinch of dried leaves), or a sage leaf or two, along with the simmering garlic and perhaps a little chopped parsley after the soup has been strained. I sometimes add a little heavy cream to give this soup richness and subtlety, but this is unnecessary. This soup is as thin as tea (which makes its bright flavor even more striking), so if you want it thicker, add the optional potato.

MAKES 6 FIRST-COURSE SERVINGS

Break the garlic bulbs into individual cloves with your fingers. Inspect the garlic carefully and throw out any cloves that are brown or soft.

Combine the garlic cloves with the broth, herbs, and potato (use for a thick-bodied soup) in a large pot with a lid. Bring to a gentle simmer over high heat, decrease the heat to low, and cover the pot. Simmer gently for 30 minutes. Make sure the soup is done by pushing the garlic and the potatoes against the inside of the pot with the back of a fork—both should crush easily.

Work the soup through a food mill. If your food mill has different size grids, use the finest one. If you don't have a food mill, strain the soup into a clean pot and puree the solids that don't go through the strainer in a blender or food processor with just enough of the soup to get them to move around. Strain the puree into the pot with the liquid.

Stir in the cream, bring the soup back to a simmer, and season to taste with the vinegar, salt, and pepper. Serve in hot bowls or cups. (A nice touch is to put a slice of toasted French bread in the bottom of each bowl before pouring over the soup.) Decorate each bowl with a pinch of parsley and miniature croutons.

6 plump bulbs garlic

6 cups broth, preferably Basic Brown Chicken Broth (page 273), or water

3 sprigs fresh thyme or marjoram, or 1 teaspoon dried

1 large (8-ounce) Yukon Gold potato, peeled and cut into 1/4-inch slices (optional)

1 cup heavy cream (optional)

2 teaspoons sherry vinegar or good-quality white wine vinegar, or more to taste

Salt and freshly ground black pepper

1 tablespoon chopped fresh parsley or chives (optional)

Miniature Croutons (page 70)

Green Garlic Soup

It may seem redundant to have a Green Garlic Soup right below Garlic Soup, but the two have little in common. Most of us wouldn't even recognize that this delicate soup is made with garlic. You'll be able to make this soup only for a short time in the spring when green garlic appears in farmers' markets; they look like scallions because the bulbs haven't formed yet.

MAKES 4 FIRST-COURSE SERVINGS

Cut most of the greens away from the garlic, leaving only about an inch of green attached to the bulb. Cut the delicate roots off the bottoms of the shoots and discard. Wash the white pieces and drain in a colander.

Put the garlic shoots in a wide, heavy skillet with the butter and cook over low heat for about 10 minutes. Pour over the broth and bring to a simmer over high heat. Turn the heat down to low and simmer gently for about 10 minutes more. Puree in a blender for 1 minute and work the soup through a strainer with the back of a ladle into a clean pot. Add the cream, bring back to a simmer, and season to taste with salt and pepper. Serve immediately.

1 1/2 pounds (about 40 shoots) green garlic

2 tablespoons unsalted butter

3 1/2 cups broth, preferably Basic White Chicken Broth (page 374), or water

1/2 cup heavy cream (optional)

Salt and freshly ground black pepper

Basil Skordalia

Skordalia and Aïoli (page 364) are the most pungent of the Mediterranean garlic pastes and sauces because they are made with raw garlic. The garlic is ground or crushed to a paste and either converted into a mayonnaise (aïoli) or worked into mashed potatoes (skordalia). Both sauces are also given a large dose of olive oil for extra flavor. When making skordalia, I break with tradition somewhat and add pureed fresh basil, which gives the skordalia a bright green color and a pungent freshness.

Skordalia is rarely if ever served alone. It is served, slightly warm or at room temperature, as a spread for crackers or little toasts or as a dip for raw or cooked vegetables. Just set out a bowl of skordalia and let guests spread it themselves. You can also serve it at the table with crusty French bread, as a sauce for artichokes, or with grilled vegetables, meats, and fish. Skordalia also makes a great substitute for mayonnaise in a sandwich. Skordalia will keep for a week, covered, in the refrigerator.

MAKES 3 CUPS; ENOUGH FOR 12 HORS D'OEUVRE SERVINGS
OR AS AN ACCOMPANIMENT TO 8 ARTICHOKES OR PLATES
OF GRILLED FOODS

Cut the potatoes into quarters and put them in a pot with enough water to come about halfway up their sides. Cover the pot and bring to a boil over high heat. Decrease the heat and simmer gently until the potatoes have completely softened and are easily penetrated with a fork, about 30 minutes. Uncover the pot and let cool for about 15 minutes. Drain and reserve the potato cooking water.

Sprinkle the basil leaves with a teaspoon of the olive oil—this prevents them from turning black—and chop very finely, almost to a paste.

Mash the potatoes with a potato masher or ricer or by working them through a drum sieve (see page 282–283 for more about mashed potatoes). Slowly work in the chopped basil, garlic, remaining olive oil, and the vinegar. If the skordalia seems too thick—it should have the consistency of mashed potatoes—work in a little of the reserved potato cooking water. Season to taste with salt and white pepper. Serve slightly warm.

1 pound russet potatoes, peeled

1 cup lightly packed basil leaves

$1/2$ cup extra-virgin olive oil

4 cloves garlic, minced and crushed to a paste

$1/4$ cup sherry vinegar or good-quality white wine vinegar

Salt to taste

White pepper

MEDITERRANEAN GARLIC SAUCES AND PASTES

Mediterranean cooks are experts at using garlic. A favorite method is to work the garlic to a paste—traditionally in a mortar and pestle but nowadays often in a food processor—with herbs, such as basil, and a thickener, such as potatoes, toasted nuts, or pieces of bread. Some of these pastes can then be spread on little toasts as a simple hors d'oeuvre, whisked into vegetable or seafood soups for a final burst of flavor, or dolloped onto hot or cold cooked vegetables.

Pesto

Most of us have encountered pesto tossed with pasta, but pesto's ability to transform a simple soup or a plate of hot vegetables is something a lot of us have never experienced.

There are all kinds of frightening rules about pesto, none of which I worry about too much, except that I always use freshly grated, authentic Parmigiano-Reggiano cheese and, of course, very fresh and bright green basil. The core of most pesto controversy is over the merits of the traditional slow grinding in a mortar and pestle or using the blender, considered by purists to be heresy. True, there is no substitute for pesto carefully ground in a huge mortar—and it's surprisingly quick and easy unless cooking for a crowd—but few of us have the requisite large mortar and pestle. So, with some hesitation, I offer a version you can make in a blender. Toasting the pine nuts is optional.

3 tablespoons pine nuts

2 cups tightly packed basil leaves

2 cloves garlic, minced and crushed to a paste

1/2 cup extra-virgin olive oil

1 cup freshly grated Parmigiano-Reggiano cheese

Salt

MAKES ABOUT 1 1/2 CUPS

Preheat the oven to 350°F.

Spread the pine nuts in a shallow pan and toast for 10 minutes. Set aside.

You can make pesto by hand or in a blender. Working aioli or another olive oil–based mayonnaise in a blender can cause the oil to turn bitter; pesto seems a bit more foregiving.

In a blender, combine the basil, garlic, pine nuts, and olive oil and puree until smooth, for about 1 minute. Scrape the sides of the blender a couple of times with a rubber spatula so no leaves escape the blender blades. Transfer to a mixing bowl and stir in the cheese and salt to taste.

To make by hand (recommended, but requires large mortar and pestle), combine the peeled cloves garlic with a good pinch of coarse salt and grind to a paste. Add the pine nuts, grind to a paste, and add the cheese. Work in enough olive oil so that you have a thick paste. Add the basil, a handful at a time, and grind until smooth. Use as soon as possible, but if you're storing the pesto, keep it tightly sealed in the refrigerator with plastic wrap pressed down on its surface to prevent contact with air.

Grinding garlic with salt.

Grinding in the pine nuts.

Grinding in the Parmigiano-Reggiano.

Working in the olive oil.

Grinding in the basil.

Pesto.

Adding pesto to a mixed vegetable soup.

Picada

One of the most exotic Mediterranean garlic mixtures is picada, used by Catalan cooks to fill out the flavors of seafood soups and stews and to give a heady satisfaction to the simplest vegetable soups (Mediterranean Mixed Vegetable Soup, page 73). There are innumerable variations of this ancient sauce, but the versions I've read about (mostly in Coleman Andrew's book *Catalan Cuisine*) contain nuts—usually almonds or hazelnuts—and sometimes pine nuts. The nuts are toasted to bring out their flavor and ground to the consistency of peanut butter in a mortar and pestle or, nowadays, in a food processor. Extra-virgin olive oil is then gently stirred into the mixture by hand. (Working the oil in a food processor turns it bitter.) Spices are sometimes added to picada, but they can be left out without the picada losing its soul. Saffron is best, but some cooks use more "exotic" spices, such as allspice, cinnamon, and cocoa powder.

Instead of using potato puree—very much the heart and soul of skordalia—picada is made with bread gently cooked in olive oil. In Mediterranean cooking, bread is the ancient predecessor to the potato (a New World import) and predates even roux, which wasn't invented until the seventeenth century.

MAKES 1 1/2 CUPS

Preheat the oven to 350°F.

Spread the nuts in a shallow pan and toast for about 15 minutes, until you can smell their fragrance. If you're using almonds, they should turn pale brown. If you're using hazelnuts with the peels, let cool slightly and rub quickly in a towel to get off most of the thin brown skin. Don't worry if a little skin is left attached to the nuts. If you're using pine nuts, only toast them for only 8 to 10 minutes because they brown faster than other nuts.

Lightly brown the bread cubes on both sides in 1/2 cup of the olive oil in a small frying pan over low heat. Don't let the pan get too hot or the olive oil will lose its flavor.

Combine the nuts, bread, garlic, and saffron with its soaking liquid in a food processor and process for about 5 minutes, scraping down the sides of the food processor several times during the grinding. If the mixture gets very stiff and won't move around in the food processor, add the cold water. The finished mixture should have the consistency of smooth peanut butter. Transfer the paste to a mixing bowl.

If you're making the picada by hand, first grind the garlic to a paste in a mortar and pestle before working in the other ingredients.

Slowly work the remaining 1/2 cup of olive oil with a wooden spoon or the pestle. Season to taste with salt. Cover and store in the refrigerator for up to a week or indefinitely in the freezer.

3/4 cup hazelnuts, blanched almonds, or pine nuts

2 slices French bread, each about 3 inches in diameter and 1 inch thick, crusts removed, cut into 1-inch cubes (about 1 1/4 cups)

1 cup extra-virgin olive oil

4 cloves garlic, coarsely chopped

1/2 teaspoon saffron threads, soaked for 30 minutes in 2 teaspoons warm water

1 tablespoon cold water (optional)

Salt

Add the remaining ingredients, except the bread, to the garlic paste.

Grind to a paste.

Add the bread cubes.

Slowly work in olive oil, by hand. Using food processor for this step will make the paste taste bitter.

Picada made the traditional way.

HEARTS OF PALM

Taken from the core of certain palm trees, hearts of palm are necessarily expensive because the harvesting process kills the tree. They have a delicate flavor and texture and can be added to salads and stir-fries. Normally hearts of palm are covered with a sheath that must be removed before cooking. Once the meaty heart is in hand, it can be cut into rings or thin little strips. You'll find canned hearts of palm in most grocery stores, but for fresh be prepared to explore Asian markets.

Hearts of palm.

Hearts of Palm and Pineapple Salad

Like so many dishes involving hearts of palm, this salad is a study in contrasts of textures and flavors. The hearts of palm provide a cool crunch while the pineapple provides a softer texture and a bracing sweetness and acidity.

MAKES 6 FIRST-COURSE SERVINGS

Gently toss together all the ingredients. Serve cool or cold.

2 cups fresh pineapple, cut into $1/2$-inch cubes

3 hearts of palm, sliced lengthwise into $1/8$-inch-thick strips

Juice of 1 lemon

$1/4$ cup crème fraîche or heavy cream

Salt and freshly ground black pepper

HERBS

Of the hundreds of herbs long used mostly for medicinal purposes, only a couple of dozen or so end up being used in the kitchen. But life without these herbs is hard to imagine as most foods, and especially vegetables, are enhanced with the gentle application of herbs.

It wasn't so long ago that the only way to get your hands on an herb was to plant it. Nowadays the basic herbs are available in most supermarkets. This brings us to the subject of dried herbs. Some herbs dry better than others. Those herbs that grow best in hot climates—thyme, rosemary, and oregano to name a few—contain a lot of flavorful oil and can be dried without distorting their basic flavors. Other herbs such as parsley, chervil, chives, and tarragon—those that require gentler climes—have their flavor contained in water. When this water evaporates, the flavor dissipates and what's left behind is only a dusty vestige of the original herb.

BASIL. There are many varieties of basil, all with a similar flavor, but with different size leaves—ranging from not much larger than pinheads, to the size of most of the basil we see in the markets.

To the surprise of many, basil is delicious in salads, used generously as a green and not stingily like an herb, and is especially good when paired with arugula. It can also be added to vegetable soups, stews, and pasta dishes, for which it should be chopped (with a drizzle of olive oil to prevent blackening) or ground to a paste (pesto) with a mortar and pestle.

Older recipes call for adding basil to a bouquet garni but basil cooked for more than a minute or two rapidly loses flavor and aroma. Basil is especially good with Mediterranean foods such as garlic, tomatoes, olives, saffron, and grilled bell peppers. When ground with garlic, Parmigiano-Reggiano, and pine nuts, it becomes pesto or the French *pistou*, added at the last minute to the vegetable soup with the same name.

Vietnamese basil.

Spicy basil.

Thai basil.

Holy basil.

While many of us associate basil with Mediterranean cooking, it's also popular in Southeast Asia. Holy basil, sacred to the Hindus, is often planted around temples. It has a rather disappointing mild flavor and is used primarily in cooking and is never used raw. Thai basi is similar to Western basil, but has a more pungent licorice note that's a little bit more wild.

Be careful when combining basil with other herbs—it goes best with Mediterranean herbs, such as oregano, thyme, and marjoram, and poorly with dill and tarragon.

BAY LEAVES. It's hard to imagine cooking, especially French cooking and much of American cooking, without bay leaves. Typically, bay leaves are included in a bouquet garni (the bundle of herbs simmered in broths, soups, and stews) in relatively small amounts, a single leaf being enough for several quarts of liquid. As the bay leaf simmers, its flavors meld with the other herbs (thyme and parsley) in the bouquet garni.

There is some confusion as to whether to use imported or domestic bay leaves. Always buy imported bay leaves because they are much more subtle than their cousins from California, which have a distinct and aggressive eucalyptus perfume.

BORAGE. This unusual herb has the vague flavor and aroma of cucumbers and can be tossed in mixed vegetable salads for a distinct herbal effect. Borage can be hard to find, and you may need to grow it yourself.

CHERVI.L This underrated and underutilized herb has a delicate licorice scent that doesn't take over in the same way as tarragon. Chervil is one of the four herbs used in *fines herbes* mixtures, the others being tarragon, parsley, and chives. Chervil's presence is better appreciated if the tarragon is left out of the mixture. Chervil has very fine delicate leaves that make it perfect for decorating salads and vegetable stews.

CHIVES. These members of the onion family can be added to almost anything delicate enough not to disguise their sometimes fleeting flavor. Chop chives very finely and toss them in vegetable stews and mixed vegetable salads. Combine them with chervil, parsley, and tarragon to make a classic fines herbes mixture that can be tossed with delicate vegetables (artichokes and salsify come to mind). Or use them alone for a delicate onion accent in sauces.

CILANTRO. Not everyone likes this aggressive herb. Cilantro looks much like flat-leaf parsley (many a student has mistaken the two) and has an aroma that to some is "chemical" or soapy. Cilantro does best when paired with hot spicy foods containing plenty of chiles; without heat, it

Borage.
Chervil.

Left to right, top to bottom:
Chive flowers.
Mexican cilantro.
Dill.
Hyssop.
Lavender.
Lovage.
Marjoram wild.
Peppermint.
Spearmint.
Corsican mint.
Oregano.

HERBS

lands rather flat. Far less known is Mexican cilantro, which has larger spiky leaves and a more delicate flavor and aroma.

DILL. Don't confuse this herb with fennel, the fronds of which it resembles. Dill is aggressive and should be used alone. It goes well on carrots, potatoes, and cucumbers. Dill doesn't dry well.

EPAZOTE. This leafy green herb is used in Mexican stews, soups, and other long-cooking dishes to which it lends a discreet flavor, reminiscent of how thyme functions in a bouquet garni.

FENNEL. Usually thought of as a vegetable and not an herb, the fronds from the top of the fennel can be sprinkled on salads and vegetables such as cucumbers. The stalks can be stored (they dry well) and be added to broths to which they add an ineffable freshness, or they can be put on the grill to scent seafood and poultry. There is also "leaf fennel," which is grown for its seeds.

HYSSOP. Mostly encountered in old French cookbooks, hyssop is rarely called for any more. This is a pity since its leaves (which look a little like tarragon) and flowers are delicious sprinkled over salads. Hyssop is never found already cut; you have to grow your own. Hyssop dries well.

KAFFIR LIME LEAVES. These leaves look like bay leaves but that is about as much as the two have in common. Kaffir lime leaves, as their name implies, have a distinct flavor of lime without the acidity. If you can't find kaffir lime leaves (usually they can be found frozen in places where they sell Thai products), use a strip of lime zest instead. They are used frequently in Thai soups and stews.

LAVENDER. While not usually thought of as a culinary herb (soap associations are hard to dispel), lavender comes into its own when paired with garlic or with other herbs such as in those little bottles of *herbes de Provence*. Try mincing lavender flowers with garlic and sprinkling the mixture over sautéed mushrooms or zucchini a minute or two before serving.

LEMON GRASS. These long stems are thinly sliced (or crushed in a mortar and pestle) and used to give Thai soups and stews a distinct lemon or, more exactly, citronella flavor. When using lemon grass, use only the bottom third of the stem. Peel off the outermost and tough outer membrane. Lemon grass is often available fresh these days, but frozen lemon grass works fine. In fact, if you find yourself with extra, don't hesitate to freeze it for up to several months.

LOVAGE. With a flavor almost identical to celery, lovage can be added to a bouquet garni (especially if no celery has been added) or chopped and tossed with cucumbers, carrots, and mixed vegetable salads. Lovage doesn't dry well.

MARJORAM. This greatly underappreciated herb has a delicate floral and perfumy aroma that pairs beautifully with Mediterranean soups, stews, grilled vegetables, and salads. Marjoram is often confused with oregano, which is nothing like it.

MINT. While mint comes in many varieties, including peppermint and spearmint, the different kinds are used in the same way. Mint can be aggressive, but when ground to a paste with a mortar and pestle (a pinch of sugar helps with the grinding), it can be used as a subtle flavoring for a vinaigrette. Mint is also good paired with cucumber and carrots. When chopped, mint turns black so it should be sprinkled with oil (which protects it somewhat from the darkening air) and chopped at the last minute. Mint can be dried, but it rapidly becomes stale.

OREGANO. Perhaps one of our most confusing herbs, oregano is often compared with marjoram with which it bears no resemblance. While oregano comes in well over a dozen varieties, the best known are from Greece and Mexico. Fresh oregano has very little flavor and must be dried—tie it up in bundles as soon as it flowers and hang them in the kitchen—for its flavor to come out. The dried-up leaves and flowers, ground between the fingers to a powder, make a delicious seasoning on all manner of grilled vegetables.

PARSLEY. Perhaps the most overused and underrated of all the herbs, parsley, when finely chopped at the last minute, lends an ineffable fragrance and subtlety to any delicate vegetable preparation. The most important thing to remember is the last-minute chopping. When chopped even 15 minutes ahead of time, parsley's delicate aroma is lost and what remains smells like lawnmower clippings. Parsley doesn't dry. Don't even think about chopping wet parsley and then wringing out the parsley in a towel just before the serving. Much is made about the differences between curly and flat parsley when in fact their flavor is identical. There are those who claim that flat parsley is somewhat more aromatic, but once chopped this is hard to determine.

RICE PADDY HERB. Looking somewhat like tarragon, as its name implies rice paddy herb is found in rice paddies. The flavor is hard to describe but it's slightly lemony and spicy at the same time. Rice paddy herb is used in soups and stews—as a garnish added at the last minute—and has a particular affinity for fish.

ROSEMARY. I find that rosemary is overused. Unless used in very small amounts or in conjunction with other herbs, it rapidly turns aggressive. Bundles of fresh rosemary can be moistened and thrown on the grill to lend a subtle smoky fragrance to grilled foods. Rosemary is delicious

Gold oregano.
Rue.

paired with pork (just a few sprigs tied to the roast, nothing chopped) and grilled foods but should be used sparingly. Rosemary dries well.

RUE. This ancient herb was popular in Roman cooking and was considered an antidote to various poisons, including mushrooms. Nowadays it is best used sprinkled on salads, to which it contributes a slightly dissonant medicinal note.

SAGE. This beautiful herb is almost overused in Europe and underused in the United States. The Italians are particularly fond of it and love to pair it with veal and pork. (A few leaves tied onto a roast are best.) It is delicious as a flavoring for ricotta- or pumpkin-stuffed ravioli that are finished with brown butter.

SALAM LEAVES. These aromatic leaves are an essential component in much of Indonesian cooking. The aroma is hard to describe, but use salam leaves in stews and soups that require long simmering.

SAVORY. Underrated in part because it is hard to find, savory comes in winter and summer varieties. Fortunately for the cook, the two are similar, even if winter savory is the more delicate of the two. Chopped winter savory is a classic accompaniment to fava beans and can trans-

Left to right, top to bottom:
Purple sage.
Variegated sage.
Summer savory.
Winter savory.
Shiso.
Tarragon.

form a salad with its delicate flavor. Savory can be used as a substitute for thyme in a bouquet garni. Savory dries well. It can also be put into a bottle of extra-virgin olive oil as a flavoring.

SAWTOOTH HERB. This herb has a similar aroma and flavor as cilantro but looks distinctively different with long pointed leaves with saw-toothed edges. Use it as you would cilantro, specifically as a garnish for Asian soups and stews.

SHISO. These spicy heart-shaped leaves are often served with raw fish in sushi restaurants as an accent flavor and for a little color. The flavor of shiso reminds me a little of cinnamon, both for its heat and for its spicy quality.

TARRAGON. It would be hard to imagine cooking without this anise-like herb. Tarragon is great when paired with poultry or seafood and can be added (abundantly) to a bouquet garni in a pot of chicken broth. It is one of the four herbs used in a classic fines herbes mixture, the other herbs being parsley, chives, and chervil. Because chervil has a similar (and more delicate) flavor than tarragon, the tarragon is often best left out of a fines herbes mixture. Chop tarragon at the last minute with a little oil sprinkled over to slow down its blackening.

THYME. Cooking without thyme would be dull indeed. Except for the delicate flowers, which can be sprinkled with dramatic effect on salads, thyme is best in slow-cooking preparations as part of a bouquet garni. Its flavor, while rather assertive in its fresh or dried state (it dries well), attenuates with long cooking and merges with other disparate elements. unifying them into an integral whole. Dried or chopped fresh thyme is a marvelous element on grilled vegetables and other grilled foods. Don't confuse thyme with lemon thyme. While lemon thyme has its aficionados, it has a distinct aroma that reminds some of furniture polish. Its flowers are more delicate; the flowers can be used in salads and omelets and the leaves in tea. Don't, however, use it as a replacement for regular thyme.

WORMWOOD. Best known as the principle ingredient in absinthe, wormwood is extremely bitter and acts as a tonic that settles upset stomachs. It can be infused with alcohol and sugar to make a bitter aperitif or amaro.

Thyme.
Wormwood.

HORSERADISH

Until recently, my own experience with horseradish was limited to spooning it out of a jar and into a Bloody Mary. Many of us have used bottled horseradish but have never encountered the actual vegetable. And while bottled horseradish is useful stuff, horseradish reveals itself only when it is fresh and raw.

Horseradish is a rather daunting-looking vegetable. Elizabeth Schneider describes it as "something that may have belonged to a male mastodon." Horseradish is a root, typically from 8 to 12 inches long, with a sort of bulbous formation at one end and tapering down to a point at the other. It has a thick, pale brown peel and irregular indented surface that makes it necessary to peel it quite deeply with a straight-bladed vegetable peeler. When shopping, look for horseradish that doesn't have too many indentations—to make peeling easier—and avoid horseradish that is limp or soft, that has any signs of mold, or that's beginning to sprout.

Horseradish.

Since usually you won't need to use more than an inch or two of the horseradish at one time, just peel the section you'll be grating. When you've used what you need, wrap the exposed part of the horseradish in plastic wrap and keep the horseradish in the refrigerator for up to a week. Horseradish can also be tightly wrapped in aluminum foil and frozen for several months. It can be peeled, grated, and preserved for several months in vinegar.

Horseradish is used mostly as a condiment—I've never encountered a recipe that suggests cooking large pieces as a vegetable—and as a flavoring in sauces.

Cutting off the hard end.

Peeling.

Grating.

Horseradish Sauce for Grilled and Sautéed Meats

This sauce is delicious with red meats and pork. If you don't want to bother, just can also stir a little grated horseradish into a simple gravy.

MAKES ENOUGH FOR 4 STEAKS OR PORK CHOPS

If you're cooking the meats on the stove, make the sauce in the pan used for sautéing the meat. Pour the cooked fat out of the pan and stir in the shallot. If you're grilling or broiling, make the sauce in a saucepan. Stir the shallots over medium heat with a teaspoon of butter until you smell the shallot's aroma, about 2 minutes.

Add the horseradish and broth, and simmer until the sauce thickens slightly, a minute or so at most. Whisk in the cold butter and season the sauce to taste with the vinegar, salt, and pepper. Serve over the meats or at the table in a gravy boat.

I shallot, minced

I teaspoon unsalted butter (if using a saucepan)

I tablespoon grated horseradish, horseradish preserved in vinegar, or bottled horseradish

1/4 cup Concentrated Broth (page 377)

3 tablespoons cold unsalted butter

2 teaspoons sherry vinegar or good-quality white wine vinegar, or more to taste

Salt and freshly ground black pepper

Horseradish Cream Sauce

This delightful little sauce will add pizzazz to any number of vegetable salads. It's especially good tossed (in moderation) with cold beets, but you can also use it to liven up leftover cooked carrots, as a sauce for cold seafood (such as shrimp), and as a condiment to pass at the table with cold leftover fish or roast meats.

  I most like to make this sauce with crème fraîche, which is stiff and rich and gives the sauce a luxurious texture. You can make crème fraîche yourself or buy it (it's expensive), or use whipped cream instead. If you're worried about the calories, you can substitute plain yogurt for half the crème fraîche or heavy cream. I sometimes add chopped dill to this sauce.

MAKES I CUP, OR SLIGHTLY MORE IF YOU USE WHIPPED CREAM

If you're using crème fraîche or half crème fraîche and half yogurt, simply whisk in the horseradish, dill, vinegar, and salt and pepper to taste.

If you're using heavy cream, beat it to medium stiffness by hand or in an electric mixer. If it's a hot day or you're in a warm kitchen, put the whisk (or beater), cream, and bowl in the freezer for 10 minutes just before you start beating. Stir in the horseradish, dill, vinegar, and salt and pepper to taste. Keep the sauce cold.

I cup crème fraîche, or I cup heavy cream, or 1/2 cup plain yogurt and 1/2 cup crème fraîche or heavy cream

2 tablespoons finely grated horseradish, horseradish preserved in vinegar, or bottled horseradish, liquid drained off

I tablespoon finely chopped fresh dill (optional)

I tablespoon sherry vinegar or good-quality white wine vinegar, or more to taste

Salt and freshly ground black pepper

VARIATIONS:

Escoffier, in his famous *Guide Culinaire,* first published in 1902, describes a horseradish sauce with walnuts. To make Escoffier's version, lightly toast 1/2 cup walnut halves in a 350°F oven for about 15 minutes. Chop them very coarsely and stir them into the sauce above. You can also make a hot sauce by adding a little concentrated broth to the heated cream sauce.

JERUSALEM ARTICHOKES

The name "Jerusalem artichoke" has such a convoluted and mysterious origin that several pages could be spent expounding various theories. Suffice it to say that Jerusalem artichokes—sometimes called sunchokes—have no relation to artichokes and aren't particularly popular in Jerusalem.

To be frank, I'd not been a big fan of these peculiar looking tubers until I started experimenting. The trick, I've found, is to use Jerusalem artichokes raw or only very slightly cooked, as in a stir-fry. When fully cooked, Jerusalem artichokes have a rather insipid flavor and texture, but when raw or undercooked they have an intriguing gentle crunch very similar to fresh water chestnuts, which are hard to find and more difficult to peel. The flavor of raw Jerusalem artichoke is similar to that of raw potato, but with less earthiness and a crisper, almost applelike texture. I've had the best luck cutting the peeled artichokes into dice and then combining them with other ingredients with similar textures (celery, apple, jicama) or contrasting textures (cheese, nuts, cubes of diced cooked meats) in a light sauce, such as lemon juice and olive oil or yogurt.

Buy Jerusalem artichokes that feel firm to the touch and avoid those that are limp or wrinkled or that have soft or moist spots. You can keep Jerusalem artichokes in the refrigerator—for up to a week—in a plastic bag with a few holes poked in it.

Jerusalem artichokes are brown and nubby with irregular bumpy protrusions that make them hard to peel with a vegetable peeler—I use a sharp paring knife instead. Peel Jerusalem artichokes just before you're going to use them. In the same way as globe artichokes, they turn dark when exposed to air.

Jerusalem artichokes about the size of small fists.
Peel with a small knife.

Jerusalem Artichoke, Apple, Gruyère, and Watercress Salad

This is a fascinating and enormously satisfying salad. The hint of mystery as to what it contains—I always challenge my guests to make guesses—keeps interest and appetites high.

MAKES 6 FIRST-COURSE SERVINGS

Combine the apples, Jerusalem artichokes, and cheese in a salad bowl with the lemon juice and oil.

Cut the bottom stems off the watercress bunches and discard. Wash and dry the top halves of the watercress and toss in the bowl with the rest of the ingredients. Season to taste with salt and pepper.

VARIATIONS:

Replace the lemon juice and oil with 1/2 cup plain yogurt drained for 3 hours in a coffee filter–lined strainer over a bowl. You can also add 2 tablespoons of freshly chopped mint to the salad immediately before serving.

2 apples, such as Granny Smith or McIntosh, peeled and cut into 1/4-inch dice

4 Jerusalem artichokes, peeled and cut into 1/4-inch dice

8 ounces Swiss Gruyère or other firm, full-flavored cheese, such as Comté, Fribourg, or English Cheddar, cut into 1/4-inch dice

3 tablespoons fresh lemon juice

3 tablespoons toasted walnut oil or extra-virgin olive oil

2 bunches watercress

Salt and freshly ground black pepper

JICAMA

Once considered exotic and found only in "gourmet" food stores, jicama now appears in even the most ordinary supermarkets. I find this somewhat mysterious, since very few people seem to know anything about it or have ever served it.

Jicama looks vaguely like a turnip but is usually larger, pale brown, and not as perfectly round. Food writers laud jicama's applelike crispiness, but I've always found it a bit dry, insipid, and in need of flavorful ingredients to provide contrast. Jicama can be cut up and simmered in soups or glazed like turnips, but I follow the advice of my Mexican food mentor Rick Bayless and prefer to serve it raw, especially in salads. Rick recommends cutting it up and serving it with a squeeze of lime juice and a dusting of chile powder, or serving it in a salad with cucumbers and oranges. I suggest it as one of the ingredients, as an alternative to cucumbers, in the Mexican-Style Vegetable Salad on page 222.

Select jicama as you would turnips—by lifting them and feeling their weight. Jicama dries out as it ages and becomes light and spongy. An average jicama weighs about 1 pound. Jicama is best peeled rather deeply with a paring knife.

Jicama.

Mexican-Style Vegetable Salad

Cilantro, hot chiles, and lime juice give this salad its Mexican flare. This salad also contains jicama, but if you have trouble finding it, use the cucumber instead.

MAKES 8 SIDE-DISH SERVINGS

Cut the tomatoes into eight to twelve wedges each, depending on their size. Slide your thumb and forefinger along the sides of the wedges to take out the seeds. (Seeding isn't essential but it helps keep the salad from getting watery.) Toss the tomato wedges with 2 teaspoons of the coarse salt and drain in a colander for 30 minutes.

Plunge the ears of corn in a pot of boiling water and simmer for about 5 minutes. Drain and let cool. (You can also grill the corn—instead of boiling or in addition to boiling—to give it a savory, toasty, smoky flavor.) Cut the kernels off each cob with a sharp knife and reserve. Thawed frozen corn can be used as is.

Slice the onion as thinly as you can—a vegetable slicer makes this easy—and rub the slices with 2 teaspoons of the remaining coarse salt. Drain the slices for 30 minutes in a colander.

Peel and slice the jicama into slices about 1/8-inch thick. (There's no need to rub the jicama with salt.) If you're using cucumbers, scoop the seeds out of the cucumber halves with a spoon and slice the halves into 1/8-inch-thick crescent shapes. Thoroughly rub the slices with the remaining 2 teaspoons of salt—until you can't feel the salt under your fingers—and let drain for 30 minutes in a colander. (You can push the onion to the side and use the same colander.)

Peel and halve the avocados and slice each half, lengthwise, into 6 strips. Sprinkle with salt and pepper and half the lime juice.

To prepare the sauce, combine the garlic, jalapeños, chipotles, and cilantro with the olive oil and the remaining lime juice.

Squeeze the cucumbers and onion, in small bunches, in your hands to get rid of as much of their liquid as you can.

Arrange the vegetables in a large salad bowl with the strips of peppers on top. Just before serving, pour over the sauce and gently toss.

VARIATIONS:

Strips of meat (leftover grilled steaks or pork chops), strips or chunks of tuna (either fresh grilled or canned and drained), cooked shrimp, or pieces of chicken (especially leftover barbecued chicken) can be added to this salad to convert it into a main course.

---

4 ripe medium to large tomatoes, peeled if desired

4 to 6 teaspoons coarse salt

1 cup corn (kernels from 3 plump ears), or 1 (10-ounce) package frozen corn, thawed

1 medium red onion

1 (8-ounce) jicama, or 1 long hothouse cucumber, or 2 regular cucumbers, peeled and halved lengthwise

2 ripe avocados, preferably Hass

Salt and freshly ground black pepper

Juice of 2 limes

1 clove garlic, minced and crushed to a paste

2 to 4 jalapeños, seeded and minced

2 chipotle chiles in adobo sauce, rinsed, seeded, and minced

2 tablespoons finely chopped fresh cilantro

1/2 cup extra-virgin olive oil or crème fraîche

2 large poblano chiles, or 2 red or 1 red and 1 yellow bell pepper, charred, peeled, seeded, and cut into 1/8-inch-wide strips

KALE

I wasn't very enthusiastic about kale until I encountered it cooked in soups, in restaurants in Italy. Unless you grow it or manage to find it in its most infantile form (leaves just a couple of inches long), it's not worth eating raw. In fact, kale needs substantial cooking, at least 20 minutes, to soften it. Kale benefits from lots of garlic and pork in one form or another—bacon fat, a prosciutto end, pancetta, or a smoked ham hock.

While most varieties of kale are members of the same species—and all are members of the cabbage family— kale comes in different colors, from green to yellow to red and purple and even black (a delicious Italian black variety, called *cavolo nero*, is starting to appear in fancy markets and at green markets), with different shaped and textured leaves. Unfortunately, many of the more brightly colored varieties are rather tough. In any case, don't buy kale meant as a decorative plant as it may have been sprayed with insecticide. Most of the kale we encounter at the supermarket is green and has very wrinkled leaves.

When shopping for kale try to find the smaller, more tender leaves and avoid kale that looks limp, is wilting, or has dark patches. Kale wilts quickly but it can be stored for a day or two, wrapped in a plastic bag, in the refrigerator.

To prepare the kale, pull the stems off in the same way as spinach by holding the two sides of the leaf forward with one hand and then peeling back the stem with the other hand. In this way, the stem is removed even where it goes up into the leaf. Once you get the stems off the leaves, the leaves should be washed and shredded or coarsely chopped so they're easier to eat. Unlike spinach, which softens as soon as it's hot, kale always retains a little texture.

If you're serving kale on its own, I recommend plunging it first in boiling salted water—blanching it—for 5 minutes to soften it; but if you're adding kale to a soup or vegetable stew, preboiling shouldn't be necessary— just make sure you cook the kale long enough to tenderize it.

Tuscan kale *(Cavolo nero)*.

Kale.

Italian-Style Kale Soup with Prosciutto

Kale is great in a soup because other ingredients can accent and balance the hearty flavor and texture of the kale. This recipe is actually a garlic soup to which shredded kale and whole boiled garlic cloves are added at the end, but don't hesitate to add other chopped vegetables—or to replace the kale with other greens, such as Swiss chard. I sometimes add cooked beans just before serving.

Several kinds of pork products can be used to flavor this soup and give it body. My favorite is prosciutto (I buy the end pieces from prosciutto di Parma, which are much cheaper), but you can also use bacon or pancetta.

MAKES 8 FIRST-COURSE SERVINGS

Break up the garlic into cloves. Peel half of the cloves and reserve. Combine the unpeeled garlic cloves, the sage, and parsley with the broth in a medium pot. Bring to a simmer over medium heat, reduce the heat to low, and simmer gently, covered, until the cloves are completely mushy when you press them against the inside of the pot with the back of a fork, about 30 minutes. Strain the broth through a food mill or by working it through a strainer with the back of a ladle into a clean pot. Press hard so you extract the creamy pulp from the garlic.

If you're using prosciutto, add the cubes directly to the strained garlic soup. If you're using pancetta or bacon, cook the cubes in a small frying pan over medium heat for about 5 minutes to get rid of some of their fat. Transfer the cubes to the broth with a slotted spoon and save the rendered fat for other recipes or discard it.

Add the peeled garlic cloves and, if they're fresh and uncooked, the shell beans to the broth and simmer gently over low heat, covered, for 15 minutes. Add the kale, remove the lid, and simmer gently, uncovered, for 20 minutes more. If you're using cooked dried beans, add them a couple of minutes before the end of cooking. Season the soup to taste with salt—it may not need any since the prosciutto is salty.

In the dining room or in the kitchen, place a slice of French bread toast in each heated soup bowl. Ladle over the soup. Grind fresh pepper over each bowl.

1 bulb garlic

2 leaves fresh or dried sage

1 small bunch parsley

10 cups broth, preferably Basic Brown Chicken Broth (page 373), Turkey Broth (page 374), Basic Brown Beef Broth (see page 375), or water

1 (8-ounce) $1/4$-inch-thick slice prosciutto end, pancetta, or bacon, cut into $1/4$-inch cubes

$1^1/2$ cups fresh shell beans, such as cranberry, or $1^1/2$ cups cooked dried beans, such as cannellini or great Northern ($1/2$ cup dried beans before cooking)

$1^1/2$ pounds kale, stems removed, or $3/4$ pound baby kale with stems left on, coarsely chopped

Salt

8 slices French bread, toasted

Freshly ground black pepper

Kale with Garlic and Sausages

The intense flavor and gentle bitterness of sautéed kale is nicely contrasted with pork, especially sausage. Feel free to experiment with a variety of sausages.

MAKES 4 MAIN-COURSE SERVINGS

Heat 2 tablespoons of the oil over medium heat in a large skillet. Add the sausages and sauté until well browned, about 15 minutes. Keep warm.

Heat the remaining 3 tablespoons olive oil over medium heat in a skillet large enough to hold the kale. When the oil begins barely to ripple, add the garlic. Sizzle the garlic for about 1 minute and add the kale. Turn the heat to high and stir around the kale until it becomes completely limp, 10 to 20 minutes. Arrange on plates and place a sausage on each serving. Sprinkle with salt and grind over pepper.

5 tablespoons pure olive oil

4 (5-inch) sausages, your favorite kind

6 cloves garlic, minced

2 bunches kale, stems removed

Salt and freshly ground black pepper

Kale with Garlic and Sausages.

KENCUR

Also called aromatic ginger, kencur, a member of the ginger family has a flavor and aroma all its own. Some say it resembles camphor more than ginger. Both the leaves and root (actually a rhizome) are eaten. It is popular in Malaysia and Southeast Asia as a flavoring for rice. The leaves are sometimes dipped in pungent sauces.

KINOME

Both the leaves and the pods of this plant, actually sprigs of an immature prickly ash, are edible. The leaves are typically used to garnish every manner of food and the pods are ground to make a kind of pepper called *sansho*. Sansho is very similar in flavor to Sichuan peppercorns and is used to season a variety of Japanese dishes, especially grilled fatty foods such as eel.

KOHLRABI

This is one vegetable you'll have no trouble spotting because it looks like an organ on life support, with spiky, veinlike stems coming out of a pale green, round base—what looks like a root but is actually a thickened stem.

Kohlrabi makes a great substitute for turnips and rutabagas, although "substitute" is the wrong word, because kohlrabi is sweeter and more delicate than most turnips and rutabagas and would probably be a first choice more often in my kitchen if it weren't sometimes hard to find. I like to cook kohlrabi by peeling the rootlike stem, slicing it between $1/8$- and $1/4$-inch thick—a vegetable slicer is best for this—and gently sautéing the slices in butter, bacon fat, or rendered pancetta fat for about 20 minutes until tender. Kohlrabi can also be boiled—peel after boiling—and mashed with butter or cream as you would rutabagas . If you find kohlrabi with fresh-looking leaves, sauté the leaves as you would Swiss chard or spinach—after cutting out the stem running along the middle—in a little olive oil with garlic.

You may use kohlrabi in any recipe calling for turnips or rutabagas.

LAMB'S QUARTERS

Lamb's quarters have heart-shaped leaves with saw-toothed edges. Describing the taste of an unknown green as resembling spinach is much like describing an unfamiliar meat as tasting like chicken. Despite its sometimes rough-and-tumble appearance, lamb's quarters are delicate both raw in salads or cooked, again, like spinach. You can apply the same methods to both greens—steaming, boiling, and sautéing—and some of the same flavorings, especially garlic. Lamb's quarters can also be creamed in the same way as spinach (page 309). Your best chance of tracking down lamb's quarters is at a farmers' market.

Lambs quarter.

LONG BEANS

While they look like giant green beans, long beans are cooked somewhat differently. They tend to be relatively tough and hence require a longer cooking time. One of my favorite methods for cooking them is sauté-steaming in a wok.

Long beans.

Long Beans with Peanuts and Garlic

This recipe uses typical Chinese flavors for cooking what is a typical Chinese food-stuff. The peanuts add crunch and a gentle flavor that acts as a foil to the more aggressive ginger and garlic.

MAKES 4 SIDE-DISH SERVINGS

Sauté or stir-fry the beans in the peanut oil over high heat for 5 minutes or until their color starts to fade. Add the ginger, garlic, and jalapeño and stir for 1 minute more. Add the water, soy sauce, sesame oil, and sherry and cover the sauté pan or wok. Boil, covered, over high heat for about 3 minutes. Remove the lid and boil down until the sauce thickens slightly and coats the beans. Sprinkle with the peanuts.

1 medium (about 1½-pound) bunch long beans, cut into 1-inch lengths

3 tablespoons peanut oil

1 tablespoon grated fresh ginger

2 cloves garlic, minced

1 jalapeño, stemmed, seeded, and minced

½ cup water

2 tablespoons Japanese dark soy sauce

1 teaspoon toasted sesame oil

⅔ cup sherry

½ cup toasted peanuts

Stir-frying the long beans.

Boiling, covered.

Boiling, uncovered, to reduce and thicken.

LOTUS ROOT

Lotus root is usually about 5 inches long, 3 inches thick, and has tunnels, arranged in flower-like patterns, that run the length of the root. This fascinating aquatic plant has a number of uses. It can be stir-fried, deep-fried, braised, or used in soups. One author, Grace Young, even candies it.

Lotus root.

Candied Lotus Root à la Grace Young

I've strayed from Grace's original recipe in her wonderful book, *The Wisdom of the Chinese Kitchen*, and have flavored these lotus root slices with orange.

MAKES 4 DESSERT SERVINGS

Blanch the orange zest in boiling water for 30 seconds to eliminate bitterness. Drain in a strainer and reserve.

Bring about 8 cups water to a boil, add the lotus root slices, and cook for about 1 minute. Drain and repeat twice more.

Combine the orange zest, lotus root, sugar, orange juice, star anise, ginger, and lime juice in a saucepan and simmer gently until the lotus root slices turn translucent, about 90 minutes. Serve cool in its syrup.

2 pieces orange zest, about 3 inches long and $1/2$ inch wide

2 medium lotus roots, peeled and sliced about $1/4$ inch thick

$2 1/2$ cups sugar

2 cups fresh orange juice, strained

1 star anise

2 slices fresh ginger

2 tablespoons lime juice, or to taste

Slicing lotus root.
Lotus root in sugar syrup.

Candied lotus root.

LUFFA

Really a kind of squash, luffffa is used in Chinese stir-fries and soups. There are two types: smooth luffa and, what's shown here, angled luffa. Smooth lufa looks a little like a hothouse cucumber, while angled luffa looks considerably more exotic with deep ridges that run the length of the vegetable.

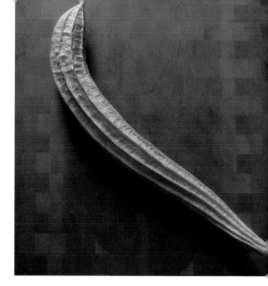

Luffa.

Luffa Stir-Fry with Enoki Mushrooms, Bok Choy, Jicama, and Water Chestnuts

One of my favorite tricks for enhancing Chinese stir-fries is to incorporate an order of boneless spareribs from the local Chinese restaurant. The little fragments of meat add savor and contrast to a mixture of vegetables.

MAKES 6 MAIN COURSE SERVINGS

Heat the oil in a wok or large skillet over medium heat and add the ginger. Let the ginger sizzle for a minute or two and add the garlic. Let the garlic sizzle for 15 seconds and add the mushrooms, bok choy, luffa, jicama, water chestnuts, bamboo shoots, spareribs. Turn the heat up to high and stir the mixture until the vegetables soften, about 10 minutes. Serve immediately.

3 tablespoons peanut oil

1 (1/4-inch) slice fresh ginger

1 clove garlic, minced

1 bunch (about 6 ounces) enoki mushrooms, gritty stems removed

1 bunch bok choy, stemmed, leaves cut into lengthwise strips

1 luffa, sliced 1/8-inch thick

1 small jicama, peeled and sliced between 1/8 and 1/4 inch thick

6 water chestnuts, peeled and quartered

1 fresh bamboo shoot, prepared as shown on page 108, or canned (optional)

1 pint take-out boneless spareribs

Luffa Stir-Fry with Enoki Mushrooms, Bok Choy, Jicama, and Water Chestnuts.

MÂCHE

These delicate green leaves have the aroma of roses and are irreplaceable in delicate salads. Typically mâche, also called "lamb's lettuce" (not to be confused with lamb's quarters) comes in small bunches. The leaves must either be separated from the bunches or the bunches very carefully washed because they often contain sand.

Mâche and Flower Salad

Most people don't realize that a large number of flowers are edible. This is not to say that you should run out to your neighborhood florist and eat whatever petals look pretty; they could be poisonous and almost always will contain insecticides. Be sure to buy flowers that are intended for eating (and usually there's no need for washing). I especially like to make this salad with rose petals.

MAKES 4 FIRST-COURSE SERVINGS

Wash your hands and gently fold together the ingredients until everything is well coated with vinaigrette. Serve on plates.

2 cups mâche

2 cups flower petals, such as roses or nasturtiums

2 tablespoons canola oil

1 tablespoon toasted hazelnut or toasted walnut oil

1 tablespoon sherry vinegar or good-quality red wine vinegar, or more to taste

Salt and freshly ground black pepper

MINUTINA

This lovely salad green may look like grass, but it has a delicate subtle flavor. It is somewhat fibrous, which means that you may want to cut it into 2-inch lengths before tossing it with a salad. Otherwise, toss minutina with other greens—its consistency becomes a little monotonous when served alone.

Minutina.

MITSUBA

Almost exclusively grown in Japan, mitsuba has finally made it to American shores. Mitsuba is a salad plant and an herb that looks much like cilantro. Its taste is a bit like cilantro, but with notes of parsley and celery. It is often included in mesclun mixes to which it adds a delightful dissonant note.

MUSHROOMS

It may have required bravery to eat the first oyster, but it was a far riskier enterprise to nibble on the first oyster mushroom. Mushrooms have long been among the most revered of all vegetables. The Romans were fond of them, and not a few Romans succumbed both literally and figuratively to their charms. The Romans ground dried mushrooms and combined them with their favorite seasoning, garum, a kind of fish sauce probably similar to the fish sauce now used in Southeast Asia. Apicius, a Roman cook who lived under the Emperor Tiberius, describes a not-bad-sounding dish for cooked mushrooms with wine, olive oil, and chopped fresh cilantro.

For centuries after the fall of the Roman Empire, mushrooms were eschewed, probably out of fear of poisoning, but also out of a suspicion toward vegetables in general. Medieval trenchermen, at least those who could afford it, preferred meat. The Italians were among the first to reaffirm an appreciation for the mushroom, but the French didn't take the mushroom to heart until the seventeenth century, as part of a trend toward using fewer spices and exotic ingredients and showing greater appreciation for indigenous foods.

While it is true that cultivated white mushrooms aren't in the same league as their wild cousins, they can still be delicious, especially if you use a few tricks to wake up their flavor. Much of the reason for cultivated mushrooms' delicate (some would say bland) flavor is that they contain a lot of water. The trick is to cook them long enough to evaporate their water and concentrate their flavor. You can also marinate raw cultivated mushrooms in oil and vinegar for several hours—both these ingredients enhance the mushroom's flavor—and serve them cold as a salad or side dish or as one of the components of a mixed crudité plate.

The common supermarket mushroom is not the only kind of mushroom that is cultivated. Italian cremini mushrooms, which look like a dark brown version of our common white cultivated mushrooms, have twice the flavor. And when cremini mushrooms grow up, they turn into large, dark portobello mushrooms, which are easy to grill and make a delicious substitute for horrendously expensive porcinis.

Avoid mushrooms that seem damp, that have wet spots, or that smell of mildew. Most of the time it's best to avoid mushrooms that look dried out or that have wrinkled caps, but some slightly dry mushrooms, such as morels, are fine and can be a bargain because they weigh less. Cultivated white mushrooms are at their freshest when the caps are tightly closed and almost perfectly white.

When you get your mushrooms home, don't wash them until you're ready to cook them (the moisture can cause them to mildew) and store them in paper bags—never plastic—in the refrigerator for up to 3 days.

There's always a great deal of debate about whether to wash mushrooms. I wash almost all mushrooms except very clean-looking morels, which absorb a lot of water. Don't leave mushrooms soaking

Assorted mushrooms to be sautéed.

in a sink filled with water, but quickly rinse the mushrooms in a colander while gently tossing with your fingers. Drain and dry immediately on paper towels. Wipe very large mushrooms, such as porcini or portobello, with a damp towel instead of washing.

Mushrooms require very little preparation before cooking. You may have to cut a very thin slice off the bottom of some mushrooms if the end seems dark, damp, or dried out. Trim any dried out, hard, or slimy patches off wild mushrooms. Shiitakes have leathery stems that never soften and should be cut off where they join the cap (these can be frozen and used to flavor broths). Cut large, cumbersome mushrooms into smaller chunks but not so small that you won't be able to appreciate their meaty, satisfying texture.

Mushrooms can be sautéed, stuffed, added to soups, baked, and used raw or marinated in salads.

TRIMMING AND CUTTING UP MUSHROOMS

Many mushrooms, especially if they're large, need to be cut into smaller pieces to make them easier to cook and, if they're being combined with other kinds of mushrooms, to ensure that all the mushrooms cook in the same time. When trimming, slicing, or cutting up mushrooms, do everything you can to show off the mushrooms at their best. Regular cultivated mushrooms and cremini mushrooms, for example, can be quartered vertically through their caps so they retain more of their texture and shape, instead of always being sliced. Wild mushrooms are best left whole or cut in such a way that they retain some of their original beauty and shape. Morels should be left whole or, if very large, cut lengthwise in half; porcini should be left in thick slices or chunks—at least 1 inch thick—to show off their meaty texture. Chanterelles should be left whole or halved or quartered lengthwise; oyster mushrooms should be cut following their beautiful convolutions.

Slicing cremini mushrooms.

WILD AND CULTIVATED MUSHROOM VARIETIES

BLACK TRUMPETS (*trompettes de la mort*). These delicious mushrooms are underappreciated, perhaps because they are sometimes called "death trumpets" after the French name. The name, however, comes from the mushroom's appearance—black and trumpet shaped—not its edibility. Because of this, black trumpets can be a good value. Black trumpets often contain grit or sand and are best cleaned by cutting off the hard base and then quickly rinsing and drying. Don't bother with dried black trumpets; they don't have much flavor. Black trumpets are best sautéed in butter or olive oil and sprinkled with a little garlic or shallot and some finely chopped fresh parsley. (Season: spring and fall.)

CAESAR'S AMANITAS (*oranges*). Bright red and orange, these mushrooms are appreciated in Europe but rarely seen in the United States. Caesar's amanitas can be gently sautéed with a touch of garlic or shallot, or they can be cut up and served with pasta and risotto. They're such a rarity that when I've encountered them in the United States (at horrendous prices in Italian restaurants), they are served raw, sprinkled with a little lemon juice and extra-virgin olive oil (Season: summer, early fall.)

CHANTERELLES (GIROLLES). Golden chanterelles are an American favorite. Chanterelles range in size from under ¹/₂ inch to 8 inches tall and several inches wide, but usually they're only about 1 inch wide and 3 inches tall. Unlike many mushrooms that release liquid when heated, chanterelles are relatively dry so they're easy to sauté. Chanterelles don't dry well, but become very hard and lose their flavor. (Season: late summer, fall, early winter, spring.)

CREMINI. Almost identical to the common cultivated mushroom except that cremini mushrooms are brown instead of white and have about twice as much flavor. Creminis were the only cultivated mushroom available in the United States until the 1920s, when the white mushrooms we're familiar with today were developed. Cremini mushrooms are still the standard cultivated mushroom popular in Italy and France and often cost the same as cultivated white mushrooms so you get more flavor for your money. Use creminis in any recipe calling for regular cultivated mushrooms when you want a more intense flavor. When cremini mushrooms grow large and their caps unfold, they are called portobello mushrooms. (Season: year-round.)

ENOKI (ENOKITAKES). Very long and thin, these mushrooms are usually sold in plastic bags. Enoki mushrooms are usually cream colored, about 5 inches tall, with tiny caps. Because of their unusual shape they tend to show up in Japanese and nouvelle cuisine restaurants in salads, soups, and as garnitures. Unfortunately, they have a rather bland taste. (Season: year-round.)

GYROMITRAS. Several species of these mushrooms are often confused with morels because they have a similar wrinkled and spongy outer surface. They don't, however, have morels' distinct cone shape but tend to be more amorphous. While some species of gyromitras can be used in the same way as morels, they don't have morel's distinctive full flavor. Because some species of gyromitras are poisonous, only use them if they have been procured from a reliable source. (Season: spring, early sunmer, fall.)

HEDGEHOG MUSHROOMS (*pieds de mouton*). These delicious mushrooms are becoming easier to find in gourmet markets and are usually less expensive than some of the better-known varieties, such as chanterelles or morels. Hedgehog mushrooms are easy to recognize because they have tiny spines on the bottom of their caps instead of gills. They have a firm, almost brittle texture and, like chanterelles, are relatively dry so they don't release much liquid during cooking—a quality that makes them good for sautéing. (Season: fall, early winter.)

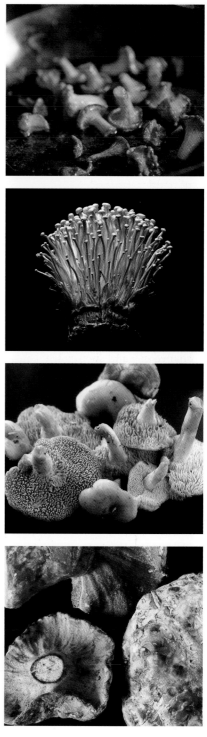

Chanterelles.
Enoki mushrooms
Hedgehog mushrooms.
Lobster mushrooms.

LOBSTER MUSHROOMS. Bright orange or yellow and peculiarly shaped, lobster mushrooms are actually a kind of parasite that attacks other mushroom species. Lobster mushrooms have firm, relatively dry flesh (which makes them easy to sauté) and grow quite large—I often see specimens weighing as much as a pound for sale in gourmet groceries. Because of their large size, lobster mushrooms almost always need to be sliced or carved following their natural contours. (Season: spring and fall.)

MATSUTAKE (PINE MUSHROOMS). These mushrooms are so prized in Japan and Korea that they're one of the few foods that approach the price of truffles. I, who have a weakness for such delicacies, have tasted them only once in a Japanese restaurant where it (I only got one) was grilled and served to me piping hot, seasoned with a little soy sauce. It was indeed delicious, with a meaty flavor reminiscent of the best porcini. Mitsutake mushrooms are now being harvested in the Northwest, so we can hope their price will make them at least occasionally accessible to mere mortals. Matsutake mushrooms are best grilled—brushed with melted butter or olive oil—or sautéed. (Season: November and December.)

MORELS. Easy to recognize because of their distinctive cone- or sphere-shaped cap and sponge-like outer surface, morels are in peak season during the spring, but they can also be found fresh other times of the year. As is true of most mushrooms, the flavor of morels emerges only when they are cooked. Morels range in size from about $1/2$ inch to 4 inches tall and $1/2$ inch to a couple of inches wide at the base of the cone.

When shopping for morels, make sure they aren't wet or soggy—you'll be paying a lot for moisture, and the mushrooms won't cook properly. In fact, look for morels that are slightly dried out; you'll get more for your money. Smell the morels and don't buy them if they have any mildew odor. Don't confuse morels with gyromitras (see above), which are irregularly shaped, aren't as tasty as morels, and should be cheaper. Dried morels are among the best of all dried mushrooms. (Season: mostly spring, but also summer, fall.)

MOUSSERONS (*St. George's Agarics*). Small and brown, these have long been a favorite in France, are only beginning to be discovered by American cooks for their delicate rich flavor. Mousserons are best when gently sautéed or cooked with a little cream and served as a side dish for red meats or game. (Season: spring, summer, fall.)

OYSTER MUSHROOMS (*pleurotes*). Fan-shaped and likely to grow on oak logs, oyster mushrooms are usually gray but occasionally brown, and grow quite large—up to 8 inches across. Oyster mushrooms are one of the easiest to find at a gourmet grocery and often the least expensive of the "wild" mushrooms. (Wild is in quotes because these mushrooms

Maitake mushrooms.
Morels.
Mousserons.
Nameko mushrooms.

are now being cultivated.) Oyster mushrooms can be delicious, but they decompose very quickly, especially if stored in a plastic bag where their moisture accumulates, and take on a slippery feel and a rank mildew odor. (Season: year-round)

PORCINI (BOLETES). Because these meaty mushrooms are usually imported from Europe, they tend to be very expensive. And to make matters worse, porcini shrink to about half their raw size when cooked. Despite all this, because of their meaty texture and full flavor, porcini are among the most prized of all mushrooms. Porcini can grow to be very large—I've seen caps as large as a foot in diameter—which makes them easy to use for dramatic presentations. However you cook porcini, don't slice them too thin or the effect of their meaty texture will be lost.

When shopping for porcini, look for ones that are firm-textured with no wet spots or signs (or odor) of mildew. And since people aren't the only creatures that like porcini, look for worm holes. If, when you get your mushrooms home, you discover a worm or two, don't panic. Heat the mushrooms in a 250°F oven for 30 minutes. The worms will crawl out and die—don't say anything to the guests. Porcini make some of the best dried mushrooms. (Season: Fresh are available mostly in the fall, but sometimes during the spring; dried are available year-round.)

PORTOBELLOS. These large cultivated mushrooms are full-grown cremini mushrooms. Portobellos have wide, flat caps and very dark brown, almost black, gills. They are delicious grilled and make a relatively inexpensive substitute for porcini. Portobellos can be served whole, much like a thick steak, or they can be sliced and cooked in the same way as cultivated white mushrooms or cremini mushrooms. One word of warning: Portobello mushrooms turn cream sauces a murky gray. (Season: year-round.)

ROYAL TRUMPETS. Why these mushrooms are called trumpets, I have no idea. They have long, thick stems that are perfectly edible and nicely rounded even tops with gills that go only down to the stem. They are delicious on the grill. (Season: spring and fall.)

SHIITAKE. Unless you're a mushroom hunter you're most likely to run into cultivated shiitakes at the supermarket, where they are now often available year-round. Shiitakes are firm (the caps feel leathery) and full-flavored and can be cooked in the same way as regular cultivated mushrooms. The only thing to watch out for is the stems, which are tough and best cut off. The stems are, however, flavorful, so I save them in the freezer and simmer them in meat broth before straining. (Season: year-round.)

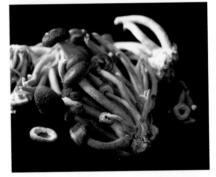

Oyster mushrooms.
Piopinnis.
Pompom mushrooms.
Porcinis.

TREE EARS. Tree ears are usually used dry. They are easily reconstituted in warm water. Tree ears are used in soups and stews to which they lend an interesting texture but little flavor. After soaking, cut away any hard pieces or stems before simmering in a soup or stew. (Season: year-round.)

DRIED MUSHROOMS

One of the great things about dried mushrooms is that you can keep them on hand for emergencies and last-minute inspirations. I keep a bag of dried porcini, tightly wrapped, in my refrigerator for flavoring simple pasta dishes or for giving an elegant and subtle savor to vegetables.

Morels, porcini, and shiitakes make the best dried mushrooms. Rinse the mushrooms under cold water. Rinse and soak dried morels and porcini for about 30 minutes—until they've plumped and softened—in enough warm water to come only halfway up their sides. Turn the mushrooms around in the water every few minutes so they soak evenly. Dried shiitake mushrooms take longer—about 5 hours in warm water or 30 minutes when barely covered with boiling water. After soaking, squeeze the mushrooms to get rid of excess water. Carefully strain the soaking water into another container (leaving any grit behind) so it can be incorporated into the dish.

Morels take especially well to drying and, in fact, have a distinctive smoky aroma that leaves some connoisseurs preferring them over fresh. When buying dried morels, inspect them to make sure you're getting whole, relatively large mushrooms, instead of small or broken mushrooms or a bag full of grit. Most dried morels come from France or India. French morels are somewhat tastier but much more expensive than the Indian variety, which are certainly acceptable and are a good value. Don't pay morel prices for gyromitras, which are less tasty and have a gnarled, irregular shape unlike the almost perfect cone-shape of most morels.

Porcini, also called cèpes, are available dried, but vary even more in quality than morels. Look for large mushrooms and thick slices instead of little bits of broken slices and try to buy dried mushrooms from a market that does a brisk trade so you're not stuck with old stale mushrooms. Excellent porcini are also available in Polish markets under the names *borowiki*, *prawdziwki*, or simply "Polish mushrooms."

Many cooks prefer the flavor of dried shiitakes to that of fresh. Dried shiitakes are available in Chinese markets under the names "black mushrooms" or "black forest mushrooms." There are two types: those with smooth caps and those with white irregular cracks or fissures on top. Those with the fissures are much tastier and more expensive.

Depending on their shape and how dry they are, dried mushrooms weigh between ³/₄ and 1¹/₂ ounces per cup.

Portobellos.
Royal Trumpets.
Shiitake.
Tree Ears.

Mushrooms "Truffle Style" (*Funghi Trifolati*)

Though the word "trifolati" literally means to cook with oil, garlic, and parsley, the effect of this dish is to create the flavor of truffles. Although there aren't any truffles in this recipe, the truffled effect comes from slicing the mushrooms paper-thin. The result is heavenly. You can also use this trifolati mixture as a delicious stuffing for ravioli.

MAKES 6 PASTA-COURSE OR 4 MAIN-COURSE SERVINGS
(2 1/2 TO 3 CUPS SAUCE)

If you are using the dried porcinis, give them a quick rinse and soak in 1/4 cup warm water until soft, about 30 minutes. Squeeze out the excess water, chop coarsely, and reserve the soaking water.

Stir the shallots, garlic, and thyme in the olive oil in a wide sauté pan over medium-low heat and sauté for 5 minutes—their aroma should fill the kitchen. Toss in the sliced mushrooms and the carefully decanted soaking liquid, turn the heat up to high, and stew the mushrooms until they release their liquid into the pan. Cook for a few minutes more to evaporate the liquid.

While the mushrooms are cooking, bring about 8 quarts salted water to a rapid boil.

Stir the butter, parsley, and cream into the mushrooms and simmer gently for about 3 minutes, until the sauce thickens slightly. Season to taste with salt and pepper.

Toss the pasta into the boiling water and cook until al dente. Check that the pasta is done by fishing out a piece with a spoon and biting into it. Fresh pasta takes a minute or two, dried pasta takes from 5 to 10 minutes. Drain the pasta, put it back in the empty pot, pour over the mushroom sauce, and toss quickly. Season to taste with salt and pepper and serve immediately on wide hot plates or pasta bowls.

I small handful dried porcini mushrooms (optional)

2 large shallots, minced

2 cloves garlic, minced

I teaspoon chopped fresh thyme leaves, or 1/2 teaspoon dried

2 tablespoons pure olive oil

1 1/2 pounds cultivated white or cremini mushrooms, sliced paper-thin (use a vegetable slicer)

2 tablespoons unsalted butter

2 tablespoons finely chopped fresh parsley

1/2 to I cup heavy cream

1 1/2 pounds fresh or I pound dried pasta, such as fettuccine, linguine, or pappardelle (1/2- to 1-inch-wide noodles)

Salt and freshly ground black pepper

Fettuccine with Dried Porcini Mushrooms

This is one of those dishes that amazes guests by its depth of flavor but is still a snap to make. It's a staple dish in my household, partly because I never get tired of it and partly because the ingredients are always on hand and there's no need for last-minute shopping. You can serve this dish as a main course (in which case, double the given amounts below) or, as the Italians do a smaller first course.

MAKES 4 FIRST-COURSE SERVINGS

Toss the porcini into 1/4 cup warm water in a small bowl and let sit for 30 minutes. Move the porcini around with their soaking liquid every 10 minutes so they soak evenly. Squeeze the water out of the porcini and reserve with the water left in the bowl. Coarsely chop the softened porcini.

Bring about 8 quarts of salted water to a boil for cooking the pasta.

1/2 to I cup (3/8 to 3/4 ounces) dried porcini

I (1/8-inch-thick) slice prosciutto, finely chopped (optional)

I clove garlic, minced

2 teaspoons unsalted butter

I cup heavy cream

Salt and freshly ground black pepper

I pound fresh fettuccine or linguine, or 12 ounces dried

Freshly grated Parmigiano-Reggiano cheese, for serving

Combine the prosciutto, garlic, and butter in a heavy-bottomed 4-quart pot and cook over medium-low heat until the aroma of garlic fills the room, about 2 minutes. Don't let the garlic brown. Add the porcini, stir for 2 minutes over medium heat, and then carefully pour the mushroom soaking liquid into the pan, leaving any grit or sand behind in the bowl. Boil until the liquid has all evaporated, then pour in the cream. Simmer gently for 2 to 5 minutes, until the cream thickens slightly. Season to taste with salt and pepper. Keep warm.

Cook the pasta in the boiling water, drain, and toss it in the pot with the sauce. Serve immediately on hot plates. Pass the Parmesan cheese at the table.

Marinated Mushrooms with Fresh Tarragon.

Marinated Mushrooms with Fresh Tarragon

My guests always assume I've done something terribly complicated to these mushrooms, but all that's involved is a quick slicing and tossing with olive oil, vinegar, and chopped tarragon. If you can't find fresh tarragon, you can substitute fresh basil or even parsley, but don't scrimp on the quality of the vinegar and the oil. If kept overnight in the refrigerator, these mushrooms will turn a bit dark but their flavor will improve. If you can find cremini mushrooms use them instead of the standard white mushrooms. I serve these mushrooms as a simple first course or hors d'oeuvre. I also sometimes serve them as a side dish for dinners of grilled foods.

MAKES 6 TO 8 SIDE-DISH SERVINGS

Slice off and discard the very bottom of the mushroom stems if they seem gritty or dried out. Slice large mushrooms vertically into slices about 1/4 inch thick. If the mushrooms are very small—with caps less than 1 inch in diameter—cut the mushrooms vertically into quarters. Toss the mushrooms gently with the oil, vinegar, and tarragon in a mixing bowl. Season to taste with salt and pepper. Cover with plastic wrap and store in a cool place for at least 1 hour, or up to 8 hours, before serving.

1 pound cultivated mushrooms with caps tightly closed

1/2 cup extra-virgin olive oil

1/4 cup sherry vinegar, balsamic vinegar, or good-quality red or white wine vinegar, or more to taste

2 tablespoons coarsely chopped fresh tarragon

Salt and freshly ground black pepper

⌒ GRILLING MUSHROOMS ⌒

Virtually any mushroom can be grilled, but the effect is most dramatic with large meaty mushrooms that can be served whole, or almost whole, like steaks. When grilling smaller mushrooms, put them on skewers, which will make for a more dramatic presentation and keep the mushrooms from falling through the grill top. If the mushrooms are somewhat large, use two wooden skewers per kebab to make them easier to turn on the grill. If you're using wooden skewers, press the mushrooms right next to each other or the wood will burn. Wrap each end of the wooden skewers with a tiny piece of aluminum foil to prevent the ends from burning.

Cultivated mushrooms.

Sautéed Mushrooms with Garlic and Parsley

Almost any mushroom, cultivated or wild, can be sautéed with delicious results. Even though ultimately this is a simple dish, some mushrooms—especially everyday cultivated mushrooms—release water when they get hot, so if you're not careful, the mushrooms will end up in a soggy little stew of their own juices. To avoid this, make sure the mushrooms are completely dry and the pan is very hot. Add the sliced or quartered mushrooms a handful at a time so the water released is immediately vaporized and doesn't accumulate in the pan. The only disadvantage to this method is that you can't use whole butter, which would burn—you'll need to use olive oil or clarified butter or some kind of rendered fat, such as duck fat. You can also deal with the moisture problem by putting all the mushrooms in the pan at once, letting them releases their liquid, and then cooking them until the liquid evaporates and is reabsorbed by the mushrooms. Some mushrooms such as chanterelles, black trumpets, and hedgehog mushrooms don't release liquid as they cook.

Sautéed mushrooms.

MAKES 4 SIDE-DISH SERVINGS

Cut large cultivated mushrooms into quarters from top to bottom or into ¼-inch-thick slices. Cut wild mushrooms into larger pieces according to their shape and size (see page 233).

Combine the garlic with the parsley.

Heat the oil over high heat in the largest sauté pan you have. When it starts to ripple (don't let it smoke), toss in just enough of the mushrooms to cover the pan in a single layer. Don't toss or stir the mushrooms until you see them start to brown, after a minute or two. Stir or toss the mushrooms every several seconds or so for a couple minutes more until they're evenly browned. Push these mushrooms to one side of the pan and toss in about the same number of mushrooms, wait a minute or two, and repeat until you use all the mushrooms. If at some point the mushrooms release water, don't add more mushrooms until the water evaporates. Continue tossing or gently stirring the mushrooms over high heat until all the mushrooms are well browned and there's no liquid left in the bottom of the pan.

Sprinkle the parsley-garlic mixture over the hot mushrooms and stir or toss for a minute or two over high heat, until the parsley mixture evenly coats all the mushrooms and the room fills with the aroma of garlic. Sprinkle with salt and grind over fresh pepper. Serve immediately. I serve these mushrooms with just about any full-flavored meat or fish dish.

1 pound cultivated or wild mushrooms, trimmed

2 cloves garlic, minced and crushed

2 tablespoons finely chopped fresh parsley

2 tablespoons olive oil, clarified butter or ghee (see page 149), or rendered goose, duck, pancetta, or prosciutto fat

Salt and freshly ground black pepper

Mushrooms growing in a cluster before being separated.

Baked Morels Stuffed with Foie Gras

I invented these little treats in my Greenwich Village restaurant when two of my most critical regular clients telephoned in advance, asking for something special. I had been having an ongoing debate with the two gentlemen about the merits of American foie gras, which was then just becoming available. I was delighted with it, but my two friends insisted that foie gras wasn't worth eating outside of France. To elicit an unbiased opinion, I disguised the foie gras and served it to them surreptitiously. With the back of a pencil, I pushed slivers of the foie gras into the hollows of large, juicy morels and served them a plate of these hot baked morels as their first course. The dish was a triumph and American foie gras was vindicated.

I admit that this is hardly an everyday hors d'oeuvre for an impromptu gathering of friends, but the results more than justify the extravagance. Through some kind of symbiosis, the morels make the foie gras taste more like foie gras, and the foie gras makes the morels taste more like morels. You can serve the hot morels by themselves or on little croutons—which offer a delightfully contrasting crunch—but warn your guests to grip morel and crouton firmly in hand as the morel is perched somewhat precariously. Otherwise, catastrophe of catastrophes, the precious mushroom may roll off onto the floor.

When selecting morels for this dish, you'll have to be especially fussy. They must be just the right size—about 2 inches long—and perfectly straight so you can slide in the foie gras. They should have a good clear opening in which to insert the foie gras.

Most of the work for this dish can be done earlier in the same day—only the final baking of the morels must be done at the last minute.

MAKES 6 HORS D'OEUVRE SERVINGS

Preheat the oven to 400°F and fire up the broiler. (If the broiler is in the same oven, don't worry about it—you'll just need a hot oven in which to finish the morels.)

If the morels look dirty or sandy, rinse them under cold running water to get rid of sand or grit. Immediately shake out any water that may have ended up trapped in their hollow centers and gently pat dry on paper towels.

Slice the foie gras into strips just large enough to fit through the morel stems and push the foie gras into the morels with the back of a pencil or chopstick.

Slice the baguette into twenty-four pieces between ⅛ inch and ¼ inch thick. You may have to cut the bread at an angle so the slices end up slightly longer than the morels. Brush the bread with the melted butter and spread them on a baking sheet. Slide the bread under the broiler and toast until the tops of the slices are golden brown. (You need only brown one side.)

Arrange a morel on each of the bread slices and gently spoon the remaining butter over each morel. Season with salt and pepper. Bake until the butter is bubbling up on the morels, about 7 minutes. Serve immediately. If you're passing the morels as an hors d'oeuvre, pass around cocktail napkins at the same time.

24 fresh morels, each about 2 inches long

1 (5-ounce) slice terrine of foie gras, (labeled *bloc* or *entier*, if French)

1 French-style baguette, at least 10 inches long

6 tablespoons melted unsaltebutter or goose fat

Salt and freshly ground black pepper

Morels with Cream

Other than a few unattainable follies made with truffles, this is one of the most luxurious of all vegetable dishes. When I do make it, which isn't often because of its expense, I serve it alone, without distraction, as a first course or with a luxurious roast. You can also spoon the morels, in their creamy sauce, over pieces of cooked meat, seafood, or pasta.

While creamed morels are best made with fresh spring morels, dried morels are also delicious in this dish.

MAKES 6 FIRST-COURSE OR SIDE-DISH SERVINGS

If the fresh morels seem gritty or sandy, rinse them quickly under cold running water and lay them on paper towels to dry.

Rinse dried morels quickly under cold running water and soak them for 30 minutes in a small bowl with just enough warm water to come halfway up their sides. Turn them around in the water every few minutes so they soak evenly. Squeeze the excess water out of the dried morels back into the soaking liquid and reserve the liquid separately.

Heat the butter in a 12-inch sauté pan (don't use a cast-iron skillet, which can turn the cream a murky gray) over medium heat until it froths. Toss the morels into the hot butter and toss or stir until the aroma of the morels fills the room and any liquid they release into the pan evaporates, about 10 minutes. Pour in the Madeira and morel soaking liquid—pour slowly, leaving any grit behind—and boil over high heat until there's no liquid left. Turn the heat down to medium-high and pour in the cream. Simmer gently until the cream barely begins to thicken and coat the mushrooms, about 5 minutes. Sprinkle with parsley and season to taste with salt and pepper. Serve immediately.

1 1/2 pounds fresh morels, or 1 1/2 ounces dried

1 tablespoon unsalted butter

1/4 cup Madeira or dry Spanish sherry

1 cup heavy cream

1 tablespoon finely chopped fresh parsley

Salt and freshly ground black pepper

MUSTARD GREENS

Because mustard greens are members of the overwhelmingly large genus *Brassica*, a genus that includes cabbages, radishes, turnips, and broccoli, there's a lot of confusion about what makes mustard mustard. This all gets especially tricky if you're shopping in a Chinese market, where the language barrier confuses things even more. There are various Chinese mustard greens, including bamboo mustard cabbage, which looks like a cross between spinach and Swiss chard (smallish with somewhat dull-green sawtooth-edged leaves and pale green stems). There is a variety lovingly described by Rosa Ross in her book, *Beyond Bok Choy*, as wrapped heart mustard cabbage.

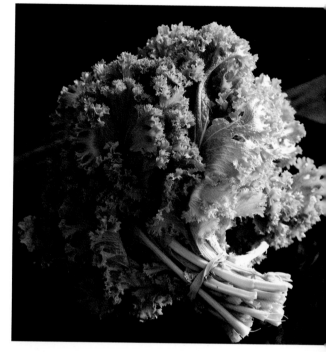

Mustard greens.

But to narrow things down a bit, unless you're in a Chinese market, you're most likely to encounter the bright green variety with leaves with scalloped edges. The leaves look somewhat like kale, except they're brighter and usually more tender.

Occasionally you may find mustard greens in other shapes (some are bunched like cabbages) and colors (red, purple). Whatever kind of mustard you do pick up, make sure that the leaves look perky with no sagging or signs of wilting or dark or slimy patches. Once you get the mustard home, you can store it for a day or two in a plastic bag with holes poked in it in a drawer in the refrigerator, but you're best off using it the day you buy it.

Fortunately, despite all the variety and confusion, except for the tiny red or green leaves sold in mesclun salad mixes, mustard greens can all be cooked in the same way. Just keep in mind that tougher leaves may take a little longer to cook. Cook the mustard greens as you would Swiss chard or beet greens, by sautéing in olive oil flavored with garlic and/or little cubes or strips of prosciutto or pancetta (page 329). You can also stew mustard greens as you would collard greens (page 179), but for half an hour to an hour instead of two hours and with bacon instead of a ham hock—a ham hock wouldn't have time to cook. You can also chop mustard greens and add them to soups during the last 15 minutes of cooking, as you would kale.

MINERS' LETTUCE

Closely related to purslane (see page 284), miners' lettuce is sometimes called winter purslane because, unlike purslane, which is in season in the summer, miners' lettuce comes in the early spring.

Miners' lettuce doesn't really look like lettuce at all but more like a cross between pea shoots and watercress. The flavor is mild and delicate so miners' lettuce makes a nice addition to any salad containing greens. It is also sometimes used in savory dishes as a garnish or even as a thickener.

OKRA

The world is divided about okra. There are those who can't resist the stuff and lick their lips as soon as they hear the word, and there are others, more numerous I fear, who have such an aversion to things slippery and slimy that they would rather not even think of okra. I don't have any methods for getting rid of the much feared slipperiness—after all, it's part of what makes okra okra—so if you're unwilling to encounter a little of that magical sliminess, go ahead and turn the page. But if you're adventurous, you may want to listen to Elizabeth Schneider, author of *Uncommon Fruits and Vegetables,* who reminds us that "there's a lot of good slippery stuff out there to try."

Okra made its way to America from Africa and has long been a staple of Southern cooking. Southern cooks use it in gumbos and are fond of serving it as a vegetable. Okra is also popular in India, where it is served as a vegetable side dish, and in Japan, where it's used as a thickener for soups.

Okra.

Purple okra.

Okra is very perishable; when shopping look for small, bright green okra and make sure there's no browning or discoloration, especially at the tips. Okra should be firm to the touch and show no signs of limpness. Avoid okra that is too large—okra is best under 3 inches long. Once you get the okra home, don't store it for more than a day or two, or it will lose its texture and may even turn moldy. If you must store it, leave it wrapped in a paper bag in the refrigerator—don't wrap it in plastic.

When preparing okra for cooking, cut off the stalk where it joins the pod. If you're cooking okra whole, be careful not to cut so far down along the pod that you expose the seeds. Trim off any brown patches around where the stem joined the pod.

Sautéed Okra

One of the simplest and most satisfying ways to cook okra is to slice it and stir it in hot fat until it softens slightly. The only problem is that no one agrees exactly what "softens slightly" actually means. Fifty years ago cookbooks recommended cooking okra for 2 hours while more contemporary recipes suggest anywhere from 5 to 30 minutes. My own experience is that 20 minutes is about right; I neither like okra gray and mushy from long cooking nor crunchy and raw.

The kind of fat you use for cooking will give okra its ethnic identity. Stirring it in bacon fat makes it distinctly Southern; cooking in peanut oil with a few chopped chiles makes the dish decidedly Asian, and sautéing with olive oil, a little prosciutto, and garlic gives it an Italian character. I sometimes add pine nuts and chopped anchovies for a specifically southern Italian accent.

MAKES 4 SIDE-DISH SERVINGS

1 pound okra

2 tablespoons bacon fat, peanut oil, or pure olive oil

2 cloves garlic, minced (optional)

1 thin slice prosciutto, cut into $^1/_8$- by 1-inch strips (optional)

2 jalapeños, seeded and minced (optional)

Salt and freshly ground black pepper

Cut off and discard both ends and slice the okra into $^1/_4$-inch-thick rounds.

Heat the bacon fat in a wide skillet or wok over medium heat and add the okra. Cook over medium to high heat—just hot enough to keep the okra sizzling but not enough to brown it right away or cause the oil to smoke. Stir every 5 minutes so it cooks evenly. After 15 minutes, stir in the garlic and prosciutto or the chiles (or all three if you want) and cook for 5 minutes more. Season to taste with salt and pepper and serve immediately.

Miso Soup with Okra and Shiitake Mushrooms

The cornerstone of miso soup is the Japanese broth, dashi, made from seaweed and flakes of dried bonito fish. Just combine the dashi with a tablespoon or two of miso to convert it into miso soup. In this recipe, shiitake mushrooms give the miso broth a spectacular woodsy flavor and the okra gives the soup a special texture. If you've got them, serve this soup in Japanese lacquer bowls—the black of the bowl makes a perfect backdrop for the rounds of green okra.

MAKES 4 FIRST-COURSE SERVINGS

If you're using fresh mushrooms, remove their stems—save them for adding to the broth—and slice the caps about $^1/_4$ inch thick. If you're using dried mushrooms, soak them in just enough boiling water to cover for about 30 minutes. Squeeze dry. Cut off the stems and slice the caps into $^1/_4$-inch-thick slices.

In a large pot, bring about 2 quarts of water to a rapid boil. Cut the ends off the okra and slice the okra into $^1/_4$-inch-thick rounds. Boil the okra for 3 minutes, drain, and reserve.

In another small pot, bring the dashi to a gentle simmer and stir 1 tablespoon of the simmering dashi into 2 tablespoons of the miso in a small bowl. Stir the soy sauce into this mixture and stir the mixture into the simmering dashi. Add the okra and sliced mushrooms to the dashi and bring back to the simmer. If the soup lacks flavor or doesn't seem salty enough, make more miso paste and stir it into the soup. Serve immediately in heated bowls.

Miso Soup with Okra and Shiitake Mushrooms.

8 fresh or dried medium shiitake mushrooms

8 ounces okra

4 cups Dashi (page 77)

2 to 4 tablespoons white, red, or brown miso

1 tablespoon Japanese dark soy sauce

ONION FAMILY

It's almost impossible to imagine cooking without onions. Most soups and stews are started by cooking chopped onions and sometimes other vegetables in a little butter or oil before liquid is added.

The onion family includes scallions, leeks, shallots, ramps, and chives, but there are over 300 species in the Allium genus, many of which are native to the New World. Most of the onions we eat are yellow onions sold loose or in bags in the supermarket. Most yellow onions are harvested in the fall and stored in special ventilated sheds so that they're available year-round. The yellow onion has no special qualities except that it is full-flavored and a reliable standby for cooking almost anything that calls for onions. White onions are also available year-round, but because they have a higher water content than yellow onions, they're slightly more perishable. When raw, white onions are slightly sweeter than yellow onions, but when the two are used in cooking it's hard to tell any difference. Spanish onions are very large yellow onions that taste very similar to regular yellow onions. Red onions, once called Bermuda onions (they don't come from Bermuda), are sweeter and milder than yellow or white onions and for that reason are better in dishes calling for raw onions. Nothing's better than raw red onions on a good thick cheeseburger.

In addition to yellow, white, and red onions, which are available year-round, there are also so-called sweet onions. Sweet onions are more seasonal—they're usually available only during the spring and summer, although a few are held in special storage until Thanksgiving. Sweet onions are more perishable and more expensive than year-round onions. Most sweet onions are named after where they are grown: Vidalia (from Georgia), Maui (Hawaii), Walla Walla (Washington), Nu-Mex (New Mexico), and Texas. Sweet onions are most dramatic in recipes calling for raw onions, such as salads and on hamburgers. Sweet onions are very perishable and should be used within a few days.

Onions come in all sizes. There are walnut-size white boiling onions and marble-size pearl onions. Pearl onions are usually solid in pint boxes or bags. The boiling onions and pearl onions that we encounter during most of the year have thin papery skins, but in the spring, fresh pearl onions with their greens still attached are easy to find in farmers' markets.

Onions.

Some people call scallions "green onions," but a green onion is any onion that has its greens still attached. Most green onions are relatively small and range from pearl onion size to the size of a hard ball. Green onions have a fresher, brighter flavor than onions that have been stored and no longer have their fresh greens. Green onions show up in markets in the spring, summer, or fall. Green onions can be cooked in the same way as older onions but require lighter peeling (a green onion's outer peel is thin and translucent) and a small amount of the green can be left attached to show off the onion's freshness and just to look pretty.

When buying green onions, scallions, leeks, or ramps, look for crisp bright greens with no signs of drooping, wilting, or wet spots. When buying regular onions, avoid those with brown, soft, or slightly translucent spots or any onions that have a peculiar odor or that have begun to sprout. You can keep green onions in the refrigerator, wrapped in a plastic bag, for up to 2 days and bulb onions loose, in a cool dry place, for up to 2 weeks.

Halve the onion for easier peeling.

Cut away the peel where it joins the root end.

Slice into the onion with the root end away from you. Don't cut all the way through the root end—leave slices attached at the root end.

Slice the onion sideways, leaving the slices attached at the root end.

Slice across the onion.

Chop finer as needed.

∾ WHAT ABOUT THE TEARS? ∾

Every cook has some idea about how to avoid tears when peeling and chopping onions. One cook I know insists that onions be frozen before peeling, others suggest peeling under water, and another says to sprinkle vinegar on the cutting board when chopping. But none of these methods works very well—the frozen onions need to thaw before they can be chopped, and the vinegar seems to do nothing at all.

The best trick I know is to have something between your eyes and the onions. Glasses help and contact lenses are even better, but if you don't use either of these, your next best bet is to get a set of cheap plastic goggles at a hardware store….Then again, we all need a good cry once in a while.

ONION FAMILY

Roasted whole red onion.

Cut off the top of the whole roast onion.

Pull out the inside of the onion.

Whole Roast Onion

Roasting an onion whole preserves its flavor. The flavor is released as soon as you cut into it and nibble on it.

MAKES 4 SIDE-DISH SERVINGS

Preheat the oven to 400°F.

Roast the onions, on a sheet pan (in case they drip) for about an hour, or until they're easily penetrated with a paring knife. Encourage your guests or family to cut off the top third of the onion (you may need to pass around a relatively sharp knife or do this ahead in the kitchen) and then scoop the flesh out of the bottom two-thirds. Serve with salt and pepper.

4 large red onions

Salt and freshly ground black pepper

Green Onion Frittata

A frittata is simply an omelet with ingredients (in this case, onions) whisked into the eggs before they are cooked. Unlike traditional omelets, a frittata is not folded but is presented like a flat pancake. To get it to cook on top, slide it under the broiler for a minute or two.

MAKES 4 FIRST-COURSE OR LIGHT MAIN-COURSE SERVINGS

Whisk together the onions, eggs, and cream (the cream keeps the omelet tender) and season with salt and pepper.

Preheat the broiler.

Heat the butter in a 12-inch nonstick skillet until frothy over medium heat. Add the egg mixture and let set over medium heat, repositioning the pan every few seconds so the bottom cooks evenly and the omelet is mostly set, about 4 minutes. Slide the pan under the broiler just long enough to set the omelet, about 30 seconds. Slide the omelet out onto a large heated plate. Cut into wedges and serve.

4 green onions, whites thinly sliced, greens discarded or reserved for use in broth

8 eggs

$1/4$ cup heavy cream (optional)

Salt and freshly ground black pepper

2 tablespoons unsalted butter

French Onion Soup

I can think of no dish more satisfying than a French onion soup on a cold winter's evening. I enjoy onion soup even in cheap restaurants, where the broth comes out of a can and the cheese is only so-so. If you've eaten only restaurant versions, homemade onion soup will be a revelation.

Most recipes for onion soup call for beef broth, a requirement that causes most people to give up before starting, but you can certainly get by using low-sodium canned beef or chicken broth, or homemade chicken or turkey broth.

To make the very best French onion soup, don't skimp on the onions or the cheese. Use really good cheese, such as authentic Swiss Gruyère or good farm cheddar without orange coloring (the coloring doesn't affect the flavor, but it looks weird). Don't use generic "Swiss" cheese, which has an insipid flavor and will make a stringy mess when it melts in the soup.

Good onion soup takes a frightful number of onions—you'll think you've sliced too many—but as you stir them over the heat, they will shrink to about one-eighth of their original volume. I usually use large red Bermuda onions because they're slightly sweet, but regular yellow onions work fine. If you like the soup very sweet, try Vidalia or Maui onions. Because this soup is baked, you'll need to use heatproof bowls or soup crocks—I use 12-ounce soufflé dishes.

MAKES 6 LIGHT MAIN-COURSE SERVINGS

6 tablespoons unsalted butter

3 pounds red or yellow onions or sweeter varieties, very thinly sliced

8 cups broth, preferably Basic Brown Beef Broth (page 375), Basic Turkey Broth (page 374), or Basic Brown Chicken Broth (page 373)

3 sprigs thyme

3 sprigs parsley

1 imported bay leaf

Salt and freshly ground black pepper

4 cups grated Swiss Gruyère or good-quality cheddar

6 (^{1}/2-inch-thick) slices French bread cut from a large loaf, toasted (the slices should just fit in the soup crocks)

Melt the butter in a large, heavy-bottomed pot over medium heat. Add the onions and cook, stirring every few minutes, until softened and browned and the juices caramelize on the bottom of the pan, 45 to 60 minutes. Watch the onions carefully during the cooking so neither they nor the sides or bottoms of the pot have a chance to burn.

When all the liquid released by the onions has evaporated and the bottom of the pot is covered with a brown glaze of natural caramel, add the broth. Tie together the thyme, parsley, and bay leaf to make a bouquet garni, add to soup, and gently simmer for 15 minutes. Scrape against the sides and bottom of the pot with a wooden spoon so the caramelized juices dissolve in the soup. Season to taste with salt and pepper. Remove the bouquet garni.

Preheat the oven to 400°F.

Ladle the hot soup into 12-ounce deep ovenproof bowls, individual soup crocks, or soufflé dishes. Sprinkle half the cheese over the soup and place a slice of toast on each one. Sprinkle with the remaining cheese. Put the bowls on sheet pans and bake them in the oven until the cheese bubbles and turns light brown, about 10 minutes. If the soup bubbles up but doesn't brown on top, slide the bowls under the broiler for a minute. Serve immediately.

French Onion Soup.

Grilled Onions

Cooks are sometimes surprised to discover how delicious grilled onions really are. Use medium or large red onions and slice them about $^1/_3$ inch thick. If the slices are too thin, you'll end up with onion rings that will be hard to manage on the grill. Lightly brush the onion slices with olive oil, sprinkle them with herbs if you like, and grill for about 6 minutes on each side, or until they darken around the edges and the rings start to separate.

You can also grill walnut-size boiling onions on skewers, but simmer the onions in water for about 10 minutes before grilling or they'll take too long to cook. With the preliminary simmering, they take about 10 minutes on the grill. Count on 2 large onions or 8 walnut-size onions for 4 servings. Serve the onions as a side dish for other grilled dishes.

Onion Tart

This is a dish that never fails to get a rise out of guests who don't expect much when I announce our first course, but who are always surprised by the tart's buttery sweetness. If you're being really elegant, you can make individual tartlets, but most of the time I just bring one big tart to the table. You can bake this tart in a regular pie pan, but I prefer to use a tart mold with a removable bottom. Don't worry about the onions—it will seem as though you have too many—but they shrink as soon as you start cooking them. This recipe makes a 10-inch tart.

MAKES 8 FIRST-COURSE SERVINGS

2 tablespoons unsalted butter

6 medium onions, very thinly sliced

1 (10-inch) Tart Shell (page 252), baked

2 cups milk

4 large eggs, beaten

1 teaspoon salt

Freshly ground black pepper

Tiny pinch of freshly grated nutmeg

Preheat the oven to 300°F.

Melt the butter in a large, heavy-bottomed pot over medium-high heat and add the onions. Stir the onions every few minutes until they soften and begin to turn pale brown, about 30 minutes. If the onions start to brown sooner, turn down the heat.

Spread the cooked onions in an even layer in the tart shell. Whisk together the milk, eggs, salt, pepper, and nutmeg and pour this mixture into the tart shell. Bake until the liquids set—you can see this by gently moving the tart back and forth and verifying that the liquid does not move—in 45 to 60 minutes. Let cool for 10 minutes. Serve in wedges.

Work the dough into a disk.

Combine all the ingredients for the dough in a food processor.

Process until the dough comes together in a lump.

Roll the dough onto the rolling pin, then unroll it over the tart mold.

Line the mold with the dough.

Add very thinly sliced onions to melted butter.

Cook the onions until they're about one-eighth their original volume.

Fill the baked tart shell with the onions.

Pour in the egg and milk mixture.

Tart Shell

MAKES ONE 10-INCH TART

Combine all the ingredients in the food processor. Process the mixture for about 30 seconds until it comes together in a ball. Flatten the dough into a disk about ³/₄ inch thick. If it's hot and the butter threatens to melt, refrigerate the dough for 10 to 15 minutes (but not longer, or it will harden and become impossible to roll).

Roll out the dough into a 12-inch round. Transfer it to a 10-inch pie or tart pan by rolling it up on a rolling pin and unrolling it over the tart pan or by folding it in half or quarters, centering it in the tart pan, and then unfolding it. Press it into the corners very thoroughly. Roll over the top of the tart shell with a rolling pan to detach the excess dough. Put in the freezer for 15 minutes.

Preheat the oven to 425°F. Place a sheet of parchment paper or aluminum foil in the pie pan, fill the pan with beans or rice to weight it, and bake for about 20 minutes, until the edges of the dough barely begin to brown. Remove the beans and aluminum foil and bake the shell for about 15 minutes, until the dough along the bottom of the pie or tart pan turns pale brown. If at any point the dough starts to get too brown, turn the oven down to 350°F.

1¹/₄ cups all-purpose flour

¹/₂ cup (1 stick) plus 2 tablespoons unsalted butter, cut into ¹/₂-inch cubes and frozen

1 egg yolk

1¹/₂ tablespoons heavy cream

¹/₂ teaspoon salt

Onion Tart.

LEEKS

Leeks are the royal members of the onion family. They have a subtle earthy flavor that's hard to get enough of and are especially delicious when cooked with cream or in soups, or when served cold in a mustardy vinaigrette.

When you consider how little is used, leeks are expensive. It's always a little discouraging to use only a small part of the whole leek, the white. In restaurants, the leek greens are tied up in bundles with herbs and used as bouquet garnis in big pots of stock, but at home, unless you have a pot of broth simmering on the stove, it can be hard to find a use for them. They are occasionally used in pureed vegetable soups.

In most parts of the country, leeks are available year-round, but they're at their peak season in the fall. Inspect leeks carefully before you buy to make sure that the greens are bright and fresh with no signs of yellowing or wilting, and make sure they stick straight out instead of hanging limply. Check the white part of the leek—the outer membrane should be pure white with no brown or slimy spots.

Cutting off the root end of leeks.

Cutting off the greens.

Leeks need to be carefully washed because sand and mud have a nasty way of hiding in between the leaves and membranes of the white. To wash leeks, cut off the greens leaving a couple of inches of pale green attached to the white. Use a sharp knife to whittle off the tough outer green membranes from the pale green end of the leek. This reveals that what was green on the outside is really white or very pale green on the inside. To rid leeks of grit, cut the leeks in half lengthwise or, if the leeks must be left whole, only down to an inch above the root end. Hold the leeks under cold running water with the green end facing down (if it's facing up the water will drive grit farther down into the leek) and fold back the membranes, one by one, rubbing between thumb and forefinger to rinse out grit. Trim off the hairy root end exactly where it joins the base of the leek. Don't cut above the bottom or the leek will fall apart.

Cutting the leek whites in half.

Rinsing sand out of each half.

Thinly sliced leeks.

Leeks in Vinaigrette

This simple first course is almost ubiquitous in inexpensive restaurants in France but relatively unappreciated in the United States. I make this dish in the fall, when I can find finger-thick baby leeks scarcely larger than scallions. If you can't find baby leeks, large leeks, while not as dramatic, also work well. Some people don't like the flavor of olive oil in vinaigrette for leeks and prefer to use a tasteless oil, such as safflower or canola oil.

MAKES 4 FIRST-COURSE SERVINGS OR SIDE-DISH SERVINGS

Bring a large pot of salted water to a boil.

Whittle any very dark green membranes off the green ends of the leeks without cutting off the pale green or white membranes in the center. If you're using baby leeks, leave them whole. If you're using medium or large leeks, cut them in half lengthwise. Rinse the leeks thoroughly to eliminate any sand or grit.

Slide the leeks into the boiling water. Simmer the leeks, uncovered, until they offer no resistance when poked with a paring knife (don't be tempted to under-cook them), 12 to 15 minutes, depending on their thickness. Drain the leeks in a colander and rinse immediately with cold water. Press the leeks gently between your hands to squeeze out excess water.

Prepare the vinaigrette in a bowl by whisking together the vinegar and mustard and then stirring in the oil. Season to taste with salt and pepper. The vinaigrette should be very mustardy and well seasoned.

Thickly coat the leeks with the vinaigrette in a mixing bowl and arrange them in neat rows on individual plates. Sprinkle with chives. Serve cool or at room temperature but not cold.

24 baby leeks, 12 medium leeks, or 8 large leeks, all but 2 inches of green removed

1 tablespoon sherry vinegar or good-quality white wine vinegar

1 tablespoon Dijon mustard

3 tablespoons canola or extra-virgin olive oil

Salt and freshly ground black pepper

1 tablespoon finely chopped fresh chives or parsley (optional)

Leek Gratin

This is the easiest and best way I know to cook leeks, but if you're on a diet, forget it—the leeks are baked in heavy cream. I admit to a certain glee when showing this dish to my students—their mouths open in horror as I pour over the cream. But once they take a bite, they all give up their scruples. This dish is delicious served with roast beef, lamb, or chicken.

MAKES 4 SIDE-DISH SERVINGS

Preheat the oven to 375°F.

Whittle off the dark green outer layers of the leeks without cutting off the pale green or white layers at the center. Cut the leeks in half lengthwise and rinse out any sand or grit.

Arrange the leek halves, flat side down, in a medium (about 8-cup) oval gratin dish or baking dish just large enough to hold them in a single layer. There's no need to butter the dish since the cream prevents the leeks from sticking. If the leeks don't quite fit, turn some of them on their sides. Pour over the cream—there should be enough to come halfway up the sides—and sprinkle with salt and pepper.

Bake for about 35 minutes, until the leeks until the cream has thickened and been almost entirely absorbed by the leeks. A couple of times during the baking, use a spoon to baste the leeks with the cream and press the leeks down into the cream to prevent those parts not submerged from browning and getting tough. Serve immediately or turn the oven down to 200°F and hold for up to 30 minutes.

SCALLIONS

These lovely greens look like miniature leeks or baby onions without bulbs. I rarely cook scallions alone, but I do thinly slice them and sprinkle them as a delicate last-minute flavoring in salads and soups (especially clear Asian soups such as dashi). Cubes of tofu, sprinkled with soy sauce and scallions, are a favorite bar snack in Japan. Some recipes call for only the whites of the scallions, but much of the time, especially if the scallions are very thinly sliced, the greens can be used, too.

SHALLOTS

Shallots are very similar to onions except that they have a more intense flavor without the harshness of onions. For this reason they can be used raw—they're delicious sprinkled over salads—but they really come into their own when used with vinegar or white wine to make rich sauces such as beurre blanc, béarnaise sauce, and seafood sauces.

Two kinds of shallots appear in American markets. The most common of the two has orange, reddish, or slightly purple skin and is almost completely round. Less common are so-called gray shallots, which are more

6 to 8 medium leeks, all but 1 inch of green removed

1 cup heavy cream, or more as needed

Salt and freshly ground black pepper

Scallions.
Scallion shoots.

continued

elongated and with paler skin than the orange variety. Gray shallots aren't really gray, but they're paler and milder and have a more subtle flavor than orange shallots; so if you have a choice, which you probably won't, go for the gray.

Inspect shallots to make sure they're not sprouting, don't have soft spots, and are not dried out.

Most of us use shallots in small amounts, usually finely chopped, but shallots can also be peeled and cooked whole—creamed or glazed—in the same way as small onions. In one of my favorite recipes, shallots are baked with crème de cassis (black currant liqueur). To pull this off, arrange the shallots in a pan just large enough to hold them in a single layer. Pour over enough crème de cassis to cover the bottom of the pan. Add water to come halfway up the shallots. Cover the pan, simmer for about 15 minutes, then uncover the pan, turn up the heat, and reduce the liquid to a glaze.

Shallots.

Add black currant liqueur (crème de cassis) to the shallots in a wide pan.

Glazing shallots in black currant liqueur.

RAMPS

Ramps look a bit like baby leeks, but while leeks may remind us of French cooking, the ramp is an all-American vegetable. Despite their similar looks, they taste completely different. Leeks are delicately earthy, probably the result of centuries of cultivation, but ramps are rambunctious, assertive, and wild tasting. Unlike all but the babiest of leeks, ramps have delicate greens that can be cooked along with the white bulbs or can even be served raw in salads. To prepare ramps, cut off the stringy root end but not too far up or the ramp will fall apart.

Ramps make great gratins. One of my favorite tricks is to bake the ramps in a little cream—the cream attenuates their aggressiveness and brings more subtle flavors into play. To pull this off, trim the roots off the ramps, cut off all but an inch or so of greens, and spread the ramps in a

Ramps with their roots.

Ramps.

Sautéeing ramps with bacon.

baking dish just large enough to hold them in a single layer. Add enough heavy cream to come halfway up their sides. Bake in a 350°F oven until the cream thickens, about 20 minutes. Stir the ramps around in the cream at least once during the baking so they cook evenly.

Ramps are especially good with smoked foods, in particular, bacon. To make ramps with bacon, cut thick-sliced bacon into $1/4$-inch cubes and render them in a large sauté pan over medium heat. When the cubes turn crispy, in about 8 minutes, add the ramps—trimmed of most of their greens and the root—and stir around over medium heat until limp and tender, about 10 minutes.

Ramps sautéed with bacon.

PARSNIPS

For many, parsnips are among those dreaded vegetables that evoke memories of school cafeterias and Dickensian images of orphanages. But like other dreaded vegetables (turnips and cabbage come to mind), when properly cooked, parsnips are a pleasant surprise. Parsnips are sweet like carrots and have a satisfying starchiness like potatoes.

The most common parsnips look like oversized pale brown carrots and, in fact, raw parsnips also smell a bit like carrots. Occasionally turnip-shaped parsnips, more popular in Europe, show up in the United States. While not essential, try to find parsnips with the greens still attached and avoid parsnips that are limp, sprouting, or have brown or soft spots. Avoid "baby" parsnips, which after peeling won't leave you with much at all. To store parsnips for a couple of days, cut off the greens, wrap the roots loosely in a plastic bag with holes poked in it, and keep in the refrigerator crisper drawer.

Parsnips.

Roasting parsnips.

Parsnips can be cooked like any other root vegetable except that they cook more quickly than either carrots or turnips, probably because of their higher starch content. You can cut up or glaze parsnips as you would carrots—in a little butter and, if you've got it, a bit of broth. You can also toss them with a little oil or melted butter and roast them. I serve roasted or glazed parsnips family style or on the same platter as a roast leg of lamb or roast beef. Parsnips are magical with red meat. Parsnips are also delicious when layered in a gratin with potatoes in the same way as turnips or when simmered with potatoes before mashing (use one part parsnips to three parts potatoes).

Maple Syrup–Glazed Parsnips

To glaze parsnips, cut them into 2-inch lengths. A more refined knife method is to treat them like carrots and cut each length into wedges. In other words, cut each piece lengthwise into wedges so that all the wedges end up the same thickness; you might make three wedges out of the thin end of the parsnip and as many as five out of the thick end.

MAKES 4 SIDE-DISH SERVINGS

4 large parsnips

2 tablespoons maple syrup

2 tablespoons unsalted butter

Salt and freshly ground black pepper

Peel the parsnips and cut them into 2-inch lengths. Cut the pieces into wedges all about the same size. Put them in a pan just large enough to hold them in a single layer. Pour over the maple syrup, put in the butter, and add enough water to come a third of the way up the sides of the parsnips. Season with salt and pepper. Partially cover the pan and bring to a simmer. Simmer over medium heat for about 15 minutes. The idea is to get the liquid to evaporate and the glaze to form at the same time as the parsnips are cooked. Check them every few minutes, poking at them with a paring knife, to know how they're doing. If they're approaching doneness and there's still a lot of liquid in the pan, uncover the pan and turn the heat to high. If, conversely, the parsnips are raw and the liquid has evaporated into a glaze, add more water, cover the pan, and cook over low to medium heat. Serve as soon as the parsnips are done and well glazed.

Cut parsnips pieces into wedges.

Parsnips prepared for boiling.

PEAS

What a pity that it's almost impossible to find tiny fresh baby peas rushed in from the farm, instead of the overgrown and starchy peas we find in most supermarkets. Like corn, peas should be cooked within hours of harvest, and they are best harvested while they're small and undeveloped. Unless you grow your own peas, or you have access to an excellent farmers' market, you're better off using frozen peas. Frozen peas lack the delicacy and sweetness of just-picked fresh peas, but they're infinitely better than the overgrown "fresh" peas we usually find at the market. The trick to using frozen peas is not to follow the directions on the package, which tell you to boil the peas. Frozen peas have already been cooked before freezing, so you're better off simply thawing the peas and heating them in something flavorful, such as butter, olive oil, or a little broth. Be sure to buy frozen baby peas (*petit pois*); some frozen peas are tough, flavorless, and too large.

When buying fresh peas, look for small peas with crispy shells. The peas should be tender and taste sweet—open a pod and taste a raw pea to be sure. Avoid peas whose pods seem limp, that have yellow spots, or that seem dried out around the edges. Cook baby peas for about 1 minute in a pot of boiling salted water, drain them, and toss them with butter, a little salt and pepper—you don't need to do anything else. Peas can be stored overnight in a plastic bag in the refrigerator, but the sooner you cook them the sweeter they'll be.

Peas in their pods.

Shelling peas.

Peas.

Basic Buttered Peas

This is the simplest and best way to cook fresh or frozen peas. There isn't much to cooking peas and serving them with butter, but it's important to remember that the peas must be hot and completely dry before they are tossed with the butter. Don't be tempted to melt the butter in the pan and then add the peas—this will cause the butter to turn oily and make the peas seem greasy instead of buttery.

MAKES 6 SIDE-DISH SERVINGS

3 pounds fresh whole baby peas, or 2 (10-ounce) packages frozen baby peas

2 tablespoons unsalted butter, thinly sliced

Salt and freshly ground black pepper

To prepare fresh peas, shell the peas. Bring about 4 quarts of salted water to a rapid boil. Boil the peas over high heat, uncovered, for 1 minute. Reach in with a spoon and quickly taste a pea to make sure it is done—if not, cook a minute more. Drain immediately in a colander. Put the peas in a wide skillet and toss them over high heat to dry them off—they should have no trace of moisture clinging to them. This drying process should take about 1 minute. Pour the hot peas into a heated serving dish and gently stir or toss them with the butter and salt and pepper to taste. Serve immediately.

To prepare frozen peas, unwrap the peas and let them thaw at room temperature in a colander set. If you're in a hurry, put the whole frozen chunk in a frying pan over medium heat and keep it moving back and forth until the peas come apart, or defrost the peas in the microwave. Don't stir the peas or you may break them.

Put the thawed drained peas in a wide skillet or frying pan—if you've thawed them on the stove, just leave them in the pan—and keep moving the pan around over medium heat until the peas are hot and there's no moisture left in the pan or clinging to the peas. Take the pan off of the heat and immediately add the butter slices. Move the pan around in a circular motion to melt the butter. Sprinkle with salt and pepper and serve immediately.

Peas with butter and parsley.

FLAVORINGS FOR FRESH AND FROZEN PEAS

Peas are so delicately flavored that they lend themselves to all sorts of variations, but be careful not to overpower them with strong-tasting ingredients, such as garlic.

Peas with cooked pearl onions and thin shreds of lettuce are a classic French combination, but the possibilities are almost limitless. Finely chopped or shredded herbs, such as tarragon, chives, sorrel, mint, parsley, or chervil (alone or in combination) are delightful when tossed with the hot peas at the last minute. Soaked and chopped dried wild mushrooms (porcini and morels are the best), chopped truffles, tiny slices of prosciutto, minced garlic (be very sparing), and anchovies also can be used as last-minute flavorings.

Fresh buttered peas with dried morels and porcinis.

SNOW PEAS

The peas in snow peas are so tiny that most of what we eat is really the pod. Snow peas have the obvious advantage of not requiring any shelling, but their flavor is entirely different from sweet peas. For many it's their crunchy texture rather than their flavor that makes snow peas a treat.

Buy snow peas that are deep green with no yellow spots or signs of drying. You can store snow peas overnight in the refrigerator in a plastic bag, but if held longer they'll lose their crisp texture. Snow peas don't require much preparation before cooking—only break off their stem end and strip away the string that runs up one side.

The easiest way to cook snow peas is simply to sauté them in oil in a skillet or stir-fry them in a wok. Snow peas can first be boiled in salted water in the same way as other green vegetables, but the boiling must be quick—no more than a minute—or the snow peas will lose their exciting crunch. Once boiled, drain the snow peas in a colander and toss with a chunk of butter or a dribble of extra-virgin olive oil. A simple final seasoning with salt and pepper is usually enough to do the trick, but a last-minute tossing with chopped herbs, such as basil, parsley, or chervil, will give the peas a burst of flavor.

Because of their crunchy texture and assertive flavor, snow peas are delicious in Chinese stir-fries and hold up well to full-flavored ingredients, such as ginger, garlic, sesame oil, pork, ham, and duck confit.

Snow Pea Stir-Fry with Cashews.

Snow peas.

Snow Pea Stir-Fry with Cashew Nuts

This dish is not only one of the most flavorful vegetable dishes I know, but the cashew nuts (you can also use peanuts) and the sesame seeds are a study in crunchiness when eaten along with the snow peas. Because this dish has a lot of flavor, I like to pass it around the table with other flavorful Chinese dishes or fish or meat.

MAKES 4 SIDE-DISH SERVINGS

Break the stem end off the snow peas and peel off the strings. Heat the ginger in the peanut oil in a wok or skillet over high heat. Let the ginger sizzle in the oil for about a minute—if the oil starts to smoke, turn down the heat—and add the nuts, garlic, sesame seeds, and ham. Cook until the garlic barely begins to turn golden, 1 to 2 minutes. Stir in the snow peas, sesame oil, soy sauce, and water. Stir over high heat for 3 minutes. Season with pepper, fish out the ginger slice, and serve the snow peas immediately.

8 ounces snow peas

1 (1/4-inch-thick) slice fresh ginger

1 tablespoon peanut oil

2 heaping tablespoons roasted cashew nuts or peanuts, salted or not

1 clove garlic, minced

1 tablespoon sesame seeds

1 (1/8-inch-thick) slice Smithfield ham, cut into 1- by 1/8-inch strips (optional)

1/2 teaspoon toasted sesame oil

2 teaspoons dark Japanese soy sauce

1 tablespoon water

Freshly ground black pepper

SUGAR SNAP PEAS

Sugar snap peas look a lot like sweet peas except that sugar snap peas are shorter, darker green, and somewhat more plump. The real difference, of course, is that sugar snap peas can be eaten whole, pod and all. When buying sugar snap peas remember that smaller is better. Buy peas that are bright green with no signs of drying.

I cook sugar snap peas in the same way as snow peas—quickly boiled and tossed with butter and herbs or stir-fried. Sugar snap peas have a string along their inner (concave) side. The stem end should be broken off and the string pulled away before cooking. Another approach, if you're desperate for something resembling fresh baby peas, is to shell the snap peas.

Sugar snap peas.

Sugar Snap Peas with Butter and Fresh Marjoram

MAKES 4 TO 6 SIDE-DISH SERVINGS

Break the stem end off the sugar snap peas and peel the end back so the string comes away at the same time. Coarsely chop the marjoram just before cooking the peas. (If it is chopped too far in advance it will turn black and lose flavor.)

Heat the butter in a skillet over medium heat. When the butter froths, stir in the peas. Turn the heat up to high and stir the peas until they cook through, about 4 minutes. Sprinkle with salt and pepper and the chopped marjoram, toss a few times, and serve immediately.

12 ounces sugar snap peas

1 tablespoon fresh marjoram leaves

1 tablespoon unsalted butter or extra-virgin olive oil

Salt and freshly ground black pepper

Sugar Snap Peas with Mushrooms, Curry, Coconut Milk, and Shrimp

These sugar snap peas make an easy one-pot dish that's substantial enough for a simple family dinner. Shiitake mushrooms are best for this dish and give it a distinctive Asian flavor, but you can also use cultivated white mushrooms. This dish has a runny (but delicious) sauce, so you may want to serve boiled rice in a separate bowl at the table to help mop up the juices and round out the meal.

MAKES 4 MAIN-COURSE SERVINGS

Heat the peanut oil in a large skillet or wok over high heat. Stir in the garam masala, garlic, ginger, and red pepper flakes. As soon as the ingredients start to froth, after about 15 seconds, add the mushrooms and peas. Stir or toss the mixture over high heat for 3 minutes. Add the shrimp and stir or toss for 2 minutes more. Pour in the coconut milk, soy sauce, and chopped fresh cilantro. Bring to a simmer and simmer for 2 minutes. Serve immediately in hot bowls.

2 tablespoons peanut oil

2 teaspoons garam masala or bottled curry powder

I clove garlic, minced

2 teaspoons grated fresh ginger

I teaspoon dried red pepper flakes

8 ounces shiitake mushrooms, stemmed, or white cultivated mushrooms, cut into 1/4-inch-thick slices

8 ounces sugar snap peas or snow peas, trimmed

I pound large shrimp, peeled and deveined

I cup unsweetened coconut milk

I tablespoon Japanese dark soy sauce

2 tablespoons chopped fresh cilantro

Sugar Snap Peas with Mushrooms, Curry, Coconut Milk, and Shrimp.

Stir-frying sugar snap peas.

PERILLA

Closely related to shiso (see pages 216 and 217), perilla is used as a wrapper for steamed foods and as a salad green. It is quite pungent so it should be balanced with gentler milder greens. Perilla is easy to recognize because of its heart-shaped leaves with a distinct saw-toothed pattern on their edges.

PLANTAINS

The first time I spotted a plantain was in a Caribbean market in New York, where I thought it was an overripe banana. But plantains are a far cry from our familiar bananas and are cooked in entirely different ways. Plantains are an important staple food in the Caribbean and are used in much the same way as potatoes. The plantain's versatility is enhanced by the fact that it can be cooked during any of the three stages of its slow ripening process. The youngest plantains (*platanos verdes*) are green, with rather tough skin. The flesh of these underripe plantains, which is starchy and contains a resin that will stain fingers and aprons, can be baked or boiled in much the same way as potatoes. In the Caribbean, plantains are served with a spicy traditional garlic and mint sauce, called *salsa de ajo*. In the north, it is served with butter, salt, and pepper. Green plantains are also used to make *tostones*—crushed and deep-fried plantain pieces—served piping hot as a savory with salsa de ajo, or as a sweet, sprinkled with sugar.

Peeling yellow plantains.   Deep-frying plantains.   Deep-fried plantains.

As green plantains ripen, they turn yellow and begin to look like regular bananas except that plantains are larger and usually more elongated. The inside of a yellow plantain is smooth, silky, and bright yellow. Yellow plantains are sometimes added to Caribbean and Indian soups and stews. They cook more quickly than the underripe green plantain, usually in about 10 minutes.

Fully ripened plantains, called *maduros*, are dark black and look like overripe bananas. It's during this stage, however, that plantains are at their softest and sweetest. The flesh of a ripe plantain is orange and so soft that it must be handled carefully. One easy and delicious method for cooking ripe plantains is simply to sauté the slices in butter—in a nonstick pan is best—and sprinkle them with a little cinnamon and lime juice. They can also be sprinkled with sugar and flambéed with some good dark rum for a delicious dessert.

POTATOES

It's hard to imagine that Europeans once thought potatoes caused leprosy. Potatoes are in fact related to belladonna (deadly nightshade), so it's indeed possible that some of the original strains imported to Europe from South America caused a mild reaction. In some places at the beginning of the nineteenth century, the potato was still considered poisonous (one writer claimed its cooking water could "poison a dog"), but by the turn of the twentieth century, Americans were eating 200 pounds of potatoes per person per year, which works out to more than a pound every two days.

Though we no longer eat a half pound a day, the potato has become an American staple. However, many of the best recipes for potatoes—those containing lots of cream and butter—have become mildly taboo. The result is that once commonplace dishes, such as mashed potatoes, have taken on the appeal of forbidden fruit.

There are many varieties of potatoes, but you need know only the basic characteristics of each to decide how best to cook them. New potatoes are by definition potatoes that still had the green tops attached when they were pulled out of the ground. New potatoes are usually small, have thin skins and firm flesh, and best served whole, unpeeled. Medium waxy potatoes are larger, with thicker skins, and are usually peeled. Waxy potatoes are best in recipes that require the potato to hold its shape—sautéed potatoes, potato salads, and gratins. Starchy potatoes, best for mashing and frying, include the thick-skinned russet and Idaho potatoes (russets grown in Idaho). The thin-skinned Yellow Finn and Yukon Gold potatoes have a medium starch content and are the absolute best potatoes for mashing.

When buying potatoes avoid those that have a green cast to their skin, which according to some is slightly poisonous. Poisonous or not, green indicates that the potatoes have been exposed to light. Buy potatoes that feel hard and have no soft or dark spots or signs of sprouting. Make sure the skins are firm and have no signs of wrinkling. Potatoes are best stored in a dark, cool place with air circulation—preferably not in the refrigerator—for up to a week. Keep new potatoes, which are a bit more perishable, in the refrigerator for 2 to 3 days, wrapped in a plastic bag with holes poked in it.

New potatoes.

A FEW POTATO VARIETIES AND DEFINITIONS

Potatoes, as of late, seem to have come into their own at farmers' markets and high-end gourmet stores where a surprising number of heirloom and unusual varieties can now be seen.

FINGERLING. Several varieties of potato are called fingerlings in reference to their fingerlike shape. Fingerling potatoes are best cooked like new potatoes, simply steamed and crushed with a little butter or olive oil.

HEIRLOOM. So many unfamiliar varieties of potatoes are appearing in farmers' markets across the country that it's almost impossible to describe and name them all. The word heirloom is used for unfamiliar species that may have been popular many years ago but that have fallen out of fashion. Many of the best heirloom varieties are small or unusually colored (for example, little purple Peruvian potatoes) and are often genetically closer to the original wild varieties from South America.

IDAHO. Refers to russet potatoes that have been grown in Idaho. Idaho potatoes are consistently starchy and make excellent baked potatoes, mashed potatoes, soup, and French fries. Unlike russets from other parts of the country, Idaho potatoes barely turn color when exposed to air.

NEW. Refers to a potato that has been pulled out of the ground while it still has greens attached. Small red and white waxy potatoes are not necessarily new potatoes. New potatoes are best cooked very simply—either steamed or gently simmered.

RATTE. When grown in the United States, this French variety is also called La Reine. Rattes are usually about 3 inches long and have an incomparable flavor and texture. They are best simply steamed or simmered and crushed with the back of a fork and topped with a pat of butter or a dribble of extra-virgin olive oil. They make excellent mashed potatoes.

Carola potatoes.
Peanut potatoes.

Below, left to right:
Superior potatoes.
Red Norland potatoes.
Ratte potatoes.

RUBY REDS. These potatotes tend to be waxy and thus are good in gratins or stews in which it's important that the potato keep its shape.

RUSSET. These are the familiar, usually large, baking potatoes with fairly dark brown, thick skins. The best-known russets are grown in Idaho—Idaho potatoes—but also are grown in other parts of the country, such as Maine and Long Island.

STARCHY. Potatoes with high-starch contents—russets are the most familiar of starchy potatoes—are best for baking or for mashed potatoes.

WAXY. Even though there are many varieties of waxy potato, the most familiar are either white or red and are sold simply as "white" or "red." Unless you go to a farmers' market, you'll rarely see the name of the variety. Waxy potatoes stay firm when they are cooked and are best in gratins and straw mat pancakes and for boiling and steaming. They are characterized by their thin, almost translucent, skin.

YELLOW FINN. Variety of medium-starch potato excellent for soups and mashed potatoes.

YUKON GOLD. Delicious, fine-grained, medium-starch potato—best used for sautéing, mashing potatoes, and simmering in soups.

Ruby red potatoes.

❧ WHEN IS NEW, NEW? ☙

Many of us think of any small potato or any red potato as a new potato, but just because a potato is small or red doesn't mean it's new. A new potato is a potato that's been pulled out of the ground while the plant is still leafy green. New potatoes usually look a little bedraggled because their skin is slightly shredded, an unavoidable occurrence because the skin of the new potatoes is so fragile.

Because their skin is so thin and delicate, new potatoes can be steamed or gently simmered whole—each guest need only crush the hot potato with the back of a fork and sprinkle it with olive oil or smear it with a pat of butter.

❧ KEEPING POTATOES WHITE ☙

Any of us who has peeled a potato and let it sit for a few minutes in the open air has seen its color turn to a depressing gray. This color change is the result of a complicated enzymatic process (oxidation) and mysteriously seems to affect some potatoes more than others. The best way to prevent the color change is to keep peeled or sliced potatoes covered with cold water before cooking. If the potatoes are very starchy and start to turn color in the water, change the water.

Baked Potatoes

Not a lot needs to be said about this easiest of all potato dishes, except that the best potatoes for baking are russets and that potatoes are best baked in just their skins instead of wrapped in aluminum foil, which makes their skins soggy. The only possible disadvantage to baking potatoes is that they require leaving a hot oven on for almost an hour—a waste of energy if you're baking only one or two and extra heat in the house during the summer.

You can cook potatoes in the microwave, but they cook unevenly. The solution is to cook them most of the way in the microwave and then finish them in the oven. If baking potatoes in the usual way, poke them in three or four places with a paring knife to prevent them from bursting in the oven. Bake in a 400°F oven for 45 to 60 minutes to an hour, until the potatoes are easily penetrated with a paring knife or skewer.

Even though the traditional baked potato topping of butter, sour cream, and chives is a combination hard to improve upon, try using the gravy or jus from an accompanying roast. Another trick is to simmer a tablespoon of chopped fresh herbs (tarragon, marjoram, and basil are best) in some Concentrated Broth (page 377), and then serve this at the table for people to help themselves. For an ultimate treat, try Truffle Butter (page 344) or the Black Truffle Cream Sauce (page 347).

MAKES 4 SIDE-DISH SERVINGS

4 large russet potatoes, well scrubbed

Preheat the oven to 500°F.

Poke the potatoes in three or four places with a paring knife, and cook in the microwave on high for 6 minutes per potato. After 2 minutes of cooking, turn the potatoes over, zap them for 2 minutes more per potato, and then turn them around, end to end, for the last 2 minutes of cooking. All of this turning is designed to get the potatoes to cook evenly.

Transfer the potatoes to the oven and bake for 10 minutes. Turn the oven off— don't open the door—and leave for 10 minutes more. Just before serving, cut the potatoes lengthwise along one side and push together the two opposing ends to get the potato to open up. Serve immediately and pass the condiments.

✺ STEAMED POTATOES ✺

Simple steamed small or new potatoes are a wonderful accompaniment to winter seafood dishes. I like to peel potatoes, even delicate ones with thin skins, but this is completely up to you. When serving steamed potatoes, serve plain butter or parsley butter at the table for guests to help themselves.

To steam potatoes, put about 3 cups of water in a steamer or a pot large enough to hold a Chinese steamer. Put the potatoes in the top of the steamer, cover, and bring the water to a rapid boil over high heat. Steam small potatoes for about 20 minutes and large potatoes for about 30 minutes. Serve immediately. Eat the potatoes by crushing them with the back of a fork and spreading over a slice of the butter.

Buttered rattes.

Basic Sautéed Potatoes

This dish is both the simplest and most complicated of potato recipes. It is simple because all you need is potatoes, some kind of cooking fat, and a sauté pan; it is complicated because the potatoes can stick to the pan, not brown evenly, or fail to take on that just-right golden and delicately crunchy crust. The sticking problem is easy to eliminate by making sure the potato slices are perfectly dry and by using a nonstick pan or a well-seasoned cast-iron skillet or sauté pan. Use a pan with a heavy bottom—so the potatoes cook evenly—but not one that's so heavy that you'll have trouble tossing the potatoes. If you're dead set against tossing the potatoes (tossing instills terror in even the most seasoned cooks), stir them instead with a wooden spoon or spatula (don't ever use a fork), or turn them with wooden tongs. In any case, be very careful not to break the crust that has formed on the outer surface of the potato. Otherwise the potatoes will release starch, and you'll have a sticky and solid mass closer to hash browns than sautéed potatoes.

I almost always cook these potatoes in butter for flavor. Some cooks use clarified butter (page 149), which can be heated to a high temperature without burning, but if you're careful not to get the pan too hot, especially at the beginning, plain butter will work fine. Olive oil also works well, and some people prefer it. You can also use rendered bacon fat, duck fat, or most sublime, goose fat.

If you want these potatoes to be perfect, use two of your largest sauté pans so you can cook all the potatoes in a single layer—and then turn the potato slices, one by one with wooden tongs (Metal tongs have little teeth that will break into the potatoes and release starch.)

MAKES 4 SIDE-DISH SERVINGS

Peel the potatoes and slice them into $1/8$-inch-thick rounds with a mandoline or plastic vegetable slicer. Put the slices in a bowl and cover with cold water. Swirl the potatoes around in the water to rinse off some of their starch. Drain in a colander, spin in a salad spinner, about one-quarter at a time, and pat dry on cloth towels. (Don't use paper towels; they tear and stick to the potatoes.)

Heat the butter in one or two 12- to 14-inch sauté pans over medium heat. When the butter starts to froth or the other fats begin barely to ripple, slide in the potatoes. Turn the heat up to high and immediately start shaking the pan back and forth to keep the potatoes from sticking to the pan. Cook until the potatoes are golden brown on the bottom, about 5 minutes, then toss them or gently turn them over, one by one, with wooden tongs. Brown on the other side for about 5 minutes more. Sprinkle the potatoes with salt and freshly ground pepper. Gently transfer them to plates or a platter with a slotted spoon so excess butter or oil is left behind in the pan. Serve immediately.

VARIATIONS:

SAUTÉED POTATOES WITH GARLIC AND PARSLEY. Mince a clove of garlic and crush it to a paste with the side of a chef's knife. Combine this paste with 2 tablespoons finely chopped fresh parsley. Two minutes before the potatoes are done, tilt the pan away from you and pull back the potatoes with a slotted

Baby potatoes.

2 pounds white or red waxy potatoes

6 tablespoons unsalted butter, olive oil, goose fat, duck fat, or bacon fat

Coarse salt

Freshly ground black pepper

spoon so some of the melted butter or oil accumulates in the corner of the pan away from you. Spoon the garlic-parsley mixture into the butter or oil and let the mixture sizzle for about 30 seconds. Toss or stir gently until the potatoes are well coated with the mixture.

SAUTÉED POTATOES FROM LEFTOVER BAKED POTATOES. Sautéing is a great way to give new life to leftover baked potatoes. In fact, when baking potatoes I always bake a few extra so I can sauté them the next day. Peel and carefully slice the potatoes (cooked potatoes are fragile) into $1/2$-inch rounds. Cook in a single layer over medium to high heat in 1 tablespoon of butter or olive oil per potato for 5 minutes on each side.

Hash Browns

Good hash browns, once a staple of even the cheapest breakfast places, seem to have gone the way of the french fry—downhill. Most of the time when I order them out they're greasy and taste of vegetable oil instead of bacon fat, which used to give them their flavor. The trick to making delicious hash browns is to use bacon fat, butter, or olive oil (not vegetable oil) and to serve them as soon as they're ready so they don't have time to get greasy and soggy. Traditionally, hash browns contain onion but they're also great with garlic.

MAKES 4 SIDE-DISH SERVINGS

1 medium onion, chopped

2 cloves garlic, minced (optional)

$1/4$ cup ($1/2$ stick) unsalted butter, bacon fat, or olive oil

$1^1/2$ pounds starchy or medium-starch potatoes, such as russet or Yukon Gold, peeled

Salt and freshly ground black pepper

Gently sauté the onion and garlic with 2 tablespoons of the butter in a 12-inch nonstick or well-seasoned sauté pan over medium heat until the onion turns translucent but doesn't brown, about 8 minutes. Set aside.

Cut the potatoes into cubes about $1/4$ inch on each side. Don't wash the cubes. In a mixing bowl, toss the cubes with the chopped onion and garlic mixture and with salt and pepper.

Heat the remaining 2 tablespoons butter over medium heat in the pan used for cooking the onion. When the butter froths, add the potato mixture all at once. Jerk the pan back and forth for the first 2 or 3 minutes of cooking to keep the potatoes from sticking. Whatever you do, don't stir the potatoes or they won't form together into a pancake. Continue cooking, uncovered, until they're well browned on the bottom, 12 to 15 minutes. After 10 minutes of cooking, carefully lift them with a spatula and peek at the bottom to make sure they aren't burning.

If you trust your flipping skills and your pan has sloping sides, you can flip the pancake. First drain off the fat and reserve. Then jerk the pan quickly toward you as you lower the pan for an instant and catch the hash browns in free fall. (A less daunting approach is to drain off and reserve any excess fat, slide the pancake onto a plate, turn the pan over the plate, turn the whole thing over.) Pour the fat back in. Cook the pancake for about 15 minutes on the second side. Near the end of cooking, press down on the pancake with the back of a spatula to help hold the pancake together. Slide the pancake onto a cutting board with a spatula and cut it into four wedges. Serve immediately.

POTATO SALADS

Few of us realize how many versions of potato salad there are in different parts of the world and how easily a potato salad can be varied and livened up with a few different ingredients—it may be the potato's relatively neutral flavor and gentle texture that make it so adaptable. Firm-fleshed potatoes, such as larger red or white waxys, are best for making potato salads. Starchy potatoes tend to fall apart. Potato salads are more successful if the potato slices are carefully layered with the sauce ingredients rather than tossed, which can cause the potatoes to break apart.

Every region of France seems to have its own potato salad with each region claiming to have the best. French potato salads differ from their American cousins in that the French use oil and vinegar (or occasionally lemon juice or cream) while Americans prefer mayonnaise. I make French versions more often than American versions, not because French potato salads are necessarily better, but because a lot of the time I'm just too lazy to make mayonnaise and I so dislike bottled mayonnaise that I never use it.

The simplest (and hence one of my favorite) of all French potato salads is the Parisian version, made by gently tossing or layering cooked potatoes with vinegar, white wine, a flavorless vegetable oil, such as canola or safflower (or more recently, extra-virgin olive oil), chopped shallots, and parsley. Versions from other regions of France contain apples and cream (Normandy); cheese, fennel and a little kirsch (Jura); shrimp and mussels (Brittany); and garlic and anchovies (Provence). In addition to these better-known "classic" potato salads, there are innumerable improvised variations made by adding leftover cooked meats or seafood, salt cod, olives, or capers to a basic potato salad with vinaigrette and herbs.

Whereas we Americans may only make potato salad to serve at an outdoor picnic or barbecue, the French serve potato salad with leftover cooked meats or with marinated or smoked fish, such as herring or smoked salmon, to serve as a first course.

Blue potatoes.
Slicing blue potatoes.

American Potato Salad

Most of us have our favorite potato salad recipe, usually containing mayonnaise, celery, sometimes hard-boiled eggs, and accent ingredients, such as capers, raw onions, or pickles. Some of us have a secret ingredient or two that we claim makes our own version better than all the others. My own trick is to make the salad sauce with homemade mayonnaise and plenty of fresh herbs, but my own "recipe" changes according to whim and what I find in the refrigerator or track down at the farmers' market. The mayonnaise is usually made with extra-virgin olive oil and garlic and from time to time a little saffron or curry powder is thrown in for flavor and color. Celery is essential for crunch and a fresh green flavor. Onions or shallots add the necessary pizzazz.

I use large red or white waxy potatoes because they're firm and won't fall apart when I'm spooning out the salad. Small new potatoes are delicious and hold up well, but they take more time to peel (of course, you can leave the peel on). Russets will do in a pinch, but you should slice them a little thicker than I suggest here because they're more fragile.

MAKES 6 SIDE-DISH SERVINGS

Put the potatoes in a 4-quart pot and add enough water to cover. Bring to a boil over high heat and immediately turn the heat down to maintain a gentle simmer. Simmer gently until the potatoes can easily be penetrated with a paring knife or skewer but still offer a little resistance, about 25 minutes. If the peels begin to crack, you're overcooking the potatoes. Drain the potatoes in a colander and let cool for about 10 minutes to make them easier to handle. Don't let them cool for too long, or they'll be harder to peel.

While the potatoes are cooking, peel the strings off the celery by snapping off the white end and peeling it back. Cut the celery stalks in half lengthwise and then slice $^1/_2$ inch thick.

Peel the potatoes by holding them in one hand with a towel and pulling off the peel in long strips with a paring knife. Slice the potatoes into $^1/_2$-inch rounds and toss gently with the vinegar in a large decorative mixing bowl. Sprinkle with salt and pepper as you're tossing.

Combine the celery, mayonnaise, onion, and cornichons with the potatoes by layering everything in a large dish or folding everything gently together so as not to break up the potatoes. Adjust the seasoning as you go with more salt and pepper or more vinegar, if needed. Gently stir the salad just before serving to redistribute any dressing that may have settled to the bottom of the bowl.

2 pounds large red or white waxy potatoes

6 stalks celery

2 tablespoons sherry vinegar or good-quality white wine vinegar, plus more to taste

Salt and freshly ground black pepper

1 to $1^1/_2$ cups homemade mayonnaise, such as Basic Mayonnaise (page 367), Aïoli (page 369), Saffron Aïoli (page 368), or Curry Mayonnaise (page 368)

1 large red onion, minced

$^1/_2$ cup coarsely chopped cornichons (French sour pickles) (optional)

$^1/_4$ cup finely chopped fresh herbs, such as chives, parsley, chervil, tarragon alone or in various combinations, or 1 tablespoon finely chopped stronger fresh herbs, such as thyme, marjoram, oregano, savory, hyssop, sage alone or in various combinations

Parisian Potato Salad

This is the simplest of all the French potato salads. It's unlike an American potato salad because a vinaigrette with white wine and plenty of shallot is used to moisten the salad instead of mayonnaise. Because it is lighter, you may find you prefer this version to American versions.

MAKES 6 SIDE-DISH SERVINGS

Put the potatoes in a 4-quart pot and add enough water to cover. Bring to a boil over high heat and then turn the heat down to maintain at a gentle simmer. Simmer gently until the potatoes can easily be penetrated with a paring knife or skewer but still offer a little resistance, about 25 minutes. Don't cook the potatoes until the peels crack, or they will be overcooked. Drain the potatoes in a colander and let cool for about 10 minutes to make them easier to handle. Don't let them cool for too long, or they'll be harder to peel.

Peel the potatoes by holding them in one hand with a towel and pulling off the peel in long strips with a paring knife. Slice the potatoes into $1/4$-inch-thick rounds.

Whisk together the wine, vinegar, olive oil, shallots, and parsley in a small bowl. Season to taste with salt and pepper.

Layer the potatoes in a square or oval glass, earthenware, or porcelain gratin or baking dish large enough to hold the potatoes in about four layers. Sprinkle each layer with a one-quarter of the wine-oil-shallot mixture, quickly stirring the mixture each time so the ingredients stay evenly distributed.

Serve at room temperature or slightly cooler but not directly out of the refrigerator. When serving the salad, be sure to reach all the way to the bottom of the dish—the dressing tends to settle to the bottom.

VARIATIONS:

While many potato salad variations are made with the simplest ingredients, don't hesitate to experiment with more interesting and exotic additions, and even leftovers.

SHELLFISH. Layer 1 pound of cooked shellfish, such as small peeled shrimp, bay scallops, lobster meat, crabmeat, or mussel meats (you'll need to steam 4 to 5 pounds of mussels to get 1 pound of meat) with the Parisian Potato Salad. This will make 8 first-course servings.

SMOKED FISH. Cut 8 ounces smoked salmon, sturgeon, sable, or other smoked fish into strips about 2 inches long and layer with the Parisian Potato Salad. Salmon roe can be used as a garnish on top of each serving. This will make 6 to 8 first-course servings.

LEFTOVER MEATS. Leftover roast meats—or even the meat leftover from making stocks—can be layered with the Parisian Potato Salad and then served as a light main course. Use about 8 ounces of leftover roast meats.

---

2 pounds large red or white waxy potatoes

2 tablespoons dry white wine

$1/4$ cup good-quality white wine vinegar

$1/2$ cup extra-virgin olive oil

3 shallots, minced

3 tablespoons coarsely chopped fresh parsley, preferably flat-leaf

Salt and freshly ground black pepper

BACON. Boil potatoes as described in the beginning of the basic Parisian Potato Salad. Cut 8 ounces thick-cut bacon into strips about $1/8$ inch wide and 2 inches long. Cook the strips in a 12-inch sauté pan over medium heat until they barely begin to turn crispy, about 8 minutes. Take the bacon out of the pan with a slotted spoon and reserve $1/4$ cup of the bacon fat (any extra bacon fat can be discarded or saved for other recipes). Pour the reserved bacon fat, $1/4$ cup extra-virgin olive oil, and $1/3$ cup sherry vinegar or good-quality white wine vinegar into the pan used for cooking the bacon.

Peel and slice the cooked potatoes. Bring the bacon vinegar mixture to a boil, add the cooked bacon strips, and spoon the bacon and vinegar mixture over the potatoes in layers. Season each layer with salt and pepper. Makes 6 to 8 first-course servings.

OLIVES, ANCHOVIES, AND CAPERS. Layer a dozen or so anchovy fillets, 2 tablespoons capers, and $1/2$ cup pitted and coarsely chopped black or green olives (don't used canned olives) with the basic Parisian Potato Salad recipe. Makes 6 to 8 first-course servings.

FRENCH FRIES

It used to be that the best fries were served in cheap restaurants, but nowadays in a lot of places you're likely to find thick and mealy potatoes that have come precooked out of the freezer. French-fry lovers are split into two camps: those who prefer thin french fries and those who prefer the thick french fries, called steak fries. I'm a loyal member of the thin french-fry school, and I prefer my fries made from peeled potatoes (a recent restaurant trend is to leave the peels on) fried in olive oil, beef suet, or duck fat, not vegetable oil.

I'd rather not make french fries at home. The hot oil scares me and the stove ends up needing a thorough cleaning, but the situation had become so desperate that I no longer rely on restaurants for a fix of crisp, salty fries.

The trick to making french fries is to fry them twice, unless you're making straw potatoes (see page 277), which need only be fried once. I use pure olive oil (not extra-virgin, which would be too expensive) for the frying, and unless I fry a lot of potatoes the first time around, I save the oil, strain it once cooled, store it tightly sealed in the refrigerator, and use it once or twice again.

French fries come in three basic sizes: tiny straw potatoes about $1/8$-inch thick; matchstick potatoes (the standard thin french fry) slightly thinner than $1/4$ inch; and thick french fries, called steak fries, which are about $1/2$ inch thick. My favorite are matchstick potatoes, which when properly fried are crusty on the outside but smooth and pureelike on the inside.

French fries.

Classic Thin French Fries

French fries are fried twice. The first (and more time-consuming) lower-temperature frying can be done an hour or two ahead, and the french fries then spread on a baking sheet until you're ready for the final frying. This will make it easier to coordinate the frying with the rest of the meal. When you start the last frying, you can accumulate the finished french fries on a paper towel–lined baking sheet in a 200°F oven until you have enough to serve—or, more casually, just serve them as they come right out off the fryer. My guests tend to hang out in the kitchen anyway and end up eating the fries faster than I can make them. Try serving french fries Belgian style with homemade Basic Mayonnaise (page 367)— something that sounds weird but makes instant converts.

MAKES 6 SIDE-DISH SERVINGS OR 8 HORS D'OEUVRES SERVINGS

Peel the potatoes. To cut the potatoes into french-fry strips about 3 inches long and slightly less than $1/4$ inch on each side, slice the potatoes lengthwise with a vegetable slicer or mandoline. Then slice each of the slices with a chef's knife. Submerge the potatoes in cold water to keep them from turning dark. Just before you're ready to fry, drain the potatoes, spin them dry in a salad spinner, and pat them dry on cloth towels (paper towels will stick and tear).

Heat the oil to 320°F in a deep-fryer or heavy pot large enough so that the oil doesn't come more than a third of the way up its sides. Start out by frying a small handful of the potatoes—it's safer to put the potatoes in a fry basket or spider than dropping them in directly, which may cause the oil to spatter on your fingers. Gently lower the potatoes into the hot oil. If you're using a pot on the stove, you'll have to turn the heat up to high to bring the temperature back up to 320°F. Fry the potatoes for 3 to 5 minutes while gently stirring with a spider or wooden spoon to keep them from sticking to each other. The fries should be cooked until puree soft (take one out, hold it in a towel, and pinch it—it should crush easily) but not long enough to brown. If the potatoes brown before 3 minutes, turn down the heat; if they're still hard after 5 minutes, turn up the heat.

When the potatoes have finished their first stage, remove them from the oil. If you have a fry basket, just hook the fry basket to the side of the pot and let the

| 2^1/$_2$ pounds russet potatoes |
| 8 cups pure olive oil or canola oil |
| Fine salt |
| Medium-coarse salt (optional) |

Thinly sliced potatoes ready for deep-frying.

First deep-frying at lower temperature.

Final frying at higher temperature.

oil drain back into the pot. If you're using a spider or slotted spoon, transfer the potatoes to a baking sheet. (You can accumulate the potatoes and keep them for up to a couple of hours on a baking sheet.)

Just before you're ready to serve the potatoes, heat the oil to 360°F and fry the potatoes in batches the same way as before, stirring with a metal spoon or spider to prevent sticking. Fry until the potatoes are golden, 1 to 2 minutes, and drain on kitchen towels. Sprinkle with both coarse and fine salt. Serve immediately or keep warm for up to 20 minutes in a 200°F oven.

VARIATION:

STRAW POTATOES: Thin and crunchy fried potatoes are easier to make than matchstick potatoes because they need to be fried only once. You need only julienne them with a mandoline (or by hand) so they're about ⅛ inch on each side. Soak for 10 minutes, drain and pat dry, and fry in 350°F oil for a minute or two until blond and crispy. In what may seem a paradox, if they turn out brown and limp, the oil is too hot. If they're too oily, the oil is too cool.

❧ POTATO CHIPS ☙

So many of us are used to potato chips out of cellophane bags that it never occurs to just make our own. If you have a French mandoline, you can also make ruffled potato chips by using the undulated waffle slicer and then giving the potato a quarter-turn after each slice. To make potato chips, slice russet potatoes as thinly as potato chips and fry in 350°F oil for 2 to 3 minutes. Drain on kitchen towels.

Roasted Potato "Chips"

These aren't the potato chips we usually think of, but rather are roughly cut cubes of potato that are baked in a roasting pan with butter or olive oil and herbs. They're simple to make and the result is a treat that requires less attention than sautéing. You can bake these potatoes alone, but I sometimes use them to surround a roast chicken and then present everything at the table together—a simple combination to deal with in the kitchen and a dramatic sight in the dining room.

MAKES 4 SIDE-DISH SERVINGS

Preheat the oven to 400°F.

Peel the potatoes and cut into ½-inch cubes. Don't worry if the cubes aren't perfectly even. Toss the cubes with the melted butter and chopped thyme. Spread the potatoes and any butter left in the bowl on a nonstick sheet pan just large enough to hold the potatoes in a single layer. A nonstick silicone pad comes in handy here. Bake for 20 minutes, and then toss the potatoes around in the pan to redistribute them. Bake for 20 minutes more, or until the potatoes are an even golden brown. Sprinkle with salt and pepper and serve immediately.

NOTE: If you're cooking the potatoes around a roast, you may be roasting at a lower temperature, so you'll need to bake the potatoes longer. If you're roasting at 350°F, count on an hour for the potatoes.

Roasted Potato Chips.

4 large starchy or medium-starch potatoes, such as russet or Yukon gold

5 tablespoons melted unsalted butter, or ¼ cup extra-virgin olive oil

2 teaspoons finely chopped fresh thyme leaves, or 1 teaspoon dried

Salt and freshly ground black pepper

Roasted New Potatoes or Turned Large Potatoes

Small new potatoes—no more than 2 inches long—roasted in their skins are an easy and natural accompaniment to roast meats. Spread the potatoes in a single layer in a baking dish, sprinkle them with a little olive oil and perhaps some chopped herbs, such as rosemary or thyme, and then just slide them into the oven about an hour before your roast is ready.

Another trick is to arrange the potatoes around the roast in the same pan so the drippings from the roast get absorbed into the potatoes and add to their flavor. When I'm roasting potatoes in the same pan as roast meat, I either peel the potatoes completely or remove a 1/2-inch strip of peel around the center of each one so they absorb more of the juices from the roast.

If you don't have small potatoes, cut larger waxy potatoes into quarters. You can also trim or turn their edges to give them the natural oval shape of whole potatoes. Count on about 5 to 8 ounces potatoes per serving and about 30 minutes in a 400°F oven.

Cutting potatoes lengthwise into quarters.

Turning the quarters.

Browning the potatoes in oil.

Adding butter to browned potatoes.

Basting with melted butter.

Brushing finished potatoes with melted butter.

French Creamy Potato Gratin (*Gratin Dauphinois*)

The gratin dauphinois is a triumph of French mountain cooking. Loaded with milk and savory cheese, it is held in low esteem by the calorie- and fat-conscious, but I would gladly go hungry all day just to look forward to a winter's dinner where this, my favorite potato dish, was being served.

It's hard to go wrong making a gratin dauphinois, but you'll have the most dramatic results if you use the best cheese. I usually use Swiss Gruyère because it has a full nutty flavor that melds deliciously with everything else, but you can substitute other firm, sharp cheeses.

Some gratin dauphinois recipes call for a lot of heavy cream, but I like the result somewhat more when I combine cream and milk or use half-and-half—which, despite its name, is somewhat less rich than half milk and half cream. Cream is too rich, and the texture when made with milk alone is too watery.

MAKES 4 TO 6 SIDE-DISH SERVINGS

Preheat the oven to 350°F. Rub the inside of a medium oval gratin dish or square or rectangular baking dish with butter.

Peel the potatoes—keep them under cold water if you're not using them right away—and slice into $^3/_{16}$-inch rounds with a mandoline, vegetable slicer, or by hand. Don't wash the rounds—the starch on their surface helps thicken the gratin.

Combine the milk and cream in a saucepan and bring to a simmer. Stir in the crushed garlic. Arrange the potatoes in layers in the gratin dish, sprinkling each layer with cheese, the milk and cream mixture, salt, pepper, and nutmeg. Save one-quarter of the grated cheese for sprinkling over the top of the gratin.

Bake for about 1 hour, or until the top of the gratin is golden brown and the potatoes are easily penetrated with a paring knife. Let cool for about 10 minutes—any runniness will disappear—before serving.

2 pounds large red or white waxy potatoes

1 cup milk combined with 1 cup heavy cream, or 2 cups half-and-half

1 small clove garlic, minced and crushed into a paste

2 1/2 cups coarsely grated Swiss Gruyère cheese

Salt and freshly ground black pepper

1/4 teaspoon ground nutmeg

Simmering the milk, cream, and garlic.

Serving the gratin.

French Creamy Potato Gratin.

Pan-Fried Straw Mat Potato Cake

Potatoes can be grated, mashed, cut into various shapes—usually julienned or cubed—and then pan-fried or baked until they hold together, either in one large cake or in individual "pancakes." Some recipes contain egg so the mixture doesn't fall apart, but most of the time the starch left clinging to the potatoes is sufficient to hold the whole thing together.

The finished cake—crispy on the outside and meltingly buttery on the inside—is hard to resist. The recipe calls for a prodigious amount of butter, but keep in mind that much of the butter isn't absorbed (in fact you can pour it off and reuse it).

4 pounds large waxy potatoes

2 tablespoons vegetable oil

1 cup (2 sticks) unsalted butter, in 4 pieces

Salt and freshly ground black pepper

MAKES 6 TO 8 SIDE-DISH SERVINGS (ONE 10- TO 12-INCH CAKE)

Peel the potatoes and cut them lengthwise into julienne strips 3 to 4 inches long and 1/8 inch on each side with a mandoline or by slicing them with a vegetable slicer and then julienning the slices with a chef's knife. Don't wash the julienned potatoes—you need the starch to hold the cake together.

Heat the vegetable oil in a 12- or 14-inch nonstick or well-seasoned sauté pan with sloping sides over high heat until the oil begins to smoke. (Because sauté

Slicing potatoes lengthwise.

Julienning potato slices.

Sautéing julienned potatoes.

Adding butter.

Pressing down during sautéing.

Flipped pancake.

pans with sloping sides are measured to the outside rim, a 12-inch pan will give you a 10-inch cake.) Add the potatoes all at once and press them down with the back of a spatula. Jerk the pan back and forth for about a minute—if you're not using a nonstick pan—to prevent sticking. Turn the heat down to medium, wait about a minute, and put the butter around the sides of the pan. Season to taste with salt and pepper. Continue cooking the pancake over medium heat, pressing down on it every few minutes with the back of a spatula, until it well browned on the bottom—gently lift a corner and peek underneath—in about 15 minutes. If you're not using a nonstick pan, continue to give the pan an occasional backward jerk to dislodge it if it's sticking.

You now need to turn the pancake over. The easiest (albeit scary) way is to flip it. This requires some daring, and if you've never done it before you should practice ahead of time by flipping a pot holder over and over again. To flip the pancake, hold it in place with the back of a spatula and pour the melted butter out into a small bowl and reserve. (This is to prevent splattering when you flip.) Take the pan off the stove and hold it in front of you at a height that's comfortable, usually at waist level. Tilt the pan away from you, at about a 20° angle, and jerk the pan rapidly toward you while jerking it up slightly at the same time. You can place a sheet pan under the pan while you're flipping so that in the event of a catastrophe you can rescue the potatoes.

If you're not up to flipping, drain the butter off in the same way, and place a plate the same size as the cake face down in the pan. Hold the plate and pan firmly together and turn the whole contraption over. Slide the cake back into the pan with the cooked side up. When you get the cake turned over, pour the reserved melted butter back in the pan, sprinkle with salt and pepper, and cook the cake over medium heat, until well browned, about 10 minutes more. Drain off the butter again and cut the cake into wedges. Serve immediately.

Cutting into wedges.

Mashed Potatoes

Though mashed potatoes are a sublime treat that remind us of home cooking at its best, fewer and fewer people make them at home. Instead, mashed potatoes are appearing more in restaurants—in corner diners and in fancy places—as an accompaniment to meats and fish.

There are several ways to make mashed potatoes—some are actually pureed potatoes—with each method producing a different effect. Everyone has a favorite approach. Some of us don't mind lumpy potatoes; others don't peel the potatoes—peels do enhance the flavor somewhat but make havoc of the texture. Some of us insist on using a ricer, while others are emphatic about using an old-fashioned hand masher. Any of these methods will work—mashed potatoes are a delight in almost any form—but I admit to a preference for mashed potatoes that are buttery and silky smooth. While a ricer comes close, the trick to smooth perfection is to use a drum sieve. A drum sieve indeed looks like a drum with a circular metal or wooden frame holding a screen. The drum sieve is placed over a large bowl and the potatoes are worked through the top with the back of a large spoon or plastic pastry scraper. While using a drum sieve when cooking for a crowd can leave you with a sore elbow, for small amounts it takes only an extra 5 minutes—and potatoes worked through a drum sieve are astonishingly good. An easy trick is to bake potatoes in the oven, cut them in half lengthwise, and just work the potatoes, held upright, back and forth against the drum sieve until the pulp works through. In this way you never need to peel the potatoes. However, if you're fanatical about your potatoes being perfectly white, you'll have to peel them and boil them—the baking method leaves tiny, almost imperceptible flecks of peel in the potatoes.

Many of us steer clear of mashed potatoes because of the large amounts of butter and/or milk or cream they contain. It is true that mashed potatoes can contain loads of butter (one of my favorite recipes calls for a stick of butter per pound of potatoes), but they can also be delicious with very little butter. If you're watching your butter intake, peel and simmer the potatoes in just enough water to come halfway up their sides (those potatoes not submerged will actually steam) in a covered pot. When the potatoes are done, the flavorful liquid left in the bottom of the pot can be added to the mashed potatoes. I like mashed potatoes on the runny side, but the final consistency is up to you. Adjust the consistency by using varying amounts of the potato cooking liquid, butter, and milk.

Almost any starchy or medium-starch potato will take reasonably well to mashing, but my favorites are Yukon Gold and Yellow Finn.

MAKES 4 TO 6 SIDE-DISH SERVINGS (3 1/2 CUPS)

Peel the potatoes, cut them in quarters, and put them in a heavy-bottomed pot with just enough cold water to come halfway up the sides of the potatoes. Cover the pot and bring to a boil over high heat. Turn the heat down to low and keep the potatoes at a low simmer until they're easy to penetrate with a knife or fork, about 25 minutes.

Drain the potatoes, reserving the liquid left in the pot. Mash the potatoes by working them through a drum sieve, ricer, or food mill or by mashing them with an old-fashioned hand masher.

1 1/2 pounds Yukon Gold, Yellow Finn, or russet potatoes

1/4 to 1/2 cup milk

4 to 6 tablespoons unsalted butter or more, sliced

Salt and ground white pepper

Heat the milk in a small saucepan. Stir in as much butter as you'll allow yourself and continue to stir until the butter melts. Stir the milk-butter mixture and as much of the reserved potato cooking liquid as needed into the potatoes to get the consistency you like. Season to taste with salt and white pepper. If the potatoes are no longer hot, put them back in the pot and stir them with a wooden spoon over medium heat to warm them up. Serve immediately.

VARIATIONS:

As wonderful as plain mashed potatoes are, potatoes have an uncanny ability to absorb and enhance other flavors without being completely taken over. Garlic, celeriac, fennel, mushrooms, herbs, and truffles can all be added to mashed potatoes to give them unique and luxurious flavors.

The easiest approach for some of these additions is simply to add the vegetable to the potatoes while the potatoes are cooking and then strain everything together through the drum sieve, ricer, or food mill. You can also cook and puree the other vegetables separately and stir them into the mashed potatoes at the end. Some ingredients—wild mushrooms—are too luxurious to strain out and can simply be stirred into the finished mashed potatoes. Try cooking a whole bulb of garlic, peeled, broken into cloves, with 2 or 3 pounds of potatoes and then straining it out by working the potatoes through a food mill or drum sieve. Other possibilities include Pesto (page 204) stirred in at the very end; 1 celeriac root simmered with 3 or so pounds of potatoes; 1 fennel bulb cooked with the potatoes; dried wild mushrooms reconstituted, chopped, and stirred in at the end; truffles added at the end; or drizzling with Truffle Butter.

Each of these preparations is based on the standard recipe given above and will produce 3 to 4 cups depending on what you add.

Assorted potatoes.

⚐ MASHED POTATO PANCAKES ☙

This is a great way to use leftover mashed potatoes. Just work a few eggs into the potatoes (about 1 egg per cup of potatoes), form the mixture into pancakes, and cook the pancakes in butter (some cooks use bacon fat or olive oil) in a nonstick pan. I sometimes flavor the potatoes with a little onion or garlic, but the ingredients you add are limited only by your imagination. If the pancakes turn out to be too loose, work in another egg. I like to dust the pancakes with flour—or better yet, freshly grated Parmigiano-Reggiano cheese—before cooking to give them a crispy (and with cheese, savory) outer coating.

PURSLANE

Purslane has thin stems and rather pulpy, succulent leaves. While it can be cooked, its pleasantly sour flavor and crunchy texture make it delicious in salads. If you do want to cook it, stir-fry it in peanut oil and flavor it with ginger, soy sauce, and toasted sesame oil.

Purslane.

Purslane and Cracked Hazelnut Salad

Here the texture and flavor of hazelnuts contrast with the juicy crispiness of purslane. If you have it, use toasted hazelnut oil.

MAKES 4 FIRST-COURSE OR SIDE-DISH SERVINGS

Preheat the oven to 350°F.

Spread the hazelnuts in a shallow pan and toast for 15 minutes, or until fragrant. Immediately transfer them to a kitchen towel, fold over the towel, and rub vigorously to eliminate (at least some of) the peel.

Remove any large tough stems from the purslane, leaving the smaller stems whole (don't remove the leaves). Crush the hazelnuts, just a little bit, under a saucepan or wrapped in a towel with a rolling pin.

Toss together the purslane, hazelnuts, oil, and vinegar. Season with salt and pepper and serve immediately.

3 tablespoons hazelnuts

2 medium (6-ounce) bunches purslane

2 tablespoons toasted hazelnut oil or extra-virgin olive oil

1 to 2 tablespoons sherry vinegar

Salt and freshly ground black pepper

RADISHES

I was not a big fan of radishes until I picked up the French habit of sandwiching the radish in a tiny chunk of crusty bread and smearing the whole thing with butter as a before-dinner hors d'oeuvre. The process is so addictive that you'll have no trouble eating a bunch of radishes and a rather shocking amount of butter. A more restrained approach is to slice the radishes and put them on miniature toasts as an hors d'oeuvre (see page 284).

Most of us are familiar with the spicy red radishes called globe radishes, but little French radishes—also called breakfast radishes—are beginning to appear in farmers' markets and supermarkets. French radishes are smaller than globe radishes and elongated rather than round, with white on their ends. Because breakfast radishes are milder tasting and smaller, they're easier to eat whole. You may also run into icicle radishes, which are all white and elongated in the same way as breakfast radishes, but somewhat larger. They have the same delicate flavor as breakfast radishes.

Giant radishes, until recently found only in Asian markets, have made their way into most produce stores and supermarkets. The best known giant radish is daikon. There are also elongated black radishes and a round variety that looks like a black turnip. Black radishes are cooked like turnips and make a nice alternative if the turnips in the market seem spongy or old.

Japanese daikon.   Cherry belle radishes.   Breakfast radishes.

Buy small red, icicle, or French breakfast radishes with fresh-looking greens with no signs of wilting or slimy patches. Avoid radishes with limp greens or cracks in the sides. Don't buy radishes in little plastic bags because it's harder to judge their age. Judge daikon and black radishes as you would turnips, by heft. They should feel heavy—light root vegetables are spongy—and firm with no sagging or limpness and no signs of sprouting. Radishes to be served raw should be eaten as soon as possible, or they'll lose their crunch, but you can get by keeping any kind of radish, loosely packed in a plastic bag with holes poked in it, in the refrigerator for up to 2 days.

Small radishes make a refreshing and crunchy addition to an hors d'oeuvre or crudités plate and don't require any work. Small radishes can be glazed in the same way as baby turnips, baby carrots, and pearl onions and are easier to find and less expensive than other baby vegetables.

DAIKON

While daikon comes in many varieties, we're most likely to see a standard white variety, typically weighing a pound or two (although some daikon can weigh as much as 50 pounds), and cylindrical in shape. Often daikon has small amounts of greens growing on one end.

Buy daikon that feels firm and that in no way is sagging. Keep it in the refrigerator but try to use it within a week so it doesn't lose its crunch.

Julienned Daikon Salad

Shredded daikon makes a light a crispy salad that's a perfect accompaniment to grilled, baked, or raw fish. I suppose that shredded daikon could be tossed with a Western-style vinaigrette, but it's hard to disassociate the flavor and crunch of daikon with the sweet and salty flavors of Japanese salad dressings. Daikon is difficult to push through a plastic vegetable slicer with its tiny shredding attachment so it should instead be very thinly sliced and the slices cut sliced into julienne.

MAKES 4 SIDE-DISH SERVINGS

Peel the daikon with a vegetable peeler and cut it into 3- or 4-inch-long pieces. Shred the pieces lengthwise by slicing first with a vegetable slicer and then thinly slicing the slices. In a small mixing bowl, whisk together the soy sauce, mirin, vinegar, sesame oil, ginger, and sesame seeds. If you're using sugar, be sure to give it time to dissolve.

Just before serving, toss the shredded daikon with the salad dressing.

1 (1 1/2-pound) daikon

3 tablespoons Japanese dark soy sauce

1 tablespoon mirin, or 2 teaspoons sugar dissolved in 1 tablespoon hot water

1 tablespoon rice wine vinegar

1 teaspoon toasted sesame oil

1 tablespoon grated fresh ginger

2 teaspoons white sesame seeds (optional)

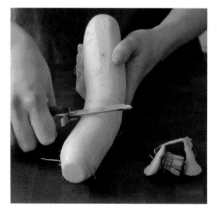

Peeling daikon.

Julienning daikon.

Julienned Daikon Salad.

⤳ RADISH TOASTS: AN EMERGENCY HORS D'OEUVRE ⤳

Radish toasts are light and tasty and literally take about 5 minutes. To make hors d'oeuvre for six people, cut eighteen thin slices from a crispy baguette and lightly toast the slices in the broiler. Lightly butter the slices and arrange very thin radish slices on top. Sprinkle with salt and freshly ground black pepper.

RHUBARB

To start out with a warning, never eat rhubarb leaves, and don't eat a whole lot of raw rhubarb stems. They contain oxalates that can cause significant irritation; eating the leaves can be fatal. On that cheery note, most of us don't remember rhubarb as the first fresh thing to come into season in the early part of spring. It is usually associated with sweet ingredients (such as sugar or maple syrup) probably because of its bracing acidity.

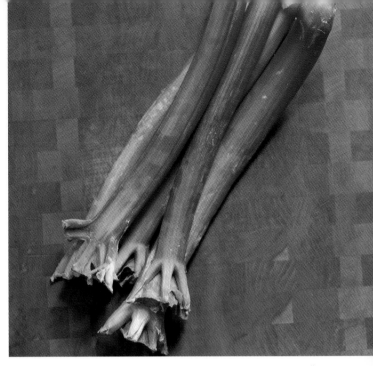

Rhubarb.

Rhubarb Gratin with Vinegar and Sugar

When preparing rhubarb, be sure to remove all the leaves and discard them as they are poisonous. The pectin in the rhubarb causes this gratin to thicken as it cooks.

MAKES 4 SIDE-DISH SERVINGS

Preheat the oven to 350°F.

Spread the rhubarb in a baking dish just large enough to hold it in a single layer. Add the vinegar, sprinkle over the sugar, and add the water. Season with salt and pepper. Bake until the liquids form a glaze on the bottom of the baking dish, about 30 minutes. If the baking dish runs dry before this, add a little more water or vinegar. Serve hot.

5 stalks rhubarb, leaves removed, stalks cut into 3-inch lengths

1/4 cup sherry vinegar, plus more as needed

1 1/2 tablespoons sugar

1/4 cup water, plus more as needed

Salt and freshly grated black pepper

Slicing the dried ends off the rhubarb.

Slicing rhubarb.

Rhubarb baked in vinegar and sugar.

RUTABAGAS

When learning to cook in France, I never encountered a rutabaga. The French are fond of turnips, but they associate the similar-tasting rutabaga with the dismal war years when there wasn't enough other food to eat. But after American friends convinced me to give rutabagas a try, I became a devoted fan.

Rutabagas look and taste like giant turnips and can be cooked in much the same way. Like turnips, rutabagas are best with something a tad sweet (glazed with port, they're marvelous) or smoky, such as bacon. They are

sometimes easier to find in good shape than turnips, which at certain times of the year become woody and spongy. This may be because they are coated with a thick layer of wax, which helps preserve them. This wax isn't a problem because they are always peeled anyway. Rutabagas can be somewhat difficult to peel because they're large and awkward to handle. I prefer a sharp chef's knife to a vegetable peeler. When buying rutabagas, judge them by weight the way you would turnips—they should feel heavy. Avoid any with soft or brown spots. They can be stored for up to 2 weeks, unwrapped, in the refrigerator or in a cool place.

Rutabagas can be cubed, sliced, or turned in the same way as turnips. Any of the recipes given for turnips will work as well for rutabagas. Consider making a gratin by making the French Creamy Potato Gratin on page 279 and substituting half rutabaga slices for half the potatoes.

Slicing the end to begin removing the peel.

Whole Roasted Rutabaga with Port Sauce

Because of its size, a whole rutabaga brought to the table and carved as you would a joint of meat makes a dramatic sight. It does need a sauce for contrast and richness.

MAKES 4 SIDE-DISH OR FIRST-COURSE SERVINGS

Makes sure that the rutabaga sits flat on the surface. If it doesn't, remove a thin slice on one end to make it even. Put the rutabaga in the oven and set the temperature at 375°F. You may notice the wax smells during the baking, but this isn't important.

While the rutabaga bakes, boil down the broth over high heat until it has the consistency of a glaze.

In a small saucepan, heat the shallot over medium heat in 1 teaspoon of butter. Add the thyme and stir it around until it smells fragrant, about 1 minute. Add the port, and the reduced broth and bring to a boil. Boil until the sauce has the consistency you like, about 4 minutes. Reserve until just before you're ready to serve.

1 large rutabaga

4 cups Basic Brown Chicken Broth (page 374), plus more as needed (canned broth will never boil down into a glaze)

2 shallots, minced

1/2 cup (1 stick) cold unsalted butter

1/4 teaspoon chopped thyme leaves, preferably fresh

1/2 cup port

Water (optional)

Salt and pepper

Start checking the rutabaga after about an hour. Insert a skewer through the top all the way into the center. Continue roasting until the skewer penetrates easily, usually 1 to 2 hours.

Bring the sauce to the simmer and whisk in the remaining butter. Thin the sauce with water or broth if it starts to get too thick.

Carve the rutabaga by first slicing off the top. Then cut along and down the sides to remove the peel or by pulling the peel away with your fingers. Hold the rutabaga in place with a fork in your left hand and use the chef's knife in your right. Continue slicing, crosswise, into $1/2$-inch slices. Transfer the slices to heated plates and spoon over a little sauce.

Peeling rutabaga using a knife.

Peeling rutabaga using your fingers.

Fully peeled and ready to slice.

Slicing crosswise.

Whole Roasted Rutabaga with Port Sauce.

SALSIFY

I delight in serving vegetables that my guests have never tried (or even heard of), and salsify (sometimes called "oyster plant") is no exception. It's easy to understand why more of us have never tried salsify. It doesn't show up in markets very often and, when it does, it's rather dull and dirty looking and frankly doesn't have a whole lot of flavor. But it does have an interesting shape and, especially when combined with other vegetables, it provides a bit of mystery and a special texture of its own.

Actually there are two kinds of salsify—salsify proper, which looks like a dull brown elongated carrot, often but not always sold with its greens, and scorzonera, a longer version—usually at least a foot—with no greens and a very dark brown or black peel.

Fortunately both kinds are prepared and cooked in the same way, and since you'll probably never see both kinds sold in the same place at the same time, you won't have to decide between them anyway. When buying either variety, just make sure they're stiff—not as stiff as a carrot but not limp either—and with no soft or moldy spots.

Salsify is easy to prepare—just peel as you would carrots—but you should wait until the last minute for peeling because, like artichokes, peeled salsify turn dark when exposed to air. If you insist on peeling ahead of time, cut the peeled salsify into short lengths and keep the pieces in a bowl of water with a little lemon juice until you're ready for cooking. My favorite way to cook salsify is to cut it into 1-inch-long pieces and then glaze it as I would carrots. I also sometimes toss the pieces with a little oil or melted butter (to keep them from darkening or drying out) and roast them with other vegetables (see Roasted Assorted Fall and Winter Vegetables, page 31)— salsify pieces take about 40 minutes. You can also add salsify to vegetable soups (give the pieces about 20 minutes) or simmer the salsify in water with lemon juice for 15 to 20 minutes, until artichoke-tender, and then sauté the pieces with butter, garlic (or shallot), and parsley. You can also add cooked salsify to vegetable stews (see French-Style Vegetable Stew, page 58) or to salads, such as the Artichoke, Morel, and Salsify Salad on page 292.

Peeling salsify.

Rubbing salsify with lemon.

Salsify and Pecan Salad.

Salsify and Pecan Salad

This simple little salad provides a good way to appreciate salsify, especially if you're cooking it for the first time. The salsify is peeled, simmered in water with lemon juice in it, and then tossed with vinaigrette. Toasted pecans are included to provide contrasting texture and flavor.

MAKES 4 SIDE-DISH SERVINGS

Preheat the oven to 350°F.

Spread out the pecans in a shallow baking pan and toast for 15 minutes, or until fragrant.

Peel the salsify and rub each root with a half a lemon. Cut the salsify into 2- to 3-inch pieces, Squeeze the lemon halves into 4 quarts of water (don't add the whole halves or the salsify will taste like lemon furniture polish) in a large pot. Add the salsify to 4 quarts simmering salted water and simmer until the salsify can be penetrated with a knife, but still offers some resistance (about the same as a perfectly cooked artichoke), about 20 minutes. Drain and let cool.

Whisk together the mustard and vinegar and then whisk in the oil. Toss with the salsify, the nuts, and the salt and pepper. If you're not serving right away, don't add the nuts until the last minute or they'll get soggy.

$^1/_2$ cup pecans

10 salsify roots

1 lemon

1 teaspoon Dijon mustard

2 teaspoons sherry vinegar

2 tablespoons canola or pure olive oil

Salt and freshly ground black pepper

Artichoke, Morel, and Salsify Salad

This luxurious salad is easy to make once you have the various elements trimmed and precooked. If you're using dried morels, there's no need to precook them but if you're using fresh, they need to be sautéed in a little olive oil. (Don't use butter or it will congeal when the mushrooms cool.)

MAKES 6 FIRST-COURSE SERVINGS

If youre using fresh morels, sauté them for about 5 minutes in the 3 tablespoons of the pure olive oil over high heat until they smell fragrant. If you're using dried morels, soak them in just enough warm water to come halfway up their sides for 30 minutes. Squeeze out the water.

Peel the salsify and rub each root with a half a lemon. Cut the salsify into 2- to 3-inch pieces. Squeeze the lemon halves into the 4 quarts of water (don't add the whole halves or the salsify will taste like lemon furniture polish) in a large pot. Add the salsify and simmer in salted water until the salsify can be penetrated with a knife, but still offers some resistance (about the same as a perfectly cooked artichoke), about 20 minutes. Drain and let cool.

Toss together the morels, salsify, artichokes, remaining 1/4 cup olive oil, vinegar, and parsley. Season to taste with salt and pepper. Serve within an hour or two.

I pound fresh morels, or I ounce dried

3 tablespoons pure olive oil

4 salsify roots

I lemon

4 large artichokes, prepared as shown on page 97

1/4 tablespoons extra-virgin olive oil, for dressing

I tablespoon sherry vinegar, plus more to taste

2 teaspoons finely chopped fresh parsley or fennel fronds

Salt and freshly ground pepper

Artichoke, Morel, and Salsify Salad.

SAMPHIRE

Also called salicorne, these crunchy and salty little green twigs grow in most parts of the world, primarily along seashores. While samphire is sometimes cooked, my own preference is to serve it raw, or barely steamed, with seafood. It can also be included in salads especially those containing something sweet, such as apple, to contrast with sampire's saltiness.

Samphire and Apple Salad

This salad is a study in contrasts between more or less crisp ingredients. You can also try using jicama, red radishes, or daikon in this salad instead of, or in addition to, the apple. Serve as a first course or side dish with seafood.

MAKES 4 FIRST-COURSE OR SIDE-DISH SERVINGS

Toss together the samphire and apples. Dissolve the sugar in the vinegar. Add to the salad along with the oil and toss. Season with salt and pepper. You can also serve this salad as a side dish with seafood. Serve on individual plates.

$1^1/_2$ cups samphire

2 crisp tart apples, peeled, cored, cut into $^1/_4$-inch dice

$^1/_2$ teaspoon sugar

1 tablespoon sherry vinegar

2 tablespoons canola oil

Salt and freshly ground black pepper

SEAWEED

When taking a leisurely stroll on the beach, it's hard to imagine eating the seaweed we see tangled on the sand. Fortunately the seaweed we buy in an Asian grocery looks nothing like the stuff swept up on the seashore. If you're adventurous and start haunting Asian markets looking for seaweed, you'll most likely encounter a dizzying variety.

Flat nori.

Wild nori.

NORI. The best-known seaweed, it is familiar as the black crispy sheets and strips that are used to wrap sushi and are sometimes shredded to decorate seafood and vegetable salads. I'm such a fan of nori that I sometimes just serve strips of it at the table for guests to dip in little bowls of soy sauce as an accompaniment to a seafood dinner. Nori comes wrapped in cellophane, in rectangles, usually about 8 by 9 inches long. If you're shopping in a Japanese grocery, you may run into a dozen different brands and most likely none will have a word of English on the package. When buying nori, look for the darkest sheets. The best nori is jet black; lesser brands will have a distinct green cast. Nori needs to be lightly toasted to crisp it slightly before it is used. This will have already been done to most nori that you buy, but if you're uncertain, ask someone in the store if the nori has been toasted. If not, just wave the nori over a gas burner—turned on high—for about 10 seconds before you use it. Nori can be kept in a kitchen cabinet for at least a year.

Kombu.

Flat kombu.

Fresh wakame.

WILD NORI. Wild nori is harvested from both the Atlantic and Pacific sides of the United States, as well as in Ireland and Wales. Unlike the nori that comes in flat rectangular sheets, wild nori is irregular and knarled. It retains its crunch even when used in soups and seafood stews. It's also good in salads.

KOMBU. This kind of kelp is popular in Japan as one of the main flavorings for Dashi (page 77), the basic broth used almost universally in Japan for soups and sauces. Like nori, kombu comes dried and wrapped in cellophane packages. The best kombu, from the northern Japanese island of Hokkaido, is almost jet black with what looks like a light dusting of salt on its surface. The kombu strips are usually 18 inches to a couple of feet long—they're sold folded over themselves—and 3 to 5 inches wide. Gently wipe the strips (never wash) before using them and gently heat in water, almost like making tea. Most of the time this infusion—called kombu dashi—is used to make dashi, which requires the addition of bonito flakes (see page 76), but vegetarian cooks sometimes use it, without the bonito flakes, as a flavorful base for vegetable soups. Kombu dashi has a lovely aroma of the sea. Kombu will keep in a dry place for at least a year. Wild kombu can be used in the same way as the familiar flat kombu.

WAKAME. Most of us have encountered this pale green seaweed floating around in miso soup. Like most familiar seaweeds, wakame is available dry. It can be quickly rehydrated and used in soups and in any Japanese-style brothy dishes containing tofu or meats or calling for seaweed. Wakame comes in two forms—as sheets and as a more shredded "instant" version. Both versions should be quickly rinsed and soaked, but if you're using the sheet version, go over it with your fingers and cut away any tough center rib sections. (Nibble a piece if you're not sure which parts are tough.)

Alaria.

Hijiki.

Fucus.

ALARIA. Harvested off both coasts of the United States, this variety of wakame tends to be somewhat saltier. It is best soaked for 30 minutes and the liquid drained off before the alaria is used. It is delicious in soups and stews.

HIJIKI. Arguably the most delicious seaweed of all, I occasionally see it fresh in Japanese markets, but most of the time it's sold in the same way as other seaweeds, dried in cellophane packages. Fresh hijiki is a beautiful green, but once dried it turns black. Hijiki is easy to recognize because it comes in bunches of thin tangles. Hijiki is never cheap, and the best brands can be quite expensive. I look for the thinnest strips, which of course cost more because any tough sections on it have already been trimmed off. To use dried hijiki, soak it in warm water for about 20 minutes to soften it. If the hijiki has thick sections or places where it feels tough, trim them off and discard them. The best way to know exactly what to trim is to cut off a piece here and there and bite into it to see if it's tough. Add the softened hijiki to Japanese-style or vegetarian soups and simmer until tender, or steamed for about 30 minutes and use in salads. Fresh hijiki should be bright green and can be kept in the refrigerator and eaten within a day or two of purchase. Dried hijiki will keep in a dry place for at least a year.

FUCUS. Also called bladderwrack, fucus is most often used to make tea-like infusions, but it can also be used in quick-cooking seafood dishes. When cooked for long periods, it becomes gelatinous and will function as a thickener.

AGAR. This is used like a kind of flavorful gelatin that remains "set up" even when warm. For this reason it is used as a culture media for growing bacteria in petri dishes. It can be used for desserts calling for gelatin and for aspics, especially those that will be made to sit out at room tem-

Agar.

Ocean ribbons.

Silky sea palm.

Sea lettuce.

perature. It should be soaked for 20 minutes before it is used—by being dissolved in boiling liquid.

SEA LETTUCE. This soft, deep green seaweed is harvested off both coasts of the United States. Use it in stir-fries or, once soaked, in salads.

OCEAN RIBBONS. This Pacific coast seaweed looks a little like hijiki but is much larger and, when dry, not quite as black. It adds a subtle flavor to soups and seafood stews.

SEA PALM. As its name implies, this variety looks vaguely like a miniature palm tree in the water. When sold, it can look like green pasta ribbons or, when more finely shredded, like hijiki. Unlike most seaweed, it is used for its crunchiness and is sprinkled on salads or warm foods as a salty garnish.

DULSE. Slightly damp and coated with salt when you buy it, dulse softens and dissolves when heated in soups, stews, and casseroles. Some cooks like to include it, right out of the package, in salads.

Dulse.

Hijiki with Sanbaizu Sauce

Sunbaizu sauce is a simple combination of dashi, soy sauce, sugar, and vinegar. The hijiki is soaked and steamed, cooled, and tossed with the sauce.

MAKES 4 FIRST-COURSE SERVINGS

To make the sauce, combine the vinegar, dashi, soy sauce, sugar. Set aside in the refrigerator.

Soak the hijiki in cold water to cover for 20 minutes, then drain.

Steam the hijiki over boiling water for 30 minutes. Let cool. Toss with the sauce and serve.

SAUCE

1/4 cup rice vinegar

1/2 cup Dashi (page 77)

2 tablespoons Japanese dark soy sauce

1 tablespoon sugar

2 handfuls dried hijiki

SHELL BEANS, FRESH AND DRIED

A shell bean is any bean with a tough and fibrous pod. Shell bean pods aren't usually eaten. Green beans, for instance, aren't shell beans, even though they're closely related, because they're immature enough that what we call the bean is actually the pod—most of us don't even notice the tiny beans inside.

Fresh shell beans are in season in the summer, but the rest of the year we must rely on dried beans, or in a real pinch, on canned. For those of us who have never tasted a bean that wasn't once dried, frozen, or in a can, fresh shell beans—which are quick and simple to prepare—are a wonderful surprise.

Flageolet beans.

Once cooked—about 15 minutes for fresh shell beans and about $1^{1}/_{2}$ hours for dried—beans are one of the most versatile of vegetables. They can be tossed into salads, cooked with flavorful meats into simple or sophisticated pork-and-bean concoctions, mashed into dipping sauces or Mexican refritos, or served simply as they are, with a dribble of olive oil or butter and a few chopped herbs.

Beans take especially well to braising. Dried beans must be cooked slowly because they take so long to soften. Fresh shell beans can be cooked on the stove for 20 minutes or so with savory ingredients, such as herbs and bacon, but dried beans take at least $1^{1}/_{2}$ hours and should be slowly baked or very gently simmered.

Home-cooked beans are a far cry from canned pork and beans. Beans that are baked or slowly simmered can be finished simply, with a few pieces of sausage, or luxuriously with duck and lamb as in the French cassoulet, or even with foie gras. Some of the best bean dishes are really meat stews, except that the liquid part of the stew is absorbed into the beans.

FRESH SHELL BEANS

Cooking most fresh shell beans is an easy process of shelling (kids love to do it) and quickly boiling the beans.

When buying fresh beans, feel along the pods to make sure they contain plump beans and avoid pods that are dried out or that have dark spots. Fresh beans can be stored in their pods loose in the refrigerator for several days, and shelled beans can be stored in the refrigerator covered with plastic wrap for a day or two before cooking. Cooked beans will keep for a day or two, covered, in the refrigerator.

Shelling lima beans.

CRANBERRY BEANS. Except perhaps for fava and lima beans, cranberry beans are the beans you're most likely to find fresh at the green market. Cranberry beans are easy to spot by their long white pods streaked with red. The beans themselves have coloring similar to the pods—white with fine reddish markings—but their color turns to pale brown during cooking.

Fresh cranberry beans always seem best simply boiled and tossed with excellent olive oil, chopped parsley, and lemon juice. They are easy to cook—just boil them for 12 to 20 minutes until they lose their mealiness. When dried, cranberry beans are sometimes called by their Italian name, borlotti.

FAVA BEANS. Fava beans are the only beans that have to be shelled and then individually peeled, a fact that discourages most of us from making them for a crowd. If you encounter them in a restaurant, you're unlikely to see more than a few sprinkled on a plate—they're too labor-intensive. But if you organize the peeling (I peel in front of late-night TV and while I'm on the phone), you'll find the process soothing and satisfying as your precious pile of shiny green beans slowly grows. In recent years, the fava bean has even acquired a certain chic (probably because they're hard to peel) as some chefs have made them the darlings of trendy restaurants.

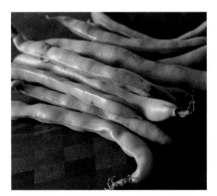

Fava beans.

When buying fresh fava beans, look for large, plump pods and run your thumb along the length of the pods to make sure they contain beans; sometimes plump-looking pods are half empty. To get the beans out of the pods, just run your thumb along the seam on one side and the beans will pop out. If you have a lot of beans to peel, plunge them in a pot of boiling water and blanch for 1 minute, drain in a colander, and rinse under cold water to loosen the peels. Peel the thick green membrane off of each shell bean with a small paring knife or a long thumbnail or by just giving each bean a gentle squeeze (see photos, right).

I cook fava beans in vegetable stews (they look pretty and I can get by serving fewer) or as accompaniments to roast meats, especially lamb.

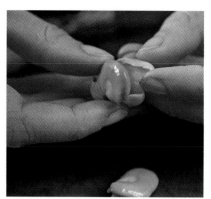

Shelling and peeling fava beans.

The classic flavoring for fava beans is fresh winter savory, but it is hard to find, so I usually use thyme, mint, or a little sage. Fava beans cook faster than other fresh beans, usually in 2 to 5 minutes.

FLAGEOLET BEANS. These pale green beans are usually found dried, but do occasionally show up fresh in farmers' markets. They're easily mistaken for green beans, but closer inspection reveals their tiny green beans on the inside. They're classically served with roast lamb, especially leg of lamb. (Try dousing them with a little jus before serving.)

EDAMAME. These shell beans are typically served whole in the pod in Japanese restaurants at the start of a meal. I never understood what the big deal is but it does seem to be all the rage. Edamame beans have an extremely delicate (some might say bland) flavor.

LIMA BEANS. It's easy to understand why most of us have never tasted fresh limas; they are hard to find. While not as time-consuming to prepare as fava beans, they still have to be shelled out of their rather tough pods. Lima beans are delicious when simply boiled, uncovered, in rapidly boiling salted water for about 10 minutes and tossed with butter or olive oil. They can also be braised with enough liquid to come halfway up their sides (water, broth, cream, and so on), a little bacon, pancetta, or prosciutto or with dried porcini mushrooms.

Edamame.
Lima beans.

Miniature Fava Bean "Cassoulet" with Foie Gras

This is by no means an inexpensive everyday dish, but it has such a sublime flavor that I can't resist including it. If you don't mention the foie gras to your guests, they'll just start going nuts over the beans without really knowing why.

MAKES 4 SIDE-DISH SERVINGS

Shell the fava beans and plunge them into boiling water for 1 minute. Drain and rinse with cold water. Peel the beans; you should have 2 cups.

Just before serving, boil the beans in 2 quarts of water with 1 tablespoon salt for about 2 minutes. Drain the beans in a colander—don't rinse them—and gently stir them with the foie gras in a small pot. Cover the pot and place it over low heat for 5 minutes, gently stirring the beans every 2 minutes. Chop the parsley, stir it into the beans, and season to taste with salt and pepper. This dish can be kept warm for up to 15 minutes in a 200°F oven before serving.

3 pounds fresh fava beans in the pod

1 (4-ounce) slice terrine of duck or goose foie gras, cut into 1/4-inch cubes

1 tablespoon finely chopped fresh parsley

Salt and freshly ground pepper

Fresh Cranberry Bean Salad

This makes a lovely vegetable side dish at a summer barbecue, but if you want to have an Italian-style dinner, serve it on an antipasto plate along with little plates of olives, sliced salami, and artichoke hearts.

MAKES 4 SIDE-DISH SERVINGS OR 6 ANTIPASTO SERVINGS

Shell the beans and reserve.

Bring about 2 quarts of salted water to a rapid boil. Add the beans. Boil the beans for 12 to 20 minutes]until, when you taste one, they are no longer mealy. Drain the beans in a colander.

Toss the beans and parsley in a bowl with the olive oil and lemon juice. Season to taste with salt and pepper. Serve slightly warm or at room temperature.

VARIATION:

Try tossing the beans with cooked shellfish such as clams, mussels, or pieces of octopus; all of these are typically Italian. A further refinement is to add the reduced cooking liquid from the shellfish to the salad sauce.

1 1/2 pounds fresh cranberry beans in their pods

1/4 cup good-quality extra-virgin olive oil

1 to 2 tablespoons fresh lemon juice, or to taste

2 tablespoons finely chopped parsley or basil

Salt, preferably coarse sea salt

Freshly ground black pepper

DRIED BEANS

Dried beans are available year-round and in much greater variety than fresh beans. They are also inexpensive and easy to store, so you can keep them on hand for sudden inspirations.

When buying dried beans, try to find those from the latest harvest. Dried beans over a year old take longer to cook and don't cook as evenly. I know of no foolproof way of judging the age of dried beans, but your chances are best of finding fresher beans in busy stores that have a lot of turnover.

❧ SOAKING BEANS ❧

It's possible to get by without soaking dried beans, but the soaking allows them to cook faster. I soak virtually all dried beans before they are cooked, sometimes overnight, but usually for only 2 or 3 hours. Before soaking, pour the beans out onto a sheet pan and pick through them to eliminate the occasional pebble or piece of debris. If you're in a hurry, soak the beans in warm water to shorten the soaking time to about an hour and a half. Soak the beans in enough water to cover by at least 3 inches, otherwise as the beans absorb the water those on top will end up above the liquid. It's easy to tell when the beans have soaked long enough because the outer skins shrivel up and wrinkle. Once dried beans have been soaked, simmer then in water or broth for 1 to 3 hours, until they soften and lose their mealiness.

Because beans absorb the flavors of the liquids they are cooked in, be sure to add one or more aromatic vegetables, such as onions, garlic, carrots, celery, or fennel to the cooking liquid, as well as some herbs, usually fresh thyme, parsley, and a bay leaf tied up with string in a traditional bouquet garni. I add salt halfway through the cooking—salt added too soon makes the beans take longer to cook and may make them tough. Salt added at the end doesn't penetrate the beans so they end up tasting flat.

Dried beans can be cooked up into stews, soups, and baked dishes using almost identical techniques—the difference is mainly in the amount of liquid that is used.

If you walk into a fancy gourmet food shop, you're likely to encounter dozens of varieties of dried beans in so many bright colors and exotic designs that unless you're careful, you'll come home with a lifetime supply. If you get into the habit of cooking beans, you may want to experiment with unusual heirloom varieties, but here's a list of more common varieties to get you started. Don't hesitate to substitute different beans in the recipes given on the next few pages.

BLACK BEANS. There are several kinds of black beans, but the most common are the black turtle bean, more commonly just called black beans, which is mostly used in Mexican and Central American cooking, and the black gram bean, popular in India for soups and stew like dishes. Black gram beans come in two forms: the whole black bean (*kali dal*) and the hulled and split beans, which are actually white (*urad dal*). Black beans, or more precisely, black turtle beans, are among the few beans that usually aren't soaked before cooking. Kali dal, however, cook very slowly and should be soaked for several hours before you cook them. Both of these black beans soften to a smooth and creamy texture.

Varieties of dried beans.

BLACK-EYED PEAS. These are easy to recognize because they are creamy white with a distinctive black spot on one side. Black-eyed peas—not really a pea—turn somewhat mealy when cooked, but they're delicious with pork and in traditional Southern cooking.

CANNELLINI BEANS. These medium-size white beans, also called white kidney beans, are the traditional beans used in Tuscany for making minestrone and *fagioli cotti al fiasco*, a slow-cooked dish made with olive oil, garlic, and fresh sage. Cannellini beans can be used in any dish calling for navy beans or great Northern.

CRANBERRY BEANS. These are among the few beans that are often available fresh, but dried cranberry beans are also delicious. Cranberry beans are very popular in Italy both fresh and dried, where they are called borlotti.

FLAGEOLET BEANS. These miniature pale green beans are a French favorite. One of the more traditional ways to serve them is with roast lamb.

GREAT NORTHERN BEANS. These small white beans have a delicate flavor and can be used for almost any dish calling for white beans, cannellini beans, or cranberry beans. Great Northern beans have the advantage of always being available at the supermarket.

MUNG BEANS. These tiny cylindrical beans come in both green and yellow. The yellow beans are simply the green mung bean with the hull removed and are popular in Indian cooking. Yellow mung beans cook very quickly and can be used as a substitute for pink or yellow lentils.

NAVY BEANS. These tiny white beans got their name because they were long a staple aboard ship. Navy beans tend to be a bit mealy; if you have a choice, substitute great Northern or cannellini.

PINK BEANS. These small beans are a uniform pink and are usually used in the same way as pinto beans in Mexican and Central American recipes.

PINTO BEANS. These beans are relatively small and pink with dark red markings, but the markings disappear during cooking. They turn slightly mealy when cooked. Pinto beans are popular in American Southwestern, Central American, and Mexican cooking.

TONGUES OF FIRE. Also called *lingua di fuoco*, tongues of fire are reddish brown with dark red markings, but they turn a uniform brown once cooked and are plump and flavorful with a smooth texture that makes them popular in Italian cooking. Tongues of fire are closely related to cranberry beans and can be used the same way.

Basic Dried Bean Recipe

MAKES APPROXIMATELY 6 CUPS, ENOUGH FOR 10 SERVINGS

Spread the beans on a sheet pan and pick through them to eliminate any debris. In a large bowl, soak the beans in enough warm water to cover by 3 inches for about 3 hours or overnight, until the skins wrinkle.

Drain the beans and combine them with the broth and vegetables in a heavy-bottomed pot. Tie the thyme, parsley, and bay leaf into a bouquet garni with string—or if you're using dried thyme, in a piece of cheesecloth—and add the bundle to the beans. Add the bacon.

Bring the beans to a gentle simmer, partially cover the pot, and simmer until the beans have lost their mealiness, $1^1/_2$ to 3 hours. Add the 1 teaspoon salt about 1 hour into the cooking. Add more broth or water as needed to keep the beans from drying out. Season to taste with additional salt. Pick out the vegetables and the bouquet garni before serving.

$2^1/_2$ cups dried beans, soaked for 3 hours in enough water to cover by several inches

$^1/_2$ stalk celery

1 medium carrot, peeled

1 medium onion, halved vertically

5 cups Basic Brown Chicken Broth (page 373) or Basic White Chicken Broth (page 374), or water, or more as needed

3 sprigs fresh thyme, or $^1/_2$ teaspoon dried

1 small bunch parsley or parsley stems

1 imported bay leaf

2 thick-cut slices bacon, cut into thin 1-inch strips (optional)

1 teaspoon salt, plus more to taste

Soaking beans.

Pork and Beans

I like to serve this dish as a main course for an informal winter dinner. My guests try their best to be enthusiastic when I announce what we're having, but they're truly delighted once they take their first bite. This recipe isn't exactly like traditional Boston baked beans because it doesn't contain any sweeteners, such as molasses or maple syrup—ingredients you're welcome to add.

Pork shoulder is the best meat to use for this dish because it's inexpensive and won't dry out during the long cooking. In this recipe, the tomatoes and wine are added an hour into the cooking. If added earlier, their acidity slows down the cooking of the beans and may leave them mealy.

Serve the beans with garlic bread or plenty of crunchy French bread and a green salad.

MAKES 8 MAIN-COURSE SERVINGS

Spread the beans on a sheet pan and pick through them to eliminate any debris. In a large bowl, soak the beans in enough warm water to cover by 3 inches for about 3 hours or overnight, until the skins wrinkle. Drain and reserve.

Trim any large pieces of fat off the pork shoulder (remove the bone if it has one) and cut the meat into 1-inch cubes.

Preheat the oven to 350°F.

Cook the bacon in a Dutch oven or heavy-bottomed pot over medium heat until the bacon renders it fat and turns crispy, about 8 minutes. Take the bacon out with a slotted spoon and reserve. Turn the heat up to high, season the pork cubes with salt and pepper, and brown them, several cubes at a time, on all sides in the bacon fat. (Unless your pot is very large and your stove produces a very high heat, brown the meat in batches, or it will release water and stew in its own juices.) Take the pork out of the pot with a slotted spoon and reserve. Discard the fat.

Return the pork to the pot. Add the garlic, onions, carrots, reserved bacon, beans, and broth. Tie the parsley, bay leaf, and thyme into a bouquet garni with string—or if you're using dried thyme, in a piece of cheesecloth—and add the bundle to the beans. Bring to a slow simmer on top of the stove and skim off any froth that floats to the top. Cover the pot and slide it into the hot oven.

Bake for 1 hour. Check inside the pot every 20 minutes to make sure that the beans are cooking only at a very gentle simmer. Adjust the oven temperature, if necessary.

Take the pot out of the oven and skim off and discard any fat or froth that has formed on top of the beans. Gently stir in the tomatoes, wine, and salt, and bake for about 1 hour more, until the beans lose any trace of mealiness.

If you find during the last 30 minutes of cooking that the beans are starting to dry out, add 1 cup more of broth or water. If, on the other hand, near the end of cooking there is a lot of liquid left in the pot with the beans, remove the lid on the pot so the excess liquid can evaporate, or drain the liquid off, boil it down on top of the stove, and pour it back over the beans. Serve immediately.

3 cups dried beans, such as cannellini, great Northern, tongues of fire, or navy

1 (4-pound) boneless pork shoulder, or 1 (5-pound) bone-in pork shoulder

2 slices thick-cut bacon or pancetta, cut into 1/4-inch cubes

Salt and freshly ground black pepper

8 cloves garlic, peeled and left whole

2 large onions, coarsely chopped

2 medium carrots, peeled and cut into 1/2-inch slices

6 cups Basic Brown Chicken Broth (page 373) or water, plus more as needed

1 medium bunch parsley

1 imported bay leaf

3 sprigs fresh thyme, or 1/2 teaspoon dried

6 medium tomatoes, peeled, seeded, and coarsely chopped, or 3 cups drained, seeded and chopped canned tomatoes (a bit less than two 28-ounce cans)

1 cup dry white wine

1 tablespoon salt, plus more to taste

Black Bean Soup

Like most beans, black beans are best when cooked with something smoked. This recipe uses bacon, a ham bone, or ham hocks, and some sherry to give it a rich, smoky flavor. You don't need to soak black beans, but the cooking time will be shorter if you do.

Give yourself a lot of time to cook this soup; black beans take longer to cook than most beans—2 hours when soaked and as many as 4 hours when not soaked.

Some people like black bean soup to be almost solid, with the consistency of chili, while others like a thinner, more soup-like puree. This depends on how much broth or water you add at the end—it's completely up to you.

This soup is great served with fresh corn bread and condiments such as coarsely chopped fresh cilantro, sour cream, chopped jalapeños, fried tortilla strips, chopped avocado, and chopped onions.

MAKES 8 FIRST-COURSE SERVINGS

Spread the beans on a sheet pan and pick through them to eliminate any debris. In a large bowl, soak the beans in enough warm water to cover by 3 inches for about 4 hours, or overnight, until the skins wrinkle. Drain and reserve.

Cover the ham hocks or ham bone with the broth or water in a large heavy-bottomed pot. Bring to a gentle simmer over medium-high heat and skim off any froth that floats to the top. Tie the parsley, bay leaf, and thyme into a bouquet garni with string—or if you're using dried thyme, in a piece of cheesecloth—and add the bundle with the beans. Cover the pot and simmer very slowly over low heat for about 1 hour. Add the salt and simmer until the beans are soft, $1^1/2$ to 3 hours more. If the beans start to run dry, add just enough broth or water during the cooking to keep the beans covered by about an inch.

While the beans are cooking, slice the bacon into $^1/4$-inch-thick slices—remove the rind if you're using slab bacon—and slice each of these into 1 by $^1/4$-inch strips. Cook the bacon strips in a 4-quart pot over medium heat until they just start to turn crispy, about 8 minutes. Remove with a slotted spoon and reserve. Do not wash the pot.

Add the onion, garlic, and jalapeños to the bacon fat in the pot. Cook the mixture until the vegetables soften and smell fragrant, about 10 minutes.

When the beans are finished cooking, remove the hocks or ham bone, trim and discard any rind, pull the meat away from the bones, and cut into $^1/2$-inch cubes. Remove and discard the bouquet garni.

Combine the vegetable mixture with the beans and puree the cooked beans (along with their cooking liquid) in a blender until smooth. Return the pureed mixture to the pot and stir in the cubes of ham and the sherry.

Bring the soup to a slow simmer over medium-high heat. Reduce the heat to low and simmer for about 5 minutes to cook the alcohol out of the sherry. If you want, you can thin the soup with a little broth or water. Season to taste with salt, if necessary.

Ladle the soup into hot bowls and sprinkle each serving with the cooked bacon strips. Pass assorted condiments.

2 cups dried black beans

2 (10-ounce) smoked ham hocks, or 1 meaty ham bone

8 cups Basic Brown Chicken Broth (page 373) or Basic White Chicken Broth (page 374), or water, plus more as needed

1 medium bunch parsley

1 imported bay leaf

3 sprigs fresh thyme, or $^1/2$ teaspoon dried

1 tablespoon salt, plus more to taste

8 ounces bacon

1 large onion, chopped

3 cloves garlic, chopped

4 jalapeños, seeded and minced

1 cup dry Spanish sherry

CONDIMENTS
(SERVE ONE OR MORE)

Fresh corn bread

Tabasco sauce

Sour cream

Chopped fresh cilantro

Chopped jalapeños

Fried tortilla strips (see page 173)

Chopped avocado

Chopped onions

LENTILS

While going to pastry school in Paris, whenever I had any money—which was rare—I squirreled away dried beans, rice, and lentils for leaner times. I remember one dinner when friends and I rushed through our sad little main course of plain stewed lentils to get to the dessert, a luxurious Gâteau Grand Marnier, which I had made that day at school. I eventually disassociated the taste of lentils with poverty, especially since they have now become chic and show up in fancy restaurants, cooked with all sorts of expensive foods, such as foie gras, goose, duck, and salmon.

Most of us are familiar with the common brown lentil, but there are several other varieties that can be more exciting. The French eat a lot of brown lentils, but they are also fond of green *de puy* lentils the size of pin heads. Because de puy lentils are firmer and hold their shape better than brown, green lentils are good in salads where they won't fall apart or turn mushy. The pink lentils popular in Indian cooking are really brown lentils with the brown hull removed. Because they have no hull, pink lentils (*masar dal*) cook more quickly than brown lentils, have a silky texture, and turn an appealing yellow once cooked. Pink lentils make delicious silk-textured soup. Egyptian red lentils also can be used in recipes calling for pink lentils. Indian cooks also use yellow lentils. There are two kinds of yellow lentil; one is our familiar brown lentil with the husk removed (the

Lentil Soup.

Lentils.

308   THE VEGETABLES: A TO Z

color of brown lentils with the husks removed ranges from pink to yellow), which cooks in the same way as pink lentils. Another variety of yellow lentil, *toovar dal*, comes from a different species and takes somewhat longer to cook than pink lentils.

Lentils are easy to cook, but I like to cook them with a certain amount of fat, to keep them from tasting flat or mealy. You can cook lentils with meat—especially pork, duck, and goose—but Indian vegetarian cooks make delicious meatless lentil dishes luxurious with butter or ghee (see page 146), cream, and sometimes yogurt. Lentils are also good with smoked foods; lentils cooked with bacon are heavenly. They can be simmered with meats, pureed or left whole, and served thick or thin as a vegetable or soup, or served cold as a salad.

Unlike most dried beans, which need to be soaked before cooking, lentils need only a quick sorting to spot the very occasional pebble and a quick rinsing to get rid of dust. They are then ready to be simmered for 20 to 30 minutes in water or broth, usually with aromatic vegetables, spices, or meats, such as a ham bone, a chunk of bacon, or a confit duck or goose leg. Lentils about triple in volume when cooked.

Lentils Stewed with Bacon

These hot lentils are a traditional winter accompaniment to game birds, such as pheasant and partridge, but they also go well with roasted red meats, chicken, and turkey. I use good-quality double-smoked slab bacon, cut into satisfyingly thick strips. If you use presliced bacon, buy the thickest you can find. Make sure the bacon is naturally smoked, not "smoke-flavored." You can also make this stew with a ham bone simmered in just enough liquid to cover for 3 hours—and use the liquid to stew the lentils.

MAKES 4 SIDE-DISH SERVINGS

Put the bacon in a heavy-bottomed 4-quart pot over medium heat. Stir the bacon every couple of minutes until it barely begins to turn crispy, about 8 minutes. Discard the bacon fat or save it for another recipe.

Put the lentils, the onion with the clove stuck in its side, and broth in the pot with the bacon. Tie the parsley, bay leaf, and thyme into a bouquet garni with string—or if you're using dried thyme, in a piece of cheesecloth—and add the bundle to the lentils. Bring to a simmer over high heat, cover the pot, decrease the heat to low, and simmer until the lentils are completely soft, about 30 minutes. Remove and discard the onion and bouquet garni.

Stir in the butter and season to taste with salt and pepper. Beat the lentils with a whisk to incorporate the butter and slightly thicken the mixture.

VARIATIONS:

Try nestling some duck confit into the lentils while they're stewing. Serve as is or pull the meat off the confit and add it to the beans.

4 thick-cut slices bacon, cut into $1/4$-inch strips

1 cup brown lentils, rinsed and drained

1 medium onion

1 whole clove

1 small bunch parsley

1 imported bay leaf

3 sprigs fresh thyme, or $1/2$ teaspoon dried

$2^1/2$ cups Basic Brown Chicken Broth (page 373), Basic Brown Beef Broth (page 375), or water

2 tablespoons unsalted butter

Salt and freshly ground black pepper

SORREL

Sorrel is underrated and hard to find. When you can find it, it's sometimes expensive, especially if your grocer thinks of it as an herb and sells it at herb prices. My local Italian grocery sells it by the pound in the summer, but as an expensive bunch in the winter. If you have a patch of garden, sorrel will grow like a weed. If you like it as much as I do, this won't be a problem. There are two kinds of sorrel—garden sorrel and French sorrel. Garden sorrel has slightly more elongated leaves, but both varieties taste and behave the same in the kitchen.

Sorrel, also called sour grass, has a tangy tartness that makes it delicious with fish. It also makes the best of all possible soups and is great, lightly creamed, alone or in combination with spinach. Sorrel, in fact, looks somewhat like spinach but with more elongated and brighter leaves.

When buying sorrel look for crisp, bright green leaves with no signs of wilting and no dark or slimy spots. Buy the sorrel with the largest leaves to make stemming go faster. Sorrel can be kept for a day or two in the refrigerator, wrapped loosely in a plastic bag. If you want to keep it longer, put the stems in a glass of water and cover it with a plastic bag attached to the glass with a rubber band. Remove the stems from sorrel leaves in the same way as spinach by pinching the leaf together between thumb and forefinger of one hand and then pulling the stem away from the back of the leaf with the other hand. For dishes that are strained, such as sorrel soup and sorrel sauce, you don't need to remove the stems—they'll be strained out anyway.

Keeping sorrel fresh.

Sorrel.

Unlike other green leafy vegetables, sorrel should never be cooked in boiling water or it will just melt away to nothing. Nothing will preserve sorrel's bright green color—it turns a rather sad shade of green as soon as it touches heat. Fortunately its dull color is well made up for in taste. I typically cook the stemmed leaves in reduced heavy cream. Boiling down the cream compensates for the liquid released by the sorrel when it gets hot. Once the sorrel is cooked, after a minute or two, I serve it as a vegetable in the same way as spinach.

Because cooked sorrel is sour, I like to serve it with fish or sometimes chicken. Cooked sorrel can also be combined with an equal amount of cooked spinach (cook the raw spinach directly in a skillet until it "melts," drain off the liquid it releases, add the sorrel, and cook for 5 minutes more) so that the muted flavor of the spinach softens the tart flavor of the sorrel.

Removing the stem.

Sorrel Sauce

Fresh sorrel cooked with a little cream and pureed makes a simple and delicious sauce for fish, chicken, and veal. If I'm being fancy, I sometimes add some reduced fish or meat broth, whichever is appropriate, but this is certainly not essential. Sorrel sauce is usually served hot, but it can also be served cold. Cold sorrel sauce is great with grilled chicken. To shred the sorrel leaves, stack and roll up several at a time and slice them into thin little strips.

MAKES 1 TO 1¼ CUPS, ENOUGH FOR 4 TO 6 MAIN-COURSE SERVINGS

Combine the wine and shallot in a small saucepan or pot and simmer over low heat until reduced by half, about 10 minutes. Stir in the cream and simmer until the sauce thickens slightly, about 5 minutes. Stir in the sorrel—you may need to add it in batches so it fits in the pan—and simmer with the cream over low to medium heat for 5 minutes. Stir in the broth and simmer the sauce, while stirring, until it reaches the consistency you like. Season to taste with salt and pepper. Serve hot or cold.

½ cup dry white wine

1 medium shallot, minced

½ cup heavy cream

10 ounces sorrel, leaves shredded or finely chopped

¼ cup Concentrated Broth (page 377), Basic Brown Chicken Broth (page 373), Basic Brown Beef Broth (page 375), or water

Salt and freshly ground black pepper

Creamed Sorrel

Creamed sorrel is especially good with fish, so good that I often make a small mound of sorrel in the bottom of the fish plate and then set the fish or shellfish directly on top.

MAKES 4 SIDE-DISH SERVINGS

Put the cream in a large sauté pan and boil it down until it thickens, about 4 minutes over low to medium heat. Season it liberally with salt and pepper. Add the sorrel, turn the heat to high, and stir until all the sorrel "melts" into the cream. Serve immediately.

½ cup heavy cream

Salt and freshly ground black pepper

1 pound sorrel, stems removed

Reduce cream until it gets very thick.

Add the sorrel all at once.

Stir until all the sorrel melts.

SPINACH

I can never get enough spinach, and if I were just a little less lazy, I'd probably eat it every night of the week. Spinach does require thorough washing and stem removal (although you can now buy it washed) and has the discouraging tendency to shrink to almost nothing when you cook it.

When shopping for spinach, you'll probably run into one of two varieties: one with flat, smooth, and rather small leaves and a variety with crinkled thicker leaves. Both have an identical flavor, but the crinkled type is fleshier and better for cooking—you get more for the same amount of work removing the stems—and the more delicate flat-leaved variety is better for eating raw in salads. But in a pinch, either kind will do for any dish calling for spinach. In any case, when making salad, look for tender small leaves and when cooking, look for the largest leaves you can find. If you buy washed spinach, you'll still have to remove the stems. Inspect spinach carefully before you buy it and avoid any with dark or slimy patches on the leaves or with leaves that look dried out, yellow, or wilted.

Spinach must be thoroughly washed, and because the stems soften very little during cooking (unless the spinach is very young and tender), they must be removed. Fill the sink—or a large mixing bowl—with cold water and then, holding the bunch of spinach in one hand, pinch each leaf together next to the stem and peel the leaf forward so the stem peels off the back of the leaf rather than just breaking off. When you get all the leaves in the water, swish them around a little—be gentle if you're using the spinach in salad—and lift them out and drain them in a colander. Rinse out the bowl or sink and repeat. At the end of the second washing, feel the bottom of the bowl or sink. If there's more than a grain or two of grit, wash the spinach one more time. If you're serving the spinach in a salad, spin it dry in a salad spinner.

Traditionalists cook spinach by plunging the cleaned leaves into a pot of boiling salted water, followed by a quick draining and rinsing; those of the modern school prefer steaming or lightly sautéing the raw leaves. Boiling cooks the spinach very quickly and preserves its color, but some of the nutrients are leached out into the boiling water. Steaming leaches out fewer nutrients than boiling, but it won't leave the spinach as bright as boiling does. Sautéing captures all the nutrients—provided you use the liquid released by the spinach—but because the spinach releases a lot of liquid into the pan, the liquid has to be drained off or boiled down, with the risk of overcooking the spinach. I boil spinach for delicate dishes, such as creamed spinach, or when I want to cook the spinach ahead of time and reheat it at the last minute. I sauté spinach when I'm in a hurry and don't want to wait for the water to boil.

Spinach.

Basic Boiled or Steamed Spinach

MAKES 4 SIDE-DISH SERVINGS

Bring 4 quarts of salted water to a boil in a large pot or 2 to 4 cups of water to a boil in a steamer (the exact amount of water to put in the steamer depends on the kind of steamer). Boil or steam the spinach until it melts—1 to 2 minutes—and drain the spinach in a colander. Press on the spinach with the back of a spoon to squeeze out excess water. Stir the spinach with butter, season to taste with salt and pepper, and serve.

3 (10-ounce) bunches spinach, stemmed, or 2 pounds loose spinach

2 tablespoons unsalted butter (optional)

Salt and freshly ground black pepper

Basic Creamed Spinach

Even for experienced spinach lovers, this dish is a treat. The cream, used in a surprisingly small amount, gives the spinach a special delicacy—the French describe it as *suavité*—without masking its flavor. The spinach can be blanched earlier the same day but should be reheated in the cream only a few minutes before serving. In this recipe the spinach leaves are left whole. If you want a smooth puree, see the recipe below.

MAKES 4 SIDE-DISH SERVINGS

3 (10-ounce) bunches spinach, stemmed, or 2 pounds loose spinach

1/3 cup heavy cream

Salt and freshly ground black pepper

Bring about 4 quarts of salted water to a rapid boil and toss in the spinach. You may have to push the spinach down into the water with a long spoon. Boil the spinach just until it "melts," about 30 seconds, and drain immediately in a colander. Rinse under cold running water until the spinach no longer feels warm to the touch.

Squeeze the water out of the spinach and reserve the spinach, covered with plastic wrap, in the refrigerator until you're ready for the last-minute creaming.

Season the cream generously with salt and pepper and boil it in a medium pot or sauté pan over high heat until it gets very thick, for about 3 minutes. Immediately stir in the spinach and turn the heat down to medium. Stir the spinach over the heat until it's hot and has absorbed all the cream, 1 to 2 minutes. Serve immediately.

VARIATION:

To make the kind of creamed spinach puree you're likely to find at a steakhouse, cook the leaves from 3 (10-ounce) bunches of spinach and combine them with a white sauce made with 1 cup half-and-half, 1 tablespoon unsalted butter, and 1 tablespoon all-purpose flour. Add a pinch of nutmeg, salt, pepper. Puree in a blender. This spinach puree can be made in advance as long as it's kept cold and reheated at the last minute (if kept hot it will turn gray).

STRING BEANS: GREEN, YELLOW, AND PURPLE

While these beans are often called string beans, "string bean" is somewhat of a misnomer because the string was bred out of the bean sometime around the turn of the twentieth century. String beans are now usually called green beans. But not all string beans are green and not all green beans are string beans.

Most "green" beans in the United States are thick, green, and round, and come in various colors, sizes, shapes, and flavors. The largest green beans are Italian Romanos—flat and meaty—and the smallest are the French haricots verts, delicate and flavorful. There are yellow wax beans and purple beans (which turn green when cooked). All of these varieties can be steamed or boiled and occasionally braised or sautéed. My favorite green beans are haricots verts, because they're thin, delicate, and bursting with flavor. Their only disadvantage is that they are usually imported, which makes them hard to find ultra fresh and also makes them expensive. You can "french" thicker green beans (see page 316) or you can cut them crosswise into halves or thirds—at an angle—to make them easier to eat.

When buying green beans, look for beans that are crisp. Avoid beans that sag, those with brown spots, or those that are slimy—you'll notice this near the ends of the beans. Once you get the beans home, you can store them in the refrigerator in a plastic bag, with holes poked in it, for at least 2 days.

Green beans are easy to prepare for cooking: Snap off the ends and peel back so that any vestiges of the original string come away at the same time. Some cooks don't bother snapping off the thin little pointed ends; the choice is yours. If you are serving green beans hot, boil them at the last minute and quickly toss with butter or olive oil. If you are serving them cold, boil them and immediately rinse with cold water—to stop further cooking. Dress them shortly before serving.

Purple green beans.

String beans.

Yellow string beans.

Kentucky Wonders.

Haricots verts next to regular string beans.

STRING BEANS: GREEN, YELLOW, AND PURPLE

Basic Boiled and Buttered String Beans with Fines Herbes

Like so many foods, green beans are best cooked simply. Here they are simply boiled and finished with a mixture of parsley, chervil (if you can find it), chives, and tarragon.

A mistake that a lot of cooks make when serving string green beans, or for that matter any green vegetable, is to heat the cooked beans in melted butter in a sauté pan so that the butter turns oily and gives the beans a greasy look and feel in the mouth. A better approach is to cook the beans in boiling water, drain them and quickly reheat them in the pot they were boiled in, without any butter.

MAKES 6 SIDE-DISH SERVINGS

Bring 8 quarts of salted water to a boil in a large covered pot. Add the beans. Don't cover the pot. Boil over high heat for 4 to 10 minutes, until the beans are cooked but retain an almost imperceptible crunch—you'll have to spoon one out and bite into it. Drain the beans in a colander—don't rinse them—and return them to the pot. Toss or gently stir the beans over high heat for about 1 minute to dry them.

Transfer the beans to a heated serving bowl and add the butter, chives, parsley, chervil, and tarragon. Sprinkle with salt and pepper and toss to coat the beans. Serve immediately.

VARIATIONS:

To make a lovely salad, rinse off the hot green beans, spin or pat dry, and toss with olive oil, vinegar, toasted slivered almonds, salt, and pepper.

If you ever start getting bored with the flavor of green beans, pep them up with a typical southern Italian approach: Gently cook 4 minced garlic cloves in olive oil and add 10 anchovy fillets that have been crushed to a paste. Stir in a teaspoon or so of red pepper flakes. Toss the hot beans (omit the butter) with this mixture and serve immediately.

I pound green beans, trimmed and halved or quartered crosswise if large

2 tablespoons unsalted butter

I teaspoon chopped fresh chives

I tablespoon chopped fresh parsley

2 teaspoons chopped fresh chervil (optional)

I teaspoon chopped fresh tarragon

Salt and freshly ground black pepper

Buttered frenched green beans.

⤳ FRENCHING GREEN BEANS ⤳

If you want your green beans to be thin, but you can't find or don't want to spring for the expensive French haricots verts, you can "french" large green beans. To french green beans, break off the ends and cut each bean in half lengthwise with a small sharp paring knife. If you want the beans even finer, cut each of the bean halves in half again.

Some electric mixers come with frenching attachments, and the ends of vegetable peelers also sometimes have a little device for frenching green beans, but both of these tend to make a mess of the beans, so you're stuck doing the frenching by hand—a task best reserved for watching TV or listening to music.

Frenching string beans.

SUMMER SQUASH AND ZUCCHINI

One lucky summer I rented a house in Tuscany with some close friends. The house was idyllic with a large vegetable garden, an olive orchard, and a gardener who brought us fresh vegetables as they came into season. But the romance inched toward panic as baskets of giant club-shaped zucchini started appearing at the back door. Determined not to let any of this wonderfully fresh food go to waste, I set out to cook zucchini in every way I could think of—sautéed with pasta, grilled, and baked—until my housemates rebelled, and I ended up desperately begging the gardener to take some of the monsters home to his wife.

Zucchini and summer squash (zucchini is a variety of summer squash) can be found year-round, but really come into their own during the summer when, as the season progresses, they keep growing to ridiculous sizes. But zucchini and summer squash are best when they're young and quite small—from babies scarcely more than a couple of inches long to the standard size, 8 inches or so.

When buying zucchini and summer squash, make sure the squash aren't dented or gashed and that they don't have any soft spots. Other than zucchini and the familiar yellow summer squash with the same shape, there are also yellow crookneck squash (shaped vaguely like a swan), straightneck squash (shaped like a zucchini but dazzlingly bright yellow with green ends), and patty pan squash, which comes in white, green, or yellow and looks like little cogged wheels.

Yellow summer squash.   White patty pan squash.   Yellow patty pan squash.

Zucchini and summer squash can be kept in a plastic bag with holes in it in the refrigerator for up to 3 days. Before cooking summer squash, scrub them thoroughly with a brush or one of those rough sponges used for dishes. Summer squash hardly ever needs to be peeled; you just have to cut off both ends.

Zucchini and summer squash are mild flavored (some might say insipid) and many argue that they must be cooked very gently with very delicately flavored ingredients so their particular flavor can come through. Others are of the school that summer squash and zucchini need bold flavors to compensate for their timid flavor and bring them to life. I'm of the second school, and I delight in zucchini with garlic and pungent herbs.

Because zucchini and summer squash contain a lot of water—one reason they don't have a bolder flavor—the best cooking techniques tend to dry them out somewhat. Sautéing, slow cooking in a gratin, grilling, and frying best concentrate the squash's flavor.

Fried Stuffed Zucchini Flowers

If you grow your own zucchini, you'll have access to plenty of their bright yellow flowers. Otherwise you'll have to snoop around farmers' markets or fancy food shops to find them. The effort is well worth it. Stuffed zucchini flowers are versatile and can be served as an hors d'oeuvre with drinks, a first course, or an accompaniment to grilled foods or roasts. The stuffing given here contains a mishmash of typically Mediterranean ingredients, all of which of course can be changed to suit your whims.

MAKES 6 HORS-D'OEUVRE, FIRST-COURSE, OR SIDE-DISH SERVINGS

Trim off any stems that may still be attached to the bases of the zucchini blossoms. Check the blossoms for dirt or bugs—you may want to brush them, but this isn't usually necessary—but don't wash them.

Heat the ¹/₄ cup olive oil in a medium sauté pan or skillet over medium heat and add the onion and garlic. Stir for about 10 minutes, or until the vegetables soften. Stir in the marjoram and zucchini, and turn the heat up to high. Continue cooking until the mixture is dry, about 10 minutes. Add the 1 tablespoon flour and stir over high heat for about 3 minutes. Add the ricotta, and stir for a minute more. Transfer this mixture to a mixing bowl, let cool slightly, and stir in the egg, anchovies, and Parmesan cheese. Season to taste with salt and pepper.

Spoon enough of the stuffing into the zucchini flowers to fill them about three-fourths full. Twist the ends of the flowers to seal in the stuffing.

To make the batter, in a medium mixing bowl, combine the remaining ¹/₂ cup flour with just enough of the water to create a paste, whisking until smooth. Gently whisk in the rest of the water.

Heat the 4 cups oil to 350°F. Dip the stuffed flowers in the batter, about three at a time, and gently lower them into the hot oil. Fry until the batter turns a pale golden brown, about 2 minutes. Drain on a plate covered with kitchen towels and serve immediately.

18 large zucchini blossoms, or more if they're small

¹/₄ cup pure olive oil

1 medium onion, minced

2 cloves garlic, minced

1 teaspoon finely chopped fresh marjoram or thyme, or ¹/₂ teaspoon dried

1 small zucchini, cut into ¹/₄-inch dice

¹/₂ cup plus 1 tablespoon all-purpose flour

¹/₂ cup ricotta cheese

1 large egg

4 anchovy fillets (optional) soaked in cold water for 5 minutes, drained on paper towels, and minced (soaking optional)

¹/₄ cup freshly grated Parmigiano-Reggiano cheese

Salt and freshly ground black pepper

1 cup water

4 cups pure olive oil or vegetable oil, for frying

Fresh zucchini flowers.

Fried Stuffed Zucchini Flowers.

Pan-Fried Sage-Scented Zucchini Pancakes

These delightful little pancakes make a great side dish any time of the year. You can substitute other herbs—marjoram, oregano, thyme—for the sage or Parmesan cheese for the flour (see variation). The zucchini mixture can be prepared ahead of time so you'll need only to form the pancakes just before cooking.

MAKES 4 SIDE-DISH SERVINGS (4 PANCAKES)

Cut off the ends of the zucchini and cut the zucchini crosswise in half so you end up with 2 pieces about 4 inches long. Using a vegetable slicer or by hand, slice each of the zucchini pieces lengthwise into 1/8-inch-thick slices. With a chef's knife, slice each of these into 1/8-inch-wide julienne strips. (If you have a French mandoline you can use the julienne blades to julienne the zucchini in one step.) Rub the salt into the zucchini strips until the salt dissolves and you can't feel the grains. Drain the zucchini in a colander for 30 minutes.

Combine the garlic, sage, and 6 tablespoons of the flour in a small mixing bowl. Stir the water into the flour mixture and work to a smooth paste with a small whisk.

Spread the remaining 6 tablespoons flour on a work surface.

Squeeze the zucchini in small batches in a tight fist to extract as much water as you can. Gently stir the zucchini into the flour-water mixture and season with pepper. Form the mixture into hamburger-shaped pancakes about 1/2 inch thick and about 4 inches across and gently flour them on both sides.

Heat the olive oil over medium heat in a large nonstick frying pan or cast-iron skillet. (If you don't have a large enough pan, you'll have to make the pancakes in two batches.) Gently slide the pancakes into the hot oil. Cook for about 7 minutes on the first side until golden brown. Gently turn the patties over with a spatula and cook for 5 minutes on the other side—flatten them from time to time with the back of a spatula to compress them and make them thinner. Serve immediately or reserve in a 200°F oven for up to 30 minutes.

VARIATION:

Replace the flour in the sage and garlic mixture and the flour for coating with the same amount of finely grated Parmigiano-Reggiano cheese. Don't add any water to the sage-garlic-cheese mixture.

4 medium zucchini

1 1/2 tablespoons coarse salt

3 cloves garlic, minced and crushed to a paste

9 fresh sage leaves, finely chopped

3/4 cup all-purpose flour

6 tablespoons water

Freshly ground black pepper

3 tablespoons extra-virgin olive oil

Flipping zucchini cakes.

Pan-Fried Sage-Scented Zucchini Cakes.

Provençal Zucchini Gratin with Tomatoes and Fresh Marjoram

This gratin is flavored with marjoram—one of my favorite herbs—but other herbs including dried or fresh thyme, rosemary (use half as much), sage, fresh parsley, or *herbes de provence* will each give this gratin its own special flavor. Fresh basil (use about 20 leaves), finely chopped just before assembling the gratin, can also be added alone, or in combination with other herbs.

MAKES 4 SIDE-DISH SERVINGS

Slice the zucchini on an angle into $1/8$-inch-thick ovals with a vegetable slicer or by hand.

Combine the garlic with the marjoram and 2 tablespoons of the olive oil in a small bowl and reserve.

Cut the tomatoes in half from top to bottom and cut each half into 4 wedges. Push out the seeds with your thumb and forefinger.

Preheat the oven to 325°F.

Rub the bottom of a medium baking dish or oval gratin dish with the remaining 1 tablespoon olive oil. Finely chop the basil and smear it over the bottom of the dish. Arrange the zucchini in a single layer, overlapping halfway up each slice. Arrange the tomato wedges, again in a single layer, over the zucchini. Brush or spoon over the garlic-marjoram-olive oil mixture and season lightly with salt (remember, the cheese is salty). Sprinkle the cheese over the gratin.

Bake for 1 hour, or until there's no liquid left from the tomatoes and the rims of the zucchini have browned slightly. Grind over some fresh pepper and serve immediately.

2 medium zucchini, trimmed

1 clove garlic, minced and crushed to a paste

1 teaspoon freshly chopped fresh marjoram, or $1/2$ teaspoon dried

3 tablespoons extra-virgin olive oil

4 medium tomatoes, peeled

20 fresh basil leaves

Freshly ground black pepper

2 tablespoons finely grated Parmigiano-Reggiano cheese or hard goat cheese

Grilled Zucchini or Summer Squash

I like to eat zucchini and summer squash sizzling hot, right off the grill. The heat of the grill dries the vegetables slightly and concentrates their flavor. I slice large and medium zucchini and summer squash lengthwise—so the slices don't fall into the grill—and then grill the slices until well browned. Baby zucchini and summer squash are also delicious on the grill, but thread them onto skewers, or they'll fall through the spaces in the grill top. Grilled zucchini are best on an outdoor grill, but you can also slide the vegetables under a broiler for about 5 minutes on each side.

MAKES 4 SIDE-DISH SERVINGS

Toss the zucchini slices or baby zucchini halves with the olive oil and garlic in a large mixing bowl. Spread the slices or halves (thread baby zucchini halves on skewers) on a baking sheet and sprinkle with the herbs. Season with salt and pepper.

Grill the zucchini for 5 to 8 minutes on each side, about 4 inches above the coals, until well browned with dark grill marks. Unless you have a very large grill, you'll need to grill the zucchini in batches. (If you're using the broiler, broil the zucchini about 2 inches from the broiler flames for 2 to 4 minutes on each side, or until golden brown.) Serve immediately.

3 medium zucchini, cut lengthwise into $1/8$-inch strips, or $1^1/2$ pounds baby zucchini and/or summer squash, halved lengthwise

$1/4$ cup extra-virgin olive oil

2 cloves garlic, minced and crushed to a paste

1 tablespoon chopped fresh herbs, such as marjoram, thyme, savory, rosemary, sage, lavender, oregano, or hyssop, or $1^1/2$ teaspoons dried

Salt and freshly ground black pepper

Zucchini ready to grill or broil.

Broiling zucchini.
Broiled zucchini ready to serve.

Stuffed and Baked Zucchini or Summer Squash

Most stuffed vegetables are stuffed with themselves. The inner part of the vegetable is carved out, sautéed with aromatic vegetables (often garlic and onion) and herbs, and then put back into the vegetable shell before baking. Usually some kind of binder—most often bread crumbs—is added, as well as flavorful ingredients such as Parmesan cheese, anchovies, mushrooms, or even truffles. Zucchini and summer squash take well to stuffing and slow baking because the prolonged heat of the oven causes some of their moisture to evaporate and concentrate their flavor.

MAKES 4 FIRST-COURSE OR SIDE-DISH SERVINGS

Cut the zucchini in halves lengthwise and scoop out the flesh with a melon baller or metal measuring spoon so that you end up with little boats with 1/3-inch-thick walls. Chop the scooped out zucchini until the pieces are about the size of baby peas. Set aside.

Heat 2 tablespoons of the olive oil in a medium sauté pan or skillet over medium heat and stir in the garlic, onion, and marjoram. Cook gently for about 10 minutes or until there's no moisture left in the pan—don't allow the onion to brown—and pour in the red wine. Turn the heat up to high and boil down the wine until only a couple of tablespoons are left. Stir in the tomatoes and cook over medium heat for about 45 minutes, stirring every few minutes to prevent sticking, until the sauce is very stiff.

Preheat the oven to 350°F.

Heat the remaining 2 tablespoons olive oil in a sauté pan over high heat and stir in the chopped zucchini. Stir or toss until the zucchini has dried out and lightly browned, about 10 minutes.

Combine the tomato sauce, chopped zucchini, sugar, 6 tablespoons of the Parmesan cheese, and the vinegar in a mixing bowl or the pan used for making the sauce. Season to taste with salt.

Fill the zucchini boats with the tomato mixture and sprinkle over the remaining 6 tablespoons of the cheese. Arrange the zucchini boats in an oiled gratin dish or baking dish and cover loosely with a sheet of aluminum foil.

Bake for 30 minutes, remove the foil, and bake for 30 minutes more. Grind over fresh pepper and serve.

4 medium zucchini or summer squash, trimmed

1/4 cup extra-virgin olive oil

1 medium onion, peeled, chopped

2 cloves garlic, minced

1 teaspoon chopped fresh marjoram or thyme, or 1/2 teaspoon dried

1/2 cup full-bodied red wine

4 ripe medium tomatoes, peeled, seeded, and chopped, or 2 cups drained, seeded, and chopped canned tomatoes (one 28-ounce can)

2 teaspoons sugar

3/4 cup freshly grated Parmigiano-Reggiano cheese

2 teaspoons balsamic vinegar or sherry vinegar

Salt and freshly ground black pepper

Sautéed Sliced Zucchini or Summer Squash with Garlic and Parsley

Because zucchini and summer squash contain a lot of moisture, they do very well in the sauté pan—the high heat evaporates their juices and concentrates their flavor. Their delicacy also makes them a perfect foil for garlic and parsley.

MAKES 4 SIDE-DISH SERVINGS

Slice the zucchini into rounds about $1/8$ inch thick. A plastic vegetable slicer is great for this.

Combine the garlic and parsley and 1 tablespoon of the olive oil in a small bowl and reserve.

Heat the remaining 2 tablespoons olive oil in a large, well-seasoned skillet or non-stick sauté pan over high heat until the oil begins to ripple. Don't let the olive oil smoke or it will lose its subtle flavor. Slide in half the zucchini slices and let them sit for about 1 minute. Toss or stir the zucchini and let sit again. The trick here is not to stir or toss the zucchini so much that you don't allow it to brown—just stir or toss it enough to prevent it from burning.

When the zucchini slices are starting to brown, add the rest of the slices and continue sautéing until all the slices are well browned and have shriveled to about half their original size, between 12 and 15 minutes. Toss in the garlic-parsley mixture and toss or stir thoroughly to break up the mixture, which tends to clump. Continue tossing or stirring until the zucchini slices are well coated and the kitchen smells of garlic, 1 to 2 minutes. Season with salt and pepper and spoon the zucchini into a hot serving dish or onto the individual plates.

4 medium zucchini, trimmed

2 cloves garlic, minced and crushed to a paste

3 tablespoons finely chopped fresh parsley

3 tablespoons extra-virgin olive oil

Salt and freshly ground black pepper

Sautéing zucchini.

SWEET POTATOES

Most of us are confused by the difference between a yam and a sweet potato. When we see "yams" at the supermarket or greengrocer, we're most likely looking at sweet potatoes. Sweet potatoes originated in South America but made their way to North America in the seventeenth century, where they quickly became popular, especially in the southeast. The sweet potato not only took a northern itinerary (actually it went to Europe first and then back over the Atlantic to North America) but also spread west to the South Pacific islands, Japan, and eventually to China—all places where, to this day, it remains a staple. Authentic yams originated in Africa and are a completely different vegetable. (See page 359 for more about yams.)

There are dozens of varieties of sweet potatoes, the best known of which is the familiar orange and sweet variety first introduced as a Louisiana yam. While this particular sweet potato has no relation to an authentic yam, the name has stuck so sweet potatoes, especially in the South, are still called yams. Apparently the orange sweet potato so beloved at our holiday feasts—and so often smothered with melted marshmallows—is a variety not found elsewhere in the world. The white sweet potato, sometimes marketed under its Spanish name *boniato*, is the sweet potato that is a major staple from South America to China.

Sweet potatoes.

Most of us have eaten orange sweet potatoes although most likely it was in an overly sweet sauce preparation. To my mind, the natural sweetness of a good sweet potato is enough; any sweeter and they're just too sweet. My favorite way to cook orange sweet potatoes is to bake them like regular potatoes, slit them open, and add plenty of butter. White sweet potatoes (*boniato*) haven't much sweetness, but they have a delicately spicy, almost floral flavor that gives them an appeal all their own. Both kinds of sweet potatoes can be cooked using almost any recipe that works for regular potatoes, except that white sweet potatoes don't take well to mashing—they tend to become gluey.

When buying sweet potatoes, make sure the potatoes feel heavy and don't have any soft spots or any signs of sprouting. Orange sweet potatoes usually have a uniformly colored skin—which isn't always orange but can vary from brown to pinkish to purple—and an elegant shape that tapers at both ends. White sweet potatoes are a little wilder looking with mottled irregular reddish-orange coloring. Check both varieties carefully for bruises or injuries that may have resulted from rough handling. Don't store sweet potatoes in the refrigerator. They do best in a cool place where the air can move. Handle sweet potatoes carefully—they bruise more easily than potatoes—and use them within a couple of days.

Baked Sweet Potatoes

Both orange sweet potatoes and the starchier white sweet potatoes are easy to bake and delicious just served with butter, salt, and pepper. The peel on some sweet potatoes turns crusty and hard during baking, which doesn't bother most people, but if you want a softer peel, wrap the potatoes in aluminum foil. To find out if sweet potatoes are done, give them a quick squeeze to see if they feel soft or poke them with a small knife to feel if the center has softened.

MAKES 4 SIDE-DISH SERVINGS

Preheat the oven to 400°F.

Scrub the sweet potatoes and poke them in several spots with a fork or paring knife. Put the sweet potatoes in a baking dish or on foil—don't put them directly in the oven because juices ooze out of the holes in the potatoes and will smolder on the bottom of the oven.

Bake for about 50 minutes. Turn the potatoes over after about 25 minutes so they cook evenly. Poke with a paring knife to see if the center is soft or give the potatoes a quick squeeze to feel if they have softened. Serve with butter.

4 medium (8 to 12 ounces each) white or orange sweet potatoes

$1/4$ cup to $3/4$ cup ($1/2$ to $11/2$ sticks) unsalted butter

Purple sweet potatoes.

Baked Sweet Potatoes.

Sweet Potato, Chile, and Turkey (or Chicken) Soup

I invented this soup one night when I had some leftover roast turkey and a couple of baked sweet potatoes from a holiday dinner. I wanted something hot and spicy to make up for the rich holiday foods. The juxtaposition of the sweet cubes of sweet potatoes against the bright red and admittedly fiery background of the soup makes this an unforgettable combination. The soup makes a great first course, but you can also serve it as a main course for a light dinner. Don't panic if you don't have all the chiles; just use more of the others or substitute other dried chiles for the anchos and other fresh chiles (even bell peppers) for the poblanos. Now, unless I have turkey around, I make this soup with chicken.

MAKES 6 FIRST-COURSE OR 4 LIGHT MAIN-COURSE SERVINGS

Soak the ancho chiles in warm water for about 30 minutes or until they are soft and pliable. Pat dry. Cut off and discard the stems. Cut them in half lengthwise and rinse out their seeds under cold running water. Combine the ancho, chipotle, and poblano chiles and finely chop.

Gently cook the chopped chiles, onion, and garlic in the butter in a 4-quart pot over medium heat until the onion and chiles soften and you can smell the fragrance of the chiles (you may cough a little), about 10 minutes. Add 2 cups of the broth and simmer gently for 10 minutes. Pour the mixture into a blender (or use an immersion blender) and puree for about 2 minutes. (Remember to never fill the blender more than a third full, use the pulse mechanism, and hold the lid firmly with a towel.) Work the puree through a medium strainer with the back of a ladle into a clean pot.

Add the remaining 2 cups of broth, the sweet potatoes, chicken, lime juice, and cream and bring to a gentle simmer—there's no need to actually cook the soup at this point; you're just reheating it. Season to taste with salt and pepper and serve immediately in hot bowls. Pass the sour cream and lime wedges at the table.

3 ancho chiles

3 canned chipotle chiles in adobo sauce, rinsed, stemmed and seeded

2 poblano chiles, stemmed and seeded

1 medium onion, chopped

2 cloves garlic, chopped

2 tablespoons unsalted butter or pure olive oil

4 cups broth, preferably Basic Brown Chicken Broth (page 373) or Basic Turkey Broth (page 374)

2 baked sweet potatoes, peeled and cut into 1/2-inch cubes

2 cups strips or 1/2-inch cubes cooked turkey or chicken (1 double chicken breast will provide enough meat)

Juice of 2 limes, or more to taste

1/2 cup heavy cream

Salt and freshly ground black pepper

CONDIMENTS

Sour cream

Lime wedges

SWISS CHARD

This lovely leafy green is often ignored by American cooks who prefer the gentler flavor of spinach. Though Swiss chard can be cooked in the same way as spinach, Swiss chard has a meatier texture and a more forthright, earthy flavor. It comes in red, yellow, and green with the red Swiss chard (sometimes called rhubarb chard) being the stronger tasting of the three. Red Swiss chard—which actually has green leaves and red stems—tastes like beets, its close relative. I sometimes combine the milder green Swiss chard (with white stems) or yellow Swiss chard with equal parts of the red-stemmed variety, but most people prefer to stick with one or the other. I especially like to serve Swiss chard as an accompaniment to red meats or grilled seafood that keep up with its flavor, or as an addition to pasta.

Swiss chard can be washed in the same way as spinach, but you may want to use a small scrub brush to get rid of any sand and grit that is likely to accumulate on the stems. Unless you're using very young Swiss chard, cut the stems away from the greens by unfolding each leaf flat on a cutting board and quickly cutting along each side of the stem with a sharp paring knife. I use the stems in most recipes, along with the leaves.

Swiss chard is usually sold in 10- or 20-ounce bunches with half the weight made up of stems and half the weight of leaves. Buy Swiss chard with large leaves, which are easier to clean and trim. Look for crisp and fresh leaves with no dark or moist patches, and avoid Swiss chard with cracked or dried-out stems. Check the stalks of tight bunches to make sure they aren't slimy. You can store Swiss chard, wrapped in a paper bag sprinkled with water, in the refrigerator for up to 3 days, or in a bowl of water— the whole thing covered with a plastic bag—for up to 5 days. Swiss chard can be boiled, steamed, sautéed, and added to soups and stuffings. It can be used in most recipes calling for spinach or kale.

Swiss chard.

Swiss chard.

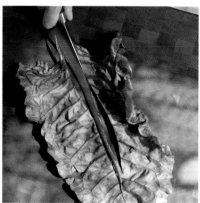

Stemming Swiss chard.

Shredding Swiss chard.

Sautéed Swiss Chard

The easiest way to cook Swiss chard is to stir it in a little oil or butter over medium to high heat until the leaves soften and turn bright green. Many cooks throw out the brittle stems, but this seems wasteful, so I sauté the stems along with the leaves.

Swiss chard has relatively tough leaves that are softened by sautéing. Because of its deep earthy flavor, it goes especially well with olive oil and garlic.

MAKES 4 SIDE-DISH SERVINGS

Wash the Swiss chard in a large bowl of cold water, lift the leaves out of the water and drain in a colander. Repeat the washing and draining until there is no sand or grit left in the bottom of the bowl. If the insides of the stems are gritty, scrub them gently with a small brush.

If the Swiss chard is fully mature—the stems are thicker than $1/4$ inch—cut the leaves away from the stems. Cut the stems in half lengthwise, and then slice them into approximate $1/4$-inch dice. Cut the Swiss chard leaves across into $1/2$-inch-wide strips. (This is easiest if you stack and roll up the leaves and then slice the roll.) If you're using baby chard, don't bother separating the leaves and stems; just cut the leaves and stems together into $1/2$-inch-wide strips. If the Swiss chard is young and tender, I slice the leaves, with their stems, crosswise into $1/2$-inch-wide strands.

Heat the olive oil in a 12- or 15-inch sauté pan over medium heat with the garlic and sauté gently for 2 minutes.

If you're using tender leaves with their stems, turn the heat up to high and stir the Swiss chard in the oil for 2 to 4 minutes, until the leaves are completely limp.

If you've cut out the stems, add the diced Swiss chard stems to the garlic mixture and stir every couple of minutes for 6 to 10 minutes, or until the cubes become translucent and tender. Turn the heat up to high and stir in the leaves. If there's not enough room for all the leaves in the pan, add only half the leaves and wait a

1 pound loose Swiss chard, or 2 (10-ounce) bunches

3 tablespoons extra-virgin olive oil

3 cloves garlic, minced

Salt and freshly ground black pepper

minute before adding the rest. Stir the leaves for 4 to 6 minutes—the exact time will depend on the age of the leaves—until the leaves soften.

Season with salt and pepper and serve immediately.

VARIATIONS:

SWISS CHARD WITH GARLIC AND ANCHOVIES. Anchovies are a delicious complement to Swiss chard. Even confirmed anchovy haters are unlikely to be bothered by them or, for that matter, to be certain they're there. If the anchovies seem strong or you're worried about your guests, soak 10 anchovy fillets in cold water for 5 minutes and pat them dry on paper towels—otherwise, just chop them without soaking. Finely chop the fillets—almost to a paste. Prepare the recipe above, but stir the chopped anchovies into the hot oil and garlic mixture a minute before adding the leaves.

SWISS CHARD WITH BUTTER AND SHALLOTS. Heat 3 tablespoons of unsalted butter in a 12- to 15-inch sauté pan over medium heat. When the butter begins to froth, stir in 2 tablespoons of finely chopped shallots and finish preparing in the same way as for the recipe above, without the garlic.

SWISS CHARD WITH BACON, PANCETTA, OR PROSCIUTTO. The smoky or cured flavor of these ingredients is a perfect match for Swiss chard. Cut 4 ounces bacon or pancetta into 1/4-inch cubes and cook in a sauté pan over medium-low heat until they release fat and barely turn crispy, about 8 minutes. If you're using prosciutto, which is leaner, sauté it gently for a minute or two in 1 tablespoon of olive oil, unsalted butter, or rendered fat from the outside of the prosciutto before adding the Swiss chard.

Scoop the cubes of meat out of the fat, drain, and reserve. Cook the Swiss chard, starting with the diced stems, as described in the recipe above, but leave out the garlic. Stir in the meat cubes just before serving.

Yellow chard.

TAMARIND

A bean that comes in a large brown pod with a flaky dried peel, tamarind is not used for the bean itself but for the sticky sour flesh that surrounds each bean. This paste is dissolved in Southeast Asian soups and sauces to give them an acidity that would probably come from lime or vinegar in the West.

To prepare tamarind, don't try to pull away the paste with your fingers—you'll end up with a gluey mess. Instead, peel the tamarind and soak it in hot liquid to dissolve the paste.

Tamarind paste.

Tamarind pod.

TARO

Closely resembling a tuber, taro is really a corm which, according to Webster's, is a kind of "underground stem." There are two varieties. One is large (or larger), cylindrical, and covered with a rough, dark brown skin. The other, smaller, is often crescent shaped—being brown, some look strikingly like croissants—and is sometimes called Chinese taro perhaps because the Chinese prefer this variety.

Taro has been a mainstay of human civilization for 10,000 years. It was used widely in Mediterranean cooking before potatoes, imported from the New World, became popular. It is still used throughout Africa, Hawaii, the Philippines, Japan, China, and the Caribbean.

Despite its off-putting appearance, taro has a very appealing aroma and flavor once cooked. Don't try eating taro raw because of the irritating oxalate crystals it contains—you'll feel like you ate a mouthful of cactus needles. In fact, it's a good idea to use gloves when handling it raw. Taro can be boiled, steamed, or fried. When boiled or steamed, it is much like potatoes but with a rich creamy—some say coconut—

Taro.

flavor and aroma. The only downside versus the potato is the rather sickly gray the taro turns after cooking.

When buying taro, make sure it is hard to the touch and that there are no moist spots or patches of mold. Keep taro in the refrigerator spread out in a way that lets air circulate.

To boil taro, peel it and simmer it for about 30 minutes in just enough water to cover. You can also leave the peel on and slip it off (or strain it out with a food mill) once the taro is cooked. Steaming takes about the same amount of time. Large taro may take a little longer. Once done, mash the taro as you would potatoes and serve it with plenty of butter. You can also make a cream soup with taro in much the same way you would make the Basic Creamed Soup on page 60, except that instead of finishing the soup with cream, finish it with coconut milk.

Peeling taro.

Taro sliced open to reveal the flesh.

TOMATILLOS

Sometimes called green tomatoes, tomatillos are a completely different vegetable (well, actually a fruit) and shouldn't be confused with underripe tomatoes. Tomatillos are related to gooseberries—a relationship easy to see because both have a thin, papery sheath enclosing the green fruit.

Tomatillos give a bright, sour tang to Mexican-style sauces and stews. They're irresistible when they're simmered with chiles, onions, garlic, and cilantro, and they make great sauces for poultry, seafood, and traditional Mexican treats, such as enchiladas.

Don't buy fully ripened tomatillos that are starting to turn purple or pale yellow or white—ripe tomatillos have less of the sourness so essential to the tomatillo's character. Buy tomatillos that are firm and a uniform pale green covered with a papery sheath. When you peel back the sheath, the tomatillo inside should feel slightly sticky to the touch. Store tomatillos in the refrigerator, in a paper bag or in a plastic bag with holes poked in it, for up to 3 days. Canned tomatillos work almost as well as fresh.

Tomatillos.

Cooked Tomatillo Salsa (*Salsa Verde*)

I never get tired of this sauce and could spoon it over just about anything, not just Mexican food. It's delicious over grilled chicken, sautéed fish or veal, and, of course, Mexican dishes, such as enchiladas or the chiles rellenos. Cool sour cream makes a delightful contrast to the stark acidity of the sauce, so I usually serve it at the table at the same time.

MAKES 1¹/₂ CUPS; ENOUGH SAUCE FOR ABOUT 6 MAIN-COURSE SERVINGS

If you're using fresh tomatillos, peel off their papery husks and rinse in a colander. If you're using canned tomatillos, just drain them. Chop the tomatillos coarsely by hand or in a food processor. (Canned tomatillos are best chopped by hand because they're so soft, the food processor may turn them to mush. Be sure to leave the tomatillos a little chunky, about the consistency of hamburger relish.

Heat the oil in a heavy-bottomed pot over medium heat and stir in the onion, garlic, and jalapeños. Cook the mixture gently, while stirring, until the onion turns translucent but doesn't brown, about 10 minutes. Add the chopped tomatillos and the broth and cover the pot. Simmer gently for 10 minutes for fresh tomatillos or only 5 minutes if you're using canned tomatillos. Strain if you want a perfectly smooth sauce, but this isn't necessary. Stir in the cilantro and season to taste with salt. Serve hot.

8 ounces fresh tomatillos or 1 (11-ounce) can, drained

2 tablespoons olive oil, unsalted butter, or rendered bacon fat

1 medium white onion, minced

3 cloves garlic, minced

3 jalapeños, seeded and minced

1 cup broth, preferably Basic Brown Chicken Broth (page 373), or water

2 tablespoons finely chopped fresh cilantro

Salt

Peeling the husks away from tomatillos.

TOMATOES

While botanists claim that tomatoes are actually fruits and not vegetables (a fruit is formed from a fertilized flower and has seeds, a vegetable is the plant itself or a part of the vegetable, like the leaves or roots), the only meaningful difference for the cook is that vegetables are savory, and fruits are sweet. While it's true that tomatoes can be quite sweet—sweeter than some fruits—I've never made a tomato dessert. While I know such a thing is possible (Alain Passard, at *L'Arpège* in Paris makes a sweet tomato confit), our associations with sliced tomatoes on hamburgers or as ingredients in salads makes tomato desserts seem odd.

Few vegetables cause as much complaining as tomatoes. Part of the problem is that we're used to eating tomatoes year-round, and we expect them always to be bright red and juicy. Out-of-season tomatoes are usually mealy in the mouth and an anemic pink to the eye. In the winter the only good (but not great) tomatoes come from distant places and are sold at the price of a good cut of beef. And they're never as good as in-season local tomatoes.

Heirloom tomato slices.

The best solution is to grow your own, but if you don't have the inclination or the space, your best bet is to buy heirloom tomatoes at a local farmers' market where the tomatoes won't have been picked prematurely in anticipation of their being shipped long distances. The best tomatoes will, at times, feel a little sticky from their natural sugars. When you give them a sniff, they will smell like tomatoes. While some, such as plum tomatoes, are meant to be firm textured, most tomatoes should feel a little soft when you give them a gentle squeeze. Tomatoes with some stem still attached are often better than tomatoes with no stem at all. Be suspicious of tomatoes that are perfectly smooth and firm to the touch.

Tomatoes come in dozens of varieties and in all shapes, sizes, and colors, Plum tomatoes are relatively firm and are best for sauces, but any tomato can be used in a sauce, and you're always better off buying a ripe in-season tomato regardless of variety. Beefsteak tomatoes are enormous and make beautiful giant slices that are great on hamburgers. Cherry tomatoes are, of course, small and are sometimes the sweetest tomatoes of all. Yellow, orange, purple, and white tomatoes and variegated heirloom tomatoes reminiscent of nineteenth-century still lifes show up at farmers' markets in the summer.

If you need to keep your tomatoes for a day or two, keep them in a brown paper bag at room temperature, which will allow them to continue to ripen without spoiling. Don't refrigerate tomatoes unless they are already overripe. Peeled tomatoes and raw tomato sauces keep for 2 days, covered, in the refrigerator. Tomato sauces can also be frozen for up to a year.

My favorite way to eat the best ripe summer tomatoes is just to slice them and sprinkle them with a little olive oil. If still feeling a bit restive, I'll add shredded fresh basil. Less-than-perfect tomatoes or tomatoes that are to be cooked should be peeled and seeded. The flavor and texture of less-than-perfect tomatoes are also improved if they're sprinkled with salt.

Tomato and Onion Salad with Fresh Basil

I serve this ultimately simple tomato salad as a first course at a simple lunch or dinner and follow it with a little pasta and some fruit and cheese to make a complete summer meal.

MAKES 4 FIRST-COURSE SERVINGS

Slice the tomatoes a little less than $1/4$-inch thick. Slice the onion as thinly as you can—a plastic vegetable slicer is great for this—and overlap the slices with the tomato slices on a platter or on individual plates. Sprinkle the basil leaves over the salad and drizzle the salad with the olive oil and vinegar. Season with salt and pepper. Serve right away.

5 medium tomatoes

1 medium red onion

About 20 basil leaves

3 tablespoons extra-virgin olive oil

1 tablespoon sherry vinegar or good-quality balsamic vinegar

Salt and freshly ground black pepper

Grilled Tomatoes with Basil and Parmesan

These tomatoes—one of my summer favorites—grab everyone's attention and are a snap to make. If it's late in the tomato season and too cold to barbecue, these tomatoes can also be baked. Here I suggest a half a tomato per person, but if your guests are big eaters, double the amounts and serve everyone two halves.

MAKES 4 SIDE-DISH SERVINGS

Prepare a hot fire in a grill. Alternatively preheat the oven to 400°F.

In a small bowl, combine the garlic paste, basil, olive oil, and Parmesan cheese and spoon the mixture into the tomato halves, fitting it into the little openings where there were once seeds.

Grill the tomatoes, flat side up, for 15 to 20 minutes, until they soften and you see them bubbling. (If you're baking the tomatoes, oil a baking dish just large enough to hold the tomatoes in a single layer. Bake for 40 minutes.)

Season with salt and pepper and serve immediately. Handle carefully as the tomatoes are very fragile.

1 clove garlic, minced and crushed to a paste

20 basil or flat-leaf parsley leaves, finely chopped

1 tablespoon extra-virgin olive oil

$1/4$ cup finely grated Parmigiano-Reggiano cheese

2 large tomatoes, seeded and halved crosswise

Salt and freshly ground black pepper

Grape tomatoes.

Heirloom tomatoes.

San Marzanoa tomatoes.

Cherry Tomato Salad

For a dramatic, albeit laborious, approach, try peeling cherry tomatoes for this exciting salad. If you don't want to peel, cut the tomatoes in half through the equator so the juice doesn't squirt out with a sudden burst in the mouth.

MAKES 4 FIRST-COURSE SERVINGS

Bring about 4 quarts of water to a rapid boil. Plunge the cherry tomatoes into the boil water and leave for 30 to 60 seconds. (Try peeling one after 30 seconds to make sure the peel will come off.) and immediately drain in a colander. Refresh with cold water. Peel.

Toss the cherry tomatoes with the basil, olive oil, and vinegar. Season with salt and pepper and serve.

2 pints cherry tomatoes

2 tablespoons chopped basil or spicy basil

3 tablespoons extra-virgin olive oil

1 tablespoon sherry vinegar

Salt and freshly ground black pepper

Slow-Baked Cherry Tomatoes with Herbs

I discovered this dish by accident, when one of my students left a tray of baked cherry tomatoes in the oven for 2 hours. Fortunately the oven wasn't turned too high and, curious, I risked tasting one of the sad and wizened little mistakes. What a revelation! These tomatoes have the intense flavor of sun-dried tomatoes with the bright taste and texture of fresh.

These tomatoes make a great cocktail party hors d'oeuvre, but you'll need to pass cocktail napkins for wiping sticky fingers. Or you can get fancy and put one or more of the tomato halves in tiny tartlet shells or spread them on croutons. This recipe is designed for the relatively large store-bought cherry tomatoes, but if you grow your own or have access to the tiny "grape" cherry tomatoes, increase the number of tomatoes to 60.

MAKES HORS D'OEUVRES FOR 15

Preheat the oven to 300°F.

Cut the cherry tomatoes in half crosswise and squeeze the seeds out of each half. Brush a baking dish large enough to hold the tomatoes in a single layer with a thin coating of the olive oil. Arrange the tomatoes, flat side up, in the dish. If the tomatoes don't stay upright in the dish, make a tiny slice on the bottom of each one so they rest flat.

Crush the minced garlic with the side of a chef's knife on a cutting board until you obtain a smooth paste. In a small bowl, combine the garlic with the remaining olive oil, the herbs, and Parmesan cheese. Use a small spoon to drizzle the olive oil mixture into each of the tomatoes.

Sprinkle the tomatoes with salt and bake for about 2 hours, or slightly less if your tomatoes are extremely small. The tomatoes should be shriveled and lightly browned around the edges. Serve as soon as they come out of the oven.

45 cherry tomatoes, stemmed

1/4 cup extra-virgin olive oil

1 clove garlic, minced

2 teaspoons finely chopped fresh marjoram, thyme, or oregano, or 1 teaspoon dried

2 tablespoons freshly grated Parmigiano-Reggiano cheese

Salt

Quick Tomato Sauce

This tomato sauce is a simple version of what the French call a *concassée*, which literally means "broken up." You can also strain this sauce, so it's perfectly smooth, and it becomes a *coulis*, from the French *couler*, meaning "to flow." If you make a coulis, you don't have to bother with peeling and seeding the tomatoes because the seeds and peels will be strained out. This pure and simple tomato sauce is quick to make and doesn't distort the flavor of the tomatoes with a lot of different ingredients.

MAKES 5 CUPS

Put the tomatoes in a wide (12- to 14-inch) heavy-bottomed nonaluminum pot and simmer gently for about 20 minutes, scraping along the bottom of the pot every few minutes with a wooden spoon to prevent sticking. If you're using canned tomatoes, just cook the sauce until it reaches the consistency you like. Season to taste with salt and pepper. This sauce will keep for 2 days in the refrigerator and at least 6 months in the freezer.

6 pounds tomatoes, peeled, seeded, and coarsely chopped, or 8 cups, seeded and drained canned tomatoes, coarsely chopped (four 28-ounce cans)

Salt and freshly ground black pepper

Chopping the tomatoes.

Cooking down the tomatoes until thick.

Scraping the bottom of the pan to prevent sticking.

Tuscan Bread, Grilled Bell Pepper, and Tomato Salad
(Panzanella)

I first saw this salad on a menu in a little village outside of Sienna, but because eating bread in a salad didn't sound very appealing, I didn't order it. In the weeks to come, I kept seeing it on other menus, and finally, figuring it was a Tuscan specialty, decided to give it a try. It wasn't bad, so I tried it in a few more places and found that every restaurant had its own version, all delicious and satisfying, but to my taste too bready. This version is similar to authentic Tuscan versions (if there is such a thing), but it contains more tomatoes. If you don't like anchovies, leave them out.

MAKES 4 FIRST-COURSE SERVINGS

Toss the bread cubes in 3 tablespoons of the olive oil in a sauté pan or skillet over medium heat until the cubes brown slightly, about 10 minutes. Set aside.

Chop the tomatoes into chunks about $1/2$ inch on each side. Toss the tomato chunks with the bread cubes, the remaining 3 tablespoons olive oil, bell pepper, basil, anchovies, olives, and vinegar. Season to taste with salt and pepper. Serve at the table in a large salad bowl.

3 ($1/2$-inch-thick) slices crusty French bread, about 6 inches in diameter, cut into $1/2$- to 1-inch cubes (3 cups cubes)

6 tablespoons extra-virgin olive oil

4 medium tomatoes, peeled (optional), halved crosswise, and seeded

1 medium red, green, or yellow bell pepper, charred, peeled, and seeded, cut into $1/4$-inch-wide strips

20 fresh basil leaves (optional)

8 to 12 anchovy fillets, soaked for 5 minutes in cold water and patted dry (soaking optional)

5 tablespoons pitted and coarsely chopped black olives (do not use canned)

2 tablespoons excellent-quality balsamic vinegar or sherry vinegar

Salt and freshly ground black pepper

Tuscan Bread, Grilled Bell Pepper, and Tomato Salad.

Twice-Baked Garlic and Tomato Soufflés

This twice-baking trick solves the whole problem of serving soufflés at the very last minute. And while these twice-baked soufflés aren't as light as traditional soufflés (these are more creamy and custardy), a traditional soufflé will fall if even slightly overcooked, but these twice-baked soufflés are practically foolproof.

The principle is easy: a relatively dense soufflé mixture is baked in individual soufflé dishes or ramekins and unmolded. Shortly before serving, a sauce—in this case a creamy tomato sauce—is poured over the soufflés and they are baked a second time in a baking pan. The whole pan can be brought to the table—guests will ooh and ah as you serve—or you can set up the plates in the kitchen. You can bake the soufflés the first time in the morning, set them up with the sauce, refrigerate, and then just put them in the oven 20 minutes before you're ready to serve. Because these soufflés are very rich, the portions are purposely kept small—but if you're feeding big eaters, make four servings and bake in 6-ounce ramekins for 30 minutes.

MAKES 6 FIRST-COURSE SERVINGS

To make the sauce, combine the tomatoes with the cream in a small saucepan and simmer over medium heat until the sauce thickens ever so slightly, about 10 minutes (the sauce should have a soupy consistency). Stir in the herbs and season to taste with salt and pepper.

Brush or rub the insides of six 4-ounce soufflé dishes or ramekins with softened butter. Chill the soufflé dishes in the refrigerator and coat a second time with more butter. Coat the insides of the molds with flour or Parmesan cheese by putting all the flour or cheese in one of the molds, rolling it around, and then transferring it to the others until you've used it all up. Keep the molds in the refrigerator until you're ready to fill them.

Melt the 3 tablespoons butter over medium heat in a small saucepan. Add the garlic and flour, and cook the mixture while gently whisking for about 3 minutes—you should be able to smell the flour and garlic. Add the milk, turn up the heat to high, and whisk the mixture until it boils and thickens. Remove from the heat.

Whisk about one third of the milk-garlic-flour mixture into the egg yolks and then whisk this back into the saucepan, off the heat. Stir half the grated cheese into the sauce and season to taste with salt and pepper.

Preheat the oven to 350°F. Add the cream of tartar to the egg whites (if you're using a copper bowl, add a pinch of salt instead) and beat the egg whites until they are stiff and fluffy. Whisk one-quarter of the beaten egg whites into the sauce, then fold in the rest of the egg whites. Fill each of the ramekins with the soufflé mixture and smooth the tops with a spatula. Hold your thumb about 1/2 inch into the mixture along the rim of the mold and carefully rotate the mold so you can form a small moat completely around the mold.

continued

4 medium tomatoes, peeled, seeded, and finely chopped, or 2 cups drained and seeded canned tomatoes (one 28-ounce can), finely chopped

1/2 cup heavy cream

1 tablespoon finely chopped fresh basil or tarragon, or 2 teaspoons finely chopped fresh marjoram

Salt and freshly ground black pepper

3 tablespoons all-purpose flour or freshly grated Parmigiano-Reggiano cheese (for coating the soufflé dishes or ramekins)

3 tablespoons unsalted butter

4 cloves garlic, minced and crushed to a paste

3 tablespoons all-purpose flour

1 cup milk

4 large eggs, separated

1/4 cup finely grated Parmigiano-Reggiano cheese

Pinch of cream of tartar (unless you're using a copper bowl)

First stage of baking the soufflés.

Arrange the soufflés on a baking sheet and bake until the mixture rises about 1 inch above the top of the molds, about 20 minutes.

Butter a square or rectangular baking dish just large enough to hold the soufflés. This is important; if the baking dish is too large, the sauce will run off the soufflés and may even burn. Hold the soufflés with a towel and turn them out into the baking dish. If they stick to the molds, run a paring knife around the inside of the molds to dislodge them. The unmolded soufflés can be kept up to 12 hours in the refrigerator, covered with plastic wrap, before the final baking.

Preheat the oven to 375°F. Spoon the sauce over the soufflés and sprinkle the top of each soufflé with the remaining cheese. Bake for about 20 minutes, until the soufflés puff up and the sauce in the baking dish is bubbling. Serve immediately on hot plates.

Unmold the soufflés.

Finished soufflés.

GREEN TOMATOES

Some green tomatoes are simply tomatoes that have been picked before they've ripened—don't confuse them with tomatillos. There are also varieties of tomatoes that are completely green even when fully ripe. Because green tomatoes are firmer and contain less water than fully ripened tomatoes they won't fall apart when cooked. To prepare fried green tomatoes, slice them, dredge them in cornmeal, and fry them in a sauté pan in bacon fat. Serve them with cooked pieces of diced bacon.

Green heirloom tomatoes.

Dredging green tomatoes in cornmeal.

Frying green tomatoes in bacon fat.

TRUFFLES

My first truffle came in a tiny can not much larger than a thimble and cost half a day's pay from my job as a short-order cook. It was a bitter disappointment and had little of the flavor that years later I've come to associate with truffles. Few canned truffles are worth the expense, so if you're going to splurge on a truffle or two, buy them fresh or frozen.

Truffles grow underground, attached to the roots of certain kinds of oak trees. Experienced truffle hunters say they can recognize an oak with truffles on its roots because the tree looks stunted. Most of us know that truffles have to be sniffed out by trained pigs or dogs, but in the south of France, dogless and pigless truffle hunters look for flies that are attracted to the truffle's odor and swarm in a patch at the base of the truffle oak trees.

Summer truffle.

If you've never tasted a truffle—or have only tasted one out of a can—it's easy to wonder what all the fuss is about and why truffles are so expensive. Although the aroma of white truffles reminds some people of garlic, there is no flavor or aroma quite like that of a truffle. Truffles have a peculiar, lurking, almost haunting perfume—like something smelled or tasted years before and forgotten. Truffles have an intriguing taste, but their real magic is in their ability to enhance the flavor of other foods. Eggs with truffles somehow taste more like eggs, chicken more like chicken, and butter more like butter. Truffles have a special affinity for rich ingredients like butter, eggs, and cream.

Most truffles come already well scrubbed, but if you encounter a dirty one, brush it with a toothbrush under cold running water and immediately dry it. Some truffle recipes say to peel the truffles with a small paring knife. Always save the peels—they can be finely chopped and added to whatever it is you're cooking.

If you manage to get your hands on fresh truffles and aren't planning to use them in the next few days, tightly wrap each one individually in plastic wrap and again in aluminum foil and freeze them in a plastic container with a tight-fitting lid. Frozen truffles hold their flavor for months, but use them as soon as you can so that none of their precious flavor is wasted. However, don't use frozen white truffles for slicing raw over pasta. Freezing compromises their brittle texture.

To get the most flavor out of the least truffle, never cook truffles for more than 10 or 15 minutes, or their flavor and aroma will evaporate. If you're cooking them longer, as when they're slid under the skin of a chicken, cover the pan with a tight-fitting lid. In the case of the chicken, wrap it tightly in aluminum foil, so all the aroma is trapped inside. One of the best tricks I know is to use truffles to flavor a simple sauce and then pour the sauce over vegetable or meat dishes just before serving, or simply pass the sauce at the table for guests to help themselves. (See Black Truffle Cream Sauce, page 347.)

One of the best ways to serve truffles is as part of a risotto. If you have white truffles, make a simple risotto (perhaps risotto alla milanese) and simply slice the truffles over the risotto, being as generous as you dare, just before serving. If you have black truffles, the best solution is to make a truffle butter by either chopping the truffles with the butter or simply storing the butter with the truffles overnight.

===

Though there are about sixty species of truffle, most of which, surprisingly, can be found on the West Coast of the United States, the three most famous come from Europe.

BLACK WINTER TRUFFLES (*Tuber melanosporum*). These famous truffles are sometimes sold as "Périgord" truffles, after one of the regions in France where they are hunted. Black winter truffles look like wizened black golf balls and vary in size from a pea to a baseball. It's important to be able to distinguish black winter truffles from the much less expensive summer truffle (see below). Winter truffles are usually blacker than summer truffles. When you slice a black winter truffle, you'll see a filigree pattern of fine marbled lines of white, whereas a summer truffle is a more homogeneous dark brown or black. Black winter truffles should be firm and have a pungent smell, although they won't smell as strongly as white Italian truffles. Black truffles (both winter and summer) are usually cooked; white truffles are usually used raw.

BLACK SUMMER TRUFFLES (*Tuber aestivum*). I first encountered fresh summer truffles in a little neighborhood restaurant in Tuscany, where well-truffled pasta and meat dishes were served at very modest prices. Later I found fresh summer truffles in an outdoor market for about a tenth the price of winter truffles.

Black summer truffles look like black winter truffles, but don't have as strong an aroma or flavor. Because they are much less expensive than winter truffles, they can be a good value. Summer truffles have a rough outer peel with a pronounced, almost reptilian, texture, similar to that of winter truffles, but coarser. The inside of a summer truffle is a uniform dark brown. Don't bother buying canned summer truffles; they're inexpensive but have no flavor.

WHITE TRUFFLES (*Tuber magnatum*). White truffles, the most expensive truffles of all, are hunted in the fall in the Piedmont region in northern Italy, and they are almost always used raw, shaved at the table over pasta and meats. White truffles have a pungent, garlicky aroma, not unlike scented natural gas—one friend who had just splurged on a white truffle thought her stove was leaking. But nothing really describes the white truffle's heavenly aroma.

SHOPPING FOR TRUFFLES

White truffles and black winter truffles are in season in the late fall and early winter; summer truffles are available during the summer. Truffles are best bought fresh, but their aroma starts to fade as soon as they come out of the ground, so it's important to buy them from a reliable importer or gourmet store where you know they've just come off the plane. Give the truffles a good sniff—you shouldn't have any trouble getting at their aroma—and a gentle squeeze to make sure they are firm, with no sponginess or soft spots.

If you can't find fresh truffles or want to use them out of season, it's best to buy frozen truffles from a reliable importer, and then keep them in your home freezer until you need them.

If you must buy preserved truffles, remember that the better preserved truffles come in small jars rather than cans. If you're buying French truffles, look for the words *première cuisson*, which means the truffles have been cooked only once instead of twice, a method used by some canners that completely destroys the truffles' flavor. Truffles marked *surchoix* are the largest and most expensive. Those marked *1er choix* are slightly smaller and less expensive. Canned summer truffles have so little flavor that I never bother buying them.

Truffle juice is sometimes sold in cans and can be excellent for flavoring sauces and salad dressings. Unfortunately the quality of truffle juice varies enormously, so you may need to try different brands—buy the smallest size—to find out which is best. The same caveat holds true for truffle oil, which can be so powerful that a drop or two will flavor a salad or a plate of pasta or so weak that most of the bottle won't do anything. Truffle oil comes flavored with either white or black truffles, but don't expect truffle oil to have the alluring subtle scent of fresh or frozen truffles. It sometimes has an aggressive quality—so use it carefully.

❧ TRUFFLE BUTTER ❧

If you have truffles that you're using in the next 2 or 3 days, put them in a large mason jar with a pound of butter—each stick unwrapped—or a dozen eggs in the shell or both. The butter and eggs will end up scented with truffles. When you use the truffles, the butter can be tightly wrapped in plastic wrap and aluminum foil and then used over the next week, or it can be frozen and kept for up to a year. Truffle butter is at its most amazing when served as a topping for mashed potatoes—let the guests help themselves. The eggs can be used over the next few days for making omelets, scrambled eggs, and soufflés.

Pasta with White Truffles

Whereas black truffles are usually cooked, white truffles are almost always served raw. In Italy in the fall, when white truffles are in season, restaurants offer to shave raw white truffles over meat or pasta at exorbitant prices. If you've splurged on a white truffle, shaving it over pasta is one of the best ways to appreciate its unique flavor and aroma. I like to take the tradition a step further and use Truffle Butter (see page 338) for flavoring cooked pasta. If you're really strapped for cash (and the home equity loan is maxed out), use a summer truffle instead of the white truffle.

Almost any kind of pasta makes a marvelous subject for the truffle treatment, but I prefer fettuccini or linguine, which I sometimes make myself. If you're using dried pasta, buy the best-quality egg pasta you can find. My favorite is made by Arrigo Cipriani (of Harry's bar in Venice), but it's expensive and not always easy to locate.

Slice the truffle into paper-thin slices with a plastic vegetable slicer or an Italian truffle slicer (see page 4) which looks nicer in the dining room. When you serve this pasta, walk around the table and shave generously over each of the guest's pasta—or better yet, pass the truffle and slicer (warn about the blade) and let your guests slice their own.

MAKES 4 FIRST-COURSE SERVINGS

Bring 4 quarts of salted water to a rapid boil and cook the pasta until al dente, between 1 and 2 minutes for fresh pasta and 4 and 8 minutes for dried (unless you're using the Cipriani pasta, which cooks in 2 minutes).

Slice the Truffle Butter into eight slices. Drain the pasta and toss it with the butter, salt, and pepper.

Serve the pasta on hot plates and shave very thin truffle slices over each serving with an Italian truffle slicer or a vegetable slicer.

VARIATION:

You can also serve this pasta with black winter truffles, chopped and tossed with the pasta (the heat of the pasta will cook them).

Pasta with White Truffles.

$^{1}/_{2}$ cup (1 stick) unsalted butter

1 white truffle or summer truffle, black or white

1 pound fresh fettuccine or linguine, or 12 ounces dried

Salt and freshly ground black pepper

1 stick Truffle Butter (opposite)

Spaghetti with Black Truffles, Garlic, and Anchovies
(Spaghetti alla Norcina)

One of the joys of traveling in Italy is unexpectedly running into dishes like this one in very modest trattorias. Because of its delicate flavor, pasta makes a perfect backdrop for the flavor of truffles. The Black Truffle Cream Sauce (opposite) makes a marvelous sauce for almost any kind of pasta, but I'm also fond of this wonderful mixture that is served throughout Umbria, a region to the southeast of Tuscany. Umbrian cooks use their local black winter truffles, but when I can find them fresh or frozen, I use summer truffles, which are much less expensive although admittedly not as tasty. I sometimes serve this sauce with fettuccine or linguine instead of spaghetti.

You can serve this dish, Italian style, as a first course, or as a main course, but don't serve this pasta as a side dish—it deserves to be the center of attention. Most of the work for the truffle sauce can be done earlier the same day.

MAKES 6 FIRST-COURSE OR 4 MAIN-COURSE SERVINGS

Bring about 4 quarts of salted water to a boil for cooking the pasta.

Brush and rinse off any dirt clinging to the truffle. Very finely chop the truffle or finely grate it with a small hand grater.

Just before cooking the pasta, heat 1/4 cup of the olive oil in a pan or pot large enough to hold the cooked pasta over medium heat. Stir in the garlic and anchovies, and heat until you can smell their aroma, about 5 minutes.

If you're using dried pasta, start cooking it; if you're cooking fresh pasta, wait until the truffle sauce is ready. Stir the chopped truffle into the garlic mixture and stir over medium heat for about 1 minute.

Cook the fresh pasta until al dente. Drain the fresh or dried pasta and stir into the pot with the sauce and the remaining 1/2 cup of olive oil. Season to taste with salt and pepper. Serve immediately.

1 medium black winter or summer truffle

3/4 cup extra-virgin olive oil

2 cloves garlic, minced and crushed to a paste

12 anchovy fillets, soaked for 5 minutes in cold water, patted dry, and finely chopped (soaking optional)

1 pound dried spaghetti, or 1 1/2 pounds fresh pasta, such as fettuccine or linguine

Salt and freshly ground black pepper

Baked Chicken with Truffles

When I had my restaurant, I made a long series of experiments cooking chicken with truffles. One method consisted of setting the chicken on a tripod inside a covered pot and then steaming the chicken with aromatic broth. But the best method turned out to be the simplest—sliding truffle slices under the skin of the chicken, wrapping the chicken in aluminum foil, and baking it. When the chicken was unwrapped in the dining room, the whole restaurant would fill with the truffles' aroma. This recipe calls for a black or white truffle, even though white truffles are rarely, if ever, cooked. But the result of using either kind of truffle is extraordinary.

MAKES 4 MAIN-COURSE SERVINGS

1 (3- to 4-pound) chicken

1 black or white truffle, as large as you dare

2 tablespoons unsalted butter

Salt and freshly ground black pepper

Pull any large chunks of fat out of the chicken and remove the giblets. The giblets can be frozen for another recipe.

Brush or rinse off any dirt clinging to the truffle. Thinly slice the truffle with a vegetable or truffle slicer (see page 4).

Carefully slide your forefinger under the skin of the chicken along the breast and thighs, gently separating the skin from the flesh. Don't try to separate the skin from where it attaches to the breast bone running between the two breasts or you'll tear the skin. Slide the truffle slices under the skin, pushing them around under the thigh skin and spreading them under the breast skin.

Butter the shiny side of a sheet of aluminum foil. Sprinkle the chicken with salt and pepper and wrap it tightly in the buttered aluminum foil, buttered side facing the chicken. Refrigerate for 5 to 12 hours.

Preheat the oven to 400°F.

Bake the chicken for 17 minutes per pound and place it on a platter—don't open the foil—and let it rest for 15 minutes in a warm place. (I use the turned off oven with the door cracked.)

Unwrap the chicken in the dining room—save any juice that runs out into the foil—so everyone can smell the truffles. Carve the chicken and spoon the juice over each portion.

Black Truffle Cream Sauce

This sauce is best made with black winter truffles, but if you don't want to mortgage the house, you can also make it with black summer truffles.

   If you make more of this sauce than you end up using, it will keep for several days in a tightly covered container in the refrigerator. I like most to serve this sauce on a simple sautéed piece of chicken, fish, or veal. You can also spoon it over baked, sautéed, or mashed potatoes; cooked green vegetables, such as spinach or chard; cooked baby artichokes or artichoke hearts; or grilled or sautéed mushrooms.

MAKES 2/3 CUP

Check the truffle carefully for dirt or grit. If it's dirty, brush quickly under cold running water with a small scrub brush or toothbrush. Slice the truffles as thinly as you can with a vegetable slicer or truffle slicer (see page 4). For the most dramatic effect, leave the slices whole or cut them into fine julienne. You can also just chop them—no one will complain.

Simmer the cream gently while whisking in a small saucepan over medium heat until the cream thickens slightly, about 5 minutes. Remove the cream from the heat, immediately stir in the truffles, and cover the pan. Let sit for 10 or 15 minutes without opening the lid. Stir once more and season to taste with salt and pepper. Bring the sauce quickly back to the simmer immediately before serving.

1 black winter or summer truffle, as large as you can afford

1 cup heavy cream

Salt and freshly ground black pepper

⁓ GREAT USES FOR THE BLACK TRUFFLE CREAM SAUCE ⁓

Once you've made black truffle cream sauce, you'll discover an infinite number of uses for it since it's good on just about anything. It works as a sauce for vegetables, seafood, and meat.

GLAZED ROOT VEGETABLES. Glazed pearl onions, turnips, and carrots can all be coated with the Black Truffle Cream Sauce just before serving. When the vegetables are ready, add 3 tablespoons of the sauce, heat for about 1 minute, or until the sauce coats the vegetables, and serve.

MASHED POTATOES. Pass the Black Truffle Cream Sauce at the table for guests to spoon over mashed potatoes or over any of the variations on page 282–283.

VEGETABLE GRATINS. Spoon $^1/_4$ cup of Black Truffle Cream Sauce over the finished gratin and slide the gratin back into the oven for 3 minutes.

SPINACH. Use Black Truffle Cream Sauce instead of cream to make creamed spinach (page 313).

GREEN BEANS. Prepare the Basic Boiled and Buttered Green Beans with Fines Herbes on page 316, but leave out the butter. Heat $^1/_3$ cup Black Truffle Cream Sauce in a wide skillet over medium heat and stir in the drained beans. Turn the heat on high and heat just long enough so the sauce coats the beans, about 2 minutes. Season with salt and pepper.

FRESH SHELL BEANS. Boil fresh shell beans until the beans are tender (see pages 299–300). Bring $^1/_2$ cup Truffle Cream Sauce to a simmer in a wide skillet over high heat. Drain the beans and add them to the truffle sauce. Heat for about 3 minutes, or until the beans are well coated with the sauce. Serve immediately.

PEAS. Prepare the Basic Buttered Peas on page 261, but leave out the butter. Bring $^1/_2$ cup Black Truffle Cream Sauce to a simmer in a wide skillet over medium-high heat. Add the drained peas and stir gently until all the peas are coated with sauce. Season with salt and pepper.

PASTA. Toss $^2/_3$ cup Black Truffle Cream Sauce with 12 ounces cooked dried or 1 pound fresh pasta. Makes 4 first-course servings.

MEATS AND FISH. Spoon 2 to 3 tablespoons Black Truffle Cream Sauce over each serving.

Sweet Truffle Sauce

When I first made this sauce, at a Christmas dinner with skeptical food fanatics, no one thought it would work—it just sounded too weird. But we all ended up spooning it over fruit (roast pears were best), pieces of cake, and dipping into it with cookies.

This sauce is a traditional crème anglaise—a sauce made by slowly cooking milk, egg yolks, vanilla, and sugar until the mixture thickens—except that truffles replace the traditional vanilla.

MAKES 2 CUPS; ENOUGH FOR ABOUT 10 SERVINGS

Brush or rinse off any dirt clinging to the truffle and finely chop.

Bring the milk to a simmer in a small nonaluminum saucepan over medium-high heat (aluminum turns eggs gray).

Whisk the yolks and sugar in a small mixing bowl until the egg yolks pale slightly, about 2 minutes. Stir half the simmering milk into the egg yolks. Remove the pan with the remaining milk from the heat. Return the egg yolk–milk mixture to the pan, then return the pan to the heat. Stir with a wooden spoon, gently but constantly, over medium-low heat. When the crème anglaise begins to thicken, immediately remove the pan from the heat and continue stirring for about 2 minutes (see note).

Stir the truffle into the hot crème anglaise and immediately cover the pan. Let sit for 30 minutes at room temperature—don't remove the lid—and for another 2 hours in the refrigerator. This sauce can be kept in the refrigerator, tightly covered, for up to 2 days.

NOTE: To know when a crème anglaise is ready, most cookbooks suggest making a horizontal line with your forefinger on the back of the spoon used for stirring. When the line stays in place, the crème anglaise is ready. I look at the ripples on the crème anglaise while I'm stirring—as soon as the fine ripples disappear and the sauce takes on a satiny consistency, it's ready. Remember never to leave the sauce on the stove even for an instant without stirring. In other words, don't stop and stare at the spoon while the sauce curdles.

1½ cups whole milk

6 egg yolks

6 tablespoons sugar

1 small black winter truffle

TURNIPS

I so dreaded turnips growing up—their reputation had preceded them—that I never even tried one until I was in my twenties. My parents must have shared a similar distaste, because we never had them when I was a child, and my only awareness of turnips came from gloomy descriptions of boarding schools in English novels.

Like so many loathed and feared foods I didn't discover that a turnip could be something good until I lived in France. A friend and I had saved several weeks' pay from our cooking jobs to eat at a famous restaurant in the French countryside. One of the early courses in a long succession of delicacies was a plate of turnips, sliced and gently caramelized in port wine and butter with a slice of hot foie gras on top—not really out of Dickens.

Turnips do seem to be at their best when served with meat or when cooked with meat juices. A note of sweetness—port is lovely, but sugar will do—also goes well, as does anything smoky, especially bacon. Of course, you must start out with a good turnip. Some cooks insist on using only baby turnips with the greens, but

Turnips.

I have nothing against the slightly bitter dissonant flavor of big greenless turnips found in the fall and during the winter. When buying turnips, large or small, make sure the greens on fresh turnips are bright and full with no traces of slime and not yellowing or limp. Larger turnips without greens should feel heavy—light turnips are spongy in the middle and probably too bitter. Avoid turnips with wrinkled skins, which means they are old, and don't buy turnips that are beginning to sprout.

Fresh turnips with greens will keep for several days in the refrigerator in plastic bags with holes poked through the plastic to allow the turnips to breathe. If you're planning to keep fresh turnips any longer than a few days, cut off the greens about an inch above where they join the turnip. (The greens are good to eat.) Larger turnips will keep for a week or two in a cool, dry place.

There are many varieties of turnip, but the one we're all used to seeing looks like a barely flattened sphere, purple on top and white on the bottom. Baby turnips are often often all white. Turnips have smooth skins and are easy to peel with a vegetable peeler (some older recipes insist on using a knife, but this isn't necessary). Very small baby turnips have such a thin skin they don't even need to be peeled. Once peeled, turnips can be sliced, cubed, cut into elongated rectangles, julienned, carved out with a melon baller, or "turned" into football shapes. Turning is a nuisance and for most vegetables rarely worth the effort, but if you're feeling conscientious, it's the best method for glazing larger turnips because it allows the turnips to roll about in the pan and glaze evenly. Cutting out turnip balls with a melon baller will also work, but you'll find that most of your turnip ends up in the trimmings (which can be saved for puree or soups).

A turnip gratin served in midwinter is a comforting and delicious accompaniment to hearty dishes, such as roast beef or lamb, duck, and calf's liver. Because winter turnips sometimes become strong and a little bitter, it's best to make a gratin like the French Creamy Potato Gratin on page 279 and substitute turnips for half the potatoes.

Trimming turnips.

Peeling turnips.

Preparing turnips for cutting into cubes.

Slicing turnips into rectangles.

Cutting turnips into julienne.

Cutting turnips into $1/8$-inch dice.

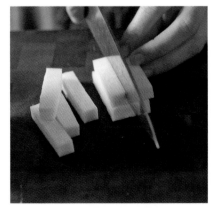

Cutting turnips into $1/4$-inch sticks.

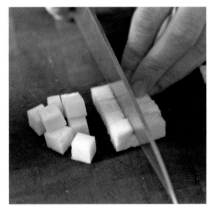

Cutting turnips into $1/4$-inch cubes.

Turnip shapes.

Port-Glazed Turnips with Hot Foie Gras

I first tasted this dish at Alain Chapel's 3-star restaurant in Mionnay, outside of Lyons. The turnips are glazed with concentrated broth, port, and a little vinegar and then topped with a slice of hot foie gras. Most cooks sauté the raw livers, but I've found that sautéing terrine of foie gras works better because a lot of the water has already been cooked out of the foie gras, making it more concentrated.

MAKES 4 FIRST-COURSE SERVINGS

2 large turnips, peeled

2 tablespoons unsalted butter

1/2 cup port

1/4 cup Concentrated Broth (page 377)

1 tablespoon sherry vinegar, plus more to taste

Salt and freshly ground black pepper

1 (12-ounce) piece terrine of foie gras (labeled *bloc* or *entier*, if French), cut into 4 slices

Preheat the oven to 200°F.

Cut two 1/4-inch thick slices out of the center of each of the turnips. The idea is to come up with four nice rounds.

Cook the turnip slices in a single layer in butter in a nonstick pan for about 8 minutes, until lightly brown on the bottom. Turn over and repeat on the other side.

When the turnips are browned, take them out of the pan and discard the fat. Return the turnips to the pan with the port, concentrated broth, and the vinegar and simmer gently until the sauce barely begins to thicken, about 5 minutes. Taste and adjust the vinegar. Season with salt and pepper. Transfer to a plate and reserve, uncovered, in the warm oven.

Heat a nonstick pan over high heat for a couple of minutes (make sure there are no birds in the vicinity—hot nonstick pans release fumes that kill birds) and add one slice of foie gras. The idea is to get the foie gras to brown before it melts, in about 30 seconds. Turn as soon as it is browned on the first side and brown the other side.

Place a round of turnip on each of four heated plates and set the foie gras slices on top. Lightly season the slices of foie gras with salt and pepper. Serve immediately.

Quick and Easy Turnip Green Soup with Bacon

In essence, the bacon is sweated and the broth and turnip greens are added, simmered a few minutes, and the soup is ready.

MAKES 4 FIRST-COURSE SERVINGS

1 pound thick-cut bacon, sliced crosswise into 1- by 1/4-inch strips

1 bunch turnip greens, washed

4 quarts Basic Brown Chicken Broth (page 374)

Salt and freshly ground black pepper

2 tablespoons sherry vinegar, plus more to taste

4 slices country bread, sliced about 1/2 inch thick, toasted

1 clove garlic, peeled

Put the bacon in a pot—large enough to hold the soup—and cook it gently, over medium heat, until it barely begins to turn crispy, about 8 minutes.

While the bacon is cooking, slice the turnip greens, stems removed, crosswise into 1/4-inch-wide strips. Add to the bacon and cook over medium heat, while stirring, until wilted, about 10 minutes. Add the chicken broth, bring to the simmer over high heat, decrease the heat to low, and simmer for 10 minutes. Season to taste with salt, pepper, and vinegar.

Rub each one of the toasts with the raw garlic and place the slices in heated soup plates. Ladle over the soup.

WASABI

Apparently most of the wasabi we encounter in Japanese restaurants is fake and is made mostly with American horseradish. To ensure you're getting the real thing, you need to have it grated to order.

Wasabi is a rhizome—a kind of underground stem—pale green and shaped like a fat stem with a small brown root end and usually stems and greens on the other end. When shopping for wasabi, make sure there are no soft spots or patches of mold on the surface.

To use wasabi, grate it on a box grater (the finest side) and put it in a bowl for 10 minutes for the flavor to develop. Be careful sniffing the stuff, or it will burn out your sinuses.

WATER CHESTNUTS

Unlike canned water chestnuts, which don't taste like anything at all, fresh water chestnuts have a delicate applelike sweetness and crunch. Nowadays fresh water chestnuts are easy to find in Asian (especially Chinese) markets.

When shopping for water chestnuts, pick over them carefully and make sure they are very firm with no soft spots. Scrub and rinse water chestnuts carefully before peeling because they're almost always coated with mud. Peel them as you would a small apple—rotating the water chestnut as you go—but use a paring knife instead of a vegetable peeler.

Water chestnuts can be thinly sliced or cubed and added to salads that include other cool and crunchy things—I use them with or as a replacement for apples and Jerusalem artichokes—or they can be sliced and stir-fried or sautéed with meats or other vegetables; their crisp freshness is an especially welcome contrast next to rich meats, such as duck or beef.

Rinsing the mud off water chestnuts.

Water Chestnut, Apple, and Watercress Salad

You're liable to confuse your guests with this study in cool crunch. Apples and water chestnuts are remarkably similar in texture so juxtaposing them results in a subtle counterpoint of textures. Watercress acts as a foil for the water chestnuts and apple. You don't have to use watercress; any salad green will do. I especially like to use purslane (see page 284).

MAKES 4 FIRST-COURSE SERVINGS

Just before serving, toss together the water chestnuts, apples, watercress, oil, and vinegar. Season to taste with salt and pepper.

1 pound water chestnuts, peeled, sliced about 1/8 inch thick

3 apples, peeled, halved, cored, halves sliced 1/8 inch thick

1 bunch watercress, large stems removed

2 tablespoons toasted hazelnut oil, toasted walnut oil, or canola oil

1 tablespoon sherry vinegar

Salt and freshly ground black pepper

WATERCRESS

There are several varieties of cress, but only one variety of true watercress. Only true watercress, which is easy to cultivate, is sold year-round in supermarkets. If you find garden cress, wild watercress (which grows near the banks of streams), or other cresses, by all means experiment by adding them to salads or using them to make the Cream of Watercress Soup on page 70.

Watercress.

When buying watercress, look closely at the leaves, which should have no dark or moist spots or lines where the leaves have folded, indicating that the watercress was badly handled. Never buy watercress that is starting to flower or that has wilted leaves or that just looks droopy. You can keep watercress, wrapped in a damp towel, in the refrigerator for up to 2 days.

Watercress is such a treat in salads that most of us forget that it is also good cooked. Most watercress sold in the United States has a slightly bitter flavor, which is great in salads but can taste out of place in cooked dishes. To get rid of the bitterness, plunge the watercress into a pot off rapidly boiling salted water, simmer for 30 seconds, drain in a colander, rinse with cold water, and leave for about 1 minute. Some recipes suggest trimming watercress by taking the leaves, one at a time, off the stems, but this is tedious and not worth the bother; just cut off and throw out the bottom half to one-third of the bunch—the part made up of mostly stems and very few leaves. Don't worry if there're some stems in your salad, a few smaller stems give everything a pleasant crunch.

Cold Cooked Watercress with Sesame and Soy Sauce

This is a delicious way to serve cold watercress during the summer months. Traditional Japanese recipes call for dashi, but as easy as dashi is to make, it's easiest to simply season the watercress with sesame oil and soy sauce. This cool dish is a perfect accompaniment to cold meats, chicken, and seafood.

MAKES 4 SIDE-DISH SERVINGS

Bring about 4 quarts of salted water to a rapid boil. Cut off the bottom half to one-third of the watercress bunches and discard. Toss in the tops of the watercress bunches, and boil for 30 seconds. Drain immediately in a colander and rinse under cold running water just long enough to cool the watercress and drain again.

Gently press the cooked watercress between the palms of your hands to eliminate excess water.

In a large bowl, stir the sugar with the soy sauce, sesame oil, and dashi until it dissolves. Toss the watercress with this mixture, sprinkle with the sesame seeds, and serve in a little plate that will catch the sauce.

3 bunches (about 6 ounces each) watercress

1 teaspoon sugar

1 tablespoon Japanese dark soy sauce

$^1/_2$ teaspoon toasted sesame oil

3 tablespoons Dashi (page 77, optional)

2 teaspoons white sesame seeds (optional)

WINTER SQUASH

I always wondered how squash could be harvested in the winter in cold, snow-covered places like New England. As it turns out, squash isn't harvested in the winter except in warm climates; it is usually picked in the fall and can be stored until spring. Winter squash's amazing ability to keep throughout the winter made it a boon before today's era of frozen, trucked, and jetted vegetables.

Unlike summer squash, which has relatively thin edible skin and small edible seeds, winter squash has thick skin and large seeds, which can be made edible by toasting but are usually discarded. (Pumpkin seeds are an exception—they're roasted and used in Mexican cooking.) But these limitations are more than compensated for by winter squash's flavor, variety, and exuberant colors—often variations on bright orange—and sometimes bizarre nonconformist shapes.

Hubbard squash.

Each variety of winter squash has its own flavor, sweetness, color, and texture. While buttercup and acorn squashes are two of my favorites, I often succumb to squash that look beautiful at the market or to some weird variety I've never seen before. Check squash carefully for soft spots, which may mean that it's been improperly stored. You can keep squash for up to a week in a paper bag in the refrigerator or in a cool airy place at about 50°F for several weeks, or for up to 3 months by hanging it in a net bag or in wire basket, which allows air to circulate. Don't store squash in plastic bags for more than a few days because the plastic traps in moisture and may encourage rot.

For some recipes, squash is simply left whole; for others it is halved or cut into pieces; and for others it is peeled (difficult if the squash is irregularly shaped) and cut into cubes. If the squash is very hard, coax the blade by tapping the back of the knife with a mallet (or rolling pin). Cut squash crosswise or lengthwise so the halves end up being more or less symmetrical. When cutting lengthwise, remove the stem first—it is impossible to cut through. Squash is best baked (either whole, halved, in pieces, or in gratins), but it can also be steamed. Squash also makes some of the best purees.

VARIETIES OF WINTER SQUASH

Winter squash shows up in fantastic variety in the fall, each with its own colors, designs, and flavor nuances.

Acorn squash.

ACORN. Perhaps because acorn squash is easy to recognize—it does in fact look like a giant acorn—and because one squash is easily cut in half to give two portions, it is one of the most popular squashes. Acorn squash comes in three colors: green, orange, and a newly developed white variety. I always choose the green—the most common variety—because it seems to be the sweetest and least stringy. An average acorn squash weighs about 1 pound.

BUTTERCUP. One of the sweetest of all squash, buttercup squash looks vaguely like a dark green turban with pale stripes running up its sides. Unfortunately this delicious squash isn't always easy to find.

BUTTERNUT. Lookings like an elongated bell with a smooth beige peel, butternut squash is one of the easiest to find and is in fact available almost year-round. Butternut squash has a creamy texture once cooked and can be halved lengthwise and baked, used in gratins, or peeled, cubed, and steamed. Once cooked by steaming or baking, it is also delicious in purees.

CARNIVAL. This brightly colored squash is best baked whole or in halves and then served with plenty of butter in the openings.

DELICATA. Shaped vaguely like an elongated football with green stripes, large delicata squash should be halved lengthwise and each half cut crosswise in half again. Delicata squash can be baked or used in gratins or purees.

DUMPLING. This squash, like acorn squash, is just the right size for splitting in half to make two servings. Sweet dumpling squash is pumpkin shaped, but is pale, almost white, with beautiful green stripes running up its sides. It is best baked in halves and then dressed with plenty of butter in the recesses.

HUBBARD. This is a delicious squash but somewhat unwieldy because of its size, which ranges from 8 to 25 pounds. Buy the smallest size and cut it into wedges before baking or steaming.

KABOCHA. This is a Japanese squash with a flattened ball shape. It is dark green with white spots and orange smudges. It can be baked, steamed, and used in gratins and purees. The Japanese like to deep-fry it in tempura.

PUMPKIN. Pumpkins can be cooked in the same way as other squash, but be sure to buy small pumpkins meant for cooking. Don't cook a large

Butternut squash.
Carnival squash.
Delicata squash.
Chinese squash.

Pumpkin.

Spaghetti squash.

pumpkin suited for a jack-o'-lantern, as I once did, because it has no sweetness. Small cooking pumpkins, on the other hand, are delicious.

SPAGHETTI. The oddball of the squash family, spaghetti squash gets its name because its flesh turns into long spaghetti-like shreds once baked. The best way to serve it is to shred it with a fork and serve as a base for low-fat pasta sauces in the same way as spaghetti.

TURBAN. This squash indeed looks like a turban and has a shape similar to buttercup squash. Unlike buttercup squash, however, it has brilliant orange coloring.

Dumpling squash.

Baked Whole or Halved Squash

This is the easiest way to cook squash because all you have to do is poke the squash in a couple of places with a paring knife and bake it. When the squash is finished baking, just cut it in half—or in quarters if it is large—and scoop out the seeds. Pass butter or olive oil at the table so guests or family can help themselves.

MAKES 4 SIDE-DISH SERVINGS

Preheat the oven to 375°F.

Rinse off the squash and poke it in a couple of places with a paring knife to let steam escape. Place the squash in a baking dish—add enough water to come about ¼ inch up the sides of the squash; this keeps the bottom from burning—and bake until a skewer or paring knife penetrate easily into its center. Turn the squash a couple of times during baking so it cooks evenly. Two 1-pound squash will take about an hour, but if you're baking a large squash, it may take as long as 1 hour and 45 minutes. When the squash is done, cut it in half or in quarters. Round squash, such as acorn squash should be cut in half crosswise, whereas oval or irregularly shaped squash should be cut first in half lengthwise and if large, each length cut in half again. After cutting open the squash, remove the seeds and place each squash piece on a platter or on plates. Pass the butter and Parmesan cheese. Set the salt and pepper on the table for guests to help themselves.

2 pounds whole squash, such as acorn, butternut, turban

Unsalted butter or extra-virgin olive oil

Freshly grated Parmigiano-Reggiano cheese, for serving

Salt and freshly ground black pepper

Halving a winter squash.

Scoop the seeds out of each half.

Baked hubbard squash halves with butter and maple syrup.

WINTER SQUASH GRATINS

Winter squash gratins are best when baked with all sorts of combinations of herbs, bread, spices, or other vegetables. Most recipes suggest peeling and cutting up the raw squash, but for some squash, especially acorn squash, peeling is a nuisance at best. Instead, I bake the squash until they soften and carefully scoop out the pulp in large chunks, cut into rough cubes, and then bake it a second time in a gratin.

Like most gratins, squash gratins are easy to make up with ingredients you have on hand. My own squash gratins tend to be based on Mediterranean ingredients, such as herbs, olive oil, bread, Parmesan cheese, and prosciutto; or Indian ingredients, especially spices, coconut milk or ghee; or they're French inspired and contain milk or cream and various firm cheeses.

Winter Squash Gratin with Heavy Cream and Gruyère

I save this rich and satisfying gratin for late fall and midwinter, when the chilly days somehow justify the richness and the calories. Be sure to use authentic Swiss Gruyère or some close equivalent (see pages 52–53). If you're using spaghetti squash, cut the squash in half lengthwise and bake it on an oiled sheet pan, flat side down, for about an hour in a 375°F oven, until easily penetrated with a skewer. Pull the spaghetti out with a fork so it separates into strands and spread these in layers, with the other ingredients, in the baking dish.

MAKES 4 SIDE-DISH SERVINGS

Preheat the oven to 375°F.

Cut the squash in half—or in quarters if you have one very large squash—and scoop out and discard the seeds. Place the squash, flesh side down, in a baking dish just large enough to hold the pieces in a single layer. Pour enough hot water into the dish to come $1/4$ inch up the sides of the squash, cover the dish with aluminum foil, and bake until the squash is soft, about 1 hour. (Or cover the dish with a lid or plastic wrap and microwave for 15 minutes. When the squash comes out, leave the oven on for baking the gratin. Let the squash cool slightly and scoop out the pulp. Cut the pulp into $3/4$-inch cubes.

While the squash is baking, cook the onion in the butter in a small skillet over medium heat until the onion turns translucent, about 10 minutes. Finely chop the sage leaves.

Spread half the onion on the bottom of an oval gratin dish or baking dish and spread half of the squash chunks in a layer on top. Sprinkle with salt, half the thyme, half the sage, half the grated cheese, the rest of the onion, and the rest of the squash. Sprinkle over the rest of the thyme and sage, the rest of the cheese, and sprinkle with salt. Pour over the heavy cream.

Bake for about 35 minutes, until a golden crust has formed on the surface. Tilt the gratin to make sure all the cream has been absorbed. If not, bake for 15 minutes more, turning down the oven if the gratin gets too brown on top. Grind over some fresh pepper and serve immediately.

2 pounds winter squash, such as acorn, buttercup, or butternut

1 medium onion, thinly sliced

1 tablespoon unsalted butter

2 fresh sage leaves

Salt

1 teaspoon finely chopped fresh thyme, or $1/2$ teaspoon dried

1 cup grated Swiss Gruyère cheese or equivalent

1 cup heavy cream or milk

Freshly ground black pepper

Squash "Spaghetti" with Tomatoes and Basil

Spaghetti squash makes a lean and unexpected alternative to regular pasta and a delightful surprise for jaded guests and family.

MAKES 4 MAIN-COURSE SERVINGS

Preheat the oven to 375°F.

Cut the squash in half lengthwise and place it on an oiled sheet pan, flat side down. Bake for about 1 hour, until easily penetrated with a skewer. Pull the spaghetti out with a fork so it separates into strands.

If the spaghetti was baked in advance and has grown cold, reheat it in a tablespoon of olive oil in a heavy-bottomed pot over medium heat. Pour over the heated tomato sauce, toss or stir gently, and serve on hot plates. Pass the Parmesan cheese at the table.

1 (2- to 3-pound) spaghetti squash

1 tablespoon pure olive oil (optional)

5 cups Quick Tomato Sauce, including the basil (page 337)

Freshly grated Parmigiano-Reggiano cheese

Squash "Spaghetti" with Tomatoes and Basil.

✺ FLAVORINGS FOR PUREED SQUASH ✺

It's easy to accent squash's delicate flavor by adding herbs, spices, or aromatic vegetables to the puree. Some flavorings, such as ground spices or finely chopped herbs—or herb butters—can be stirred into the puree before serving, while vegetables, such as onions or fennel, should be cooked with the squash and then pureed and strained at the same time. Turn squash puree into a soup by adding broth, milk, or coconut milk and adjusting the seasoning. To make it into a custard, add a beaten egg to each $2/3$ cup of puree and bake in a 275°F oven until set, about 2 hours.

GINGER. Combine 2 teaspoons grated fresh ginger with the squash pulp before pureeing.

CURRY POWDER. Gently heat 1 teaspoon garam masala or curry powder in the butter called for in the squash puree recipe over low heat until the curry smells fragrant. Stir into the squash puree.

FENNEL AND CORIANDER. Chop 1 small fennel bulb (8 ounces), stalks removed, and combine with $1/2$ cup water in a heavy-bottomed pot. Sprinkle over 1 tablespoon of whole coriander seeds, cover and simmer gently for 20 minutes, or until the fennel has softened. Check to be sure there's enough liquid in the pot so the fennel doesn't burn. Shake the pan from time to time to redistribute the fennel. When the fennel is done, if there's still liquid left in the pot, remove the lid and boil down the liquid until only 2 tablespoons remain. Puree the cooked fennel and cooking liquid in a blender or food processor with the squash. Work the puree through a food mill with the finest grid attachment or through a strainer with the back of a ladle.

PORCINI. Rinse $1/2$ cup (about $1/2$ ounce) dried porcini mushrooms and combine with 3 tablespoons warm water and let the mushrooms soften for about 30 minutes. Move the porcini around in the water every few minutes so they soak evenly. Squeeze the water out of the porcini—save it—and coarsely chop the porcini. Gently sauté the porcini in 2 teaspoons butter over medium-high heat for about 5 minutes. Carefully pour in the mushroom soaking liquid, leaving behind any grit, and cook gently for 1 to 2 minutes, until all the liquid evaporates. Stir this mixture into the squash puree. Season to taste with salt and pepper.

Squash Puree

Squash puree has a natural sweetness and texture and is at its best when seasoned and served very simply. The easiest way to puree squash is in a blender or food processor.

MAKES 4 SIDE-DISH SERVINGS

Preheat the oven to 375°F.

Rinse off the squash and cut in half lengthwise with a heavy chef's knife. Scoop out the seeds and place the squash halves, flesh side down, in a baking dish just large enough to hold them. Pour over enough water to come about $1/4$ inch up the sides of the squash and cover the dish with aluminum foil.

Bake for about 1 hour, or until a skewer or paring knife penetrates easily into the center of the squash. Let the squash cool for a few minutes and scoop out the pulp. Puree the pulp in a blender or food processor.

Stir the butter, sugar, salt, and pepper into the puree. You may find that squash takes a lot of salt. Reheat the puree by stirring it gently in a heavy-bottomed saucepan over medium heat.

2 pounds winter squash, such as butternut or acorn

2 tablespoons unsalted butter, plus more to taste

1 teaspoon sugar, or more or less to taste

Salt and freshly ground black pepper

Asian-Style Squash Gratin

Coconut has a mild and lovely sweetness that makes it especially good with spices, such as cinnamon, cloves, cardamom, and saffron.

MAKES 4 SIDE-DISH SERVINGS

Preheat the oven to 375°F.

Cut the squash in half—or in quarters if very large—and scoop out and discard the seeds. Place the squash, flesh side down, in a baking dish just large enough to hold it. Pour enough hot water to come 1 inch up the sides of the squash and cover with aluminum foil.

Bake for 1 hour, until the squash is soft. (Or cover with plastic wrap and microwave for 10 to 15 minutes, until soft.) Leave the oven on.

Let the squash cool slightly and scoop out the pulp. Cut the pulp into rough cubes about $3/4$ inch on each side. In a mixing bowl, toss the squash with the sugar, cardamom, saffron with its soaking liquid, and coconut milk. Season with salt. Spread the mixture in a 6-cup or large gratin dish so it forms a $3/4$-inch layer. Sprinkle with the almonds.

Bake for 30 minutes, or until bubbling and the almonds are golden brown. If the almonds start to brown too quickly, reduce the heat to 325°F and bake slightly longer. Serve immediately.

2 pounds winter squash, such as acorn or buttercup

2 teaspoons sugar

$1/2$ teaspoon ground cardamom

$1/4$ teaspoon saffron threads, soaked for 30 minutes in 1 tablespoon warm water

1 (14-ounce) can unsweetened coconut milk

Salt

$1/2$ cup unblanched whole almonds, coarsely chopped

Pumpkin Ravioli with Walnuts, Butter, and Sage

There's a secret to making your own ravioli quickly: use wonton wrappers. So that the wrappers don't dry out as you're using them, cover them with a damp towel.

MAKES 6 SERVINGS (ABOUT 60 RAVIOLI)

Combine the pumpkin and ricotta and season lightly with the nutmeg—a small pinch should do. Finely chop 4 of the sage leaves and mix in. Season to taste with salt and pepper—it's fine to taste it at this stage—and spread out about 10 wonton wrappers. Spoon or pipe about 1 tablespoon of the pumpkin mixture into the center of each wrapper, leaving at least a $^1/_2$-inch border all around the mixture.

Brush the exposed borders of the wrappers with cold water. Brush a second set of 10 wrappers on one side with cold water and place over the squares with the pumpkin mixture. Press the sides to push out any air that might be trapped with the stuffing. Pinch the sides to seal as securely as possible. Repeat with the remaining wrappers.

Bring 8 quarts of salted water to a boil and gently add the ravioli (a spider is good for this). Simmer the ravioli gently—don't boil or they'll burst open—for about 5 minutes. (Taste one for doneness.)

While the ravioli are cooking, in a large skillet heat the butter until it froths. Add the walnuts and the remaining 12 sage leaves and continue cooking, over medium heat, until the butter barely begins to brown.

Drain the ravioli and add them immediately to the pan of butter. Pull the pan back and forth to coat the ravioli with sauce. Spoon the ravioli into heated pasta or soup plates. Season with salt and pepper and serve.

1 (15-ounce) can pumpkin puree

1 (15-ounce) container ricotta

Ground nutmeg

16 fresh sage leaves

Salt and freshly ground black pepper

60 square wonton wrappers

1 cup (2 sticks) unsalted butter

$^1/_2$ cup coarsely chopped walnuts

Pipe the puree on square wonton wrappers.

Pumpkin Ravioli.

Pumpkin Ravioli with Walnuts, Butter, and Sage.

YAMS

If you've gone to the supermarket and brought home what you think are yams, what you probably have in hand are sweet potatoes. Even though yams are an important food crop in Africa where they originated, and in Indonesia, the Caribbean, China, Korea, and India, yams rarely appear in American markets outside of cities with large ethnic populations.

Because yams have very little taste (some say none), they are best as a foil for other foods. Yams can be baked or boiled like potatoes, but whereas potatoes are best served with rich but relatively subtle accompaniments like butter, cream, and sour cream, the bland yam needs more aggressive treatment. Sauces with lots of spices, chiles, and garlic, or one of the flavorful mayonnaises on page 368, are a good place to start.

There are so many varieties of yam that it's impossible to give a description to fit all. Some varieties do in fact look vaguely like sweet potatoes, but some yams are cylindrical and look like little logs, while others are more wildly shaped and have rougher skins. I've seen almost perfectly cylindrical yams, bear claw–shaped yams, round yams (in Japanese markets), carrot-shaped yams, and yams that look very much like horseradish. Yam skins are usually a rather dark brown, rough, and a bit shaggy looking.

When shopping—best done in a Latin market—look for yams that are heavy and very hard without cracks, obvious bruises, or soft spots. Avoid yams that seem withered or shrunken, which may mean they're old and have had a chance to dry out. Store them in a cool place with plenty of air circulation for up to a week.

Peel yams with a knife; a vegetable peeler isn't strong enough. Yams are one of those vegetables—like artichokes and potatoes—that once peeled turn dark when exposed to air. The best way to avoid this is to keep peeled yams submerged in cold water.

Yams.

APPENDIX

Butters and Sauces

Butters

One of the best ways to preserve herbs is to chop them up into butter and then refrigerate the butter or even freeze it. Once you have the butter in hand, it's great atop hot vegetables, meats, or seafood.

HERB BUTTER

Herb butter make a delicious accompaniment to hot sautéed, grilled, or fried vegetables and is a great last-minute flavoring for vegetable soups. Herb butters are easy to make and can be made ahead of time and frozen.

If you're making a small amount of herb butter—4 ounces or so—just use a wooden spoon to work a stick of softened unsalted butter with 2 tablespoons of finely chopped fresh herbs, such as basil, tarragon, parsley, chervil, or cilantro. If you're making herb butters with more powerful herbs, such as rosemary, sage, marjoram, or thyme, use only 1 tablespoon of the chopped herbs.

Slicing butter.

Combining chopped garlic and parsley to the butter.

Rolling garlic-parsley butter.

Opposite: Slicing garlic-parsley butter.

If you're making a large amount of herb butter, you can use the paddle blade of an electric mixer instead of working the butter by hand.

Herb butter can be rolled into a cylinder and cut into disks, or you can whip the butter shortly before serving and let guests dollop it on hot vegetable or into soups.

GARLIC-PARSLEY BUTTER. To make a delicious garlic-parsley butter, combine 1 finely chopped and crushed garlic clove, 2 tablespoons chopped fresh parsley, and $1/2$ cup (1 stick) unsalted butter.

GREEN BUTTER. This butter doesn't have a lot of flavor other than that of butter, but it is an attractive bright green. To make this butter, you must first extract pure chlorophyll from spinach. The chlorophyll can be preserved under a layer of olive oil for several days.

Combine the leaves from a pound of raw spinach with as little water as you need to get the leaves to turn around in a blender and blend until you obtain a green, frothy liquid. Put this liquid in a kitchen towel and ring out the juice into a small saucepan. Discard what doesn't go through the towel. Put the saucepan on low heat and watch it closely until the chlorophyll coagulates, usually just as the water gets warm. Strain through a fine-mesh strainer or kitchen towel. Work this chlorophyll into 1 cup (2 sticks) unsalted butter. Store tightly wrapped in the refrigerator for 2 weeks or in the freezer for 3 months.

MONTPELIER BUTTER. This is one of the more complicated of the flavored butters but is more than worth the effort. Use it atop cold and hot vegetables alike.

Blanch 1 cup of a mixture of equal parts watercress, parsley leaves, chervil (or tarragon), and $1/2$ cup spinach leaves for 30 seconds. Drain and rinse. Finely mince 1 shallot, combine with the blanched greens, and grind to a paste in a mortar and pestle or chop as finely as you can. Add 3 cornichons (French sour dill pickles), 1 heaping tablespoon capers, and 1 small clove garlic. Grind or finely chop the mixture. Combine with 1 cup (2 sticks) unsalted butter and work until smooth. Work in 3 cooked egg yolks and 2 raw egg yolks (you can leave out the raw egg yolks, if you wish). Slowly work in $1/2$ cup extra-virgin olive oil or canola oil. Work the mixture through a drum sieve or strainer and whip until fluffy. Store, covered with plastic wrap, in the refrigerator for up to 2 weeks. Allow to come to room temperature before serving.

TITLE: 1001 old-time garden tips : tim
el
BARCODE: 30339434839284
DUE DATE: 07-22-13

TITLE: Every day with Rachael Ray.
BARCODE: 40339123981478
DUE DATE: 07-22-13

TITLE: Vegetables : the most authorita
ti
BARCODE: 30339444032458
DUE DATE: 07-22-13

Horseradish Butter

This butter is easy to whip up and is delicious on grilled, sautéed, or roast meats and fish. If you make more than you need, wrap it in plastic wrap, and then aluminum foil and freeze. Horseradish butter keeps well in the freezer for up to a year.

MAKES 4 OUNCES; ENOUGH FOR 6 TO 8 SERVINGS

Work together the butter, horseradish, salt, and pepper in a mixing bowl with a wooden spoon or in an electric mixer with the paddle blade. The butter can be used as is, or you can roll it into a cylinder and then slice it into disks. To do this, spread the butter along the short side of a 6 by 12-inch rectangle of aluminum foil, leaving about an inch of foil and twist the two ends of the foil in opposing directions until the butter forms a tight cylinder. Let the butter harden in the refrigerator or freezer before slicing it into disks.

1/2 cup (1 stick) unsalted butter, softened

2 tablespoons freshly grated horseradish, horseradish preserved in vinegar, or bottled horseradish, liquid drained off

1/2 teaspoon salt

1/4 teaspoon freshly ground pepper

Mayonnaises and Vinaigrette

Those who have only tasted mayonnaise from a jar are amazed the first time they taste the real thing. Not only is plain mayonnaise more tasty than its bottled equivalent, it's easy to make and can be flavored with spices, herbs, flavorful pickled things (such as capers and little dill pickles), garlic, and myriad other ingredients limited only by your imagination.

Basic Mayonnaise

Mayonnaise is a snap to make, either by hand or in a blender. This is the blender or food processor method; for the hand method, see Aïoli, page 364. Just remember to add the oil slowly to the yolks, especially at the beginning. If the mayonnaise suddenly thins (meaning it has "broken"), gradually beat it into a new egg yolk or 4 tablespoons bottled mayonnaise.

Mayonnaise made in a blender or food processor is every bit as good as mayonnaise made by hand, unless you're using extra-virgin olive oil, which turns bitter when beaten hard. If you want to include extra-virgin olive oil in a mayonnaise made in a blender or food processor, use half canola or safflower oil (add these to the egg yolks in the blender or food processor) and then slowly stir in the olive oil by hand.

Mayonnaise can be kept in the refrigerator for up to 3 days, but it may separate. If it does separate, allow it to come up to room temperature and then slowly beat the broken mayonnaise into a fresh egg yolk or a couple of tablespoons of bottled mayonnaise in the same way as when making mayonnaise from scratch.

MAKES 1/2 CUP

2 egg yolks

2 tablespoons bottled mayonnaise

1 tablespoon fresh lemon juice, or 2 teaspoons white wine vinegar, plus more as needed

2/3 cup canola or safflower oil

2/3 cup extra-virgin olive oil, or 2/3 cup canola or safflower oil

Salt and freshly ground black pepper

Combine the egg yolks, bottled mayonnaise, and lemon juice in a food processor or blender. Turn the food processor or blender on low and pour in the canola oil in a thin, steady stream. If you're finishing the mayonnaise with olive oil, transfer the mayonnaise—which should now be somewhat stiff—into a glass or stainless steel mixing bowl and slowly work in the olive oil, a tablespoon at a time, with a wooden spoon. If you're finishing the mayonnaise with canola or safflower oil, just continue to add it while the mayonnaise is still in the blender or food processor. Season the mayonnaise to taste with salt and pepper and if needed, more lemon juice.

NOTE: If while you're adding the oil, the mayonnaise becomes very stiff, add a teaspoon of water from time to time to keep it at the consistency you like.

⤳ FLAVORED MAYONNAISES ⤳

APPLE AND HORSERADISH MAYONNAISE. Add a tablespoon of grated horseradish and a diced apple to ¹/₂ cup mayonnaise. The French call this mayonnaise *sauce suedoise*, or Swedish sauce.

CHILE MAYONNAISE. Grill poblano chiles, peel, seed, finely chop, and combine them with the ¹/₂ cup mayonnaise. For further complexity (I'm referring to the flavor, not the amount of work involved), add soaked and chopped dried chiles for different nuances of flavor.

CURRY MAYONNAISE. Stir 1¹/₂ tablespoons curry powder or garam masala in 1¹/₂ tablespoons vegetable oil in a small saucepan over medium heat until you smell the fragrance of the spices, about 1 minute. Be careful not to burn the curry. Stir this mixture, a bit at a time to taste, into ¹/₂ cup mayonnaise made with all vegetable oil. As you're working in the curry mixture, you may notice the mayonnaise getting very stiff. Work in a teaspoon more of water to thin the mayonnaise. If the mayonnaise gets too stiff, it may break. Curry mayonnaise is delicious with grilled vegetables or with cold leftover meats or seafood.

MOREL OR PORCINI MAYONNAISE. Soak ¹/₂ cup (about ¹/₂ ounce) dried morel or porcini mushrooms in barely enough warm water to cover for about 30 minutes. Squeeze the excess liquid out of the mushrooms and finely chop. Stir into ¹/₂ cup mayonnaise. Thin the mayonnaise, if necessary, with a little of the mushroom soaking liquid. This mayonnaise is fantastic with grilled vegetables.

SAFFRON AÏOLI. Make the Aioli (opposite). Add a pinch of saffron, soaked first for 30 minutes in a teaspoon of water. Be sure to add the soaking liquid along with the saffron.

Soak saffron threads in water. Add the egg yolks, bottled mayonnaise, and saffron to the garlic paste.

TRUFFLE MAYONNAISE. Stir a tablespoon of chopped black or white truffle or 1 tablespoon of truffle oil into ¹/₂ cup mayonnaise.

Aïoli

Aïoli has become so popular that it has lost some of its original meaning. I see "pepper aioli," "mint aioli," and any number of flavorings or ingredients that have nothing to do with the real thing. Authentic aïoli is mayonnaise made with extra-virgin olive oil and raw garlic. Aïoli is the one mayonnaise version that you can't make in a food processor or blender because the rapid action of these machines turns the oil bitter. If you want to avoid the (sometimes tedious) slow adding of the oil at the beginning, make the mayonnaise substituting half the olive oil with canola oil. Prepare this in the food processor, and add the olive oil by hand.

MAKES 2 CUPS

Combine the garlic with the salt and crush it to a paste on a cutting board or in a mortar and pestle. In a mortar or bowl, add the egg yolks, the bottled mayonnaise, and the lemon juice. Use a wooden spoon or the pestle for the mortar and work in the extra-virgin olive oil about a tablespoon at a time. When the mayonnaise begins to thicken, add it in a slow but steady stream. Season with pepper.

NOTE: If at any point the mayonnaise starts to get too thick, thin it with a teaspoon or two of water.

1 large clove garlic, minced

Pinch of coarse salt

2 egg yolks

2 tablespoons bottled mayonnaise

1 tablespoon lemon juice

1 1/2 cups extra-virgin olive oil

White pepper

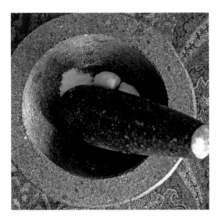

Grind the garlic together with the salt.

Grind the garlic to a paste.

When the base mixture is smooth, work in olive oil a tablespoon at a time.

Finished Aïoli.

Vinaigrette

The proportions of oil to vinegar in a vinaigrette vary wildly depending on the vinegar—you have to add the vinegar to taste. When dressing a salad, just pour over a little vinegar, about about three times as much oil, and a little salt and pepper, and toss.

MAKES I CUP

Gently stir together the vinegar, garlic, and extra-virgin olive oil in a small bowl and season to taste with salt and pepper. Don't try to get these two liquids to mix—they won't. If you decide to use vegetable oil, combine the mustard and vinegar and salt and pepper with the garlic in a small mixing bowl. Slowly beat in the vegetable oil with a whisk or fork. Taste and adjust.

$^1/_4$ cup good-quality red or white wine vinegar, balsamic, or sherry vinegar

I small clove garlic, minced and crushed to a paste (optional)

$^3/_4$ cup extra-virgin olive oil, canola oil, or safflower oil

4 teaspoons Dijon or other flavorful mustard (optional)

Salt and freshly ground black pepper

Butter Sauces

Butter sauces are delightful atop simply cooked green vegetables, such as broccoli or asparagus. Try them also with grilled vegetables. They are a bit too rich for fried foods—you're better off using a mayonnaise-based sauce.

Hollandaise Sauce

Even though you can toss it together in 10 minutes and don't have to make anything in advance, hollandaise makes a lot of people nervous. The only thing you can do wrong is to overheat the sauce at some point so the egg yolks curdle. But hollandaise is so easy to make that it's no big deal to grab another egg and start again. And once you've blown it, you'll have learned to gauge the heat.

A common mistake when making hollandaise is to use a double boiler. Double boilers are hard to control and may cause your sauce to curdle. It's easier to make hollandaise in a medium stainless steel mixing bowl held directly over the stove on medium-low heat. Standard saucepans don't work because the egg yolk hides in the corners, where it can't be reached by the whisk, and curdles. If you make hollandaise a lot, you may want to invest in a Windsor pan, which is a saucepan with sloping sides.

$1^1/_4$ cups ($2^1/_2$ sticks) unsalted butter

3 egg yolks

3 tablespoons cold water

I tablespoon fresh lemon juice

Salt and white pepper

MAKES $1^1/_2$ CUPS

Heat the butter in a small, heavy-bottomed saucepan over medium heat until it melts and froths up. Simmer it for about 5 minutes, or until the froth subsides and the butter looks clear with coagulated brown milk solids clinging to the bottom and sides of the pan. Don't let it burn. Immediately plunge the bottom of the pan into a bowl of cold water to stop the cooking. Strain the butter through a fine-mesh strainer, a triple layer of cheesecloth, or a coffee filter. Let the butter cool for 5 minutes—if the butter is too hot, it will curdle the egg yolks.

Combine the egg yolks and water in a medium stainless steel mixing bowl or Windsor pan and beat, off the stove, for 1 minute with a hand whisk until the egg yolk is frothy. Place the bowl directly on the stove over low heat or over a bowl of barely simmering water (hold the bowl with a towel) while whisking. When the egg yolks get frothy and stiffen slightly—the bowl should feel too hot to touch—take it off the heat, continue beating for 10 seconds, and slowly pour in the butter while whisking. Stop whisking as soon as you've added all the butter. Stir in the lemon juice, salt, and white pepper. Keep warm for up to 2 hours. (Don't store and reheat as this sauce is very perishable.)

VARIATIONS:

BÉARNAISE SAUCE. Simmer together $1/2$ cup wine vinegar, 5 crushed peppercorns, and 15 fresh tarragon leaves until there are only 2 tablespoons remaining. Strain and add to a hollandaise sauce that was made without the lemon juice.

MALTAISE. This orange-flavored hollandaise is the ultimate sauce for asparagus. Simmer the finely julienned zest of $1/4$ orange with the juice of 1 orange until there are only 2 tablespoons of juice remaining. Substitute 2 tablespoons of this liquid for the water called for in the hollandaise recipe. Stir the rest of the liquid and the cooked zests into the finished sauce.

MOUSSELINE. Essentially a hollandaise made light and airy with whipped cream, mousseline can be substituted in any recipe calling for hollandaise. Whisk $1/3$ cup heavy cream to medium peaks and fold it into $1^1/2$ cups hollandaise before serving.

Beurre Blanc

Beurre blanc is scary to people who aren't used to whisking loads of butter into a small amount of liquid. The beginning cook typically stands over the stove, adding butter a bit at a time in minute pieces, nervously stirring with a whisk. A better technique, and the one used by professionals, is to add the butter, which should be cold and cut into large cubes, and whisk it constantly over high heat until it's all integrated into the sauce.

MAKES 4 SERVINGS

1 shallot, minced

$1/2$ cup white wine

$1/4$ cup white wine vinegar

$3/4$ cup ($1^1/2$ sticks) unsalted butter, chilled and cut into 1-inch cubes

Salt and white pepper

Combine the shallot, wine, and vinegar in a small saucepan over medium heat and cook down to about 3 tablespoons. Add the butter, turn the heat to high, and immediately start whisking. Continue whisking (don't stop for a second or the butter will turn oily) until all the butter is incorporated and the sauce is hot but not boiling hot. If it boils, take it off the heat. Boiled beurre blanc can break. Strain if the shallots bother you. Season to taste with salt and white pepper.

Broths and Concentrated Broths

MANY COOKS GET FREAKED OUT when they run into a recipe that calls for broth, and even more so when the recipe calls for stock. Don't worry about the difference between broth and stock, there really isn't any. The word "stock" just implies that it's being saved (stocked) for use in other dishes.

It's true that most broths take at least a couple of hours, but this is cooking time not actual working time. And you needn't be fussy about carefully peeling and chopping vegetables. I usually just cut carrots and onions in half without even bothering to trim or peel them, and the only essential vegetables are onions—you can wing it without the others.

There are two kinds of broth—white and brown. White broth is made by just putting meat or fish and vegetables in a pot, barely covering everything with cold water, and then simmering. Brown broth is made by first roasting meats with vegetables before everything is put in the pot. It is usually worth the extra roasting step because it has a deeper color, a fuller flavor, and, if simmered gently, is always clear. Because the meats shrink during the roasting, you can also use less water so the broth ends up more concentrated. The only time that white broth is preferable to brown is when you're making creamed soups or sauces that you'll want to appear pure white or ivory.

Most home cooks use chicken broth instead of beef or veal broth, which require longer simmering and more expensive ingredients.

BROTH DO'S AND DON'TS

1. Never let broth come to a hard boil. If it boils, fat and proteins released by the meat will be churned back into the broth and make it cloudy and greasy. Simmer it with the pan moved to one side of the burner so fat and scum move to the other side where you can skim them off.

2. Don't add too much water. Add only enough liquid to barely cover the meat and/or bones. If you add too much water, the broth will be too diluted.

3. Don't overcook. Many cooks assume that the longer the broth is cooked, the better. True, gelatin contained in meat and bones is released during prolonged simmering, but much of the fresh savor of the meats is lost.

4. Skim often. Use a ladle to skim off fat and impurities that float to the top of the broth.

5. Don't add salt to broth. If you later decide to cook the broth down (reduce it) the salt will concentrate and become overbearing.

Basic Brown Chicken Broth

One of the great tricks for making perfectly clear broth is to brown the bones and/or meat before adding liquid. This preliminary browning also gives the broth more "punch" such that it's a good idea to use brown broth for most recipes calling for just broth, except for cream soups and other white or very pale dishes.

MAKES 3 QUARTS

Preheat the oven to 450°F.

Spread the chicken and vegetables in a heavy-bottomed roasting pan or large skillet. Roast for 45 to 60 minutes, until everything is well browned. Do not let the bottom of the roasting pan burn.

Remove the roasting pan from the oven, transfer the chicken and vegetables to a to 10-quart pot, and pour off or ladle off any grease in the bottom of the roasting pan. Discard the grease. Pour 2 cups of the water into the roasting pan and scrape the bottom with a wooden spoon to dissolve the juices adhering to the bottom.

Tie together the parsley, bay leaves, and thyme with a piece of string (or with cheesecloth if you're using dried thyme). Put the bouquet garni in the pot with the chicken and vegetables and pour over the contents of the roasting pan. Add the remaining 3 1/2 quarts of the water, or slightly more or less if necessary to barely cover the chicken.

Cook over medium heat until the water comes to a simmer. Decrease the heat to keep the broth at a slow simmer. Cook the broth, uncovered, for about 1 1/2 hours. Every 30 minutes, skim off any fat or froth that comes to the surface.

When the broth is done, strain it into a clean pot or heat-resistant plastic container. Let cool, uncovered, before putting it in the refrigerator.

6 pounds chicken wings or legs, or 2 (3-pound) chickens, cut up

1 medium onion, quartered

1 medium carrot, halved lengthwise

1 1/2 cups fennel stalks, cut into 3-inch pieces (optional)

1 stalk celery, coarsely chopped

4 quarts cold water, or enough to cover

1 bunch parsley

2 imported bay leaves

5 sprigs fresh thyme, or 1 teaspoon dried thyme

Basic White Chicken Broth

While I prefer the Basic Brown Chicken Broth (opposite) for most recipes calling for broth, there are times when a perfectly pale broth is called for, such as when making pale cream soup.

MAKES 3 QUARTS

Put the chicken and vegetables in a 10-quart pot. Tie together the parsley, bay leaves, and thyme with a piece of string (or with cheesecloth if you're using dried thyme). Add to the pot and pour over enough water to barely cover.

Cook over medium-high heat until the water comes to a simmer. Decrease the heat to keep the broth at a slow simmer. Cook the broth, uncovered, for $2^1/_2$ hours. For the first 30 minutes, skim off any fat or froth that comes to the surface.

When the broth is done, strain into a clean pot or heat-resistant plastic container. Let cool, uncovered, before refrigerating.

6 pounds chicken wings or thighs, or 2 (3-pound) chickens, cut up

1 medium onion, quartered

1 medium carrot, halved lengthwise

$1^1/_2$ cups fennel stalks, cut into 3-inch pieces (optional)

1 stalk celery, chopped

1 bunch parsley

2 imported bay leaves

5 sprigs fresh thyme, or 1 teaspoon dried

4 quarts cold water, or enough to cover

Basic Turkey Broth

Although the best broth is made by starting out with raw ingredients, I make a delicious broth from the turkey carcass left over from holiday feasting. Turkey broth can be used as a substitute for chicken or beef broth. (I use it to make the French Onion Soup on page 249.)

MAKES 3 TO 5 QUARTS

Break up the main part of the turkey with a cleaver or heavy knife—the back and breast bones—so it will fit in a 12-quart pot without taking up too much room. Put it in the pot with the onion, carrot, fennel, and celery. Tie together the parsley, bay leaves, and thyme with a piece of string (or with cheesecloth if you're using dried thyme). Add the bouquet garni and enough cold water to barely cover the bones.

Cook over medium heat until the water comes to a simmer. Decrease the heat to maintain a slow simmer, uncovered, for 3 hours. Skim off any fat or froth that floats to the top with a ladle.

When the broth is done, strain into a clean pot or heat-resistant plastic container. Let cool, uncovered, before refrigerating.

Leftover carcass from a cooked 12- to 20-pound turkey

1 medium onion, coarsely chopped

1 medium carrot, coarsely chopped

$1^1/_2$ cups reserved fennel stalks, cut into 3-inch pieces (optional)

1 stalk celery, chopped

1 bunch parsley

2 imported bay leaves

5 sprigs fresh thyme, or 1 teaspoon dried

4 quarts cold water, or enough to cover

Basic Brown Beef Broth

One of the reasons people hesitate to make beef broth is the expense and the prospect of a number of meals based on boiled beef. If you use beef shanks, which are usually sold in rounds about 1 inch thick, and if you're careful never to let the broth come to a hard boil—which will make the meat dry and stringy—you can eat the cooked shanks either hot (surrounded with a little of the broth) or cold, with a little mustard or horseradish.

MAKES 4 QUARTS

Preheat the oven to 400°F.

Combine the beef, bones, onions, carrots, fennel, and garlic in a heavy-bottomed roasting pan. Roast for about 45 minutes, stirring every 15 minutes, until the meat and bones are well browned and the juices on the bottom of the pan have caramelized.

Transfer everything to a large pot. Add 2 cups of hot water to the roasting pan and scrape the bottom of the pot with a wooden spoon to dissolve any juices. Pour this liquid into the pot. Add enough cold water to the pot to cover the meat and bones. Tie together the parlsey, bay leaves, and thyme with a piece of string (or with cheesecloth if you're using dried thyme). Add the bouquet garni, bring to a gentle simmer, and simmer, uncovered, for 6 hours, skimming every 30 minutes. If the water level drops below the top of the meat and bones, add more to cover.

Strain into a clean pot or heat-resistant plastic container. Let cool, uncovered, before refrigerating.

2 pounds stewing beef, cut into 1-inch chunks, or 3 pounds beef shank, cut into 1- to 2-inch-thick rounds

3 pounds cracked beef bones or veal knuckle bones

2 medium onions, halved

2 medium carrots, halved lengthwise

$1^1/_2$ cups fennel stalks, cut into 3-inch pieces (optional)

1 bulb garlic, halved crosswise

4 quarts cold water, or enough to cover

1 bunch parsley

2 imported bay leaves

5 sprigs fresh thyme, or 2 teaspoons dried

✺ COOLING AND STORING BROTH ✺

When your broth is done, strain it into a clean pot or heat-resistant plastic container and let it cool, uncovered, for an hour before putting it in the refrigerator. If it's hot in your kitchen, you may want to set the container of broth in a bowl of ice water to cool it more quickly. It's important that the broth not be warm (between 40°F and 140°F) for more than a couple of hours, because it's at these temperatures that bacteria begin to grow and may cause your broth to sour.

When you look at your broth the next day, it should be gelled and will probably be covered with a thin layer of fat (unless you skimmed it constantly while it was cooking). Before you use the broth, remove this fat with a spoon, but don't remove the fat any earlier than you need to because it helps preserve the broth. Broth can be stored for at least 5 days in the refrigerator and reboiled, allowed to cool, and stored for another 5 days. You can repeat this reboiling and cooling indefinitely. Broth can be frozen for at least 6 months.

To save space in your refrigerator or freezer, you can make Concentrated Broth (page 377).

Vegetable Broth

The trick to making a tasty vegetable broth is to brown the vegetables in the oven and use a little wine. Mushrooms also do wonders for a vegetable broth, but because they're expensive, they're listed here as optional. Remember to freeze unused mushroom stems—especially the stems from shiitake mushrooms, which are too tough to eat—for use in making broth.

MAKES 3 QUARTS

Preheat the oven 450°F.

Toss the onions, carrots, fennel, garlic, celery, and tomatoes with the olive oil and spread out in a heavy-bottomed roasting pan or large skillet just large enough to hold them in a single layer. Roast for 45 to 60 minutes, until the vegetables are well browned. If the bottom of the roasting pan starts to burn, turn down the heat and pour in about $1/2$ cup water. If you're using fresh mushrooms or frozen mushroom stems, sprinkle them over the vegetables, and roast for 10 minutes more.

Remove the roasting pan from the oven and scrape the vegetables into an 8- or 10-quart pot. Pour 2 cups of water into the roasting pan and scrape the bottom with a wooden spoon to dissolve the juices adhering to the bottom.

Tie together the parlsey, bay leaves, and thyme with a piece of string (or with cheesecloth if you're using dried thyme). Put the bouquet garni in the pot with the vegetables and pour over the contents of the roasting pan. Add the dried porcini mushrooms, if using, and the remaining $3 1/2$ quarts of the water, or slightly more or less if necessary to barely cover the vegetables.

Cook over medium heat until the water comes to a simmer. Decrease the heat to keep the broth at a slow simmer and simmer, uncovered, for 1 hour.

Strain the broth into a clean pot or heat-resistant plastic container. Let cool, uncovered, for an hour before refrigerating.

3 large red or white onions, washed, but not peeled (peels color the broth a rich brown), and quartered

3 medium carrots, cut into 1-inch pieces

$1 1/2$ cups reserved fennel stalks, cut into 3-inch pieces (optional)

5 cloves garlic, unpeeled and crushed

1 stalk celery, halved (optional)

5 tomatoes, halved crosswise, and seeded

3 tablespoons pure olive oil

1 pound mushrooms, sliced, or 1 pound (or less) frozen mushroom stems, or 1 cup ($3/4$ to $1 1/2$ ounces) dried porcini mushrooms, rinsed (optional)

4 quarts cold water, or enough to cover

1 bunch parsley

2 imported bay leaves

5 sprigs fresh thyme, or 1 teaspoon dried

Concentrated Broth

Some sauces are especially intense and delicious if the broth used to make them is slowly cooked down—sometimes to a fifteenth its original volume—into a syrupy glaze. Cooking broth down in this way makes it easy to store (you'll have only a thirtieth as much) and to use for making sauces. Concentrated broths are easy to make, but they take a lot of time on the stove, so you may want to save the process for a rainy stay-at-home weekend. Don't try to make concentrated broths out of canned broths—the broth will become far too salty; never add salt to a broth that you plan to concentrate.

3 quarts Basic Brown Chicken Broth (page 373), Basic Turkey Broth (page 374), or Basic Brown Beef Broth (page 375)

MAKES ABOUT 1/2 CUP

Bring the broth to a gentle simmer in a 4-quart pot. Carefully slide the pot to one side of the burner so that the broth simmers on one side of the pot only. This causes fat and froth released by the broth to stay on one side of the broth's surface so it's easier to skim off.

Every hour or so use a ladle to skim off and discard scum and fat. Rinse the ladle between uses or keep a bowl of water next to the broth for holding the ladle. When the broth has cooked down to about one-fourth its original volume—after about 3 hours—strain it through a fine-mesh strainer into a 1-quart saucepan and continue to simmer it down to 1/2 cup.

Strain the concentrated broth thorough a fine-mesh sieve into a clean plastic storage container. Let cool and refrigerate.

Index

Kombu, 76, 295
  Dashi Soup, 77
Koon Chun Sauce Factory brand hoisin
    sauce, 118

L

Lambs quarters, 227
Lan Chi brand "Chilli paste with Garlic
    and Soybean," 118
Lard for deep-frying, 17–18
La Reine potatoes, 267
L'Arpège, Paris, 334
Lavender, 213, 214
Leeks, 246, 253–255
  Basic Creamed Soup, 64
  Gratin, Leek, 255
  Miso Soup with Vegetables, 77–78
  Mixed Salade Grecque, 44–45
  Vinaigrette, Leeks in, 254
  washing techniques, 253
Leftovers
  baked potatoes, sautéed potatoes from, 271
  Parisian Potato Salad, meats in, 274–275
Lemon grass, 214
  Thai Hot and Sour Soup, 79
  Thai Red Curry, 176
  Thai-Style Fussy Melon Soup, 201
Lemons and lemon juice
  Basic Pan-Steamed or Boiled Broccoli
    with Lemon and Parsley, 121–122
  with deep-fried vegetables, 21
  Steamed Amaranth with Lemon and Olive
    Oil, 94
Lentils, 308–309
  Bacon, Lentils Stewed with, 309
  Indian-Style Vegetable Stew, 59–60
  salads, 45–47
  soups, 75–76
  varieties of, 308
Lentil Salad, 47
Lettuce. *See also* Frisée
  for green salads, 39
  peas cooked with, 261
  Romaine lettuce, 39
Lima beans, 300
  Mediterranean Mixed Vegetable Soup, 73–74
Limes. *See also* Kaffir lime
  Coconut Tapioca Pudding, Lime-
    Flavored, 145
Lingua di fuoco, 304
Linguine
  Dried Porcini Mushrooms, Linguine with,
    238–239
  with green vegetables, 80
  Northern Italian-Style Pasta with Mixed
    Vegetables, 61–62
  "Truffle Style" Mushrooms, 238
Lobster in Italian-Style Summer Vegetable
    Salad, 42
Lobster mushrooms, 235

Long beans, 227–228
  Peanuts and Garlic, Long Beans with, 228
Long-Cooked Collards with Ham Hocks, 179
Lotus root, 229
  Candied Lotus Root à la Grace Young, 229
Louisiana yams, 324
Lovage, 213, 214
Luffa, 229
  Stir-Fry with Enoki Mushrooms, Bok Choy,
    Jicama, and Water Chestnuts, 230

M

Macaroni
  with green vegetables, 80
  Mediterranean Mixed Vegetable Soup, 73–74
  pasta salads with, 48
Macédoine salads, 48–49
Mâche, 231
  Salad, Mâche and Flower, 231
Madeira
  Asparagus and Morel Salad, 104
  Cream, Morels with, 242
Maduros, 265
Ma Ling brand hoisin sauce, 118
Maltaise sauce, 371
Manchego in Pan-Fried Cheese-Stuffed
    Chiles, 172
Mandolines, 4
Manioc. *See* Cassava
Maple Syrup-Glazed Parsnips, 259
Margarine, 15
Marinades for grilling, 25
Marinated Bell Peppers, 114
Marinated Mushrooms with Fresh Tarragon, 239
Marjoram, 213, 215
  in creamed soups, 65
  Fiddleheads with Marjoram and Garlic
    Butter, Sautéed, 200
  Sugar Snap Peas with Butter and Fresh
    Marjoram, 263
  Zucchini Gratin with Tomatoes and Fresh
    Marjoram, Provençal, 320
Masar dal, 308
Mashed Potatoes, 282–283
Matchstick potatoes, 275
Matsutake mushrooms, 235
Maui onions, 246
Mayonnaise. *See also* Aïoli
  Artichoke and Morel Salad with Hazelnut
    Mayonnaise, 98
  artichokes with, 96, 98
  Basic Mayonnaise, 367–368
  flavorings for, 368
  Morel Mayonnaise, 96, 368
Meats. *See also* specific types
  Black Truffle Cream Sauce with, 348
  lentils with, 309
  in mixed vegetable soups, 71
Mediterranean Mixed Vegetable Soup, 73–74
Menon, 146
Metal steamers, 11

Mexican Chile and Tomato Soup, 173–174
Mexican cilantro, 213
Mexican Salad, 43
Mexican-Style Chickpea Salad, 157
Mexican-Style Creamed Corn with Bacon,
    Chiles, Tomatoes, and Cilantro, 182
Mexican-Style Vegetable Salad, 222
Microwaving beets, 110
Milk and cream
  in Béchamel Sauce, 53
  Black Truffle Cream Sauce, 347–348
  Corn, Creamed, 183
  Dried Chile Cream Sauce, 176
  with glazed vegetables, 35
  in gratins, 51
  Horseradish Cream Sauce, 219
  Mexican-Style Creamed Corn with Bacon,
    Chiles, Tomatoes, and Cilantro, 182
  Morels with Cream, 242
  in pureed vegetables, 90
  in salad dressings, 38
  Spinach, Creamed, 313
  Sweet Truffle Sauce, 349
  Winter Squash Gratin with Heavy Cream
    and Gruyère, 358
Miller, Mark, 168
Mincing techniques, 2–3
Miner's lettuce, 243
Miniature Croutons, 70
Miniature Fava Bean "Cassoulet" with Foie
    Gras, 301
Mint, 215
  peas with, 261
Minutina, 231
Mirin
  with dashi, 76
  in Japanese salad dressings, 50
Miso, 76
  Okra and Shiitake Mushrooms, Miso Soup
    with, 245
  Salad Dressing, 50
  Vegetables, Miso Soup with, 77–78
Mitsuba, 231
Mixed Salade Grecque, 44–45
Mixed Vegetable Grill, 28
Mixed vegetable salads, 41–43
Mixed vegetable soups, 70–74
  liquids for, 71
  meats in, 71
  Mediterranean Mixed Vegetable Soup,
    73–74
  oils and fats for, 71
  starchy ingredients in, 72
  texture enhancers for, 72
Monterey Jack cheese
  Mexican Chile and Tomato Soup, 173–174
  Pan-Fried Cheese-Stuffed Chiles, 172
Montpelier Butter, 366
Morels, 232, 235. *See also* Artichokes; Madeira
  Baked Morels Stuffed with Foie Gras, 241
  Cream, Morels with, 242

dried morels, 237
Mayonnaise, Morel, 96, 368
peas with, 261
Moroccan Spicy Carrots, 142–143
Mortar and pestle for Thai curries, 176
Mousseline sauce, 371
Mousserons, 235
Mozzarella cheese. *See also* Buffalo milk
    mozzarella
    Chile, Anchovy, and Olive Pizza, 175
    Eggplant Parmesan, 194–195
    in gratins, 54
Mulato chiles, 168
    Beef Stew with Beer, Chiles, and Sometimes
        Beans, 170–171
Mung beans, 304
    Mushrooms, 232–242. *See also* Morels;
        Porcini mushrooms
    Artichoke, Mushroom, Rice, Raisin,
        and Chicken Salad, 49
    Cream of Mushroom Soup, 67
    deep-frying techniques, 23
    dried mushrooms, 237
    duxelles, 84
    Fettuccine with Dried Porcini Mushrooms,
        238–239
    grilling, 239
    Luffa Stir-Fry with Enoki Mushrooms, Bok
        Choy, Jicama, and Water Chestnuts, 230
    Marinated Mushrooms with Fresh
        Tarragon, 239
    Mashed Potatoes with, 283
    Napa Cabbage, Bok Choy, and Wild
        Mushroom Stir-Fry, 132
    peas with, 261
    Sautéed Mushrooms with Garlic and
        Parsley, 240
    sautéing techniques, 13
    stuffed pasta with, 84
    Sugar Snap Peas with Mushrooms, Curry,
        Coconut Milk and Shrimp, 264
    trimming and cutting, 233
    "Truffle Style" Mushrooms, 238
Mussels
    Dried Bean and Mussel Salad, 45–46
    in potato salad, 272
Mustard
    Celeriac Rémoulade, 151
    Salsify and Pecan Salad, 291
    wasabi, 353
Mustard greens, 243

N

Napa cabbage. *See* Chinese cabbage
Nasturtiums. *See* Flowers
Navy beans, 304
    Dried Bean and Mussel Salad, 45–46
New Mexico chiles, 168
New potatoes, 267, 268
    Roasted New Potatoes, 278
Nightshade, 266

Nopales. *See* Cactus pads
Nori, 294–295
    Japanese Cucumber Salad with Vinegar, 188
    wild nori, 295
Northern Italian-Style Pasta with Mixed
    Vegetables, 61–62
Nu-Mex onions, 246
Nutmeg in creamed soups, 65
Nut oils
    for salad dressings, 38
    storing, 38
Nuts. *See also* specific types
    Pistachios, Brussels Sprouts with Raisins
        and, 127
    salads with, 40
    toasting, 40

O

Ocean ribbons, 297
    Oils and fats. *See also* Butters; Olive oil;
        Sesame oil
    argan oil, 153
    for deep-frying, 17–18
    for mixed vegetable soups, 71
    reusing, 18
    storing, 18
Oil seed rape, 117
Okra, 244–245
    Sautéed Okra, 245
Olive oil, 15
    Arracacha Simmered with Butter or Olive
        Oil, 94
    Beets with Olive Oil, Garlic, and Parsley,
        Sautéed, 112
    Braised Broccoli with Garlic and Olive Oil, 34
    for deep-frying, 17–18
    for French Fries, 275–276
    green beans with, 316
    for salad dressings, 38
    Steamed Amaranth with Lemon and Olive
        Oil, 94
Olives
    Broccoli Rabe with Olive Oil and Garlic, 15
    Chile, Anchovy, and Olive Pizza, 175
    Grated Carrot Salad with, 143
Onion rings, 23
Onions, 246–252. *See also* Leeks; Shallots
    in Béchamel Sauce, 53
    chopping techniques, 2–3, 247
    deep-frying techniques, 23
    French Onion Soup, 249
    Grilled Onions, 250
    Tart, 250–251
    tears, avoiding, 247
    Tomato and Onion Salad with Fresh Basil, 335
    varieties of, 246
    Whole Roast Onion, 248
Oranges and orange juice
    Endive, Orange, and Walnut Salad, 159
    Fennel, Orange, and Walnut Salad, 199
    Maltaise sauce, 371

Sautéed Radicchio, Orange, Bacon, and
    Pecan Salad, 164
wedges or slices, cutting into, 159
Orange sweet potatoes. *See* Sweet potatoes
Orecchiette
    Broccoli Rabe or Swiss Chard, Orecchiette
        with, 125
    with green vegetables, 80
    Mediterranean Mixed Vegetable Soup, 73–74
    pasta salads with, 48
Oregano, 213, 215
Oronges, 233–234
Oskard lettuce, 39
Overcooking vegetables, 10–11
Oxalates in rhubarb, 287
Oyster mushrooms, 235–236
Oyster plant. *See* Salsify
Oyster sauce, 118
    Napa Cabbage, Bok Choy, and Wild
        Mushroom Stir-Fry, 132

P

Pancakes
    Mashed Potato Pancakes, 283
    Zucchini Pancakes, Pan-Fried
        Sage-Scented, 319
Pancetta, 32
    in Béchamel Sauce, 53
    Broccolini with Pancetta, Anchovies,
        and Raisins, 123
    in mixed vegetable soups, 71
    Swiss chard with bacon, pancetta or
        prosciutto, 329
Pan-Fried Cheese-Stuffed Chiles, 172
Pan-frying
    pans or woks for, 13
    techniques, 14, 15
Panko and beaten egg batter for deep-frying,
    20–21
Pans. *See* Pots and pans
Panzanella, 338
Parisian Potato Salad, 274–275
Parmesan cheese
    Eggplant Parmesan, 194–195
    Fennel Salad with Shaved Parmesan, 198
    grated amounts of, 54
    for gratins, 52
    Grilled Tomatoes with Basil and Parmesan,
        335
    Italian Escarole Soup with Garlic and
        Parmesan Cheese, 160
    Mashed Potato Pancakes with, 283
    in stuffed pasta, 81
Parsley, 215. *See also* Garlic-Parsley Butter
    Basic Pan-Steamed or Boiled Broccoli with
        Lemon and Parsley, 121–122
    Beets with Olive Oil, Garlic, and Parsley,
        Sautéed, 112
    Carrots with Parsley, Baked, 143
    in creamed soups, 65
    deep-frying techniques, 23

Acknowledgments

While producing a second edition of a book like *Vegetables* requires the work of innumerable people—almost too many to thank adequately—there is one person, Sara Kaluzshner, who deserves special acknowledgment. She worked directly with me, producing all the images. And although I hired her as an assistant and hand model, she became so much more—stylist, muse, and friend.

Once the manuscript went to the publisher, it was labored over by a dedicated team for many months before it went to press. I especially want to thank my editors, Jenny Wapner and Veronica Randall, who relentlessly pursued and rectified falsehoods, redundancies, inconsistencies, and errors, and took care of the hundreds of details that go into the creation and production of a cookbook. In a job that requires obsession, my copyeditor Andrea Chessman was an obsessive's obsessive, driving me insane (in a good way) with seemingly unending queries. My skilled proofreader, Jean Blomquist, was also indispensable, as was my speedy indexer, Katherine Stimson. Without their help, *Vegetables* would never have come to fruition. Art director Nancy Austin, with her wonderful eye, is responsible for the beautiful design. Chloe Rawlins and Colleen Cain also contributed invaluable production assistance. In addition to all these hard-working people, I thank my very talented and hard-working publisher, Aaron Wehner.

There are also those in my private life who not only kept the book moving, but kept me moving. My agents Elise and Arnold Goodman have stood behind me for more than twenty years, and in addition to doing a great job with my books, they have become close friends. Thanks also to Joel Hoffman for his guidance and professionalism. Then there is my husband, Zelik Mintz, who is always there, encouraging and kind, without whom none of this would be possible.

Copyright © 2012 by James Peterson

Published in the United States by Ten Speed Press, an imprint of the
Crown Publishing Group, a division of Random House, Inc., New York.
www.crownpublishing.com
www.tenspeed.com

Originally published in the United States by William Morrow and
Company, Inc., New York, in 1998.

Ten Speed Press and the Ten Speed Press colophon are registered
trademarks of Random House Inc.

Library of Congress Cataloging-in-Publication Data

Peterson, James.
  Vegetables / by James Peterson. — Rev. ed.
      p. cm.
  Includes bibliographical references and index.
  1. Cooking (Vegetables) I. Title.
   TX801.P49 2012
   641.6'5—dc23
                        2011027973

ISBN 978-1-60774-026-1
eISBN 978-1-60774-205-0

Printed in China

Design by Nancy Austin

10 9 8 7 6 5 4 3 2 1

First Ten Speed Press Edition

MEASUREMENT CONVERSION CHARTS

VOLUME

U.S.	Imperial	Metric
1 tablespoon	$1/2$ fl oz	15 ml
2 tablespoons	1 fl oz	30 ml
$1/4$ cup	2 fl oz	60 ml
$1/3$ cup	3 fl oz	90 ml
$1/2$ cup	4 fl oz	120 ml
$2/3$ cup	5 fl oz ($1/4$ pint)	150 ml
$3/4$ cup	6 fl oz	180 ml
1 cup	8 fl oz ($1/3$ pint)	240 ml
$1^{1}/4$ cups	10 fl oz ($1/2$ pint)	300 ml
2 cups (1 pint)	16 fl oz ($2/3$ pint)	480 ml
$2^{1}/2$ cups	20 fl oz (1 pint)	600 ml
1 quart	32 fl oz ($1^{2}/3$ pint)	1 l

TEMPERATURE

Fahrenheit	Celsius/Gas Mark
250°F	120°C/gas mark $1/2$
275°F	135°C/gas mark 1
300°F	150°C/gas mark 2
325°F	160°C/gas mark 3
350°F	180 or 175°C/gas mark 4
375°F	190°C/gas mark 5
400°F	200°C/gas mark 6
425°F	220°C/gas mark 7
450°F	230°C/gas mark 8
475°F	245°C/gas mark 9
500°F	260°C

LENGTH

Inch	Metric
$1/4$ inch	6 mm
$1/2$ inch	1.25 cm
$3/4$ inch	2 cm
1 inch	2.5 cm
6 inches ($1/2$ foot)	15 cm
12 inches (1 foot)	30 cm

WEIGHT

U.S./Imperial	Metric
$1/2$ oz	15 g
1 oz	30 g
2 oz	60 g
$1/4$ lb	115 g
$1/3$ lb	150 g
$1/2$ lb	225 g
$3/4$ lb	350 g
1 lb	450 g